The Neuropsychology of Individual Differences

A Developmental Perspective

PERSPECTIVES ON INDIVIDUAL DIFFERENCES

CECIL R. REYNOLDS, *Texas A&M University, College Station*
ROBERT T. BROWN, *University of North Carolina, Wilmington*

PERSPECTIVES ON BIAS IN MENTAL TESTING
Edited by Cecil R. Reynolds and Robert T. Brown

PERSONALITY AND INDIVIDUAL DIFFERENCES
A Natural Science Approach
Hans J. Eysenck and Michael W. Eysenck

DETERMINANTS OF SUBSTANCE ABUSE
Biological, Psychological, and Environmental Factors
Edited by Mark Galizio and Stephen A. Maisto

THE NEUROPSYCHOLOGY OF INDIVIDUAL DIFFERENCES
A Developmental Perspective
Edited by Lawrence C. Hartlage and Cathy F. Telzrow

A Continuation Order Plan is available for this series. A continuation order will bring delivery of each new volume immediately upon publication. Volumes are billed only upon actual shipment. For further information please contact the publisher.

The Neuropsychology of Individual Differences

Individual Differences

A Developmental Perspective

Edited by

Lawrence C. Hartlage
Medical College of Georgia
Augusta, Georgia

and

Cathy F. Telzrow
Cuyahoga Special Education Service Center
Maple Heights, Ohio

Plenum Press • New York and London

Library of Congress Cataloging in Publication Data

Main entry under title:

The Neuropsychology of individual differences.

(Perspectives on individual differences)
Bibliography: p.
Includes indexes.
1. Neuropsychology. 2. Developmental psychology. 3. Individuality. I. Hartlage,
Lawrence C. II. Telzrow, Cathy F. III. Series.
QP360.N496   1985   612′.8   85-12481
ISBN 0-306-41986-6

© 1985 Plenum Press, New York
A Division of Plenum Publishing Corporation
233 Spring Street, New York, N.Y. 10013

Printed in the United States of America

"Men are what their mothers made them"
—Ralph Waldo Emerson

And this volume and volumes unwritten and
unsaid we dedicate to our mothers.

Mary Louise Pierron Hartlage (1912–1984)
Phyllis Duerr Fultz (1915–1985)

Contributors ✗

JOHN F. BOLTER, Clinical Psychology Service and Internship Training Program, Silas B. Hays Army Community Hospital, Ft. Ord, California.

RAYMOND S. DEAN, Department of Psychology, Teacher's College, Ball State University and Indiana University School of Medicine, Muncie, Indiana

CHARLES J. GOLDEN, Department of Psychology, University of Nebraska Medical Center, Omaha, Nebraska

WALTER HARRELL, Department of Neurology, Baylor College of Medicine, Houston, Texas

LAWRENCE C. HARTLAGE, Department of Neurology, Medical College of Georgia, Augusta, Georgia

PATRICIA L. HARTLAGE, Division of Pediatric Neurology, Medical College of Georgia, Augusta, Georgia

MARLIN L. LANGUIS, Department of Educational Theory and Practice, Ohio State University, Columbus, Ohio

ELAINE Z. LASKY, Department of Speech and Hearing, The Cleveland State University, Cleveland, Ohio

CHARLES J. LONG, Department of Psychology, Memphis State University, Memphis, Tennessee

ESTHER C. MELAMED, Department of Curriculum and Instruction, Kent State University, Kent, Ohio

LAWRENCE E. MELAMED, Psychology Department, Kent State University, Kent, Ohio

PAUL J. NAOUR, Department of Special Education, Muskingum College, New Concord, Ohio

FRANCIS J. PIROZZOLO, Department of Neurology, Baylor College of Medicine, Houston, Texas

MICHAEL I. POSNER, Department of Psychology, University of Oregon, Eugene, Oregon

MARY K. ROTHBART, Department of Psychology, University of Oregon, Eugene, Oregon

ROBERT F. SAWICKI, Lake Erie Institute of Rehabilitation, Erie, Pennsylvania

CATHY F. TELZROW, Cuyahoga Special Education Service Center, Cleveland, Ohio

PHILIP A. VERNON, Department of Psychology, University of Western Ontario, London, Ontario, Canada

Preface

The Neuropsychology of Individual Differences: A Developmental Perspective was designed to survey the complexities and subtleties of neurologically based differences in human beings. By conceptualizing and presenting subject matter in a developmental sequence, we hoped to emphasize the inseparable union between the science of neuropsychology and the study of human behavior.

Following a brief introductory chapter, the volume opens with chapters concerning critical preliminary questions, such as establishing a foundation and rationale for a neuropsychological basis for individual differences and consideration of important methodological issues. It proceeds with discussions of the role of neuropsychology in the individual's efforts to organize the world via such basic means as perception and temperament. Three chapters follow that discuss individual differences in higher cortical functions: cognitive ability, language, and learning. Neuropsychological differences between the sexes and in the expression of psychopathological and neurological conditions comprise the topics for the next three chapters. The final topical chapter provides a discussion of rehabilitation of neurological disorders in children, and the volume concludes with a synthesis of all contributions.

A project such as this, on completion, requires celebration and thanks to a number of persons who provided invaluable support in seeing it through. Among those deserving of such recognition are Cecil Reynolds and Robert Brown, editors of the Plenum Press series on individual differences, who helped us conceptualize and nurture this project. We extend special thanks and renewed respect for our contributing authors, who shared our enthusiasm in the developing product and captured this excitement in their work. As any editor is aware, the mechanics of typing and retyping represent a major investment of time in the volume's unfolding, and we give hearty thanks to typists Irene Friedel and Jean Woolley for enabling us to complete these activities with relative ease. Finally, we thank our publisher, and particularly Plenum Senior Editor Eliot Werner, for grand cooperation throughout the project.

At one stage of this volume's development, we received with a draft manuscript a letter from one of our authors, Charles Long. His letter said, in part, "I have learned several things about developmental brain–behavior issues: (1) I do not understand it, (2) it is questionable if anyone understands it . . . (3) this area may be too complex for anyone to understand." Charles's words, written in his usual dry wit, capture for us a valuable attitude of appreciation and respect for the enormous complexity of this subject matter. It is from that posture that we offer this volume, in the hope that through recognition of the intricacies of the science of neuropsychology we can better understand the individual differences in human beings.

LAWRENCE C. HARTLAGE
CATHY F. TELZROW

Contents

1 INTRODUCTION TO THE NEUROPSYCHOLOGY OF INDIVIDUAL
   DIFFERENCES... 1

   Lawrence C. Hartlage

2 FOUNDATION AND RATIONALE FOR NEUROPSYCHOLOGICAL BASES OF
   INDIVIDUAL DIFFERENCES 7

   Raymond S. Dean

   Individual Difference Approach 8
   Neurological Development 10
   Development of Hemispheric Lateralization of Functions 23
   Localization of Cerebral Functions in Adulthood 28
   Neuropsychological Sex Differences 31
   Conclusions 32

3 METHODOLOGICAL ISSUES IN RESEARCH IN DEVELOPMENTAL
   NEUROPSYCHOLOGY 41

   John F. Bolter and Charles J. Long

   Age-Related Effects of Cerebral Pathology 42
   Patterns of Recovery after Cerebral Trauma during
   Childhood 43
   Ontological Aspects of Recovery/Deficit Patterns 45

Factors Contributing to the Pattern of Impairment
Observed 47
Mechanisms of Recovery 53
The Problem of Chronogenetic Localization 55
Conclusions 56

4 NEUROPSYCHOLOGY OF PERCEPTION 61

Lawrence E. Melamed and Esther C. Melamed

Background Issues 61
Two Key Areas of Perceptual Development Research for
Child Neuropsychology 72
Using Constructs from Perceptual Science in
Neuropsychology 77
A Strategy for Perceptual Assessment in
Neuropsychology 84

5 TEMPERAMENT AND THE DEVELOPMENT OF SELF-REGULATION 93

Mary K. Rothbart and Michael I. Posner

Introduction 93
Models of Temperamental Self-Regulation 94
Framework for Self-Regulation 95
Ontogeny of Self-Regulation 104
Conclusions and Applications 116

6 INDIVIDUAL DIFFERENCES IN GENERAL COGNITIVE ABILITY 125

Philip A. Vernon

Three Stages of Intelligence Theories 125
Returning to Stage 1 127
Summary and Conclusions 145

7   PERSPECTIVES ON LANGUAGE DEVELOPMENT 151

    Elaine Z. Lasky

        Current Approach 152
        Language Development 154
        Conclusion 177

8   THE NEUROPSYCHOLOGY OF LEARNING DISABILITIES 183

    Francis J. Pirozzolo and Walter Harrell

        What is a Learning Disability? 183
        Pathophysiology of Learning Disabilities 184
        Biochemical Theories of Learning Disabilities 186
        Hemispheric Asymmetries in Learning Disabilities 187
        Electrophysiological Correlates of Learning Disabilities 188
        Perceptual and Information Processing 190
        Eye Movements and Reading Disabilities 194
        Summary 196

9   NEUROPSYCHOLOGICAL BASES OF PSYCHOPATHOLOGICAL
    DISORDERS 203

    Charles J. Golden and Robert F. Sawicki

        The Schizophrenic Syndromes 203
        Neuropsychological Investigations of the Schizophrenic
        Syndromes 206
        Neuroanatomical Markers of Schizophrenia 212
        The Affective Disorders 217
        Neuropsychological Investigations of Affective Disorders ... 219
        Neuroanatomical Indicators of Affective Disorders 221
        Discussion 222
        Summary and Conclusions 229

10 SEX DIFFERENCES IN NEUROPSYCHOLOGICAL FUNCTION: A VECTOR
MODEL 237

Marlin L. Languis and Paul J. Naour

A Perspective on Sex Difference 237
Critical Variables Influencing Expression of Male-Female
Gender Role Behavior 240
Patterns and Disorders in Language and Spatial
Learning 242
Phylogenetic Development of Sex Differences 247
Conclusion 248

11 A SURVEY OF DEVELOPMENTAL NEUROLOGIC CONDITIONS:
IMPLICATIONS FOR INDIVIDUAL NEUROPSYCHOLOGICAL
DIFFERENCES 253

Patricia L. Hartlage

Introduction 253
Congenital Influences on Neuropsychological
Differences 253
Postnatal Influences on the Developing Brain 260
Biochemical Influences on Behavior 262
Conclusion 263

12 THE SCIENCE AND SPECULATION OF REHABILITATION IN
DEVELOPMENTAL NEUROPSYCHOLOGICAL DISORDERS 271

Cathy F. Telzrow

Introduction 271
Specific Learning Disabilities 272
Epilepsy 280

Head Injuries 290
Summary 299

13 SYNTHESIS OF NEUROPSYCHOLOGICAL BASES OF INDIVIDUAL
    DIFFERENCES 309

    Lawrence C. Hartlage and Cathy F. Telzrow

AUTHOR INDEX 317

SUBJECT INDEX 327

CHAPTER 1

Introduction to the Neuropsychology of Individual Differences

LAWRENCE C. HARTLAGE

The scientific study of psychology has paralleled the study of individual differences. To a considerable extent, scientific psychology has been based on the study of individual differences. From the time of Galton's research on interindividual variation on such variables as reaction time, there has been a recognition that whereas we may search for psychological rules that apply to behavior in general, any theory of human behavior needs to allow for individual differences. The progression from the perceptual approaches of Weber to Fechner, Stevens and Helson reflected a shift from purely stimulus variables to more attention to subjective and contextual aspects of these phenomena, and this trend has continued in the more current signal detection research developed from recent technological advances in electronics and computer sciences. Similar progress in conceptualizations of human learning is to some extent reflected in the shift from early Hullian S-R (stimulus-response) theorizing to the subsequent S-O-R (where O stands for organism's internal intervening variables) model and later theories concerning relevance of the reinforcer to the organism. Once again, these paradigm shifts typified the increased focus on individual differences as the constant that scientific psychology needed to consider.

The scientific study of individual differences has followed one of three generic models. The earliest scientific model, dating at least to the recorded differences between Maskelyne and his assistant Kinnebrock in time required for transit plotting, was followed by Galton (1869) into the

LAWRENCE C. HARTLAGE • Department of Neurology, Medical College of Georgia, Augusta, Georgia 30902.

1

early work of Simon and Binet (1905), and is reflected today in work by Jensen (Jensen &. Munro, 1979) involving group differences in reaction time. This model was predicated on some apparently inherent individual differences in rate of processing and reacting to stimuli, of a nature that was presumably resistant to environmental intervention and thus represented stable characteristics that could be used to classify or describe individuals over extended periods of time.

Another model, perhaps most parsimoniously classified as intrapsychic, was reflected in the work of such scientists as Freud and Jung. This model described individual differences in reaction to psychological events occurring early in life—or in earlier events involving the species—which in turn manifested themselves in individual differences in perception, belief, or emotion. Because this model did not lend itself to objective measurement, it did not receive major emphasis as a research approach to the quantitative study of individual differences. However, it has had a profound and lasting influence on theoretical inferences concerning possible determinants of human differences and on intervention approaches in psychiatry, nursing, social work, and psychology, and for childrearing practices espoused by writers with a substantial lay following.

Perhaps the model that has most influenced American thinking concerning individual differences has been the behavioral approach, with its heavy emphasis on environmental and situational determinants of various aspects of behavior. Thorndike's early postulates that adult personality can be shaped by controlled environmental manipulatives gave rise to extensive research concerned with the extent to which individual differences were influenced or determined by prior schedules, types, and orders of reinforcement. This approach did not influence research in other countries to the extent it did in the United States, where it represented essentially the most important conceptual base in psychology for many years. It is interesting that Skinner, the most prominent proponent of contemporary behaviorism, has progressively moved from his early strict behaviorist orientation to one much more sympathetic to possible mediating effects of neural events on manifest behavior.

Perhaps due to the importance of the behavioral model on American psychology during the first half of the present century, the possibility of neurological determinants of certain individual differences did not figure prominently in conceptualizations of most American psychologists, educators, or others concerned with individual differences. Although nineteenth century European neurologists had identified adaptive behavioral deficits resulting from defects or dysgenesis of certain cortical areas, in the United States this body of knowledge was not viewed as having relevance as a possible basis of individual differences. It was the election

of a neurophysiological psychologist (Donald Hebb) to the presidency of
the American Psychological Association in the mid-twentieth century that
appeared to make legitimate the study of the central nervous system as
a determinant of individual variation, and to again focus on intraindividual
factors such as neurological organization as being proper topics for scientific psychological study. It was in this context that neuropsychology
began to flourish as a subset of clinical psychology, at first limited to the
study of how brain lesions affected adaptive behavior. Refinements in
both research methodology and psychometric measurement projected
neuropsychology into a role at once clinical and experimental, and the
dual roles coalesced to produce findings that suggested that normal variations in neuropsychological organization, which were found to exist in
the majority of humans, could offer parsimonious and cogent explanations
for many of the observed differences among individuals that had previously been attributed to intrapsychic or environmental phenomena. Autopsy findings of cerebral cortex asymmetry in approximately 77% of
adults (e.g., Geschwind & Levitsky, 1968), with even greater incidence of
asymmetry on computed tomography scan (e.g., Deuel & Moran, 1980)
gave rise to speculation that, if behaviorally relevant, such findings could
have important implications for the study of individual differences. Further, the finding that the unborn neonate had essentially the same incidence and extent of cerebral cortex asymmetry as that found in adults
(e.g., Chi et al., 1977; Galaburda et al., 1978) raised the further possibility
that behavioral differences related to incidence and extent of cerebral
asymmetry might be dependent on events present at birth, a remaining
fairly constant throughout the developmental span (e.g., Hartlage, 1981).
This possibility of a cerebral asymmetry basis for at least some individual
differences in adaptive behavior received conspicuous, if tangential, support from split-brain research, such as that reported by Sperry (Sperry,
1964, 1973). The fact that Sperry's work was recognized by the award of
a Nobel Prize added further confirmation to the possibility that attention
to the central nervous system and its role in individual differences might
represent a fruitful area for the study of individual differences.

This volume is addressed to exploring the ramifications of cerebral
organization for behavior and the implications of differential cerebral organization for individual differences in behavior. The extensive material
relevant to this field, and the variety of research emphases to addressing
these areas of relevance, requires a careful consideration of those aspects
having greatest implications for clarifying the issues involved. The contributors represented in the volume were selected according to the dual
criteria of expertise in a special area of relevance to the topic addressed
by the volume and of recognized excellence of scholarship within that

area of expertise. Rationale for the neuropsychological bases of individual differences is the topic of the first chapter, which sets in context the work to follow. The next chapter, dealing with methodological issues in developmental neuropsychology, leads through the tortuous and potentially treacherous path of issues that have hampered development of a compelling science in this field and offers glimpses of the imaginative and creative approaches that offer promise for meeting this goal. Because preception and learning have figured so prominently in the field of individual differences since the earliest work in the field, the first topical area chapter deals with the neuropsychological bases of these phenomena. This chapter is followed by one focused on temperament, which represents one of the issues of interest since the time of Freud and the earliest intrapsychic-oriented researchers. Cognitive ability, a major dimension of individual differences and the subject of an incredible body of research over the past 80 years, follows. The next three chapters, dealing respectively with language development, learning disorders, and psychopathological disorders, involve important subject areas for the neuopsychology of individual differences, since they deal with the implications of late nineteenth century neurologists and neuropsychiatrists (e.g., Broca, Wernicke, Dax, Hinshelwood, Stanley, Freud) for the study of the abnormal or deviant as a focus for understanding normal variation. Recent work on sex differences in neuropsychological organization puts into context yet another ramification of the utility of neuropsychological approaches for the explanation and understanding of phenomena that have traditionally been explained by cultural/environmental explanation. Pursuing the biomedical implications of neuropsychology as an explanatory concept in numerous individual differences, the survey of neurologic conditions affecting neuropsychological functioning addresses genetic and biochemical substrates of neuropsychological aspects of individual differences. The chapters are concluded with one dealing with the implications of neuropsychology for rehabilitation, with a final synthesis attempting to integrate the diverse contents and perspectives into a heuristic model.

It is anticipated that, as a scholar of individual differences, the individual reader may find different portions, aspects, and foci of the book to be of individually applicable relevance. For this reason, every attempt has been made to preserve the integrity and focus of each chapter as a free-standing unit of individual reference merit, while at the same time trying to smooth the transition between and among the diverse topic areas by editorial efforts focused on providing continuity of style and readability. Hopefully, this light editing will help preserve the richness of individual style that is so appropriate in a book dedicated to the neuropsychology of individual differences.

REFERENCES

Binet, A., & Simon, T. Methodes nouvelles pour le diagnostic du nivean intellectual des amormaux. *L' Année Psychologigue*, 1905, *11*, 191–244.

Chi, J. G., Dooling, E. C., & Gilles, F. H. Gyral development of the human brain. *Annals of Neurology*, 1977, *1*, 86–93.

Deuel, R. K., & Moran, C. C. Cerebral dominance and cerebral asymmetries on computer tomogram in childhood. *Neurology*, 1980, *30*, 934–938.

Galaburda, A. M., LeMay, M., Kemper, T. C., & Geschwind, N. Right-left asymmetries in the brain. *Science*, 1978, *199*, 852–856.

Galton, F. *Hereditary genius: An inquiry into its laws and consequences.* London: MacMillan, 1869.

Geschwind, N., & Levitsky, W. Human brain: Left-right asymmetries in temporal speech region. *Science*, 1968, *161*, 186–187.

Hartlage, L. C. Neuropsychological assessment techniques. In C. R. Reynolds & T. Gutkin (Eds.), *The handbook of school psychology.* New York: Wiley, 1981.

Jensen, A. R., & Munro, E. Reaction time, movement time, and intelligence. *Intelligence*, 1979, *3*, 121–126.

Sperry, R. W. The great cerebral commissure. *Scientific American*, 1964, *210*, 42–52.

Sperry, R. W. Lateral specialization of cerebral function in the surgically separated hemispheres. In F. J. McGuigan (Ed.), *The psychophysiology of thinking.* New York: Academic Press, 1973.

CHAPTER 2

Foundation and Rationale for Neuropsychological Bases of Individual Differences

RAYMOND S. DEAN

Neuropsychology involves attempts to relate observable behavior to the functional efficiency of the central nervous system. Research that has begun to outline the parameters of the field has grown geometrically during the past four decades. Although the antecedents of neuropsychology may be followed some 2,000 years in the past, only since the late nineteenth century has public evidence begun to accumulate regarding brain functioning (e.g., Broca, 1865; Jackson, 1874). Of course, the luxury of retrospect allows the criticism of early case study methodologies that drew conclusions concerning normal cortical functioning from the remnants of diseased brains (Broca, 1865; Jackson, 1874). However, these initial reports represent the foundation and stimulus of our current appreciation for the behavioral expression of higher order operations of the brain. More recent research has provided evidence of a correspondence between the functioning of the adult brain and cognitive, sensory-motor, and affective constellations of behavior. Continued success in articulating adult brain–behavior relationships has stimulated the neuropsychological study of the developing child. As such, child neuropsychology is a far more recent pursuit. The intent of the present chapter is to examine neuropsychological aspects of cortical development that may offer insights into individual differences observed in children's behavior. Following a review of a number of the critical issues in the area, the neuropsychological aspects

RAYMOND S. DEAN • Department of Psychology, Teacher's College, Ball State University and Indiana University School of Medicine, Muncie, Indiana 47306.

of the child's physical development will be examined with particular emphasis on functional asymmetries.

INDIVIDUAL DIFFERENCE APPROACH

The roots of neuropsychology lie in behavioral neurology and elements of both clinical and experimental psychology. This conclusion becomes unmistakable in a review of the research base that unites the field (Dean, 1983; Reitan, 1974). The most salient influence in the evolution of neuropsychology had been the emphasis on the behavioral effects resulting from focal brain damage (e.g., Reitan, 1955). Scientific attention, in the main, has focused on the localization of specific functions to distinct areas of the cerebral cortex, (Boll, 1981; Hartlage & Hartlage, 1977). Although most neuroscientists have rejected a one-to-one correspondence between behavior and microstructures of the brain (see Reitan, 1974), an empirical approach that attempts to relate behavior to macrostructures of the cerebral cortex remains. In character with the empirical emphasis in psychological research beginning in the decade preceding World War II, neuropsychology in North America has taken on a rather quantitative, atheoretical complexion (Dean, 1983). This emphasis has been argued to be the result of the attempt to gain credibility in the medically oriented neurosciences and the polemics that existed in psychology over the past two decades (Boll, 1981). A recent "paradigm shift" in American psychology to a more flexible, cognitive approach to behavior has certainly been more fertile ground for the growth of neuropsychology (Dean, in press, a). This conclusion is evidenced in the phenomenal growth in the number of systematic investigations since the early 1970s that have begun to outline the neurological correspondence of complex human behaviors.

The research methodology most often employed has involved the examination of psychological functions for groups of patients with unambiguous, localized brain lesions (e.g., Reitan, 1955). Data gleaned in this fashion are compared with those resulting from the evaluation of normal controls. Thus, this research design involves the determination of which functions are disturbed when a particular structure of the brain is damaged. The hazardous, yet often made, conclusion resulting from such a paradigm involves causative links between localized areas of the brain and behavioral deficits. The reader will recognize, of course, that although one may predict behavioral impairment resulting from damage to specific areas of the brain with clinical confidence, to infer that a specific anatomical feature is functionally responsible for a given behavior goes beyond the nature of these data (Reitan, 1974).

In sum then, human neuropsychological research has relied upon a "natural-experimental" approach in which the behavioral deficits for patients with cortical damage are used to infer impaired brain function. Although this approach relies on serendipity rather than ablation, the experimental paradigm followed in the study of brain functions resembles laboratory efforts with lower forms of life (Dean, 1983). While this approach reflects the rather primitive level of knowledge of the functioning of the brain and the lack of noninvasive measurement procedures, such as research methodology has served the fledgling science of neuropsychology well. That is to say, while inferences concerning normal cerebral functioning are tenuous from this data base, without knowledge of the neurological significance of specific behaviors, the study of neuropsychology is untenable. Thus, correlational as it may be, without a direct access to the brain, any argument that examines behavior in isolation is a tautological pursuit at best (Dean, 1983).

This approach to the study of neuropsychology has a number of factors that recommend it; however, neuropathology is clearly at its base. Hence, normal variation in brain function and resulting behavior are seen as moderating variables to be obviated by random assignment of normal individuals to control groups. Thus, this experimental design attempts to control for naturally occurring individual differences rather than to elucidate them.

The study of individual differences with its foundation in biology is concerned more directly with "naturally" occurring variation in behavior and brain function than differences observed through manipulation or the examination of neuropathology. Sometimes referred to as a correlational or differential view of neuropsychology, attention is directed to the understanding of naturally occurring variations in the behavioral expression of brain functions. The objective in the examination of individual differences in neuropsychology is the portrayal of variation in brain function which can more heuristically be attributed to an interaction of genetic and environmental factors than to neuropathology. Of obvious importance with adults, this emphasis seems crucial with children, whose rate of neurological development would appear to differentially predispose the organism to environmental influences (Sperry, 1968). Indeed, research in the area suggests that age-related differences in the psychological sequelae of childhood brain damage may be due in part to the child's premorbid neurological developmental level (Dean, 1982). Crockett, Klonoff, and Bjerring (1969) and Dean (in press, b) have stressed the increasing complexity necessary to describe children's performance on neuropsychological measures with age. That is to say, the ongoing anatomical changes in the child's nervous system call into question neuropsychological conclusions based on adult subjects (Boll, 1981; Dean, 1982; Hartlage &. Reynolds, 1981). Moreover, the greater opportunity to validate adult brain–behavior relationships with subsequent surgery or autopsy in conjunction with the large number of neurological referrals during the post World War II era has led to greater sophistication in our neuropsychological knowledge of adults than what is available with children. The naive application of behavioral constellations associated with adult neurological disorders (e.g., encephalitis) to children with similar aberrant behavioral patterns (e.g., Strauss &. Lehtinen, 1948) may well be responsible for the premature rejection of neuropsychological understanding of children's cognitive functioning (e.g., Dean, 1983).

Although specific behavioral patterns have continuous support as reliable predictors of adult cortical impairment, the evidence that these same behaviors reflect on underlying cerebral dysfunction in children is less than convincing (Dean, 1982; Satz &. Fletcher, 1981). For example, some forms of children's problems in learning are related to neurological dysfunction (Hartlage &. Hartlage, 1977). This conclusion is as obvious as the fact that many childhood learning problems may more heuristically be related to an interaction of environment and individual differences in development (see Dean, 1982). Neurologically then, children are not merely small adults. Only with an understanding of neurodevelopment comes an appreciation for the complexity of childhood brain–behavior relationships. The remainder of this chapter examines aspects of neuroanatomical and related development in function that would seem to be the taproot of individual differences in child neuropsychology.

NEUROLOGICAL DEVELOPMENT

GENERAL CONSIDERATIONS

The structural antecedents of the human nervous system are evident within the first month following conception (Minkowski, 1967). Although the embryo is less than 5 cm in length (rump to crown), the embryonic neural plate that gives rise to all future divisions of the adult nervous system may be seen. Following this meager beginning, development of the nervous system proceeds at a phenomenal rate. During some 40 weeks of gestation, the fetal brain grows to an average of 350 g. This rate of growth continues postnatally with the infant's brain weight increasing by a factor of two during the first year of life, representing approximately 70% the size of a normal adult brain (1,500 mg—male brain) (Himwich, 1970). The remaining gain in brain weight is accomplished over the next 10 to 12 years. Following the first year of life, the maturation of functional capacities is far more remarkable than changes in structure or size of the brain (Folch, 1955).

The enlargement of the postnatal brain is more the function of continued nerve cell development than an increase in the number of cells (Davison, Dobbing, Morgan, & Wright, 1959). In fact, the complement of neurons in the cerebral cortex has been shown to be near complete prior to birth (Folch, 1955; Schulte, 1969). While multiplication and migration of cells (glial, cerebellar granule cells) continue during infancy and childhood, as important in the growth of postnatal brain is the myelination of axons and arborization of dendrites (Schulte, 1969). Myelination involves the growth of a fatty sheath around the axons which may be seen to facilitate synaptic activity (Davison *et al.*, 1959; Flechsig, 1901; Peiper, 1963; Schulte, 1969). The increase in the thickness of the myelin sheath seems to be a necessary condition for the development of complex behavior and early intellectual functions. Myelination may be viewed as a measure of the maturity of the individual cell and the ability to transmit messages efficiently (Himwich, 1970). At birth, axons resemble long, thin strands capable of the transmission of impulses at a slow rate compared with the efficiency after myelination. Although the rate of myelination slows with age, the process has been followed into the fifth and sixth decade of life (Folch, 1955; Schulte, 1969). The slow, awkward responses of the infant may in part be attributed to the lack of myelination in higher order control areas (Dodge, 1964).

The patterns of myelin development of the nervous system are rather uneven; but, they follow a consistent course across individuals (Minkowski, 1967). Primary projection areas (rather large pathways of neurons) such as those required in vision, audition, as well as the thalamocortical pathway and the corticospinal tract are myelinated soon after birth (e.g., Peiper, 1963). However, axonal myelination of pathways between association areas of the cerebral cortex follows a much slower course that corresponds to the development of functional behavior in the child (Dodge, 1964). Thus, whereas the complement of the cerebral cortex seems near complete before birth, the lack of myelination reduces the functional efficiency of these cells. From this point of view, deviations from normal myelination may be reflected in behavior reminiscent of primitive subcortical functions. The process of myelination in general is a necessary but not a sufficient condition for the functional development of the brain. Dendritic arborization, or the formation of axodendritic synapsis, is often viewed as important as myelination in the early development of the nervous system (Sperry, 1968). The growth of neuronal dendrities involves the formation of efficient axodendritic synapses that form the basis of impulse transmission between neurons (Gazzaniga, 1975). This process is complete in the spinal cord and some subcortical structures in the full-term newborn, but continues at a high rate in early postnatal development for the upper subcortical and cortical structures (Sarsikov, 1964). During these periods of rapid perinatal growth, the brain is particularly susceptible to injury by a variety of toxic and metabolic substances.

The anatomical and functional development of the brain proceeds in an orderly and predictable fashion (Gazzaniga, 1975; Sperry, 1968). Although it is necessary to rely in part on research with lower forms of life, the movement from undifferentiated to specialized seems to be an invariant trend in both cortical and subcortical human development. The formation of higher order abilities (e.g., language, thought, etc.) in children is determined by the degree of maturation in the cerebral cortex which in turn is dependent on lower levels of the nervous system during development (Luria, 1973). While development favors increased localization of functions, the interdependence of all components of the nervous system cannot be minimized (Gazzaniga, 1975; Luria, 1973). Hence, in evaluating sophisticated aspects of neuropsychological functioning, subcortical aspects must be considered (Dean, 1983). Because components of the brain develop at contrasting rates and systems are interdependent, greater care needs to be taken not to attribute localized dysfunction from behavioral inadequacies established with adult subjects (e.g., Dean, in press, a).

From conception, the anatomical and functional development of the nervous system follows a sequence that has been argued to reflect the evolutionary past of the species (e.g., Green, 1958; MacLean, 1970; Penfield, 1958). Theoretically, the present configuration of the human brain evolved by the addition of increasingly complex structures which in turn allowed the species to function in the environment more effectively. With the addition of each component came increased capacity for reason and the potential for more sophisticated motor functions. Support for this notion comes both from the hierarchical organization of the human nervous system and sequential development of successively more complex adaptive mechanisms.

MacLean (1970) has portrayed these evolutionary changes in a subdivision of the human nervous system. In this scheme, MacLean characterized the upper spinal and areas of the midbrain, basal ganglia, and diencephalon as the "protoreptilian brain." The second evolutionary stage, or the "paleomammalian brain," includes components of the limbic system together with those of the protoreptilian brain. The propensity for analytic thought corresponding to upper cortical structures was distinguished as the neomammalian brain. This theoretical conception has neuroanatomical and neuropsychological support when the neurological development of the child is examined (Goldman, 1972). A good deal of evidence suggests nonfunctioning of the cerebral hemispheres of the brain of the neonate such as found with hydranencephalic and anencephalic infants cause few aberrations in the postnatal neurological examination (Dodge, 1964). Moreover, these gross abnormalities in structure are not exhibited behaviorally until later in development and congruent with the developmental sequence associated with neocortical functioning (Goldman, 1972). This phenomenon is also portrayed by Ford (1976) in a study that showed normal neurological evidence in newborns who later exhibited spastic cerebral palsies from defects present at birth.

The remainder of this section concerns the neuroanatomical and related neuropsychological developmental changes. The phases of development presented in Table 1 are offered more as an aid to the exposition than an indication of a qualitative change in the process. That is, the anatomical and functional maturation of the child's nervous system is viewed as a continuous refinement rather than discrete stages with invariant age correspondence.

PERINATAL—INFANT DEVELOPMENT

The differentiation of cells into the neural plate is evident during the third week after conception. Areas that mark the limits of developing structures can be observed on the surface of this plate (Minkowski, 1967). Cell division in the embryo is such that early hemispheric pairing may be observed by the end of the second month of gestation. Into the third month, the early beginnings of the hemispheres of the brain are clearly present, and the thalamus and cerebellar structures are distinguishable (Himwich, 1970).

The lateral ventricles of the brain are seen as separate structures by the beginning of the fourth gestational month. The major divisions of the cerebral and cerebellar hemispheres are recognized by the end of this fourth month of development. Unlike the valleys (sulci) and plateaus (gyri) of the adult brain, the surface of the embryonic nervous tissue is rather smooth. Into the fourth month of postconceptional development, fissurization begins. This is first observable with the early indications of what will become the sylvian fissure (which serves to separate the temporal lobe from the cerebrum). Fissurization in the posterior-lateral fissure of the cerebellum also becomes clearly demarcated during this period. Small fissures (sulci) that give the brain a convoluted appearance do not develop until the last trimester of gestation and are completed during the first two years of postnatal life (Sperry, 1968). This process of fissurization increases greatly the surface area of the cerebral cortex while allowing containment within a reasonable-sized skull vault.

TABLE 1

Neuropsychological Development Related to Gestational Age

Behavior	Age in weeks					
	24	28	32	34	36	40
Head turning to light	Absent	Absent	Present	Present	Present	Present
Pupil reaction	Absent	Absent	Present (29)	Present	Present	Present
Muscular tone	Absent	Absent	Poor	Fair under stimulation	Good	Good
Tone–recoil	Hypotonic	Hypotonic	Some recoil of legs	Good recoil of arms	Recoil	Recoil
Tone–head lag	Absent	Pendular head	Attempts to flex head	Less lag	Lag-sudden flex	Good tone with head righting
Posture	Limbs extended and rolls onto side	Limbs extended	Flexion of legs	Strong flexion of legs	Flexion of all limbs	Strong flexion of all limbs
Neck righting	Absent	Absent	Absent	Trunk follows	Rotation of head	Rotation of head
Ventral suspension	Floppy	Floppy	Poor flexion of legs	Fair arms and legs	Fair arms and legs	Good flexion of arms and legs
Waking–sleeping patterns	Absent	Absent	Periods awake	Periods awake	Periods of alertness	Patterns
Cry	Absent	Absent/weak	Good with hunger	Good with hunger	Good with hunger or disturbed	Good
Sucking reflex	Absent	Poor lacks endurance	Strong	Strong synchronized with swallowing	—	—
Moro reflex (startle)	Absent	Present-exhaustable	Present	Present	Present	Present
Grasp	Absent	Barely perceptible	Present	Present	Present	Present

Corresponding to MacLean's (1970) notions of the protoreptilian brain and the median brain (Yakovlev & Lecours, 1967), the structures of the basal ganglia, brain stem, and other subcortical motor nuclei develop at a faster rate than higher order areas (Yakovlev & Lecours, 1967). In fact, within the 12 months following conception, these areas are more nearly functionally matured than any other area of the brain (Gazzaniga, 1975). Overall, these structures are concerned with "large" behavioral patterning of overt responses of the entire body. These areas would seem to serve simple integration of functions and those necessary for life maintenance (Himwich, 1970). Early lesions of basal ganglia produce gross behavioral defects in posture, posture control, equilibrium, and locomotion (see Freeman & Brann, 1977). The brain stem reticular system and accompanying motor nuclei seem responsible for level of activation and gross movements of the head, eyes, and trunk (Freeman & Brann, 1977).

Specific functional capacities remain unclear in the fetus because of its inaccessibility. Prior to the age of viability (that point which life-support systems are developed to the extent that the fetus can function independently of the mother), much of our knowledge is based on anatomical research and localized for more mature organisms. The age of viability is usually considered to occur some 30 weeks after conception. Information concerning early functional development is gleaned from premature births in which gestational age may be followed (e.g., Watson & Lowrey, 1954). Therefore, information concerning functional capacities would seem to be lower bound. This is true because the effects of a premature birth on the child's development are not clear. Table 2 is offered as an overview of the development of neurologically related behaviors as a function of the premature child's age since conception.

Many of the early-appearing reflexes have little adaptive value for the infant, but rather provide evidence of the child's basic neurological development. The absence of these reflexes at an early age provides evidence of aberrations in normal neurological development (Dodge, 1964). Clearly, behavioral development reflects movement toward functional organization of subcortical structures and developing myelination of primary projection areas involved in vision, audition, and those in the thalamocortical area. For example, the visual pathway is developed to the extent that after one month of postnatal life (40 weeks gestational age), the normal infant is briefly able to follow an object. As mentioned previously, injury to the cerebral cortex may not be evident in behavior due to the general lack of integration of these areas in the early development (Penfield, 1958). Without unequivocal evidence of damage, a prognosis from the absence of the behavioral signs is a hazardous pursuit. Constellations of behavioral abnormalities (e.g., spasticity, hyperreflexia) at this point of development,

TABLE 2

Developmental Aspects by Chronological Age

Developmental aspect	Chronological age					
	0–18 mo	18 mo–4 yr	4 yr–7 yr	7 yr–12 yr	12 yr–15 yr	+ 15 yr
Piaget's stages of development	Sensory motor	Preoperational		Concrete operations	Formal operations	
		Preconceptual	Intuitive			
Gibson's reading	Orthographic—symbol discrimination				Cognitive phase—complex linguistic manipulation	
Related stages			Decoding phase—speech sound/visual stimuli			
General language	No symbols	Elementary symbolism	Symbolic intergration	Second signal system	Language without environment	
		Language as labels				
Cognitive thought	Egocentric thought	Cause and effect thought	Verbal mediation	(Logical thinking)		(Analytic)
				Simple concept formation		
	Mental combinations (stimulus-response)			Rigid rules		Abstract thought-deductive reason
	Walks alone					

Motor development milestones	Sits alone		Balance on 1 foot[10 Sec]	
	Follows object past midline	Kicks ball	Perceptual motor integration	
MacLean's evolutionary related maturation	Protoreptilian	Paleomammalian	Neomammalian	Cerebral cortex
Focus of Neurological development	Midbrain, paramedial zone	Limbic/cerebellar; (impulsive inhibition); fissurization complete; loss of primitive reflexes	Myelination of Tertiary Areas	Myelination of projection
	basal ganglia, diencephalon, motor nuclei, upper spinal		Terminal Zones	Association of hemispheres
			Functional lateralization	

although increasing the probability of neurological abnormality over a single sign, still remain inconclusive (Dodge, 1964; Freeman & Brann, 1977).

Neurological development during the perinatal period can be characterized as progression of areas of the brain involved with functions necessary for survival and arousal of the organism. Piaget (1952) had characterized development here as sensory-motor in nature. The emergence of cooing (prior to 3 postnatal months) and babbling (above 4 postnatal months) are seen as more motoric exercises than early emergence of language development (Molfese, Freeman, & Palermo, 1975). In fact, there is some neuropsychological and developmental evidence that only after some 48 months of postnatal life is the child neurologically able to move from the simple stimulus–response elements of language toward verbal thought (Vygotsky, 1962). Aspects of learning within this early stage of development amount to little more than simple response patterns and some early indications of discrimination learning (Sarsikov, 1964).

EARLY CHILDHOOD DEVELOPMENT

Aspects of development characterized by MacLean (1970) as paleo-mammalian and rudiments of the neomammalian brain are of primary interest during the early childhood years (12 to 50 postnatal months). During this phase of development, the undifferentiated impulsive behavior seen in the infant begins to be inhibited. This period is characterized by the increasing acquisition of skills requiring cerebellar and cortical control (see Table 1). The rather primitive reflexes (e.g., Moro, tonic neck responses; see Table 2) indicative of control at lower levels are repressed, with control moving to higher structures (Van der Vlugt, 1979; Yakovlev & Lecours, 1967). This fact is evident in the neurological examination of the child's reflexive responses. Here, the patient's level of neurological development is inferred by the presence of these reflexes in light of the chronological age since conception (Dodge, 1964; Freeman & Brann, 1977). The rapid pace of development in the early months of life dictate the use of age since conception rather than the time since birth as a measure of age. This fact is of considerable importance in evaluating the premature child's development. Therefore, a 3-month-old infant born at the 28th week of gestation should be more similar developmentally to an average full-term newborn than to a 3-month-old child.

As may be gathered from the foregoing, lesions to the paleomammalian structures may be observed behaviorally in a general lack of inhibition of more primitive responses indicative of lower levels (Peiper, 1963). Although some of these behaviors may continue to be elicited during infancy, most are not present during early childhood. These behaviors hold significance as developmental markers both from their time of appearance and the degree to which they are repressed during early childhood. The neurological development of the infant is characterized by the loss of reflexes (e.g., Moro and tonic neck response) and the disappearance of flexor tone (Dodge, 1964; Prechtl, 1965). The lack of these behaviors in early childhood is seen as movement of functional organization from the diencephalon or midbrain level to those skills that are more indicative of cerebellar and lower cortical control.

The paramedian zone or, if you will, the paleomammalian brain, is the developmental focus in the full-term infant. This, a most active developmental period, involves myelination and cell migration (Robinson, 1969). In tandem with development of the paramedian zone, maturation of cortical structures increases (Prechtl, 1965), although functional expression and general level of maturity of these areas lag behind lower structures (Schulte, 1969).

In what may be seen as the first move toward self-awareness, control begins to move to the limbic zone (Isaacson, 1974). Still visceral components, structures involved here compose what is termed in the adult brain as the limbic system. With direct projections to the hypothalamus, these areas are often seen to suppress more primitive behavioral sequences. In general, the development of the limbic system "opens" the way for the learning of new temporary associations. This conclusion is evident in children who have experienced a lesion in this area (Pribram & Isaacson, 1975). It seems with a lack of appropriate functioning in this area, the limbic system may serve to intensify behavioral patterns arising at a more primitive level.

At central position in the limbic system, the hippocampus is involved in the integration of information from the septal areas and external information from sensory systems. Thus, the structure serves to filter continuous sensory input of the auditory and tactile/kinesthetic systems. In this way, the overall level of attention, concentration, and arousal is involved (Pribram & Isaacson, 1975). In lower forms of life with lesions inflicted to the hippocampal formations, rather hyperactive behaviors are displayed (Kimble, 1968). Although concluding there is correspondence between hyperactive behaviors in children and developmental aberrations in this area is tempting, such behavioral excesses are not observed in adults with lesions to the hippocampus (see Douglas, 1975). Specific stimulation of the hippocampus, which is central in the limbic system, has been reported to cause a suppression in ongoing behaviors (see Isaacson, 1974; Kimble, 1968).

Research that has involved the behavioral effects of lesions to the hippocampus suggests its importance in learning. Bilateral lesions to this structure are seen behaviorally in gross impairments in new learning to all but simple stimulus responses (Ford, 1960). Although unilateral lesions to the hippocampus produce few lasting effects in adults, a rather catastrophic effect on subsequent adult behavior control is observed when the lesion occurs prior to maturation of the limbic system (see Isaacson, 1974). Pate and Bell (1971), using a spontaneous alternation paradigm, present some inferential evidence that elements of these structures reach a developmental plateau after some 48 months of postnatal life. Jones (1970) argues in favor of the development of response flexibility and the reduction of perseveration associated with development in the hippocampal area. Thus, the role of this structure in learning may well relate to attentional control and at best retrieval of functions.

The precursors of higher level cognitive functions associated with the neomammalian brain may be seen to develop during the early years of childhood (Peiper, 1963; Robinson, 1969). Geschwind (1968) points out that primordial zones of the neomammalian brain, which begin to mature during this time in development, have the more efferent and afferent connections with subcortical structures. He portrays rather succinctly the gradual invariant evolution of cortical control from lower, more primitive areas to those responsible for higher order cognitive functions that characterize human behavior. Thus, as would be expected, myelination of "terminal zones" (e.g., left angular gyrus) and corticocortical (within cerebral cortex) connections occur at a slower rate than myelination of subcortical and subcorticocortical areas mentioned above (Schulte, 1969). It would appear that corticocortical pathways that serve in the mediation of complex language and thought processes are not functionally efficient during early years of childhood. It should be mentioned that myelination of axonal pathways between some association areas of the cerebral cortex continues for some five to six decades of life. Development of asymmetrical localization of functions within cerebral hemispheres will be examined at length later in this chapter; but, it suffices to say although postnatal specialization exists, functions in early childhood are rather diffusely represented within hemispheres (Peiper, 1963).

The fine-grained analysis of the external environment seen in later years is not present during early childhood. Neurologically, this seems true because control of functions is served by lower neurological regions (Robinson, 1969). However, this conclusion is not meant to discount the role of subcortical function in the total behavior of the mature organism. One needs to appreciate that higher level functioning is determined by the maturity of both the cerebral cortex and subcortical formations (Sarsikov, 1964). This view stresses the critical importance of subcortical development as a prerequisite to more refined functions of the neocortex.

Although obvious within the present context perhaps, clinical applications of neuropsychology are often given to focus on cerebral functions in isolation and fail to appreciate the interdependence on more caudal structures (Luria, 1973).

Increasing development of neocortical structures and successively more refined adaptive mechanisms in early childhood are integrated in a rather complex fashion later in development (Hartlage & Telzrow, 1983). This process is exhibited in the child's development of fine-grained movement of the extremities corresponding to increasing control over subcortical brain stem regions (Isaacson, 1974). Thus, as motor control passes from more caudal areas of the brain, the child reaches for objects first with the entire hand and then with increasing pincer movements of the fingers and thumb. Haaxma and Kuypers (1975) offer evidence that with damage to primary motor areas of the neocortex, the development of the fine-grained movements is lost, resulting in motor behavior that is indicative of subcortical control. Integration of these motor functions also is displayed with the child's crossing of midline to transfer objects from hand to hand, sitting, standing, and beginning to walk. Such skills also depend to increasing degrees on the relatively early myelination that has occurred in the primary projection areas (e.g., vision, auditory), the corticospinal tract, and thalamocortical sensory pathways. However, skills that require the integration of functioning areas are still lacking and continue to develop through late adolescence (Robinson, 1969). As one would gather, learning at this state is more efficacious when sensory integration or cross modality responses to stimuli are minimized (Dean & Rothlisberg, 1983). This observation would seem to hold for the motor control necessary for speech development. Although some 24 months of postnatal development are required for rudimentary speech, the integration with other higher order areas is necessary for human speech. In sum, the neurological development during early childhood corresponds quite closely to Piaget's (1952) notion of a preoperational stage of behavioral development and Bruner's (1968) conception of the enactive representational base.

LATER CHILDHOOD—ADOLESCENT DEVELOPMENT

Later childhood is marked more by functional development in the brain than observable structural changes (Robinson, 1966). In fact, by gross anatomical, biochemical, and physiological measurements, the human brain has reached adult parameters after but some 15 years of life (e.g., Freeman & Brann, 1977). The commissural (connective pathways between hemispheres) and associative systems (outermost or supralimbic cerebral cortex) have the longest maturational cycle (Sperry, 1968). Sperry's (1968, 1969) evidence suggests that a relatively slow maturation of these areas may well be responsible for the selective consolidation of functions by the hemispheres of the brain and the late onset of symbolic thought. Hence, maturation of these formations, which continues beyond the first two decades of life, may be responsible in part for the progressive asymmetrical lateralization of visual perception, thought, and language. This slow consolidation may vary in relation to the myelination of the corpus callosum (bundle of transverse nerve cells that connect the hemispheres), projectional, and association axons of the cerebral hemispheres. Thus, the commitment to the consistently reported left hemispheric specialization for language may be viewed in a progression congruent with development in these secondary areas.

Some 5 to 7 years of life mark a shift in processing that has been clearly documented in the developmental psychology literature. Referred to by various terms, this shift represents a neuropsychological potential for concrete thought (Bruner, 1968; Ingram, 1970; Piaget, 1952; White, 1965). Vygotsky (1962) portrays this period as that point in which speech and hence language become distinct from early motor dependence and may become integrated into verbal thought. Moreover, the child gains facility with the use of language as a tool in learning and understanding the environment. This shift may well relate to maturation of tertiary areas of sensory integration and terminal zones (parietal lobe) in conjunction with continuing myelination of corticocortical connections (Geschwind, 1968). In normal children, neuropsychological evidence suggests this shift corresponds to increased visual-spatial, symbolic integration (Ingram, 1970; Peiper, 1963). This conclusion seems related to Van der Vlugt's (1979) findings of a sharp decrease in perceptual rotation and position reversals of letters between the ages of 6 and 8 years. These changes were attributed to both brain development associated with visual-verbal integration and natural language mediation that is present during this period.

Gibson (1968) has outlined cognitive stages in reading development that coincide closely with the evolving maturation of the child's brain. The first cognitive stage necessary in the early reading process is seen to involve the child's ability to discriminate orthographic symbols. This skill would seem to develop in the early childhood phase of neurological maturation, but not until the age of 5 to 8 years would this ability be firmly established (e.g., Vygotsky, 1962). The second stage, according to Gibson, concerns the decoding process in which visual stimuli are transformed to their speech–sound component. This process requires increased maturation of the associative areas of the cerebral cortex. The utilization of complex, linguistic units that approach the adult reading process characterizes Gibson's third cognitive phase of the reading process. The maturation of prefrontal lobes of the brain and intercortical connections that are functional in a period of from 12–15 years (see Doty & Overman, 1977; Peiper, 1963) would seem to facilitate this process. The functional progression associated with this final cognitive stage translates behaviorally to what Piaget (1952) has portrayed as formal operations and is characterized by cognitive-abstract thought. As Piaget points out and what is clear from the research in this area, both the maturation of the brain and the quality of environmental stimulation are important to the development of such cognitive skills (see Sparrow & Satz, 1970).

Development of sophisticated verbal abilities also seems tied to the increased lateralization of cognitive functions within the hemispheres of the brain (e.g., Satz & Van Nostrand, 1973). The rather diffuse representation of language and spatial perceptual abilities that are indicative of early development gives way in childhood to increasing lateralization of functions. The extensive degree to which functions are lateralized in the human brain lacks correspondence in other species (Sperry, 1968). With the renewed experimental vigor of the past two decades concerning hemispheric specialization of function and its importance in the development of normal higher order processing, it may be of interest to examine the evolution and research concerning hemispheric lateralization.

DEVELOPMENT OF HEMISPHERIC LATERALIZATION OF FUNCTIONS

The large oval mass of the brain is clearly divided by a longitudinal fissure into two distinct structures. From a gross anatomical examination, these hemispheres appear similar in their patterns of convolutions. Nevertheless, anatomical and neurophysiological differences have been shown to exist as early as the 30th week of gestation (Chi, Dooling, & Gilles, 1977; Molfese et al., 1975; Wada, Clarke, & Hamm, 1975; Witelson & Pallie, 1973). Structures of the left hemisphere, most often seen as responsible for speech (left temporal planum), are significantly, although less than obviously, larger than those same structures found in the right hemisphere prior to birth (Geschwind & Levitsky, 1968). Although less observable, Yakovlev & Rakic (1966) provide evidence favoring a developmental, structural difference between hemispheres in the rate that the pyramidal tract develops projections ("connecting fibers"). Generally, Yakovlev and Rakic have shown projections, which emanate from the left hemisphere, cross significantly earlier in development than those of the right hemisphere. Reports such as these provide evidence favoring early physical differences between hemispheres that may represent the genesis of the functional hemispheric differences of the human brain (see Geschwind, 1974). The force of these data cause one to seriously question early notions that portrayed cerebral hemispheres as having an equal potential for developing hemispheric dominance (see Satz & Fletcher, 1981). Although hemispheric asymmetries are observable in the neonate, complex patterns of dominance have been shown to develop progressively throughout childhood (Satz, Bakker, Tenuissen, Goebel, & Van der Vlugt, 1975).

The notion of dominance of one hemisphere originally was conceptualized as localization of language functions (e.g., Jackson, 1874) and only recently has taken on the more global connotation associated with control functions. Summarizing his clinical observations of brain-injured patients, Jackson (1874), late in the nineteenth century, argued in favor of the existence of two different, yet coexisting, modes of cognitive processing that followed hemispheric lines of the brain. These conclusions were consistent with Broca's (1865/1960) observations that control of many aspects of speech and language were localized in the left cerebral cortex (third left frontal convolution). Although microstructural localization of cognitive functions has been rejected by most neuroscientists in favor of more broad organizational portrayals (Dean, in press, a), notions of hemispheric specialization have gained scientific respectability during the last 30 years. Acknowledging consistent hemispheric differences, neuropsychologists continue to debate whether processing (e.g., Geschwind & Levitsky, 1968), attention (e.g., Kinsbourne, 1975), or storage (e.g., Hardyck, Tzeng, Wang, 1978) are responsible for the functional differences found in cerebral hemispheres.

Whereas most investigators have inferred specific hemispheric processing differences to exist, the evidence of Hardyck et al., (1978) concerning lateralized memory storage and Kinsbourne's (1970) data regarding the lateralization of attention between hemispheres need to be seriously considered when making conclusions concerning the underlying neurological process. With this caveat in mind, laboratory and clinical research involving split-brain patients (surgical section of the corpus callosum which links hemispheres) (Bogen, 1969; Sperry, Gazzaniga, & Bogen, 1969) and investigations using perceptual asymmetry tasks (measure of hemispheric efficiency in verbal, nonverbal, etc., tasks) (e.g., Dean & Hua, 1982; Kimura, 1966) indicate that although interhemispheric communication exists, each cerebral hemisphere selectively serves rather distinct cognitive functions. Generally, studies with right-handed subjects lead one to conclude that the left cerebral hemisphere is more adept at complex, linguistic functions than that of the right which is more closely linked to a representation of nonverbal reality (see Dean, 1982; Sperry,

1968). Research that has examined the electrical activity of the brain (electroencephalographic research) reinforces a bimodal notion of cerebral processing,. The majority of studies show less activity (alpha and beta waves greater than 13 Hz) is present in the postcentral area of the right hemisphere when processing linguistic information and on the left in the presence of visual-spatial processing (see Dean, 1983). In concert with the work of Sperry *et al.*, (1969), it generally has been concluded that the left hemisphere is superior to the right in tasks involving speech, language, and calculation. As important, information seems more efficiently processed by the left hemisphere in an analytical, logical, sequential, or temporal fashion. In contrast, the right hemisphere most often is portrayed as relatively more adept at the simultaneous processing of nonverbal gestalts, visual-spatial transformations, and the comprehension of complex visual patterns. Typically, the differences in behavior attributable to hemispheric functioning appear to be less related to the specific stimuli or modality of representation than the mode in which information is processed (Brown & Hécaen, 1976).

The extent to which functions are progressively lateralized within hemispheres is still much disputed (e.g., Kinsbourne & Hiscock, 1977; Reynolds, 1978; Satz, 1976). However, neurological and psychological development of the child both seem to favor progressive differentiation in growth and organization (Bruner, 1974; Gardner, 1968; Kendler & Kendler, 1962; Piaget, 1952). Therefore, by analogy, a hypothesis favoring progressive asymmetrical lateralization of functions would seem to hold considerable appeal. However, arguments of early and specific specialization continue to deserve consideration (Kinsbourne, 1975).

The hypothesis of the equal potential of cerebral hemispheres at birth, succinctly articulated by Lenneberg (1967), has gained little support from the robust evidence of early specialization of hemispheres (Molfese *et al.*, 1975; Wada *et al.*, 1975). The rejection of equipotentiality does not, however, discount the possibility that lateralization of functions follows a progressively more refined, more firmly consolidated pattern congruent with the child's neurological development (Bryden & Allard, 1978; Dean, in press, c; Satz *et al.*, 1975). Here, it would seem that language may become more firmly lateralized to the left hemisphere with the continuing maturation of the secondary associative areas of the brain (Peiper, 1963). Therefore, progressive facility in the use of language as a tool may well have neurological underpinnings in the maturation of structures necessary for the lateralization of functions (Sperry, 1968). A considerable data base also exists to suggest that the rate of lateralization varies with the specific function under study (Dean & Hua, 1982; Ramsay, 1979; Satz *et al.*, 1975; Waber, 1977).

The degree of plasticity (function taken over by one hemisphere with the damage of the other) in the development of cerebral hemispheres recently has come under dispute (see Satz & Fletcher, 1981). However, a number of reports suggest that damage to the left hemisphere before adolescence is less severe and language effects more transient than similar lesions in adults (Chelune & Edwards, 1981; Dax, 1865). Although alternative explanations exist (Chelune & Edwards, 1981; Isaacson, 1975; Fletcher & Satz, 1983), numerous researchers have proposed what amounts to a "critical period" (5 to 7 years of life) in which functions normally relegated to the left hemisphere may be subsumed by the right cortex following early damage to the language areas (e.g., Dikman, Matthews, & Harley, 1975; Pirozzolo, Campanella, Christensen, & Lawson-Kerr, 1981). This conclusion is consistent with Sperry's (1968) data suggesting that the role of the right hemisphere in language decreases with the child's neurological development. Interestingly, the degree of "transfer of functions" has been portrayed to vary with the severity of the damage (Chelune & Edwards, 1981; Golden, 1981; Pirozzolo et al., 1981). This point of view relies on data of patients who have undergone the removal of the entire left hemisphere. Removal before this critical period is portrayed as less devastating in terms of later language skills than that seen when less extensive damage to the left hemisphere has occurred (see Pirozzolo et al., 1981). This observation is hypothesized to occur because with the removal of the left hemisphere, "competition for language" functions does not exist to the extent as would be the case in damage that was less obvious (Dennis & Kohn, 1975; Smith & Sugar, 1975).

The failure to establish asymmetrical lateralization of functions within the cerebral hemispheres of the brain has long been argued to be an etiological factor in the development of children's language disorders (e.g., Orton, 1937). Although the theoretical underpinnings of this notion have shown considerable evolution during the recent past, most authors hypothesize interference or confusion for linguistic skills consistent with the more diffuse lateralization of language hemispheres of the child's brain (Geschwind, 1968; Semmes, 1968). The theories concerning the cause of this lack of normal lateralization in the developing child have involved genetic components (Levy & Reid, 1976), developmental aberrations (Satz et al., 1975), early insult (Geschwind, 1974), and interactions of these factors.

Orton's (1937) early notions of dyslexia were based on observations of a higher incidence of mixed hand and hand/eye preference for chidren with reading disorders. Because hand preference, like other purposeful motoric activities, is served by the contralateral hemisphere of the brain, confusion at this behavioral level often has been hypothesized to reflect the lack of complete lateralization of functions at the cortical level (Annett, 1970; Orton, 1937; Zangwill, 1962). Consistent with early observations, Zangwill (1960) reported data suggesting that as high as 88% of congenital dyslexics present with some form of mixed-hand tendency.

After five decades since Orton's (1937) original hypothesis, it has become obvious that the relationship between measures of laterality based on simple hand preference and linguistic performance is slight at best (see Beaumont & Rugg, 1978; Dean, 1982; Satz, 1976). This conclusion should not be surprising when the environmental and social variables that shape hand preference are examined. Specifically, early hypotheses that held simple handedness as a nominal measure of cerebral lateralization (right, left, mixed) appear naive in light of our present knowledge. Moreover, lateral preference seems better understood as an individual difference variable and therefore more heuristically represented in a continuous fashion (Dean, 1978; Whitaker & Ojemann, 1977). In fact, Dean (1978) and Dean, Schwartz, and Smith (1981) present data favoring the conceptualization of motoric lateralization as a factorial complex variable, best represented on a continuum from entirely right to entirely left preference. Clearly, although language is served by the left cerebral cortex and the right side of the body is most often preferred for motor tasks, both are complex systems that may be lateralized to varying degrees (Dean & Hua, 1982). Dean (1982) has hypothesized that inconsistencies in reports, which have examined lateral preference for patients with various disorders, may well relate to methodologies that have summed across motoric activities with little more than intuitive support. Dean argues that although simple hand preference is demonstrated early in neonatal life (Caplan & Kinsbourne, 1976; Petrie & Peters, 1980), the specific task selected to demonstrate this preference is of considerable importance (Dean, 1982).

Recently, using a multifactor measure of lateral preference, Dean (in press, c) offered evidence favoring the development of more consistent preference (hand, eye, etc.) in young children as a function of age and varying with sex. Interestingly, age differences varied also as a function of the specific preference factor (i.e., visually guided motor). Therefore, while children did not differ in simple hand preference, when tasks required visual guidance in their performance, 10-year-old children showed more consistent patterns of performance than that exhibited in 8-year-olds.

Beaumont and Rugg (1978) have offered an interesting hypothesis that bears directly on the notion of confused hemispheric dominance and children's learning disorders. Representing a refinement of earlier theoretical formulations (e.g., Geschwind, 1974; Pizzamiglio, 1976), Beaumont and Rugg proposed a functional disassociation in language lateralization of visual and auditory cerebral systems for many childhood language disorders. The assumption here is that the problems in language utilization correspond to a failure to integrate visual-verbal systems due to atypical lateralization of these functions, despite normal auditory–verbal functional integration. Findings for auditory-verbal (dichotic listening) (Hynd, Obrzut, Weed, & Hynd, 1979) and visual-verbal measures of lateralization (visual half-field techniques) (Kershner, 1977) with linguistically disabled children are in line with what one would predict if these children were normally lateralized for auditory-verbal functions and relatively confused for visual–verbal functions (Dean & Rothlisberg, 1983).

Although debate in this area will continue, it seems that the functions consistently seen as served by hemispheres of the brain are more clearly evidenced in right-handed individuals. Apparently, a more complex state of affairs exists for left-handed subjects. Zangwill (1960) offers data favoring left-hemispheric dominance for speech in approximately 95% of normal right-handed and 70% of left-handed adults. Therefore, for 30% of left-handers, a rather confused picture of linguistic dominance exists, with these individuals displaying either right-hemispheric or bilateral (both hemispheres) organization of speech. Clinically then, there may be good reason to assume left-hemispheric speech functions for the right-handed individual. Whereas such an inference is more tenuous for the individual displaying a left or mixed premorbid hand preference, fewer errors in prediction would be made if all the individuals were assumed to be left-hemispheric dominant for language. Differences between left-handers in language lateralization may relate to the etiology of left-hand preference. That is to say, for the majority of individuals, left-hand preference arises out of genetic factors (Hicks & Kinsbourne, 1976; Levy & Nagylaki, 1972). Satz (1972, 1973), however, argues convincingly in favor of a pathological form of left-handedness which may be more heuristically related to early damage or developmental anomaly in the left side of the brain.

LOCALIZATION OF CEREBRAL FUNCTIONS IN ADULTHOOD

The success over the past century in defining the behavioral effects of brain damage has allowed some appreciation for the functional correspondence of macroanatomical areas of the brain (Dean, 1983). It is the intent of the following section to provide a brief summary of the neuropsychological correspondence to major subdivisions of the adult cerebral cortex. This overview is offered more as a portrayal of the end point of the maturational process than a description of the developmental trends. Although some structural divisions of the brain are somewhat arbitrary, an appreciation of the individual differences in neuropsychological functioning depends on a sensitivity to such neuroanatomical relationships.

FRONTAL REGION

Because the frontal region occupies the major portion of the cortex, it had been assumed to be primarily concerned with higher level intellectual functioning unique to humans (e.g, Morgan, 1943). However, numerous surgical sections of the frontal lobe have failed to produce obvious intellectual impairments, *per se* (Hebb, 1949). More timely reports lead to the conclusion that the majority of the anterior regions of the frontal lobe (anterior prefrontal area) seem to be involved in functions more closely concerned with selective perception and sustained attention. Damasio's (1979) recent findings suggest that this formation in the frontal lobe is important in inhibiting impulsive motor responses. Damage restricted to this region in adults most often results in a considerable change in affective functioning that varies in severity with the nature and extent of the lesion (Valenstein, 1973). Generally, problems in making cognitive shifts in attention, which are expressed behaviorally in rigid cognitive styles or perseveration in applying strategies, have been linked with frontal lobe dysfunction (Ochs, 1965).

Involved in the integration of sensory information from other regions of the brain, the motor strip, which may be seen on the posterior portion of the frontal lobe, is responsible for coordination of muscle movements. Organization is such that the motor strip on one side of the frontal region serves functions of the contralateral side of the body. Early on, Penfield and Boldrey (1937) showed that the premotor areas (just anterior to the motor strip) coordinated intentional movements of the body and damage produced impairment of various motor skills.

PARIETAL REGION

The parietal lobe seems most clearly concerned with body sensations—kinesthetic and tactile perceptions (Ochs, 1965). Lesions in this area most frequently result in difficulty in identifying objects by touch or lack of tactile perception to one or both sides of the body. However, dysfunction here rarely occurs without some degree of language disturbance (Penfield, 1958). The left parietal lobe has been shown to mediate elements of verbal memory, calculation, and construction. This region of the left hemisphere is also involved to various degrees in the functions necessary for normal reading, writing, and other skills requiring the integration of stimuli (Penfield & Roberts, 1959). Examining localized right hemispheric lesions, Reitan (1964) showed damage in the parietal area to be expressed clinically in difficulties in constructing puzzles, copying designs, and complex visual-spatial manipulations. In this same report, Reitan offered evidence that problems in full appreciation for the steps needed to construct a block pattern or puzzle were more likely to be expected in left parietal damage than those of the right side.

OCCIPITAL REGION

The occipital lobe is located at the posterior pole of each hemisphere. The primary visual region of the cerebral cortex, this area is responsible for perception and to a lesser extent the comprehension of visual stimuli. Damage in the occipital region produces disturbances that may range from visual field blindness (no visual perception in the left or right line of sight) to disability in the association of visually presented stimuli with corresponding verbal or nonverbal knowledge (visual agnosia) (Luria, 1965). These more anterior visual associations of the occipital lobe seem less involved in visual perception than they are in the recognition of elements as familiar or naming them.

TEMPORAL REGION

The temporal lobe forms a flap that extends over portions of the frontal and parietal lobes. This structure is primarily involved in audition. Cortical damage to the right temporal lobe is more likely than not to be expressed behaviorally in problems with comprehension and recognition of nonverbal sounds (Milner, 1962). Although varying with premorbid language lateralization, patients rarely suffer language disorders following right temporal damage, but rather they apparently find it difficult to fully appreciate the subtleties of music or rhythmic patterns (Shankweiler, 1966) and often present problems in the integration of incomplete auditory presentations (Lansdell, 1970).

Milner (1962) offers rather convincing data that the functions of the left temporal lobe are closely tied to language comprehension and production. Damage here most often results in dysfunctions in verbal memory, comprehension, or the manipulation of abstract concepts depending on the implicated area (Luria, 1965). Penfield and Roberts (1959) have shown lesions near the temporal occipital juncture produce a devasting effect on the individual's ability to read which varies with the individual and the extent and localization of the damage.

As mentioned earlier in discussing the development of the hippocampus, the temporal area of the brain seems to be involved in triggering complex memories. A substantial amount of research has shown that ablation of the hippocampus affects the ability to consolidate memories or transfer them to long-term storage. Moreover, the bilateral sectioning of the hippocampus most often results in the inability to learn other than elementary motor functions (Barbizet, 1963). Because of its proximity to the hippocampus, the temporal area of the cortex appears closely involved in this process. Thus, this area is involved in an intricate interplay between the cerebral cortex and subcortical structures of the brain.

NEUROPSYCHOLOGICAL SEX DIFFERENCES

The inaccessibility of the healthy brain is undoubtedly the most predominant difficulty in the study of individual neuropsychological differences. This conclusion is unmistakable in the area of neurological sex differences. Obvious genetic, morphological, and hormonal differences exist between males and females from conception. However, functional neurological differences have been more difficult to document. This state of affairs has prompted neuroscientists to rely on the study of lower life forms and naturally occurring neuropathologies in the investigation of functional and structural neurological sex differences. Radiological investigations and those based on autopsies reveal few, obvious structural differences in the central nervous system of males and females (see MacLusky & Naftolin, 1981). Moreover, consistent neuropsychological sex differences are more heuristically attributed to functional neuro-organizational differences than those of gross anatomy (Kolata, 1979; MacLusky & Naftolin, 1981).

Sex hormones clearly have striking effects on the structure and functioning of the developing organism (Bardin & Catterall, 1981; McGill, Anselmo, Buchanan, & Sheridan, 1980). Because these rather potent chemicals are free to cross the blood–brain barrier to the nervous system early in gestation, these hormones have been seen as having dramatic effects on the function and development of the nervous system.

Evidence favoring such a conclusion emanates primarily from the study of lower animals. Research with androgens has shown this sex hormone to affect both the structure and functions of the hypothalamus (MacLusky & Naftolin, 1981) and preoptic, septal areas (Schmeck, 1980), to a lesser extent various structures of the limbic formation (Baum, 1979), and areas of the neocortex (Weintraub, 1981). Importantly, many of these organizational effects on the nervous system occur before birth when rates of development heighten sensitivity to such hormones. Additionally, androgens are so structured as to enable rapid access to the nervous system and therefore may produce rapid changes in the functional characteristics of the nervous system. Goy and McEwen (1980) suggest androgens may be manifestly related to the proclivity to rely upon specific cues (e.g., verbal) in learning and some evidence of slower rates of acquisition.

The extent to which genetic-hormonal sex differences are related to the consistently reported verbal superiority for females and spatial ability in males (see Maccoby, 1966) remains unclear. However, Witelson (1976) reports earlier right-hemispheric specialization for spatial processing in males than with females, who exhibit more bilateral representation until early adolescence (> 13 years). Women also generally show less consistent evidence of hemispheric specialization for language than that reported for males (e.g., Levy, 1973). Although such differences have been argued to relate to the increased developmental rates for females (Waber, 1976), as convincing are differences in functional organization that may be attributed to genetic-hormonal differences (MacLusky & Naftolin, 1981).

Whatever the etiology of this more secure lateralization of verbal and nonverbal functions in males, it does not come without a price. Apparently, the price seems to be exacted in terms of the risk of malfunction of language abilities (Nottebohm, 1979). Benton (1975) reports a ten times greater risk for developmental language disorders in boys than girls. Specific disorders involving expressive and receptive language elements hold a marked increase risk for males when compared with female cohorts (Brain, 1965; Dean, 1983).

Interestingly and without clear explanation, although females show less secure hemispheric lateralization for verbal and nonverbal processing, they also exhibit *more* consistent patterns of lateral preference (handedness, eyedness, etc.) than do males (Annett, 1970; Dean, in press, c; Levy, 1973). Conclusions that attempt to reconcile such differences in neuropsychological functions will remain speculative until the research base in this area is expanded.

CONCLUSIONS

The intent of this chapter was to provide an overview of the neuroanatomical and neuropsychological developmental changes that may hold implications in the study of individual differences. Clearly, although our knowledge of the structure and function of the adult brain is far from complete, our understanding of developmental aspects is far more primitive. Neuroanatomical and related development of function are seen as crucial in the understanding of individual differences in childhood neuropsychology. Development of the brain occurs in an orderly invariant process that can best be understood from an evolutionary point of view. While the gross anatomical features of the nervous system are established prior to 16 years of life, functional differentiation continues for a number of decades. The establishment of asymmetrical lateralization of function within cerebral hemispheres of the brain is a recent event in the evolutionary development of the species which holds implications for individual differences in neuropsychological functioning. Investigating the etiological bases of disorders related to the organization of higher order cortical functions may facilitate further understanding of individual neuropsychological differences. In light of the primitive state of our knowledge in this area, the most compassionate activity would seem to be continued research.

REFERENCES

Annett, M. Handedness, cerebral dominance and the growth of intelligence. In D. J. Bakker & P. Satz (Eds.), *Specific reading disability*. Rotterdam: Rotterdam University Press, 1970.

Barbizet, J. Defect of memorizing of hippocampal-mammillary origin: A review. *Journal of Neurology, Neurosurgery, and Psychiatry*, 1963, 26, 127–135.

Bardin, C. W., & Catterall, J. F. Testosterone: A major determinant of extragenital sexual dimorphism. *Science*, 1981, 211, 1285–1294.

Baum, M. J. Differentiation of coital behavior in mammals: A comparative analysis. *Neuroscience and Biobehavioral Reviews*, 1979, 3, 265–284.

Beaumont, J. G., & Rugg, M. D. Neuropsychological laterality of function and dyslexia: A new hypothesis. *Dyslexia Review*, 1978, 1, 18–21.

Benton, A. L. Development dyslexia: Neurological aspects. In W. J. Freidlander (Ed.), *Advances in neurology*. Vol. 7. New York: Raven Press, 1975.

Bogen, J. E. The other side of the brain III: The corpus callosum and creativity. *Bulletin of the Los Angeles Neurological Societies*, 1969, 34, 191–220.

Boll, T. J. The Halstead–Reitan neuropsychology battery. In S. B. Filskov & T. J. Boll (Eds.), *Handbook of clinical neuropsychology*. New York: Wiley, 1981.

Brain, L. *Speech disorders*. London: Butterworths, 1965.

Broca, P. Remarks on the seat of the faculty of articulate language, followed by an observation of aphaesia. In G. von Bonin (Trans.), *Some papers on the cerebral cortex*. Springfield, Ill.: Charles C Thomas, 1865/1960.

Brown, J., & Hécaen, H. Lateralization and language representation. *Neurology*, 1976, 26, 183–189.

Bruner, J. S. The course of cognitive growth. In N. S. Endler, L. R. Boulter, & H. Osser (Eds.), *Contemporary issues in developmental psychology*. New York: Holt, Rinehart, & Winston, 1968.

Bruner, J. S. *Beyond the information given*. London: George Allen & Unwin, 1974.

Bryden, M. P., & Allard, F. Dichotic listening and the development of linguistic processes. In M. Kinsbourne (Ed.), *The asymmetrical function of the brain*. New York: Cambridge University Press, 1978.

Caplan, P. J., & Kinsbourne, M. Baby drops the rattle: Asymmetry of duration of grasp by infants. *Child Development*, 1976, *47*, 532–534.

Chelune, G. J., & Edwards, P. Early brain lesions: Ontogenetic-environmental considerations. *Journal of Consulting and Clinical Psychology*, 1981, *49*, 777–790.

Chi, J., Dooling, E., & Gilles, F. Gyral development of the human brain. *Annals of Neurology*, 1977, *1*, 88–93.

Crockett, D., Klonoff, H., & Bjerring, J. Factor analysis of neuropsychological tests. *Perceptual and Motor Skills*, 1969, *29*, 791–802.

Damasio, A. The frontal lobes. In K. M. Heilman & E. Valenstein (Eds.), *Clinical neuropsychology*. New York: Oxford University Press, 1979.

Davison, A. N., Dobbing, J., Morgan, R. S., & Wright, G. Metabolism of myelin: The persistence of (4 – ^{14}C) cholesterol in the mammalian central nervous system. *Lancet*, 1959, *1*, 658–660.

Dax, M. Lesions de la moitié gauche de l'encéphale coincidant avec l'oubli des signes de la pensée—lu au congrés méridional tenu á Montpellier en 1836, par le docteur Mark Dax. *Gazette Hebdomadaire de Medicine et de Chirurgie*, 1865, *35*, 259–262.

Dean, R. S. Cerebral laterality and reading comprehension. *Neuropsychologia*, 1978, *16*, 633–636.

Dean, R. S. Neuropsychological assessment. In T. Kratochwill (Ed.), *Advances in school psychology*. Vol. 2. Hillsdale, N.J.: Erlbaum, 1982.

Dean, R. S. Neuropsychological assessment. In Staff College (Ed.), *Handbook of diagnostic and epidemiological instruments*. Washington, D.C.: National Institutes of Mental Health, 1983.

Dean, R. S. Perspectives on the future of neuropsychological assessment. In B. S. Plake & J. C. Witt (Eds.), *Buros series on measurement and testing: Future of testing and measurement*. Hillsdale, N.J.: Earlbaum, in press. (a)

Dean, R. S. Psychiatric aspects of neuropsychological assessment. In J. D. Cavenar, R. Michels, H. K. H. Brodie, A. M. Cooper, S. B. Guze, L. L. Judd, G. L. Klerman, & A. J. Solnit (Eds.), *Psychiatry*. Philadelphia: J. B. Lippincott, in press. (b)

Dean, R. S. Dual processing and cerebral laterality with preadolescent children. *Clinical Neuropsychology*, in press. (c)

Dean, R. S., & Hua, M. S. Laterality effects in cued auditory asymmetries. *Neuropsychologia*, 1982, *20*, 685–690.

Dean, R. S., & Rothlisberg, B. A. Lateral preference patterns and cross-modal sensory integration. *Journal of Pediatric Psychology*, 1983, *8*, 285–292.

Dean, R. S., Schwartz, N. H., & Smith, L. S. Lateral preference patterns as a discriminator of learning difficulties. *Journal of Consulting and Clinical Psychology*, 1981, *49*, 227–236.

Dennis, M., & Kohn, B. Comprehension of syntax in infantile hemiplegics after cerebral hemidecortication: Left hemisphere superiority. *Brain and Language*, 1975, *2*, 472–482.

Dikman, S., Matthews, C. G., & Harley, J. P. The effect of early versus late onset of major motor epilepsy upon cognitive intellectual performance. *Epilepsia*, 1975, *16*, 73–77.

Dodge, P. R. Neurologic history and examination. In T. W. Farmer (Ed.), *Pediatric neurology*. New York: Harper & Row, 1964.

Doty, R. W., & Overman, W. H. Mnemonic role of forebrain commissures in macaques. In S. Harmad, R. W. Doty, L. Goldstein, J. Jaynes, & G. Krauthamer (Eds.), *Lateralization in the nervous system*. New York: Academic Press, 1977.

Douglas, R. J. The development of hippocampal function: Implications for theory and for therapy. In R. L. Isaacson & K. H. Pribram (Eds.), *The hippocampus, Vol. II. Neurophysiology and behavior*. New York: Plenum Press, 1975.

Flechsig, P. Developmental (myelogenetic) localization of the cortex in human subjects. *Lancet*, 1901, 1027–1029.

Fletcher, J. M., & Satz, P. Age, plasticity and equipotentiality: A reply to Smith. *Journal of Consulting and Clinical Psychology*, 1983, *31*, 763–767.

Folch, J. Composition of the brain in relation to maturation. In H. Waelsch (Ed.), *Biochemistry of the developing nervous system*. New York: Academic Press, 1955.

Ford, B. Head injuries—What happens to survivors. *Medical Journal of Australia*, 1976, *1*, 603–605.

Ford, F. R. *Diseases of the nervous system in infancy, childhood and adolescence*. Springfield, Ill.: Charles C Thomas, 1960.

Freeman, J. M., & Brann, A. W. Central nervous system disturbances. In R. E. Behrman (Ed.), *Neonatal-perinatal medicine*. St. Louis: C. V. Mosby, 1977.

Gardner, E. *Fundamentals of neurology* (5th ed.) Philadelphia: Saunders, 1968.

Gazzaniga, M. S. Brain mechanisms and behavior. In M. S. Gazzaniga & C. Blakemore (Eds.), *Handbook of psychobiology*. New York: Academic Press, 1975.

Geschwind, N. Neurological foundations of language. In H. R Myklebust (Ed.), *Progress in learning disabilities* (Vol. I). New York: Grune & Stratton, 1968.

Geschwind, N. The anatomical basis of hemispheric differentiation. In S. J. Dimond & J. G. Beaumont (Eds.), *Hemispheric function in the human brain*. New York: Halstead Press, 1974.

Geschwind, N., & Levitsky, W. Human brain: Left-right asymmetries in temporal speech region. *Science*, 1968, *161*, 186–187.

Gibson, E. J. Learning to read. In N. S. Endler, L. R. Boulter, & H. Osser (Eds.), *Contemporary issues in developmental psychology*. New York: Holt, Rinehart & Winston, 1968.

Golden, C. J. A standardized version of Luria's neuropsychological tests: A quantitative and qualitative approach to neuropsychological evaluation. In S. B. Filskov & T. J. Boll (Eds.), *Handbook of clinical neuropsychology*. New York: Wiley, 1981.

Goldman, P. S. Development determinants of cortical plasticity. *Acta Neurobiologiae Experimentalis*, 1972, *32*, 495–511.

Goy, R. W., & McEwen, B. S. *Sexual differentiation of the brain*. Cambridge: M.I.T. Press, 1980.

Green, J. D. The rhinencephalon and behavior. In G. E. W. Wolstenholme & C. M. O'Connor (Eds.), *Ciba foundation symposium on the neurological basis of behavior*. London: J. & A. Churchill, 1958.

Haaxma, R., & Kuypers, H. G. J. M. Intrahemispheric cortical connections and visual guidance of hand and finger movements in the rhesus monkey. *Brain*, 1975, *98*, 239–260.

Hardyck, C., Tzeng, O. J. L., & Wang, W. S-Y. Lateralization of function and bilingual judgments: Is thinking lateralized? *Brain and Language*, 1978, *5*, 56–71.

Hartlage, L. C., & Hartlage, P. L. Psychological testing in neurological diagnosis. In J. Youman (Ed.), *Neurological surgery*. Philadelphia: Saunders, 1977.

Hartlage, L. C., & Reynolds, C. R. Neuropsychological assessment and individualization of instruction. In G. W. Hynd & J. E. Obrzut (Eds.), *Neuropsychological assessment and the school-age child*. New York: Grune & Stratton, 1981.

Hartlage, L. C., & Telzrow, C. F. Neuropsychological assessment. In K. D. Paget & B. A. Bracken (Eds.), *The psychoeducational assessement of preschool children*. New York: Grune & Stratton, 1983.

Hebb, D. O. *The organization of behavior*. New York: Wiley, 1949.

Hicks, R. E., & Kinsbourne, M. Human handedness: A partial cross-fostering study. *Science*, 1976, *192*, 908–910.

Himwich, W. A. *Developmental neurobiology*. Springfield, Ill.: Charles C Thomas, 1970.

Hynd, G. W., Obrzut, J. E., Weed, W., & Hynd, C. R. Development of cerebral dominance: Dichotic listening asymmetry in normal and learning disabled children. *Journal of Experimental Child Psychology*, 1979, *28*, 445–454.

Ingram, T. T. S. The nature of dyslexia. In F. A. Young & D. B. Lindsley (Eds.), *Early experience and visual information processing in perceptual and reading disorders.* Washington, D.C.: National Academy of Sciences, 1970.

Isaacson, R. L. *The limbic system.* New York: Plenum Press, 1974.

Isaacson, R. L. The myth of recovery from early brain damage. In N. G. Ellis (Ed.), *Aberrant development in infancy.* New York: Wiley, 1975.

Jackson, J. H. On the duality of the brain. *Medical Press,* 1874, *1,* 19. Reprinted in J. Taylor (Ed.), *Selected writings of John Hughlings Jackson* (Vol. II). London: Hodder and Stoughton, 1932.

Jones, S. J. Children's two-choice learning of predominantly alternating and predominantly non-alternating sequences. *Journal of Experimental Child Psychology,* 1970, *10,* 344–362.

Kendler, T. S., & Kendler, H. H. Inferential behavior in children as a function of age and subgoal constancy. *Journal of Experimental Psychology,* 1962, *64,* 406–466.

Kershner, J. B. Cerebral dominance in disabled readers, good readers, and gifted children: Search for a valid model. *Child Development,* 1977, *48,* 61–67.

Kimble, D. P. Hippocampus and internal inhibition. *Psychological Bulletin,* 1968, *70,* 285–295.

Kimura, D. Dual functional asymmetry of the brain in visual perception. *Neuropsychologia,* 1966, *4,* 275–285.

Kinsbourne, M. The cerebral basis of lateral asymmetries in attention. *Acta Psychologica,* 1970, *33,* 193–201.

Kinsbourne, M. Cerebral dominance, learning and cognition. In H. R. Myklebust (Ed.), *Progress in learning disabilities.* New York: Grune & Stratton, 1975.

Kinsbourne, M., & Hiscock, M. Does cerebral dominance develop? In S. J. Segalowitz, & F. A. Gruber (Eds.), *Language development and neurological theory.* New York: Academic Press, 1977.

Kolata, G. B. Sex hormones and brain development. *Science,* 1979, *205,* 985–987.

Lansdell, H. C. Relation of extent of temporal removals to closure and visuomotor factors. *Perceptual and Motor Skills,* 1970, *31,* 491–498.

Lenneberg, E. H. *Biological foundations of language.* New York: Wiley, 1967.

Levy, J. Lateral specialization of the human brain: Behavioral manifestations and possible evolutionary basis. In J. Kirger (Ed.), *The biology of behavior.* Corvallis: Oregon State Universtiy Press, 1973.

Levy, J., & Nagylaki, T. A model for the genetics of handedness. *Genetics,* 1972, *72,* 117–128.

Levy, J., & Reid, M. Variations in writing posture and cerebral organization. *Science,* 1976, *194,* 337–339.

Luria, A. R. Neuropsychology in the local diagnosis of brain damage. *Cortex,* 1965, *1,* 2–18.

Luria, A. R. *The working brain: An introduction to neuropsychology.* London: Penguin Press, 1973.

Maccoby, E. E. *The development of sex differences.* Stanford, Calif.: Stanford University Press, 1966.

MacLean, P. D. The triune brain, emotional and scientific bias. In F. O. Schmitt (Ed.), *The neurosciences: Second study program.* New York: Rockefeller University Press, 1970.

MacLusky, N. J., & Naftolin, F. Sexual differentiation of the central nervous system. *Science,* 1981, *211,* 1294–1302.

McGill, H. C., Jr., Anselmo, V. C., Buchanan, J. M., & Sheridan, P. J. The heart is a target organ for androgen. *Science,* 1980, *207,* 775–777.

Milner, B. Laterality effects in audition. In V. B. Mountcastle (Ed.), *Interhermispheric relations and cerebral dominance.* Baltimore: Johns Hopkins University Press, 1962.

Minkowski, A. *Regional development of the brain in early life*. Philadelphia: F. A. Davis, 1967.

Molfese, D. L., Freeman, R. B., & Palermo, D. The ontogeny of brain lateralization for speech and nonspeech stimuli. *Brain and Language*, 1975, *2*, 356–368.

Morgan, C. T. *Physiological psychology*. New York: McGraw-Hill, 1943.

Nottebohm, F. Origins and mechanisms in the establishment of cerebral dominance. In M. S. Gazzaniga (Ed.), *Handbook of behavioral neurobiology: Vol. 2. Neuropsychology*. New York: Plenum Press, 1979.

Ochs, S. *Elements of neurophysiology*. New York: Wiley, 1965.

Orton, S. T. Specific reading disability—strephosymbolia. *Journal of the American Medical Association*, 1937, *90*, 1095–1099.

Pate, J. L., & Bell, G. L. Alternation behavior in children in a cross-maze. *Psychonomic Science*, 1971, *23*, 431–432.

Peiper, A. *Cerebral function in infancy and childhood*. (Translation by B. & M. Nagler from the German 3rd rev. ed.). New York: Consultants Bureau, 1963.

Penfield, W. *The excitable cortex in conscious man*. Liverpool: Liverpool University Press, 1958.

Penfield, W., & Boldrey, E. Somatic motor and sensory representation in the cerebral cortex as studied by electrical stimulation. *Brain*, 1937, *60*, 389–443.

Penfield, W., & Roberts, L. *Speech and brain mechanisms*. Princeton, N.J.: Princeton University Press, 1959.

Petrie, B. F., & Peters, M. Handedness: Left/right differences in intensity of grasp response and duration of rattle holding in infants. *Infant Behavior and Development*, 1980, *3*, 215–221.

Piaget, J. *The origins of intelligence in children*. New York: International Universities Press, 1952.

Pirozzolo, F. J., Campanella, D. J., Christensen, K., & Lawson-Kerr, K. Effects of cerebral dysfunction on neurolinguistic performance in children. *Journal of Consulting and Clinical Psychology*, 1981, *49*, 791–806.

Pizzamiglio, L. Cognitive approach to hemispheric dominance. In R. M. Knights & D. Bakker, (Eds.), *The neuropsychology of learning disorders*. Baltimore: University Park Press, 1976.

Prechtl, H. F. R. Prognostic value of neurological signs in the newborn infant. *Proceedings of the Royal Society of Medicine*, 1965, *58*, 3–4.

Pribram, K. H ., & Isaacson, R. L. Summary. In R. L. Isaacson & K. H. Pribram (Eds.), *The hippocampus*. New York: Plenum Press, 1975.

Ramsay, D. S. Manual preference for tapping in infants. *Developmental Psychology*, 1979, *15*, 437–442.

Reitan, R. M. An investigation of the validity of Halstead's measures of biological intelligence. *Archives of Neurology and Psychiatry*, 1955, *73*, 28–35.

Reitan, R. M. *Manual for administering and scoring the Reitan–Indiana Neuropsychological Battery for Children (aged five through eight)*. Indianapolis: University of Indiana Medical Center, 1964.

Reitan, R. M. Methodological problems in clinical neuropsychology. In R. M. Reitan & L. A. Davison (Eds.), *Clinical neuropsychology: Current status and applications*. New York: Wiley, 1974.

Reynolds, C. R. Latency to respond and conjugate lateral eye movements: A methodological and theoretical note. *Perceptual and Motor Skills*, 1978, *47*, 843–847.

Robinson, R. J. Cerebral function in the newborn. *Developmental Medicine and Child Neurology*, 1966, *8*, 561–567.

Robinson, R. J. Cerebral hemisphere function in the newborn. In R. J. Robinson (Ed.), *Brain and early behavior*. New York: Academic Press, 1969.

Sarsikov, S. The evolutionary aspects of the integrative function of the cortex and subcortex of the brain. In D. P. Purpura & J. P. Schade (Eds.), *Growth and maturation of the brain. Vol. 4. Progress in brain research.* Amsterdam: Elsevier, 1964.

Satz, P. Pathological left-handedness: An explanatory model. *Cortex*, 1972, 8, 121–135.

Satz, P. Left-handedness and early brain insult. *Neuropsychologia*, 1973, 11, 115–117.

Satz, P. Cerebral dominance and reading disability: An old problem revisited. In R. M. Knights & D. Bakker, (Eds.), *The neuropsychology of learning disorders.* Baltimore: University Park Press, 1976.

Satz, P., Bakker, D. J., Tenuissen, J., Goebel, R., & Van der Vlugt, H. Developmental parameters of the ear asymmetry. A multivariate approach. *Brain and Language*, 1975, 2, 71–85.

Satz, P., & Fletcher, J. M. Emergent trends in neuropsychology: An overview. *Journal of Consulting and Clinical Psychology*, 1981, 49, 851–865.

Satz, P., & Van Nostrand, G. K. Developmental dyslexia: An evaluation of a theory. In P. Satz & J. Ross (Eds.), *The disabled learner.* Rotterdam: Rotterdam University Press, 1973.

Schmeck, H. M., Jr. His brain, her brain. *Science and Living Tomorrow*, 1980, 8, 23–24.

Schulte, F. J. Structure-function relationships in the spinal cord. In R. J. Robinson, (Ed.), *Brain and early behavior.* New York: Academic Press, 1969.

Semmes, J. Hemispheric specialization: A possible clue to mechanism. *Neuropsychologia*, 1968, 6, 11–26.

Shankweiler, D. Effects of temporal lobe damage on perception of dichotically presented melodies. *Journal of Comparative and Physiological Psychology*, 1966, 62, 115.

Smith, A., & Sugar, O. Development of above normal language and intelligence 21 years after left hemispherectomy. *Neurology*, 1975, 25, 813–818.

Sparrow, S., & Satz, P. Dyslexia, laterality, and neuropsychological development. In D. J. Bakker & P. Satz (Eds.), *Specific reading disability: Advances in theory and method.* Rotterdam: Rotterdam University Press, 1970.

Sperry, R. W. Plasticity of neural maturation. *Developmental Biology*, Supplement 2, 1968 (27th Symposium). New York: Academic Press, 1968.

Sperry, R. W., Gazzaniga, M. S., & Bogen, J. H. Interhemispheric relationships: The neocortical commissures: Syndromes of hemisphere disconnection. In P. Vinken & G. W. Bruyn (Eds.), *Handbook of clinical neurology* (Vol. 4). New York: Wiley, 1969.

Strauss, A. A., & Lehtinen, L. E. *Psychopathology and education of the brain-injured child.* (Vol. 1). New York: Grune & Stratton, 1948.

Valenstein, E. S. *Brain control.* New York: Wiley, 1973.

Van der Vlugt, H. Aspects of normal and abnormal neuropsychological development. In M. S. Gazzaniga (Ed.), *Handbook of behavioral neurobiology: Vol. 2. Neuropsychology.* New York: Plenum Press, 1979.

Vygotsky, L. S. *Thought and language* (E. Haufmann & G. Vakar, Eds. and trans.). Cambridge and New York: MIT Press and Wiley, 1962.

Waber, D. P. Sex differences in cognition: A function of maturation rate? *Science*, 1976, 192, 572–574.

Waber, D. P. Sex differences in mental abilities, hemispheric lateralization, and rate of physical growth at adolescence. *Developmental Psychology*, 1977, 13, 29–38.

Wada, J., Clark, R., & Hamm, A. Cerebral hemispheric asymmetry in humans. *Archives of Neurology*, 1975, 32, 239–246.

Watson, E. H., & Lowrey, G. H. *Growth and development of children.* Chicago: Year Book Medical Publications, 1954.

Weintraub, P. The brain: His and hers. *Discover*, 1981, 2, 14–20.

Whitaker, H. A., & Ojemann, G. A. Lateralization of higher cortical functions: A critique. In S. J. Dimond & D. A. Blizard (Eds), Evolution and lateralization of the brain, New York: *New York Academy of Sciences*, 1977, 299, 459–473.

White, S. H. *Evidence for a hierarchical arrangement of learning processes. Advances in child development and behavior.* (Vol. 2). New York: Academic Press, 1965.

Witelson, S. F. Sex and the single hemisphere. Right hemisphere specialization for spatial processing. *Science,* 1976, *193,* 425–427.

Witelson, S., & Pallie, W. Left hemisphere specialization for language in the newborn: Neuroanatomical evidence of asymmetry. *Brain,* 1973, *96,* 641–646.

Yakovlev, P. I., & Lecours, A. R. The myelogenetic cycles of regional maturation of the brain. In A. Minkowski (Ed.), *Regional development of the brain in early life.* Oxford: Blackwell, 1967.

Yakovlev, P.I., & Rakic, P. Patterns of decussation of bulbar pyramids and distribution of pyramidal tracts on two sides of the spinal cord. *Transactions of the American Neurology Associations,* 1966, *91,* 366–367.

Zangwill, O. L. *Cerebral dominance and its relationship to psychological junction.* London: Oliver and Boyd, 1960.

Zangwill, O. L. Dyslexia in relation to cerebral dominance. In J. Money (Ed.), *Reading disability.* Baltimore: Johns Hopkins, 1962.

CHAPTER 3

Methodological Issues in Research in Developmental Neuropsychology

JOHN F. BOLTER and CHARLES J. LONG

The purpose of this chapter is to present an overview of issues and problems associated with neuropsychological studies of brain-injured children. We are primarily concerned with factors that influence the relationship(s) between acquired cerebral pathology and the development of human abilities—factors that must be considered in both clinical practice and research. Many of those factors are simply qualified generalizations of hard-learned lessons from neuropsychological studies of adults. Others seem to be more or less unique for studies of developmental pathologies.

Our approach is rather general. For example, we do not prescribe a list of tests to be used in developmental neuropsychodiagnosis. We do, however, describe areas of human ability that should be assessed, as well as a temporal framework for comprehensive evaluation. We also touch on topics covered by other chapters in this volume, at least to the extent that theoretical concerns and epidemiological data bear on method. We begin by considering a common assumption about the factor "age at onset" relative to "cognitive" impairment and recovery of function. Next we consider neuropathological/cognitive differences between adults and (developing) children. Then we review the modifying factors known to influence brain–behavior relationships. Finally, we briefly address the problems of localizing dysfunction when dealing with a nervous system in transition.

JOHN F. BOLTER • Clinical Psychology Service and Internship Training Program, Silas B. Hays Army Community Hospital, Ft. Ord, California 93941–5000.   CHARLES J. LONG • Department of Psychology, Memphis State University, Memphis, Tennessee 38152.

AGE-RELATED EFFECTS OF CEREBRAL PATHOLOGY

Neuropsychological studies of adults have suggested two general postulates regarding the effects of brain damage on behavior relative to time (Chelune & Edwards, 1981; Johnson & Almli, 1978). First, long-term deficits following brain damage are rarely as severe as those seen initially. Thus, some degree of recovery is normally expected following brain damage in children and adults alike (Stein, Rosen, & Butters, 1974). Second (the Kennard principle), brain damage sustained early in life is associated with less deleterious effects than similar damage sustained by a mature brain. That is to say, the earlier the age at onset, the better the chances of recovery. It now seems, however, that these two postulates cannot be generalized uncritically to studies of children. The second postulate in particular has been severely questioned (Hécaen & Albert, 1978; Isaacson, 1975; Rourke, Bakker, Fisk, & Strang, 1983; St. James-Roberts, 1979, 1981; Satz & Fletcher, 1981; Schneider, 1979; Stein et al., 1974).

One of the earliest research efforts addressing age-related effects in brain damage are dated to the work of Margaret Kennard (1936, 1938, 1940, 1942). In a series of studies on the effects of unilateral and bilateral precentral cortical ablations, she reported that monkeys who sustained lesions early in life revealed much less locomotor and postural impairment than those who were similarly lesioned later in life. From these findings, Kennard concluded that there existed a direct relationship between age and the capacity for neural reorganization following cortical injury. This reorganization potential was not seen as restricted to infancy, but developmentally determined in that it progressively diminished with advancing maturation. Numerous subsequent studies with both animals and humans have reported similar findings (Braun, 1978; Hécaen & Albert, 1978; Kertesz, 1979; Milner, 1974, 1982; Rosner, 1970; Rutter, 1982; Rutter, Graham, & Yule, 1970; St. James-Roberts, 1979, 1981; Stein et al., 1974; Teuber, 1974, 1975). The results of these and other studies have been generalized to clinical populations and often are taken to mean that the effects of brain damage in children are less devastating than the same damage in adults.

Despite the authority with which the Kennard principle usually is stated, a great deal of evidence argues against the assumption of preferential recovery in young brains (Boll, 1978; Boll & Barth, 1981; Hécaen & Albert, 1978; Hutt, 1976; Isaacson, 1975; Johnson & Almli, 1978; Rourke et al., 1983; Rutter, 1982; St. James-Roberts, 1979, 1981). Although often overlooked by investigators citing her work, even Kennard (1940, 1942) noted that functional restoration in motor processes was never complete for the early-lesioned monkeys. In fact, she reported that some deficits persisted throughout the animal's life while others appeared only with increasing development and maturation (e.g., contractures and exaggerated tendon responses developed during the second and third postoperative month and marked spasticity was observed by the end of the first year).

PATTERNS OF RECOVERY AFTER CEREBRAL TRAUMA DURING CHILDHOOD

Kennard's work with monkeys suggests that injury to an immature brain presents unique possibilities with respect to the developmental pattern of cognitive-behavioral deficits. The findings of Kennard are extended to humans and greatly expanded in research by Teuber and Rudel (1962). The significance of their research suggests the need for closer investigation. They have noted three possible "deficit" patterns following childhood onset of cerebral pathology: (a) some deficits are initially present but resolve; (b) some deficits may persist; and (c) some deficits appear only later in development.

In this now classic paper on the effects of early damage with respect to perceptual abilities, Teuber and Reudel clearly demonstrated the need for examining cognitive impairment from a developmental perspective by establishing evidence for each of the deficit patterns outlined above. Using three separate position sense tasks, they compared normal and early-onset brain-damaged children representing a 10-year span from 5 to 15 years.

Early Impairment with Rapid Recovery

To examine the effects of early brain damage on self-righting (position self-righting), Teuber and Rudel (1962) blindfolded each child and, using a special tilting chair, inclined each either left or right from a vertical sitting position for periods ranging from 30 seconds to 2 minutes. The children then were rotated slowly toward the original vertical position until they reported feeling upright. Due to habituation in the tilted position, the normal response is to underestimate slightly the amount by which the chair must be rotated. Teuber and Rudel reported that the magnitude of the undershooting error is not significantly different for brain-damaged and normal adults. However, brain-damaged children between the ages of 5 and 9 years revealed a significantly greater self-righting error than normal children of similar ages. As the children grew older, the difference between the brain-damaged and normal children narrowed until by age 11 to 15 years there was no longer a discernible difference. This task, which fails to differentiate normal from brain injured adults, can distinguish brain-damaged children from normal children, although the effects of brain damage on this task were manifested only until the age 11 years, subsequent to which no performance deficits were observed.

The mechanisms that account for the early appearance and eventual disappearance, such as those in self-righting, are not known. Rudel (1978) has suggested that this phenomenon represents rearrangements in circuitry via new synaptic connections. It is important to note, however, that such rearrangements in an immature brain can also lead to anomalous connections (Schneider, 1973).

PERSISTENT DEFICITS

A second task in Teuber and Rudel's (1962) study was designed to assess the magnitude of a starting position effect. With the subject sitting in an upright position, a sound source was gradually moved toward midline until the subject reported it was on midline. Although all the normal and brain-damaged children tended to localize the sound source on the same side as the starting position (as seen with adults), the magnitude of the misalignments was found to be significantly greater in the brain-damaged children throughout the age span evaluated. Early brain damage thus would appear to be associated with persistent impairment on this task regardless of the child's age at testing. Moreover, because this task also differentiates brain-injured adults from normals, it would appear to bring out the effects of brain injury regardless of age. An interesting implication of this finding is that the persistent impairment among brain-injured children suggests a failure in "take over" by noninjured neural structures that may be less efficient for the function than the injured genetically determined one.

DELAYED ONSET OF DEFICITS

The third task in Teuber and Rudel's (1962) study, the constant error effect, involved an auditory midline task in which the subject was required to localize the source of a clicking sound while being tilted 28 degrees to the right or left. The sound source was moved radially in the coronal plane at a constant distance of 12 inches from the occipital pole. The subjects were required to indicate when the sound source was immediately above the midline of their heads. The normal response to this task is a small displacement error opposite to the side of body tilt. The displacement error is virtually zero at about 5 years of age, and it increases gradually until reaching a constant value during adolescence. Brain-injured adults, especially those with frontal lobe involvement, tend to make a significantly larger displacement error than normal adults. With children, however, Teuber and Rudel found that this task is insensitive to the effects of brain damage prior to the age of 11. With increasing age, the brain-damaged children became progressively worse than similarly aged normals. By 11 years of age, this task could be used effectively to discriminate the brain-damaged from normal children. Interestingly, the same results were observed for a visual midline task under body tilt conditions.

Whereas delayed manifestations of early brain injury have been reported in several studies (Goldman, 1971, 1972, 1974; Johnson & Almli, 1978; Lawrence & Hopkins, 1972; Lenneberg, 1967), the underlying mechanisms are not understood. One possible explanation is that the lesioned area is either functionally immature or not utilized at the time of insult. When the function assumes dependency on the damaged neural region at a specific point in developmental maturation, the weakness in the system becomes apparent through the appearance of a functional deficit. This supposition does appear consistent with our knowledge regarding the development of the central nervous system (CNS).

Regardless of the mechanisms underlying delayed deficits, researchers should be attuned to this developmental pattern of deficits associated with brain damage in childhood. An investigative approach, one commonly employed with adult brain-damaged patients, that merely asks whether or not impairment is present at a single point in time would be less than adequate for child neuropsychological research. In order to properly ascertain the injurious effects of early brain trauma, it would appear necessary to investigate the *longitudinal course* of development following early brain insult. This research strategy in child neuropsychological studies is especially important in light of our limited knowledge regarding brain structural-functional development and intervening elements in that development. A second consideration, implicit in Teuber and Rudel's report, is the need for a comprehensive evaluaton. Although most neuropsychological evaluations do not, and probably never will, include position sense measures, Teuber and Rudel's conclusions should be replicable with other tests provided that a comprehensive assessment of human abilities has been made.

ONTOLOGICAL ASPECTS OF RECOVERY/DEFICIT PATTERNS

Except for normal degenerative changes accompanying aging, the adult's brain is assumed to be developmentally static and the effects of injury can often be readily determined by measuring an individual's capacity to perform a particular function. Injury to various brain regions in the adult are thereby seen as having generally agreed upon effects with respect to sensory, motor, language, perceptual, memory, and cognitive functions (see Filskov & Boll, 1981; Hécaen & Albert, 1978; Heilman & Valenstein, 1979). A child's brain, however, is characterized by growth and differentiation that extends from conception into young adulthood (Renis & Goldman, 1980; Rourke et al., 1983), and much less is known concerning the cognitive-behavioral effects of lesions in different brain foci.

At birth, neurons appear no longer capable of mitotic cell division and thus the brain has largely achieved its full complement of neurons. The immature brain does, however, continually reveal both structural and biochemical changes throughout the developmental age span. For example, changes in axon and dendritic organization, degree of myelination, synaptogenesis, carbohydrate metabolism, neurotransmitter concentration, and lipid, protein, and nucleic acid production have all been identified as accompanying postnatal brain maturation. Postnatal brain growth is illustrated dramatically by changes in weight. At birth, the brain weighs approximately 20% of its adult weight, at 4 years 80%, at 8 years 90% and at 16 years nearly 100%.

The maturational pattern, although generally progressing from phylogenetically older to newer structures, is complex, multilevel, and intrahemispherically and interhemispherically variant. For instance, within each cerebral hemisphere the development of association areas appears to lag behind corresponding primary ones and the development of the primary regions (motor, somatosensory, visual, and auditory) varies within and between each other. Unfortunately, little is known regarding the relationship between structural-brain and functional-behavioral development. Research in this area is rendered more complex by the recognition that development of brain structures and behavior are mutually interactive. Which is to say, neural maturational processes are influenced by those functions to which they give rise (Gottlieb, 1976).

Luria (1963) emphasized levels of development according to different systems in the brain. He considered (a) the arousal unit as consisting of the reticular formation and lower brain structures, (b) the posterior cortex and related structures as the sensory unit, and (c) the frontal cortex as the motor-integrative unit. Development involves a progression from the lower or arousal unit to the motor–integrative unit with operation of the first unit occurring between birth and 1 year of age, the second unit during the first 5 to 8 years of life, and the motor-integrative unit developing later between 8 and 12 years of age, possibly extending into young adulthood.

If such a progression is followed in CNS development, then it is clear that damage to different neurological systems will affect behaviors differently and the effects of such damage will occur at different stages of development. Damage to the frontal-integrative system in a young child may not become apparent until they reach 8 to 12 years of age because their system has not yet become functional. On the other hand, damage to the sensory systems may result in problems earlier and may in fact extend its influence to later developing systems. Finally, from Luria's model it is also possible that systems damaged early in life may be compensated by later developing systems (e.g., brain stem damage may produce hyperactivity early in life which disappears when the frontal-integrative system develops).

FACTORS CONTRIBUTING TO THE PATTERN OF IMPAIRMENT OBSERVED

There exists a variety of independent factors similar to those specified by Parsons and Prigatano (1978) that most child neuropsychologists would agree contribute to the pattern of deficits observed in children following brain injury. It is important that each be considered as only one in an array of variables, each of which interacts with the others in determining the pattern of deficits. A thorough investigation will consider the potential relationship each plays in contributing to experimental outcomes. Experimental designs formulated to control for each where applicable would seem to be requisite for drawing meaningful conclusions from research data. Although not conclusive, the most important among these factors would appear to be the age of the child at injury onset, locus of injury, nature of the injury, task employed to measure the injurious effects, sex of the child under study, and pre-injury and postinjury experience.

Age at Insult

As already mentioned, it is important that studies that attempt to demonstrate cognitive-behavioral deficits in children following brain damage take into account the age at which the lesion is acquired. Research from several sources (Isaacson, 1975; Sameroff & Chandler, 1975; St. James-Roberts, 1979; Stein et al., 1974; Stewart & Reynolds, 1975) illustrates the complex role age of onset may play in the pattern of deficits that emerge following early brain insult and as yet no definite statement can be made. Moreover, the test used and the time elapsed determine in part whether or not impairment is found in association with lesions acquired at the same point in ontogeny (Hutt, 1976). It is thus essential for the child neuropsychologist to understand and approach assessment from a developmental perspective such as that outlined by Luria.

LOCUS OF INJURY

Among adults, the locus of brain injury appears to have well-known implications with respect to sensory, motor, perceptual, language, and various cognitive processes (see Filskov & Boll, 1981; Hécaen & Albert, 1978; Heilman & Valenstein, 1979; Lezak, 1976). Much less, however, is known about the cognitive-behavioral implications of lesions in different brain foci occurring in children. Additionally, a child's brain is not homologous across the developmental age span and within any given age varying degrees of maturity across regions will be revealed (Yakovlev & Lecours, 1967). Thus, the structural-functional maturity of the injured locus can be expected to interact with the consequences of brain damage. For instance, Milner (1982) has noted that recovery of language functions following early left hemisphere injury arises only when the damage occurs prior to the age of 5 years *and* involves one of the two critical language zones in that hemisphere (i.e., Broca's or Wernicke's). Injury anywhere else in that hemisphere in a young child would, however, be expected to give rise to language-related deficits similar to those of an adult brain-damaged patient. Also, evaluating a damaged brain region during a prefunctional stage in its development may lead to the erroneous conclusion that the region is functionally intact, when in fact, an evaluation at the terminal stage in the region's development could reveal deficits associated with the early injury that were not previously apparent (Johnson & Almli, 1978).

NATURE OF THE DAMAGE

The impact of early brain injury cannot be understood adequately as similar or different from that observed in adult patients without taking into account the nature of the injury. Such factors as the severity, etiology, and chronicity of the damage have all been implicated as influential in the pattern of deficits found and the course of their subsequent recovery (Boll, 1978; Hécaen & Albert, 1978; Heilman & Valenstein, 1979; Satz & Fletcher, 1981). Despite this caveat, little progress has been made toward controlling for these factors when contrasting the effects of early versus late brain lesions.

This problem may be due, in part, to major neuropathological differences between children and adults that preclude making valid comparisons. For instance, the usual criterion of head injury severity in adults [posttraumatic amnesia (PTA)] does not generalize readily to children (Lishman, 1978). Posttraumatic amnesia cannot be determined accurately in children, and it is not yet certain that it carries the same implications of severity as it does with adults. It is widely recognized that among adult head-injured patients, those suffering mild injury reveal a dispropor-tionately higher incidence of psychiatric sequelae when contrasted with those suffering more severe trauma. Among children, however, this inverse relationship between head injury severity and psychiatric sequelae has not been supported (Rutter, 1982). Similarly, the type of brain damage experienced in childhood generally differs from that of adulthood, making valid comparisons between adults and children based on etiologies dif-ficult (Boll & Barth, 1981).

NEUROPATHOLOGICAL FACTORS

Neuropathological processes arising during childhood differ from those typically seen in adulthood. This difference reflects both variations in the topography and histological nature of the disorders found between the two age groups. For instance, CNS neoplasms are most commonly found between the ages of 30 and 50 years (Escourolle & Poirier, 1978). Within that age range, the majority of lesions are supratentorial and are classified as glioblastomas, astrocytomas, meningiomas, and metastatic. In children, however, neoplasms tend to be infratentorial and are classified as cerebellar medulloblastomas, astrocytomas, or fourth ventricle epen-dynomas. Similarly, the vast majority of cerebrovascular accidents occur in individuals above the age of 40. Moreover, the pathological processes underlying cerebrovascular disorders in children are usually not the typ-ical occlusive conditions of older patients (i.e., arteriosclerosis, thrombosis, embolism, hypertensive encephalopathy), but rather are more charac-teristically due to congenital disorders such as aneurysms and vascular malformations. Whereas CNS infections may strike any age, the type and pathogens responsible reveal age specificity (Kleiman & Carver, 1981). For example, 50–65% of acute purulent meningitis cases are found in children younger than 5 years of age and the offending pathogen appears to vary with age. Certain degenerative and demyelinating conditions (e.g., Alz-heimer's, Pick's, paralysis agitans, progressive chorea, multiple sclerosis, etc.) rarely occur prior to adulthood whereas a variety of disorders are predominantly seen in children (e.g., epilepsy, inborn errors of metab-olism, metachromatic leukoencephalopathy, etc.). Perhaps the most fre-quent cause of neurological problems in childhood is closed head trauma.

In general, it seems reasonable to assume that pathological brain states in children tend to be generalized rather than focal, less subject to strict anatomical localization and not usually subject to immediate inspection (Boll & Barth, 1982). Thus, in contrasting the effects of brain disturbances in children with those observed in brain-injured adults, we must take into account differences between the nature and topography of the pathological processes responsible for the dysfunction.

TASK-DEPENDENT EFFECTS

The nature of the task used to assess the effects of early brain damage remains a known influential variable that has yet to be classified. As previously noted, Teuber and Rudel (1962), using variants of a simple perceptual motor task, observed that deficits following early brain damage can persist, recover, or emerge only with the passage of time, depending on the tasks used to evaluate mental functioning. They concluded that the effects of early lesions differed according to the type of task involved, as well as the age at which the child is tested. Isaacson (1975) similarly concluded that lessened debility following early brain damage reported in the literature was not a general phenomenon, but occurred only in relation to some specific aspect of behavior. For instance, frontal lesions in an adult rhesus monkey will impair its ability to perform a variety of delayed response tasks, but similar damage in an infant monkey will not lead to such a deficit. However, with more complex tasks (e.g., an oddities learning set), both mature and immature rhesus monkeys will reveal noticeable deficits (Rudel, 1978).

Studies such as these corroborate what we already know to be true—namely, neuropsychological assessment must sample a broad range of human abilities, including at least basic sensory processes, basic motor functions, perceptual motor functions, basic language skills, memory (immediate and delayed), and intelligence (including both verbal and nonverbal reasoning) in order to evaluate the effects of brain damage at any age.

Although neuropsychologists typically attempt a comprehensive examination, two significant task-related problems are easily identified with neuropsychological tests commonly used with children. First, the tests in the Halstead–Reitan test batteries for children are not psychometrically adequate due to the fact that they have not been standardized appropriately. Second, and as a consequence, the children's and midrange versions of the Halstead–Reitan are not comparable. Therefore, the results of serial or longitudinal evaluations that cross the (arbitrary) ageline are difficult if not impossible to evaluate. Obviously a need exists for well-standardized lists of human abilities that cover the development life span that can be formulated into a standardized assessment tool.

Although a battery constructed in such a manner would be desirable, it is realized from the above discussion that there are limits to such an approach. There remain neurological systems that develop more slowly (e.g., frontal lobes) whose functional-behavioral implications are apparent only with maturation.

SEX DIFFERENCES

The effects of early brain damage may differ among males and females. In particular, evidence from several sources (Mathura, 1979; Rudel, 1978) suggests that males may be more vulnerable to the effects of early brain damage than females. For example, the incidence of minimal brain dysfunction, dyslexia, stuttering, and cerebral palsy are at least five times greater among boys than girls. Similarly, various pathological processes of the CNS (e.g., tumors, febrile convulsions, viral infections) are found more often in boys than girls.

What appears to be a greater vulnerability for the male nervous system to early insult may reflect differential patterns of neural maturation and behavioral propensities for males and females. For instance, language functions develop earlier in girls whereas boys appear to develop right-hemisphere perceptual functions earlier than girls (Buffery, 1971). Corresponding hemispheric myelination and dendritic differences have been associated with these behavioral differences between boys and girls (Mathura, 1979). Gender must be considered as a classification variable in developmental neuropsychological research.

EXPERIENCE

The cognitive-behavioral sequelae of adult-age brain disturbances represent a loss or alteration of brain functions in a previously healthy and psychologically developed system. In children, however, the matter is more complex since most neurological anomalies arise before psychological development is complete. The orderly development and appearance of cognitive skills in children, as outlined by Piaget, is dependent on normal brain growth and differentiation. Lesions that disrupt the brain's normal pattern of growth will interfere with future psychological development and the acquisition of specific skills. Thus, brain lesions in children have both primary and secondary functional effects associated with losses as well as acquisitions of psychological functions.

Because children, especially prior to 12 years of age, manifest considerable quantitative and qualitative year-to-year changes in psychological functioning, establishing the effects of brain injury is complicated for at least two reasons. First, the effects of brain injury in a child must be clarified when the prediction of premorbid capacities is most unreliable. With adults, however, an accurate picture of premorbid abilities can be derived on the basis of educational, occupational, and social history. Second, whereas injury to a child's brain may lead to deficits at the onset, it can also potentially alter the order, rate, and level of future psychological development. Moreover, this can occur in ways not only specific to the pathological process involved, but also dependent on the current and future developmental task at the time of injury (Boll & Barth, 1981).

The experimental background of the brain-injured child may interact with the pattern of cognitive-behavioral changes accompanying the injury (St. James-Roberts, 1979). Although not as yet clearly established in humans, the results of experiments with animals suggest that both preinjury and postinjury experience can influence the course of emerging deficits and subsequent recovery following early brain damage (Bakker, 1984; Greenough, Faas, & DeVoogd, 1976). In general, the data indicate that appropriate preinjury experience facilitates postinjury recovery. The enhanced behavioral sparing associated with an enriched prelesion experience, however, appears to be quite specific. In particular, the more closely the preinjury experience approximates the postinjury test, the greater the appearance of recovery. Similarly, studies reporting significant effects in postlesion experience on recovery indicate that the relationship between effective postinjury experience and recovery is task dependent.

There now appears to be little reason to believe that preinjury and postinjury experiences act in a general way on the cognitive-behavioral sequelae of early brain damage. Rudel (1978) argues, however, that the effectiveness of some experiences following early brain damage may not be realized fully until alternative neural structures capable of subsuming the lost function mature. Accordingly, she maintains that remedial efforts following early brain injury should continue even in the absence of apparent improvement because early experience with a task is critical in determining the eventual level of recovery a child is likely to achieve. Until experimentally tested, however, this remains only a plausible hypothesis regarding the role experience may play in recovery following early brain damage. In either case, because familiarity with a task can influence the emerging pattern of cognitive-behavioral deficits following early brain damage, it would seem well advised to control for this possibility, especially with single-case designs that appear currently in vogue.

SOCIOECONOMIC AND ETHNIC FACTORS

We list these factors only as a matter of completeness. We prefer to believe that no practicing neuropsychologist needs to be reminded that psychometric test performance is associated with socioeconomic background and ethnic origin.

EMOTIONAL ADJUSTMENT, COPING, AND ADAPTIVE SKILLS

Neuropsychological research with adults has indicated a strong relationship between acquired cerebral dysfunction and problems in emotional adjustment. A similar relationship has been suggested for children. Although the research evidence is inconclusive, clinical experience has convinced us that the child's emotional state and environmental situation must be weighed in both neuropsychodiagnosis and research classification. Our clinical experience has revealed considerable variability in effective level of day-to-day functioning in children with similar neuropsychological profiles. While many factors must be considered in the final analysis, coping and adaptive skills play an important role.

MECHANISMS OF RECOVERY

As mentioned earlier, it has long been recognized that functional deficits following brain damage generally show considerable improvement with the passage of time (Luria, 1963). Although the precise limitations of this improvement are unknown, the fact that it does occur has generated prodigious speculation regarding the underlying mechanisms responsible for it. Most theories regarding mechanisms of recovery have been advanced for brain damage sustained by mature organisms. There is, however, an assumption often made that such mechanisms are more efficacious in cases where brain injury is sustained by the immature organism. Because these theories have been discussed at length elsewhere (See Finger, 1978; Isaacson, 1975; LeVere, 1980; Luria, 1963; Rosner, 1970; St. James-Roberts, 1979), they will be presented here only briefly.

Among the various theoretical mechanisms of recovery are (a) *diaschisis*, the early notion of von Monakow that holds that recovery is associated with the freeing of neural systems from transient inhibitory influences; (b) *regeneration*, for which recovery follows the regrowth of damaged neurons; (c) *collateral sprouting*, which maintains that recovery arises when undamaged neurons adjacent to the site of injury sprout axon collaterals that innervate those areas left vacant by the damaged neurons (Edds, 1953); (d) *denervation supersensitivity*, suggesting that recovery occurs when denervated neurons become hypersensitive to the action of neural transmitters (Rosner, 1970); (e) *equipotentiality*, which maintains recovery reflects the mass action of remaining areas' equipotential for the lost function (Lashley, 1929); (f) *vicarious functioning*, arguing that recovery follows the "take over" of the damaged function by a separate brain region that was previously unemployed or functionally dormant, or whose function was sacrified to fulfill the role of the damaged area (Greenough *et al.*, 1976); and (g) *substitution or compensation*, which states that recovery follows the use of new neurophysiological and behavioral processes capable of achieving the original end through different means (LeVere, 1980; Luria, 1963).

The extent to which these various mechanisms operate in functional recovery is a subject of current debate (Hécaen & Albert, 1978; LeVere, 1980; Stein *et al.*, 1974). Moreover, they may not be mutually exclusive or independent of each other. For instance, the mechanisms responsible for resolution of acute transitory effects may interact with those responsible for long-term recovery (e.g., neural regeneration, vicarious functioning, etc.). Also age *per se* has not been of primary importance for most of these models and research has not been systematically directed at age-related effects. Despite the paucity of research, however, it is often assumed that age somehow directly influences these mechanisms of recovery. For example, Teuber (1974) stated that "differences in susceptibility to diaschisis and in the rates in which it seems to pass off might play a role in the differential capacity for recovery of function after lesions in young versus old brains" (p. 198).

Given that these mechanisms underlie the pattern of cognitive-behavioral changes found over time following brain damage, it has seemed reasonable to expect them to operate differentially throughout an organism's life span (Johnson & Almli, 1978). In that sense, the young developing nervous system, which is characterized as dynamic with respect to growth and differentiation, may have an advantage over the mature one. Thus, injury to a developmentally dynamic brain region could be associated with greater recovery when compared with developmentally mature regions. If, in fact, dynamic brain areas have an enhanced capacity for recovery, the mechanisms responsible would seem to involve some form of neural reorganization (e.g., regeneration, collateral sprouting, vicarious functioning). While this issue remains to be resolved in future research, attempting to clarify the potential role mechanisms of recovery have in determining cognitive-behavioral changes subsequent to brain injury in a child undoubtedly will prove useful in establishing efficacious approaches to remediation and prognostic formulations.

The nature of the problem may relate in part to the difference between recovery of function (implying some type of neuronal reorganization) and compensation (working alternative methods to accomplish a task). It appears likely that the young brain has a greater potential for neuronal reorganization or recovery of function but is less adept at compensation due to lack of prior experiences, with the converse holding true for an older brain. Thus, differences observed in recovery may relate, in part, to the degree to which recovery or compensation is accomplished.

THE PROBLEM OF CHRONOGENETIC LOCALIZATION

The extent to which child neuropsychologists can adequately predict the effects of brain injury in children is critically dependent on the degree to which they understand the development of structural-functional brain relationships. Chronogenetic localization, as first conceptualized by Vygotsky nearly 50 years ago (Luria, 1965), concerns the dynamic changes in functional systems of behavior correlated with brain integration and maturation across the developmental age span. Vygotsky concluded from making comparative analyses of symptoms accompanying focal brain lesions in children and adults that similar syndromes can arise in both cases as the result of different lesions and that identical lesions also can lead to very different syndromes. In order to account for these findings, one would have to conclude that the relationship between various brain regions subserving a particular behavioral function can change over the course of development. It is the clarification of this dynamic structural-functional organization associated with childhood that remains a task for future researchers.

For the present, even our limited understanding of chronogenetic localization can serve to improve the assessment and remediation of neurologically impaired children. Whereas for most individuals, normal psychological development may be simply characterized as changing strategies to solve old problems, Vygotsky (1965) maintained that it reflected changes in the component elements responsible for the mediation of the task in question. For instance, prior to the age of 10, children rely heavily on language in the performance of spatial or nonlanguage-related tasks (Rudel, 1978), after which such tasks do not appear to be verbally mediated. Along these same lines, there is apparently a transition in education from presentation of material in discrete steps to a more abstract problem-oriented approach to learning. It is perhaps for this reason that some children reveal problems in learning in later years or may reveal initial problems that are compensated for later.

The differential effects of cortical and subcortical lesions on spatial delayed and alternation tasks at different stages in development in monkeys provides strong support for a theory of chronogenetic localization (Goldman, 1974, 1978). The results of several investigations have clearly indicated that removing the dorsolateral prefrontal cortex in an adult monkey will impair the animal's capacity to perform delayed-response tasks. A similar lesion in an infant monkey will not, however, have a demonstrable effect on this ability. One possible explanation for this age difference is that the dorsolateral cortex (or its interconnections with subcortical structures) is not functionally mature and hence not used by the infant monkey to solve delayed-response patterns. Anatomically, it is known that the anterodorsal sector of the head of the caudate nucleus is the major efferent projection site for the dorsolateral prefrontal cortex. Lesions of this sector during infancy are also known to produce severe deficits in delayed-response learning that are relatively greater than those seen in adults with identical lesions. Thus, there appears to be a shift in cortical-subcortical relationships in mediating delayed-response functions with advancing development. That is, subcortical structures participate in the mediation of delayed-response learning prior to cortical development. With the development of cortical influence, however, the relative contribution of subcortical mechanisms in mediating delayed-response learning diminishes. Taken together, these findings would attest to the importance of understanding the chronogenetic localization of functions in order to predict adequately the effects of early brain injury.

CONCLUSIONS

Effective assessment of the nature and extent of the consequences of brain damage in children is a more difficult and challenging task than with adults. As with adults, eventual outcome is influenced by organic factors (type of pathology, locus, extent, etc.) and nonneurological factors such as emotional adjustment and sociological/environmental influences. Although these factors render assessment of neurological systems difficult at any age, it is further complicated in children by developmental changes. The child, unlike the adult, progresses from limited functioning of basic neurological systems to more integrated functioning of higher systems. This transition is not uniform, but may be fraught with developmental lags or influenced by nonneurological factors. It is essential to incorporate a developmental model into the diagnostic system when assessing neurological functioning of children.

Children "grow out" of some early acquired deficits but not others. In some cases dysfunction may not appear until later in development. Research is rather convincing that age of onset, location, and nature of the deficit interact to determine final deficits later in life. An understanding of chronogenetic localization of function is necesary to assess, treat, and predict outcome in neurologically impaired children effectively.

Perhaps Luria's model provides the best general plan for considering chronogenetic localization in assessment and remediation. Care should be taken to establish that arousal functions are operating at an optimal level. Deviation in arousal from such levels can impair functioning and limit accurate assessment. Between 5 and 8 years of age, primary assessment and remediation should be directed toward basic sensory-motor processing largely within a given modality. Complex integrative functions are not likely present and cannot be assessed reliably during this period. Between the ages of 8 and 12, higher order (frontal) systems should develop, and thus only at this time can such functions be evaluated effectively. Such an approach may explain how higher systems may develop later and provide a means of compensating for earlier deficits. Furthermore, this approach better explains the observations of Teuber and Rudel (1962) that "deficit" patterns may appear initially and later resolve, persist, or appear subsequently in development.

Acknowledgments

The authors sincerely thank W. L. Hutcherson for his critique and editorial assistance on an earlier draft of this chapter.

REFERENCES

Bakker, D. J. The brain as a dependent variable. *Journal of Clinical Neuropsychology*, 1984, 6, 1–16.

Boll, T. J. Diagnosing brain impairment. In B. B. Wolman (Ed.), *Clinical diagnosis of mental disorders*. New York: Plenum Press, 1978.

Boll, T. J., & Barth, J. T. Neuropsychology of brain damage in children. In S. B. Filskov & T. J. Boll (Eds.), *Handbook of clinical neuropsychology*. New York: Wiley, 1981.

Braun, J. J. Time and recovery from brain damage. In S. Finger (Ed.), *Recovery from brain damage*. New York: Plenum Press, 1978.

Buffery, A. W. H. Sex differences in the development of hemispheric asymmetry of function in the human brain. *Brain Research*, 1971, 31, 364–365.

Chelune, G. J., & Edwards, P. Early brain lesions: Ontogenetic-environmental considerations. *Journal of Consulting and Clinical Psychology*, 1981, 49, 777–790.

Edds, M. V. Collateral nerve regeneration. *Quarterly Review Biology*, 1953, 28, 260–276.

Escourolle, R., & Poirier, J. *Manual of basic neuropathology*. Philadelphia: W. B. Saunders, 1978.

Filskov, S. B., & Boll, T. J. (Eds.). *Handbook of clinical neuropsychology*. New York: Wiley, 1981.

Finger, S. *Recovery from brain damage*. New York: Plenum Press, 1978.

Goldman, P. S. Functional development of the prefrontal cortex in early life and the problem of neuronal plasticity. *Experimental Neurology*, 1971, 32, 366–387.

Goldman, P. S. Developmental determinants of cortical plasticity. *Acta Neurobiologica Experimentalis*, 1972, 32, 495–511.

Goldman, P. S. An alternative to developmental plasticity: Heterology of CNS structures in infants and adults. In D. Stein, J. Rosen, & N. Butters (Eds.), *Plasticity and recovery of function in the central nervous system*. New York: Academic Press, 1974.

Goldman, P. S. Development of frontal association cortex in the infrahuman primate. In *The neurological basis of language disorders in children: Methods and directions for research*. NIMCDS Monograph No. 22, 1978.

Gottlieb, G. Conceptions of prenatal development: Behavioral embryology. *Psychology Reviews*, 1976, *83*, 215–234.

Greenough, W. T., Fass, B., & DeVoogd, T. J. The influence of experience on recovery following brain damage in rodents: Hypothesis based on developmental research. In R. N. Walsh & W. T. Greenough (Eds.), *Environments as therapy for brain dysfunction*. New York: Plenum Press, 1976.

Hécaen, H., & Albert, M. L. *Human neuropsychology*. New York: Wiley, 1978.

Heilman, K. M., & Valenstein, E. *Clinical neuropsychology*. New York: Oxford University Press, 1979.

Hutt, S. J. Cognitive development and cerebral dysfunction. In V. Hamilton & M. D. Vernon (Eds.), *The development of cognitive processes*. New York: Academic Press, 1976.

Isaacson, R. L. The myth of recovery from early brain damage. In N. G. Ellis (Ed.), *Aberrant development in infancy*. New York: Wiley, 1975.

Johnson, D., & Almli, C. R. Age, brain damage, and performance. In S. Finger (Ed.), *Recovery from brain damage*. New York: Plenum Press, 1978.

Kennard, M. A. Age and other factors in motor recovery from precentral lesions in monkeys. *American Journal of Physiology*, 1936, *115*, 138–146.

Kennard, M. A. Reorganization of motor functions in the cerebral cortex of monkeys deprived of motor and pre-motor areas in infancy. *Journal of Neurophysiology*, 1938, *1*, 477–496.

Kennard, M. A. Relation of age to motor impairment in man and in subhuman primates. *Archives of Neurology and Psychiatry*, 1940, *44*, 377–397.

Kennard, M. A. Cortical reorganization of motor function: Studies on a series of monkeys of various ages from infancy to maturity. *Archives of Neurology and Psychiatry*, 1942, *8*, 227–240.

Kertesz, A. Recovery and treatment. In K. M. Heilman & E. Valenstein (Eds.), *Clinical neuropsychology*. New York: Oxford University Press, 1979.

Kleiman, M. B., Carver, D. H. Central nervous system infections. In P. Black (Ed.), *Brain dysfunction in children: Etiology, diagnosis, and management*. New York: Raven Press, 1981.

Lashley, K. S. *Brain mechanisms and intelligence*. Chicago: University of Chicago Press, 1929.

Lawrence, D. G., & Hopkins, D. A. Developmental aspects of pyramidal motor control in the rhesus monkey. *Brain Research*, 1972, *40*, 117–118.

Lenneberg, E. H. *Biological foundations of language*. New York: Wiley, 1967.

LeVere, T. E. Recovery of function after brain damage: A theory of the behavioral deficit. *Physiological Psychology*, 1980, *8*, 297–308.

Lezak, M. D. *Neuropsychological assessment*. New York: Oxford University Press, 1976.

Lishman, W. A. *Organic psychiatry: The psychological consequence of cerebral disorder*. Oxford: Blackwell Scientific, 1978.

Luria, A. R. *Restoration of function after brain injury*. New York: Macmillan, 1963.

Luria, A. R. L. S. Vygotsky and the problem of localization of functions. *Neuropsychologia*, 1965, *3*, 387–392.

Mathura, C. B. The vulnerability of the male CNS to early trauma: Implications for clinical neuropsychology. *Clinical Neuropsychology*, 1979, *4*, 34–35.

Milner, B. Functional recovery after lesions of the nervous system. 3. Developmental processes in neural plasticity. Sparing of language functions after early unilateral brain damage. *Neurosciences Research Program Bulletin*, 1974, *12*, 213–217.

Milner, B. Personal communication, Jackson, Miss. 1982.

Parsons, O. A., & Prigatano, G. P. Methodological considerations in clinical neuropsychological research. *Journal of Consulting and Clinical Psychology*, 1978, *46*, 608–619.

Renis, S., & Goldman, J. M. *The development of the brain.* Springfield, Ill: Charles C Thomas, 1980.

Rosner, B. S. Brain functions. *Annual Review of Psychology*, 1970, *21*, 555–594.

Rourke, B. P., Bakker, D. J., Fisk, J. L., & Strang, J. D. *Child neuropsychology: An introduction to theory, research, and clinical practice.* New York: Guilford Press, 1983.

Rudel, R. G. Neuroplasticity: Implications for development and education. In J. S. Chall & A. F. Mirsky (Eds.), *Education and the brain.* Chicago: University of Chicago Press, 1978.

Rutter, M. Developmental neuropsychiatry: Concepts, issues and prospects. *Journal of Clinical Neuropsychology*, 1982, *4*, 91–115.

Rutter, M., Graham, P., & Yule, W. *A neuropsychiatric study in childhood.* Clinics in Developmental Medicine (Vols. 35/36). London: Heinemann Medical/SIMP, 1970.

Sameroff, A. J., & Chandler, M. J. Reproductive risk and the continuum or caretaker casualty. In F. D. Horowitz (Ed.), *Review of child development research* (Vol. 4). Chicago: University of Chicago Press, 1975.

Satz, P., & Fletcher, J. M. Emergent trends in neuropsychology: An overview. *Journal of Consulting and Clinical Psychology*, 1981, *49*, 851–865.

Schneider, G. E. Early lesions of superior colliculus: Factors affecting the formation of abnormal retinal projections. *Brain Behavior and Evolution*, 1973, *8*, 73–109.

Schneider, G. E. Is it really better to have your brain lesion early? A revision of the "Kennard principle." *Neuropsychologia*, 1979, *17*, 557–583.

Stein, D. G., Rosen, J., & Butters, N. (Eds.), *Plasticity and recovery of function in the central nervous system.* New York: Academic Press, 1974.

Stewart, A. L., & Reynolds, E. D. R. Improved prognosis for infants of very low birth weight. *Pediatrics*, 1975, *54*, 724–735.

St. James-Roberts, I. Neurological plasticity recovery from brain insult and child development. In H. W. Reese (Ed.), *Advances in child development and behavior* (Vol. 14). New York: Academic Press, 1979.

St. James-Roberts, I. A reinterpretation of hemispherectomy data without functional plasticity of the brain: I. Intellectual function. *Brain and Language*, 1981, *13*, 31–53.

Teuber, H. L. History and prospects. *Neurosciences Research Program Bulletin*, 1974, *12*, 197–211.

Teuber, H. L. Effects of focal brain injury on human behavior. In D. B. Tower (Ed.), *The nervous system, Vol. 2: The clinical neurosciences.* New York: Raven Press, 1975.

Teuber, H. L., & Rudel, R. G. Behavior after cerebral lesions in children and adults. *Developmental Medicine and Child Neurology*, 1962, *4*, 3–20.

Vygotsky, L. S. Psychology of localization of functions. *Neuropsychologia*, 1965, *3*, 381–386.

Yakovlev, P.I., & Lecours, A. R. The myelogenetic cycles of regional maturation of the brain. In A. Minkowski (Ed.), *Regional development of the brain in early life.* Oxford: Blackwell Scientific, 1967.

CHAPTER 4

Neuropsychology of Perception

LAWRENCE E. MELAMED and ESTHER C. MELAMED

BACKGROUND ISSUES

Perceptual science occupies a rather interesting position within the cognate areas of neuropsychology. It is perhaps the only discipline that is, at once, both widely applied in neuropsychology and yet seems to have had no major impact in the way of producing a transfer of constructs and influencing the conceptual basis of neuropsychological assessment. Consider how current constructs from memory research such as "depth of processing" or "episodic memory" have worked their way into neuropsychological analysis. Parallels from perception are hard to find. Given the long history of research and theory construction in perception and, indeed, its central position in the history of psychology, one would expect a tremendously active and very current use of perceptual constructs in neuropsychology. Perhaps one source of perceptual science's lack of vigorous input into neuropsychology is the immediacy of the content, the apparent face validity of any construct that one uses, at any level of analysis. Consider the example of "visual closure." People do tend to fill in open forms as the Gestalt law of closure aptly demonstrates. It is not surprising, therefore, that Colarusso and Hammill (1972) examine this "basic" skill as one of five types in their Motor-Free Visual Perception Test. Here the child must choose the correct (closed) form from various figures drawn incompletely with gaps within one or more line elements.

If one attempts to characterize the task of the child on these visual closure items in a more fundamental way, a second source of inertia in

LAWRENCE E. MELAMED • Psychology Department, Kent State University, Kent, Ohio 44242.   ESTHER C. MELAMED • Department of Curriculum and Instruction, Kent State University, Kent, Ohio 44242.

61

using perceptual science becomes evident. The pertinent theories generally are quite abstruse and often are mathematical or physiological in orientation. Principles of contour enhancement through lateral inhibition or a quantitative specification of information content are difficult to apply to these stimuli. Further sources of difficulty would have to do with the nature and purpose of assessment of perceptual factors. Crude constructs aside, if a child cannot copy forms or discriminate them at age level, one has very useful information for school placement. The idea of *diagnosing* anomalous perceptual behavior more fundamentally has never been well developed in neuropsychology. This is so, in spite of the fact that intervention based on traditional levels of analysis generally have not been very helpful (Kavale & Mattson, 1983).

The purpose of the present chapter is to introduce those interested in perceptual assessments within the domain of child neuropsychology to the major issues, theories, and formal constructs in selected areas of perceptual science. The focus will be primarily on visual perception, given the practical limitations of this chapter. In addition, an example of an assessment procedure derived from basic research in form perception will be presented. Some of the potential benefits as well as the difficulties in attempting to create such construct-valid instruments will be discussed.

DEFINITIONS OF PERCEPTION AND PERCEPTUAL LEARNING

There are, as would be expected, many different definitions of perception current today. Although the source of these differences can be related to philosophical issues that have long been a part of the field of perception, the differences in emphasis and content also point to current deliberations on the role of perception in this age of neuroscience and cognitive psychology. It is simplest to identify perception with the operation of lower order cognitive skills that are employed in carrying out executive functions. Most compatible with this viewpoint of perception is Rock's (1975) focus on the manner in which perception specifies the external environment, the *distal* stimulus to the observer.

> In perception, the interest is in the representation of the world of objects and events that constitute our physical environment. Thus the concern is with the perceived shape, size, distance, direction, orientation, and state of rest or movement of objects. (p. 24)

Rock represents what might be termed a traditional and functional point of view where microtheories serve as explanatory vehicles for the various phenomena studied by perceptionists. Eleanor and James Gibson, on the other hand, represent the macrotheory level of analysis. The Gibsons' approach to perceptual theory has been of such importance in the developmental area that it will be discussed more thoroughly in a later section of this chapter. The most concise definition of perception offered by this approach is perhaps that found in Gibson and Levin (1975): "Perception is the process of extracting information from stimulation emanating from the objects, places, and events in the world around us" (p. 13). The apparent simplicity of this definition is misleading in that this approach involves a very novel and complex specification of stimulus information and the process of perception.

Perceptual learning from this point of view is a process of differentiating more and more useful information from the optic array:

> Perceptual learning is learning to extract the relevant information from the manifold available stimulation, that is, the invariant information that specifies the permanent layout of the environment, and invariants of events that enable us to predict outcomes and detect causes. . . . It is, rather, an increase of specificity of discrimination to stimulus input, an increase in differentiations of stimulus information. It is extraction or 'pulling out' rather than adding on. The modification is in *what* is perceived. (Gibson & Levin, 1975, p. 13)

Probably the most integrative definition of perception is that created by Uttal (1981). This statement resulted from the massive intellectual task of surveying current theories, constructs, and research in perception and cognate disciplines and then using this information in establishing a taxonomy of visual processes. Uttal's definition is as follows:

> Perception is the relatively immediate, intrapersonal, mental response evoked as a partial, but not exclusive, result of impinging multidimensional stimuli, as modulated by the transforms imposed by the neural communication systems, previous experience, and contextual reasonableness. Each percept is the conscious end product of both simple computational transformations and more complex constructionistic 'interpretations.' However, the underlying neural and symbolic processes are not part of the observer's awareness. (Uttal, 1981, pp. 13–14)

The present authors' view is very similar to Uttal's in the belief that constructs from both neuroscience and psychology must be integrated into any current metatheory of perception given the paradox that all mental processes involve neural mechanisms, yet most perceptual phenomena are too complex to be explained by neuroreductionistic models. that is most unique in Uttal's approach is the belief that the percept is influenced by the structural characteristics of the physiological processors as well as experience and context.

FUNDAMENTAL ISSUES IN PERCEPTION IN THEIR HISTORIC AND PRESENT FORM

Probably no other area of psychology has issues that have remained in contention for as long as some in the area of perception. The importance of these controversies lies first in the fact that different "schools" and methodological orientations in perception are directly or indirectly based on particular resolutions of one or more of these. A second and related point is that the same perceptual phenomenon, for example, size constancy, can be examined from different perspectives using quite different experimental manipulations depending on the theoretical orientation of the investigator.

Nativism versus Empiricism. One major axis that separates current approaches to perception is the ancient controversy over the innate (nativist) or learned (empiricist) origin of the perceptual experience, the percept. John Locke, in the early 18th century, proposed that there is nothing to the mind except what was first in the senses and that the mind is at birth a clean sheet or tabula rasa. This could be considered the prototypical empiricistic model. Contention concerning the proper sensory elements has existed from the time of Locke (1632–1704) through that of the 19th century German structuralists, until the present information-processing models of perceptual phenomena. A problem for the empiricistic point of view is the origin of integrated or organized percepts that involve more than single, unitary experiences. Some sort of associative learning process induced by temporal or spatial contiguity has been the historical solution. Nativism is the philosophical antithesis of empiricism. Consider the belief of Kant in the *a priori* concepts of objects. For Kant, sensations did not cluster spontaneously by association into percepts (Durant, 1959). Space and time as *a priori* perceptual processing agencies of the mind established the selection and coordination of sensations into organized percepts. It should be emphasized that the modal nativist position is broad enough to allow for the consideration of maturational factors in perceptual development.

The nativism/empiricism issue is very alive within developmental psychology, particularly in the area of infant perception. One recent review of this area (Acredolo & Hake, 1982) has well over 300 references. These findings indicate that the infant seems to have greater initial perceptual skills, that is, in the first few months of life, than had been anticipated previously. Such findings do not really cause an abatement of the nativism/empiricism controversy. If anything, they complicate it in two ways. They necessitate an evaluation of the role played by the novel methodologies employed in these discoveries. Second, they focus attention on physiological precursors of such behavioral capabilities. Neither of these issues would have been preeminent in the recent past.

The Role of Cognitive Concepts as Explanation. Consider the relative veridicality of the adult in reporting his or her percept of the external or distal stimulus. Changes in the proximal (retinal) stimulus are seemingly ignored in the production of perceptual constancies. How does this come about? How do we perceive objects at constant size even though their retinal image undergoes constant size transformations? Helmholtz (1924) proposed a taking-into-account mechanism of "unconscious inference." In the present example, distance information would be taken into account in evaluating size transformations in the proximal stimulus. This necessitates learning. Helmholtz's rule as specified by Hochberg (1979) is that: "We perceive just those objects and events that would under normal conditions be most likely to produce the sets of effective sensory stimulation that we are receiving" (p. 104). Although there is some controversy over whether these unconscious inferences are cognitive mediations, for example, compare Hochberg with Pastore (1971), they do imply a role for mental structures in perception.

At the present time, the role of cognitive concepts, or mental structure as Hochberg prefers, is being argued vehemently between those who identify themselves as cognitive psychologists and take an information processing approach to perception and the followers of Gibson's (1979) approach. This controversy will be discussed at length in a later presentation of Gibson's theory in this chapter. Basically, Gibson proposed that perception is *direct* and unmediated, arising from available stimulus information. His opponents can be viewed as constructivists (Reed & Jones, 1979) who have the perceiver actively creating representations of the distal stimulus from information that, in itself, may be quite incomplete.

Neurophysiological Reductionism. Neurophysiology has been an area of immense innovation and discovery in the past quarter century. Such findings as the organizational aspects of receptive fields for sensory neurons, the specificity of stimulus-coding mechanisms within the sensory nervous systems, and the lateral interactions between adjacent sensory nerve fibers have led to such an infatuation with neurological explanations for perceptual phenomena that even William James would probably think it overdone. Uttal (1981) in particular thinks this sort of model building is basically inappropriate for explaining perceptual phenomena beyond the level of basic psychophysical responses. Although he makes concrete arguments against specific classes of models such as those using single cells to explain complex percepts, it is his general remarks that are particularly cogent. His first point concerns the complexity of the brain, with perhaps 10 trillion neurons, each with thousands of synaptic connections. The resulting neural networks are beyond present conceptual and technical analysis. A related point is that current discoveries, even those of Hubel and Wiesel, have really been about what Uttal (1981) calls the peripheral communication system of the brain, rather than about the "central integrative system where the true psychoneural equivalents reside"

(p. 668). Finally, and most problematic, is the realization that there are limitless, equivalent formal models one can build for describing the activity of neurons in order to explain various perceptual phenomena (cf. Stork & Levinson, 1982).

THEORIES OF PERCEPTION AND PERCEPTUAL DEVELOPMENT

Gestalt. Probably no theory in visual perception has had more of an influence on assessment in neuropsychology than that of the Gestalt psychologists. This remark is not specifically directed toward the continued widespread, if perhaps inappropriate (Bigler & Ehrfurth, 1981), use of the Bender-Gestalt Test. Rather, it is directed toward the continuing vitality of the concept that it is the organization of the percept or perceptual-motor behavior that is the preeminent factor to be evaluated in judging the intactness and maturation of perceptual skills. A close second in influence has been another Gestalt concept, that of figure–ground, in which it is proposed that an essential aspect of any perceptual experience is the dissociation of a figure with its attached contour and relative proximity from a background that appears at a greater distance and has an amorphous organization. Many "perceptual" instruments specifically assess for this skill, for example, the Motor-Free Visual Perception Test (Colarusso & Hammill, 1972) and the Developmental Test of Visual Perception (Frostig, 1963).

The introduction of Gestalt theory in psychology was akin to an intellectual revolution. The dominance of the structuralist point of view in perception ended rather abruptly when the Gestalt approach appeared during the World War I era. While structuralists argued about the nature of elementary sensations and the manner in which they were combined through experience into percepts, Gestalt psychology began with the percept as an unanalyzed but organized entity. The proper data of perception were the *phenomenological* experiences of the observer. The answer to the question—"Why do things look as they do" (Koffka, 1935)—was not to be found in an analytic decomposition of the observer's experience into more basic component sensations. The answer was basically neurological. Perception really was a window on cortical functioning in this approach. Perceptual experiences were said to be isomorphic to autonomous brain processes. The latter served to organize sensory input into good Gestalten following a master principle, variously called *the law of pragnanz* or *minimum principle,* in which simplification and regularity were the observed outcome. Other Gestalt "laws," for example, *closure,* in which the observer tends to perceive partially incomplete forms as closed, are instances of the operation of the minimum principle. *Figure–*

ground fits in here as the simplest of mental configurations where a form "becomes a quality" (Koffka, 1935). Pomerantz (1981) makes the point that grouping is logically prior to figure–ground and must represent an earlier stage of information processing. One further aspect of Gestalt theory that should be emphasized is that it is a nativist position that leaves little room for an effect of experience on perception other than in the formation and consolidation of neurological trace systems.

Koffka (1935, 1951) has presented the Gestalt viewpoint on perceptual development. Most of his comments concern infancy. He argues that initial perceptual experience is not ambiguous or chaotic, à la William James. The simplest perceptual situation for an infant is an organized homogeneous visual field where the child is in some state of sensory equilibrium. The child can experience figure–ground when a light (a quality) is introduced. Koffka further asserts that the infant's movement is correlated with phenomenal experience. We can therefore study the movement of the child as evidence of his or her perception of a figure. The explanation of perceptual constancies such as of shape and size is cumbersome. An object will be seen veridically only when its perspective is such as to favor a phenomenal configuration that is veridical. A corollary is that once this veridical organization has been aroused, it somehow maintains itself even when the stimulus is subsequently presented at a different perspective.

Modern commentary on Gestalt theory takes two forms. The first consists of a search for a less circular and phenomenologically based set of principles for specifying and predicting perceptual organization. One approach has been that of Attneave (1954, 1955, 1957), who viewed the Gestalt laws as representing ways in which redundancy, in the formal sense of information theory (Shannon & Weaver, 1949), could be imposed on the stimulus. As an example of this approach applied to pictorial stimuli, one could be receiving redundant information from an area of homogeneous color or brightness, or second, from a contour of homogeneous direction or shape. A different approach, one in which Gestalt laws are contrasted with organizing principles more explicable from current neuroscience, is represented by the work of Beck (1966), who found that the Gestalt organizing principle of physical similarity was not as good a predictor of the grouping of pattern elements as was the similarity in spatial orientation of these same elements.

The second aspect of contemporary commentary on Gestalt theory is that of a critical analysis. Perhaps the most apparent problem with Gestalt theory is the need to operationalize its constructs, for example, similarity, good figure, pragnanz, and so forth. On the other hand, Pomerantz and Kubovy (1981) point out that the use of phenomenological reports can be productive as guides for experimental research. The focus of current arguments with Gestalt theory concerns pragnanz. Thus, Hochberg (1981) argues that this concept either refers to a process for organizing the entire stimulus field or it has no meaning. He points out that certain stimuli such as impossible figures (drawings that are seen as three dimensional objects yet such objects could never be constructed) are perceived in a way that shows the operation of *local* depth cues rather than the global organizing principles of pragnanz.

   Eleanor and James Gibson. James Gibson has a position in perceptual theory that is akin to that of Piaget in cognitive development. He is a theorist of originality and depth whose work is taken seriously, either in support or contention, by an increasing number of perceptual scientists. The name of Gibson's last book (1979) is *The Ecological Approach to Visual Perception.* It concerns the perception of places, objects, and substances rather than color, form, space, time and motion, as one ordinarily would expect of a perceptual theory. In perceiving places, objects, and so forth, one perceives what Gibson calls *affordances.* These are whatever the environment provides, whether positive or negative in effect. An elongated elastic fiber thus affords fiber, thread, and weaving. Perceiving affordances, like any perceptual event for Gibson, is a matter of extracting the appropriate invariants from the ambient optic array. For affordances, these are higher order invariants. Invariants are structural elements or features in the ambient optic array that are perceived as stable or "persistent" in the midst of the perspective changes that occur with the observer's movement. Such information is merely detected or "picked up." It is not transmitted or cognitively derived. This is a theory of *direct perception*, that is, unmediated neurally or cognitively. As Reed and Jones (1979) express it: "Perception comes first; it is not a composite of sensations with memory or with anything else. Literally, for Gibson, the perception of danger would be a far more direct and primary epistemic occurrence than sensing a patch of red" (p. 192). It is instructive to examine the manner of explanation Gibson offers for size constancy. He believes that size is perceived directly without any cognitive mediation using features of the optic array that are invariant with changes in the distance of the stimulus. One such invariant could be the number of texture elements in the optic array occluded by the object. This number would stay the same no matter the distance of the object if uniform texture elements exist throughout the array.

   There is much criticism of the theory of direct perception from "constructivists" of all types. A common complaint (Hayes-Roth, 1980; Ullman, 1980) is that mediating processes are necessary since no perceptual system could provide all the unique "invariants" for the infinite number of perceptual experiences we can have. However, Jones and Pick (1980) think otherwise, locating the information in the optical flow pattern. Some cognitive psychologists attempt to come to grips with Gibson's ideas by assigning his constructs a role in information processing. Thus Ullman has the information content analysis of ecological optics as the highest function of the visual system. Rock (1980), who thinks of mediation in the Helmholtzian manner of unconscious inferences, chooses to attack Gibson with situational evidence that does not conform to the tenets of direct perception. One particularly troublesome finding is size constancy in a situation where only the object is visible and only oculomotor "cues" to distance, such as accommodation of the lens of the eyes, are available. Other than in taking this distance information into account, it is unclear how the observer could produce accurate size judgments since there are no invariants here (Rock, Hill, & Fineman, 1968).

Eleanor Gibson is the major theorist of perceptual development. Consistent with the general approach of James Gibson, her view is that perceptual learning is learning to extract the appropriate invariants from the optical stimulation in order to adapt to our environment. This learning is facilitated by concurrent maturation of attention processes. According to Gibson and Levin (1975), other aspects of this learning are that it is active (in that the child searches for information), selective, and progresses toward better differentiation of the available information. What is learned perceptually is structure which ranges from learning the *distinctive features* of objects and forms to detecting the invariants underlying our perception of the higher order structures involved in comprehending language. As an example of the use of distinctive features analysis (Gibson, 1969), consider the capital letter *A*. This can be thought of as a stimulus containing a horizontal line, intersection of elements, symmetry, and vertical discontinuity.

One particularly interesting component of Gibson's approach is her concern with the motivational basis for perceptual learning and development. She favors the idea of intrinsic motivation, that is, innate curiosity. Mention also should be made of the three trends that Gibson and Levin see occurring in perceptual development. The first is a growing correspondence between percepts and stimulus information as the former become more and more differentiated with experience. The second is an optimization of attention in which the child becomes more competent in using behaviors that focus attention toward the most relevant aspects of the structure being examined. Finally, there is an increasing economy of information pickup such as when children show an increasing ability to use only a minimum number of distinctive features in differentiating stimuli.

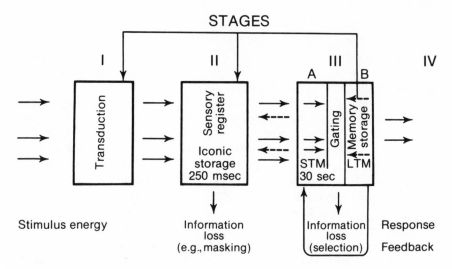

FIGURE 1. A representative information–processing model for perception. (From Forgus & Melamed, 1976.)

Information-Processing Approaches. Certainly one of the most active domains within experimental psychology during the past two decades has been the information-processing (or "cognitive") area. This area now encompasses a very broad range of approaches extending from the computational approach favored by computer scientists interested in artificial intelligence (e.g., Marr & Nishihara, 1978) to the information flow-chart model of mental structure favored by many psychologists. Although formal mathematical representations of psychological processes are likely to be found only in the computational approaches, most all information-processing models seem to have processes dictated by discoveries in neurosciences—particularly from the single-cell research on feature detection.

A representative information-processing model is presented in Figure 1. For this model, it is assumed that there are cognitive structures that underlie perceptual tasks. In this diagram, the arrows represent the transfer of information. Most of the processing within the various stages involves memory functions ranging from a brief registration of the stimulus lasting about 250 msec to a relatively permanent long-term memory. Higher stages ("knowledge") influence lower ones. Essentially, perception is viewed as a process of active construction using both internal and external cues.

Information-processing models are fairly silent on developmental issues. However, many studies have been conducted examining the viability of constructs from these models as explanations for performance differences on perceptual tasks between groups of children who differ in age or some measure of achievement.

CURRENT USE OF PERCEPTUAL CONSTRUCTS IN NEUROPSYCHOLOGY

Although traditional constructs from perceptual science are generally not being used, perceptual skill assessments nevertheless play a central role in child neuropsychology. Even comprehensive batteries such as the Halstead Neuropsychological Test Battery for Older Children and the Reitan-Indiana Neuropsychological Test Battery For Younger Children have primarily a sensory or perceptual content. Selz (1981) provides a worksheet for the Halstead battery. It is interesting to note that of the 21 measures remaining after those concerned with IQ and aphasia are removed, 12 are sensory-perceptual. These are tests such as the Tactual Performance Test where the primary component of the task is a perceptual discrimination involving the haptic sense. In fact, the majority of perceptual measures for this test involve the haptic sense. The Reitan–Indiana, dealing with younger children, does assess visual functions to a greater extent than the Halstead. The Luria-Nebraska Children's Battery (Golden, 1981), perhaps reflecting the greater intended age range (6–14), assesses somewhat more visual and auditory (including speech) skills than the Halstead or Reitan-Indiana.

The most widely used assessments considered perceptual are, of course, those involving visual forms, most often geometric or related to those from the earlier Gestalt literature. Form copying (e.g., Bender-Gestalt Test, Procedure C of the Benton Visual Retention Test, Draw-a-Design of the McCarthy Scales, and the Developmental Test of Visual Motor Integration), form discrimination using a matching to sample procedure (e.g., Motor-Free Visual Perception Test and the Recognition-Discrimination Test of the Florida Kindergarten Screening Battery), and immediate or short-term memory (e.g., Benton Visual Retention, Motor-Free, and the Visual Sequential Memory Test of the Illinois Test of Psycholinguistic Abilities) are the most commonly assessed skills. Comparable tests can be found in the auditory area (e.g., Wepman Auditory Discrimination Test).

There are many problems associated with these perceptual assessments. The central one is that there is no fine analysis of the variables or skills involved. Forms are used for historical reasons or because they work well in developing age norms. Even within the narrow confines of a comparatively simple task such as form copying, there is ordinarily no way to distinguish the perceptual sources of any difficulty that a child may have with the task. Belmont (1980) does a marvelous job of task analyzing the Bender-Gestalt Test and demonstrating the larger number of perceptual as well as higher order functions that could contribute to errors. Copying tasks often have a unique problem of their own in that scoring procedures are often based either on a "common sense" analysis of the form features or an appraisal of historical signs for brain damage such as perseveration. Such criteria are not very useful for diagnosing perceptual skills.

Perceptual constructs also are actively used in child neuropsychology in describing subgroups of dyslexia or learning disabilities. As examples of such subtyping for reading disorders, Mattis, French, and Rapin (1975) have a visual-spatial perceptual disorder group, Boder (1973) a dyseidetic, and Lyon, Stewart, and Freedman (1982) a visual perceptual group. Given that the tests used to form these groups are generally elements of the Halstead-Reitan instruments or standard ones such as the Developmental Test of Visual-Motor Integration, little progress has been made in characterizing the nature of the perceptual deficits that group membership represents. Satz and Morris (1981) provide a cogent critical evaluation of the various procedures that have been employed in producing these subtypings.

TWO KEY AREAS OF PERCEPTUAL DEVELOPMENT RESEARCH FOR CHILD NEUROPSYCHOLOGY

Given the limited space available here for reviewing research in perceptual development, it seemed best to focus our review on two areas that have received particular attention in neuropsychological assessment: (a) form and object perception and (b) spatial coding and representation. The literature reviewed has been selected to demonstrate the promising sources of information that exist for child neuropsychology and that can be used in interpreting present assessment procedures and in developing new ones. No attempt has been made to offer comprehensive coverage of any particular issue.

FORM AND OBJECT PERCEPTION

No area of research in perceptual development is more active than that of infant perception. The lure may still be the nature–nurture question, but the driving force seems to have been the invention of acceptable methodologies for evaluating perceptual skills. One of the most widely used of these is the habituation-dishabituation procedure in which the infant is presented with a stimulus or series of stimuli until some response measure such as visual fixation declines to some arbitrary level. Then either a novel stimulus condition is presented or the original one is continued. The expectation in using this procedure is that the dependent measure should recover, that is, dishabituation should occur, only for the novel condition if the infant is capable of discriminating the source of the novelty.

The habituation-dishabituation paradigm has been put to use by Eleanor Gibson and her co-workers in an attempt to find evidence for the use of invariant stimulus information in young infants and thus support for the theory of "direct" perception. In Gibson, Owsley, and Johnston (1978) and Gibson, Owsley, Walker, and Megaw-Nyce (1979), the looking time of infants recovered when the *substance* of an object was novel on the dishabituation trials. Originally the foam rubber objects employed underwent a rigid motion. A deforming motion was used in producing dishabituation. In Gibson et al. (1978), 3-month-old infants appeared to be able to differentiate invariants for both substance and shape from the same stimulus exposure, a skill that is surprising at this age. In a later study, Walker, Owsley, Megaw-Nyce, and Gibson (1980) demonstrated the detection of elasticity as an invariant property of these same objects by the 3-month-old infants. Ruff (1982) has found evidence that certain types of movement in habituation trials, particularly translation, facilitated the apparent recognition of these objects on dishabituation trials. The argument made is that certain movements are effective in providing the invariants that infants need for these perceptual achievements. Schwartz and Day (1979), using a dishabituation procedure, found that infants as young as 2 months are sensitive to relations between pattern elements. They argue that the ability to abstract such information is probably innate. Ruff (1980) has offered a set of principles that relate Eleanor Gibson's theory of perceptual development to object recognition in infancy. The first principle is that the earliest invariants differentiated are those for general aspects of an object's structure whereas specific aspects are perceived later. Secondly, invariants are detected partly because of their involvement or use in the infant's activity. As activities broaden, so does detection of invariants. Finally, Ruff believes that object recognition develops from being context bound to being context free.

Form perception was the initial area of exploration in infant perception. The basic findings have not changed since the pioneering work of Fantz (1958, 1963): (a) infants prefer to look at more complicated forms than simpler ones and (b) particular preferences may change with development. The central problem in this research has always been to determine the source of those preferences, that is, to determine whether infants are truly responding to "form" and not to selected, even primitive

74 LAWRENCE E. MELAMED AND ESTHER C. MELAMED

features. Young infants do show such preferences as curvature over straight lines (Fantz & Miranda, 1975) and for pattern elements of a certain size (Maisel & Karmel, 1978). Bornstein and his co-workers (Bornstein, Ferdinandsen, & Gross, 1981; Fisher, Ferdinandsen, & Bornstein, 1981) have shown that 4-month-old infants respond to vertical symmetry as an organizational aspect of visual patterns.

One area of perceptual development research in which there has been a strong influence from work with adults is that on the development of sensitivity to the structural elements of form. Chipman and Mendelson (1975) had children judge which of two patterns was simpler using patterns equated for contour but differing in complexity as judged by adults. They found that young (4–5 years) children were as capable as older ones (7–10 years) of detecting and responding to structure for *low contour* patterns. Although the older children responded to structure in patterns of greater contour, adults weighted the structure even more. In a later study, Chipman and Mendelson (1979) used specific types of structure, for example, vertical symmetry, in comparing judgments of visual complexity across elementary grade levels. The two developmental trends found were (a) that structural variables become increasingly important compared with contour measures with increasing age, and (b) the relative importance of different types of structure changes with age. These findings are similar to those of Aiken and Williams (1975), who used a sorting task with the multidimensional forms of Brown and Owens (1967). The major finding was the gradual increase in the size of the feature set used in sorting the stimuli, from two to three aspects, from Grade 2 to Grade 5. Using three features is similar to adult strategies. Although not specific to form perception, a very important area of research to consider is that of integral and separable stimulus dimensions. Garner (1974) has proposed that some combinations of stimulus dimensions, for example, saturation and brightness, are integral and stimuli produced from these dimensions are perceived in a holistic manner by adults, whereas others, for example, color and form, are separable and are readily perceived as separate entities from the same stimulus. Developmental research has been used to argue that children start out perceiving many dimensions of stimuli as integral that later become separable with experience. However, Smith and her associates (Kemler & Smith, 1979; Smith, 1980; Smith & Kilroy, 1979) have shown that the developmental picture is complicated. One finding is that the integral perception of children also seems to have some separable properties. In comparing kindergarten and fourth graders, Smith (1980) found that there is not a constant ordering of stimulus dimensions by their relative separability throughout development. Older children can separate color and form better than younger, but neither group could separate saturation and brightness and were also similiar in their responses to the dimensions of length and orientation. It seems that developmental trends are specific to the stimuli involved. Aschkenasy and Odom (1982) made a similar point in showing that children as young as 4 years can perceive dimensions as separable if they are sufficiently high in what is termed predisposed and distinctiveness-based salience.

SPATIAL CODING AND REPRESENTATION

Spatial perception is clearly evident in the infant. The classic study by Gibson and Walk (1960) on the "visual cliff" showed that 7- to 9-month-old infants would avoid crawling to adults located at the perceptually "deep" side of the apparatus. Subsequent research with this paradigm (Walk, 1978, 1979) reveals the complexity of research in perceptual development. For instance, changing from a checkerboard pattern to a homogeneous gray at the deep side causes a large number of 7- to 9-month-old infants to cross to this side but very few 10- to 13-month-olds. With the checkerboard pattern, age differences were not found. Either the older infants had greater visual acuity or more fear, or both.

The use of visual cues to depth is in evidence in very young infants. Banks (1980) has found accommodation at near-adult levels in 2-month-old infants. Binocular convergence, which may be present at birth, undergoes much development in the first 6 months of life (Aslin, 1977). Incredibly, Yonas, Pettersen, and Grandrud (1982) found evidence that 7-month-olds are sensitive to familiar size as a cue to distance when photographs of faces were used as stimuli. Thus young infants seem capable of encoding depth information both with sensory-based biological mechanisms and as learned, abstract cues—as do adults.

Two areas of research in perceptual development within the spatial domain will be reviewed here: (a) the oblique effect (Appelle, 1972) and (b) the cognitive representation of spatial layout. Both are thought to represent important markers in perceptual or cognitive development. Difficulties with either are diagnostically significant with adults and their assessment with children, especially in dealing with oblique orientations, is not uncommon. The oblique effect occurs when there is superior performance on some task for stimuli that are horizontally or vertically (H-V) oriented compared with those at an oblique orientation. Essock (1980) believes there are two classes of such effects. Class 1 oblique effects are said to reflect the basic functioning of the visual system. An example would be decreased visual acuity for oblique stimuli compared with those of H-V orientation. Class 2 oblique effects are revealed in paradigms in which encoding and processing of the stimulus are required. Generally, the effect is enhanced when a memory requirement exists in the task.

In examining the oblique effect in children, Class 2 effects are readily obtained. Harris, LeTendre, and Bishop (1974) found that 5-year-olds are better at remembering H-V orientations than obliques. Corballis and Zalik (1977) feel that the difficulty for these young children involves both a right-left orientation problem and a specific difficulty in discriminating line orientation for obliques. In our own research, we have found evidence for this view. Children can readily copy a 50-degree line at 5 years, but even at 9.5 years have difficulty with 30-degree lines. Children at 5 or 6 have a further difficulty in discriminating oblique lines in a matching to sample task. Rudel (1982), in an excellent review of the "oblique mystique," also argues for a processing difficulty explanation of the phenomenon. She points out that the differentiation of opposite obliques demands retention of a compound spatial label such as "up to the right," a dual representation, rather than the simpler "vertical" or "horizontal" for these stimuli. The real difference apparently between children and adults on the Class 2 oblique effect is that one must increase the level of difficulty of the processing requirement for adults in order for the effect to be apparent.

Examining children's representation of spatial layout or "cognitive mapping" is a relatively new area of empirical research in space perception (Pick & Rieser, 1982). Acredolo and Hake (1982) review the infant literature which primarily shows that the infants rely on an egocentric frame of reference in locating objects and events in their environment. The effect seems strongest in infants less than 1 year of age and can be mitigated by their being in a familiar setting or there being salient landmarks in the environment. In children a few years older, it can be shown that Euclidean properties of the spatial layout can be apprehended. This knowledge is apparently not dependent on visual experiences. Landau, Gleitman, and Spelke (1981) had a congenitally blind 2 ½-year-old child as well as sighted but blindfolded children of comparable age determine the appropriate path between two objects after walking to each of these objects from a third object. All subjects could successfully establish the new path. These data are very similar to those of Kosslyn, Pick, and Fariello (1974) who found that 4- to 5-year-olds learned the relative proximity of ten locations although they only had experience going from home base to each location individually.

The major variables investigated in spatial representation in young children are familiarity and activity. Acredolo (1982), in her review of research on the role of familiarity in the development of spatial knowledge, lists three conclusions found in the literature—namely, that (a) knowledge of an evironment begins with the noticing of landmarks and the development of memory of connections between them by means of action sequences called routes; (b) the landmark–route combinations form clusters with knowledge of intracluster spatial relationships occurring earlier than intercluster knowledge; and (c) familiarity breeds accurate metric knowledge as described earlier. Acredolo lists a large set of variables that have been shown to be important in "breeding familiarity." These include characteristics of the observer such as age and personality variables; factors related to the structure of the environment, such as visibility and redundancy within the layout; affective factors such as the feeling of security that knowledge of the environment can provide the child; and activity factors. The latter have been reviewed by Cohen (1982). It seems that factors like effort, amount of active movement, and the number of different perspectives explored are all important in spatial representation, especially in younger children.

This rather limited review of empirical research in just two areas of perceptual development should indicate the wealth of material that exists for the clinician who wishes to develop further insight into the specific factors that perceptual assessments are tapping in a neuropsychological examination. It may be an empirical question as to whether such a deep probing can further the effectiveness of neuropsychological analysis in the understanding and remediation of specific disorders, but it is necessary to approach this question (Rourke, 1982) in that neuropsychological knowledge seems to be currently evolving as an amalgam of neuroscience and cognitive psychology. In the next section, the use of findings from basic perceptual research in the development of assessment instruments is explored.

USING CONSTRUCTS FROM PERCEPTUAL SCIENCE IN NEUROPSYCHOLOGY

At this point, perception and perceptual development have been defined, fundamental issues and theories introduced, and empirical data and constructs within two areas of perceptual development provided. It is imperative to show how this information can be used in creating assessment procedures.

A TAXONOMY OF PERCEPTUAL-PROCESSING FUNCTIONS

Table 1 represents an attempt to develop a taxonomy of perceptual-processing skills that could serve as a guide for both developing perceptual-assessment instruments and for conducting such assessments. This taxonomy is not meant to be exhaustive of all functions currently explored in perceptual research. The coverage is nevertheless reasonably broad

TABLE 1
A Taxonomy of Perceptual Processing: Functions for Neuropsychological
Assessment

Processing functions	Response functions (examples)
Level 1: sensory encoding	
1. Sensory discrimination or detection	Absolute or difference thresholds; d'
2. Sensory attending	Orienting or defensive reflex
3. Sensory organization	Feature development (e.g., contour development)
Level 2: perceptual integration	
1. Perceptual organization	Pattern discrimination
	Pattern matching
	Pattern copying
2. Perceptual relation	Constancy production (e.g., size constancy)
3. Spatial patterning	Locus (radial direction and/or depth) discrimination
	Locus matching
	Locus placing
Level 3: memorial classification and retrieval	
1. Pattern Classification	Pattern recognition
a. Intra-modal	Delayed pattern reproduction
b. Inter-modal	Pattern matching
2. Naming (Verbal Coding)	Pattern identification
	Pattern reproduction (from verbal code)
	Pattern grouping (from verbal code)
Level 4: cognitive abstraction	For all domains:
Manipulation of:	
1. Verbal constructs	Comprehension
2. Mathematical constructs	Application
3. Perceptual constructs (not involving explicit verbal or mathematical constructs)	Problem solving
	Concept development

and pertinent to performance in the school achievement areas of interest in child neuropsychology.

In this scheme there are four levels of perceptual-processing functions. Successful performance of higher level functions implies adequate performance of pertinent lower level functions. Conversely, and most important for neuropsychological assessment, unsuccessful performance of a processing function at a particular level indicates a need to evaluate pertinent lower level functions that represent antecedent or current sub-components of the failed higher level function. It should be stressed that Table 1 represents a taxonomy and not an information-processing model. Regardless of terms used, no stand is taken in favor of any particular "top-down" or "bottom-up" model from cognitive psychology. The present approach can be viewed as a modification of Luria's (1966) functional system proposal in which a particular cognitive task requires the momentary organization of a set of component skills that differ in complexity. Here *each level* represents one or more perceptual-processing type of functional systems that differ in complexity from lower level to higher level.

Within each level of this taxonomy, there are processing functions and response functions. The former can be thought of as the types of tasks that are accomplished within each processing level, whereas the latter are examples of ways in which the success of the processing function can be evaluated. An attempt is made here to use response functions that comprise the type of response variables that have been developed within perceptual science. Generally, each of these response functions could be evaluated several different ways as they would be in an experimental investigation. Thus, orienting responses as measures of sensory attending in Level 1 could be evaluated through the use of several autonomic indices as well as behavioral alerting. Ideally, more than one response mode would be used if performance deficits were detected for any processing function.

As a concrete example of using this taxonomy, let us assume that a child performs well below age level on the Developmental Test of Visual Motor Integration, a form-copying test. Since the child copied some of the forms correctly and seemed to understand the instructions, we can rule out deficits at Levels 3 or 4 except perhaps in the area of motor planning. In order to ensure that the problem involves perceptual organization, a Level 2 processing function, one has to evaluate other perceptual organization response functions such as pattern discrimination tasks that do not involve the same sort of motor skills. It is important, of course, that these tasks be comparable in difficulty to the drawing task. If the child does adequately on these tasks, then the problem is in motor planning and execution. However, if the child performs poorly on other tests of perceptual organization, then the adequacy of relevant Level 1 processing functions, such as sensory attending, must be determined before one can determine conclusively that the child has a deficit in the Level 2 perceptual processing function.

A CONSTRUCT VALID ASSESSMENT INSTRUMENT

Even if one were to use the taxonomic approach to specify the level and type of processing function disorder, one would still have the remaining problem of specifying, at the construct level, what it was about perceptual processing that was disordered. In the example above, we would want to know what it was about the child's perceptual organization skills that the pattern-copying task had revealed. It would then be possible to plan a more exact and honed intervention strategy whether strength matched or compensatory (Hartlage & Telzrow, 1983). The perceptual assessments made by neuropsychologists typically do not allow for this deeper probing of the perceptual disorder. This is particularly true in the visual domain. The purpose of this section is to demonstrate how a more probing perceptual assessment instrument can be derived from constructs used in basic research in visual perception.

Derivation of the Instrument. Our research so far has focused on two processing functions from the taxonomy, sensory organization and perceptual organization. The work that is reported here concerns the development of two tests for investigating perceptual organization. These are the Kent Perceptual Processing Inventory Copying Test (KPPI-C), a form-copying test, and the KPPI-D, a form-discrimination test. Both tests use the same forms. The major reference used in establishing a strategy for selecting these forms was Zusne's (1970) comprehensive review of the visual form perception literature. Zusne divides form parameters into two major types, *transpositional* and *transitive.* The former includes such parameters as rotation and reflection which do not produce changes in the information content of a stimulus. Transitive parameters are of two types: (a) informational, such as number of sides or turns, and (b) configurational, such as the elongation of a stimulus. To ensure the relevance of the forms developed for the KPPI, form features were selected from the experimental literature on letter perception (Geyer, 1970; Gibson, 1969; Kuennapas & Janson, 1969; Laughery, 1971). These features were then used to create test forms in which they served as the transitive parameters. Rotation and reflection of these forms served as the transpositional parameters.

The initial version of the KPPI-C had three component tests that differed in the complexity and number of forms. In each test, one or two figures appeared in a panel immediately below which there was a similar-sized area for copying. KPPI-C1 used figures in which the transitive parameters had minimal information or configurational complexity, for example, straight lines and simple open curves while many different degrees of rotation of these stimuli were employed. Figures in KPPI-C2 had a larger information content in that they were produced from two intersecting lines. Configurational parameters involved point and angle of intersection as well as relative size of the two lines. The transpositional parameter was again the degree of rotation of the form. KPPI-C3 had figures in which the information load and configurational parameters were greatly increased over KPPI-C2. Lines and curves were combined in figures and configurational features involved those from KPPI-C2 plus horizontal and vertical symmetry, openness versus closure, parallelness, and so forth. The KPPI-D test required the child to match a standard stimulus to one of five or six alternatives. The forms were evenly chosen from all three KPPI-C.

A total of 215 children from 5.0 to 9.11 years of age were given the KPPI-C and KPPI-D. An objective scoring system was used with the KPPI-C that was much more specific than those found with other instruments of this type (cf. Rugle & Melamed, 1984). Each form was evaluated by examining the proportion of children at each successive 6-month age interval passing an item. Perhaps the most important finding in this entire project to date is the discovery that when objective criteria are used, children really are not very good at copying forms even at 10 years of age. One only needs to employ very basic, uncomplicated forms to get clear age-related differences in performance. This finding promises to

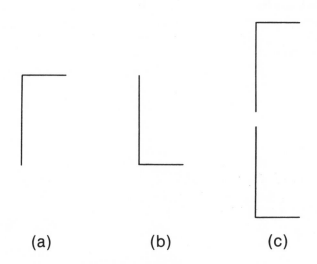

(a)   (b)   (c)

FIGURE 2. Three sequential panels from the KPPI-C2; (a) Has an age equivalent of about 5 years, 8 months; (b) of about 5 years, 2 months; and (c) 9 years, 8 months.

make the problem of the interpretation of skill deficits fairly straightforward for this instrument. Figure 2 applies these points. It contains three sequential panels from KPPI-C2. The majority of children 5.5 to 5.11 and 5.0 to 5.5 years of age could successfully copy (a) and (b), respectively. However, (c) could only be copied by a majority of children in the 9.6 to 9.11 age group even though these two forms were scored independently and with the same criteria as in (a) and (b).

The present version of KPPI-C contains 42 items chosen from the original three parts of the test. These are mostly items that showed sharp age divisions in performance level while being representative of the types of items in the original battery. The KPPI-D at present contains 26 items but is undergoing further development. Representative items for KPPI-C can be found in Figure 3.

Initial Validation Data. One fortuitous by-product of the rather sizable amount of time this project has taken is that considerable achievement data are now available for the children tested at the beginning of the project. A total of 73 first-, second- and third-graders were given the original KPPI-C and KPPI-D in the 1978 and 1979 school years. As standard procedure, children at this school received the Metropolitan Achievement Test (MAT) in the first and second grades and the Iowa Achievement battery in the third and fifth grades. Thus not only were concurrent achievement data available for all children, but also the following: one-year posttest MATs and two-year posttest Iowas (for first-graders at original testing), one-year posttest Iowas (for second-graders at first testing), and two-year posttest Iowas (third-graders, initially).

The basic question to be asked here is as follows: If one builds a perceptual skills test from the ground up in a manner attuned to the

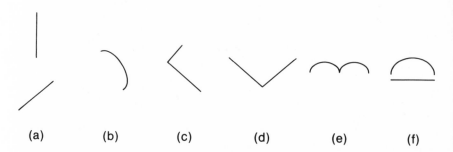

  (a)   (b)   (c)   (d)   (e)   (f)

FIGURE 3. Representative items of the reduced (current) version of the KPPI-C; (a) and (b) are from KPPI-C1; (c) and (d) from KPPI-C2; and (e) and (f) from KPPI-C3.

perceptual science literature, will it predict academic achievement more successfully than other perceptual instruments apparently do (Larsen & Hammill, 1975)? It must, of course, be taken into account that only limited aspects of perceptual processing are being evaluated by these two tests. This perhaps puts a floor on the ability of the KPPI to serve as a predictor.

The answer to the above question appears to be yes, at least for the admittedly limited and incomplete concurrent and predictive validation analyses accomplished so far. A sampling of these analyses from Rugle and Melamed (1985) will be presented here. The predictor variables used were the reduced versions of KPPI-C and KPPI-D. The former was divided into three component copying tests based on the original part of the KPPI-C that provided the final 42 items—KPPI-C1 (18 items), KPPI-C2 (12), and KPPI-C2 (12). All relationships described here were statistically significant.

For first-graders (6 and 7 years of age), the total MAT score was predicted with a multiple correlation coefficient, R, of .62 concurrently and .61 one year later. An R of .58 was obtained in predicting concurrent MAT reading score. On the Iowas two years subsequent to the KPPI, the total score was correlated .70 with these perceptual assessments, whereas reading score produced an R of .68. For math and spelling, the Rs were .56 and .57, respectively. These data resemble those of Fletcher and Satz (1980), in which perceptual factors measured in kindergarten explained more of the variance in second grade reading performance than verbal-conceptual skills. The latter were the better concurrent predictors in fifth grade.

The second-graders' (7 and 8 years of age) concurrent MAT reading ($R = .53$) and total score ($R = .47$) were correlated somewhat lower with the KPPI subtests than were those of the first-graders. Their Iowa performance one year later on math ($R = .64$) and total score ($R = .59$) were successfully predicted unlike reading and spelling achievement. Surprisingly, some of the strongest concurrent relationships for the KPPI were those for the third-graders (8 and 9 year olds). When Iowa reading was being predicted, R was .72, where it reached .56 for Iowa math and .62 for Iowa total. In a finding again consistent with Fletcher and Satz's data, our third-graders' subsequent performance on the Iowas in the fifth grade was not predicted successfully by their third-grade KPPI performance.

It is expected that future research will include not only cross-validation studies but also an analysis of the types of errors at each age or grade level in order to relate them to the constructs used in producing the items for these instruments.

A STRATEGY FOR PERCEPTUAL ASSESSMENT IN NEUROPSYCHOLOGY

For the psychologist whose milieu is the school or who is primarily concerned with children of school age, neuropsychology becomes a resource through which a more thorough evaluation of abilities and a more precise diagnosis of current functioning can be ascertained. Through it, one is provided with an enriched analysis of particular skills and an increased understanding of their various interrelationships which determine academic performance. The subsequent effect is that the child practitioner gains insight into fundamental processing abilities, difficulties that can be degenerative or require medical attention, and individual styles of processing academic material; the practitioner is in general able to glean information that assists in creating individualized programs toward remediation and the advancement of learning.

Two "ideological" considerations are particularly relevant for designing assessments. One is that conducting diagnostic assessment demands keeping mindful of Luria's concept that a specific cognitive behavior reflects the activity of an existing functional system which in turn represents an organized composite of variously complex skills. Accepting this conception of a performance task, for example, reading, necessitates an analytic assessment paradigm designed to examine processes that culminate in the productive act of reading. The second consideration provides a perceptual focus for the actual procedure of assessment. Substantial current research findings suggest that perceptional intactness is necessary for even basic conceptualization on which learning is predicted. Perceptual sensitivity or concentrated attention to relevant stimulus information seems to be required for more abstract conceptualization to occur. Furthermore, perceptual skills that compose this sensitivity are purported to be developmental and therefore hierarchical in acquisition, distinct, and capable of independent description, for example, sensory organization, spatial patterning, and perceptual organization (Fletcher & Satz, 1980; Gibson & Levin, 1975; Weber, 1980; West & Odom, 1979).

Recent studies argue that perceptually dependent skills are essential to academic achievement. West and Odom (1979), for example, report that among children of kindergarten age perceptual training in suspected deficiency areas produced more effective conceptualization with subsequent increases in problem-solving behavior. Further, Miccinati (1981) found that training in attention to the perception of distinctive orthographic features and their sound pattern relationships makes the act of reading possible for previously disabled readers. In relation to early achievement, it has been asserted that auditory-acoustic and visual-spatial attributes of academic material may appear more dominant, commanding more attention than higher order linguistic ones and are therefore substantially more important in the early learning process (Fletcher, 1980; Wohlwill, 1973).

It is evident that there must be specificity of diagnosis in order to have fruitful remediation for learning problems. This specificity can often be achieved through neuropsychological assessment with a perceptual focus. In conducting this assessment, it is judicious to keep in mind that patterns of response that are certain or clearly indicative of common disabling conditions and causative factors do not presently exist (Rourke, Bakker, Fisk, & Strang, 1983). Therefore, no ready battery of evaluative measures can be stipulated for general clinical study. Each child needs to be considered as an atypical instance or as having a particular presenting problem and an individual constellation of interrelated abilities. In order to appropriately diagnose and recommend remediation in each case, the clinician must create a comprehensive portrait through the design of an individualized assessment procedure.

It is useful for the development of an assessment battery to make choices that reflect both Luria's conceptualization of cognitive behavior and the import of perceptual processes in determining the effectiveness of that behavior. An assessment of cognitive functioning, for example, needs to examine the host of coordinated abilities that culminate in intelligent behavior in order that their interplay be observed for intimations of difficulties and strengths for further investigation. An intellectual assessment, such as the Wechsler Intelligence Scale for Children—Revised (WISC-R), provides a format for developing hypotheses concerning the underlying contributors to any currently experienced problems in adaptive cognitive functioning. These hypotheses then need to be pursued through the administration of various detailed assessments that include an evaluation of perceptual processes.

There are myriad ways in which these evaluative assessments can proceed and, therefore, carefully formulated hypotheses are required. Suppose an instance of a child's exhibiting relatively poor performance on a *cognitive* assessment subtest for which successful task completion involves visual sequencing and visual memory. The difficulty in making a conclusive diagnosis from the cognitive assessment data alone is that performing the task involves an integration of several abilities that confounds identification of particular deficits. Not only are visual sequencing and visual memory deficits not distinguishable in performance here, but each consists, of course, of component skills. A series of questions need to be asked in order to focus understanding of the functional limits of deficits observed on the task. Questions that might arise include: Is visual sequencing with tactual props affected? Are both short- and long-term memory involved? Can a memory deficit be differentiated from a sequencing one? Does attention affect sequencing? Would an auditory assist increase visual accuracy? How does verbal cuing affect the deficit?

A number of evaluations within the visual processing domain could be conducted while addressing assessment to the types of questions posed previously. An administration of Knox's Cube Test allows for the observation of sequencing skills based on short-term visual memory, the child's ability to maintain directed attention, and whether a tactual medium affects performance. To investigate the influence of auditory cuing on the same task, the McCarthy Tapping Sequence can be administered. In order to discern sequencing capability without a visual memory factor, Reitan's Progressive Figures Test, Porteus Mazes, or Reitan's Target Test would be appropriate measures. Use of the Benton Visual Retention Test would permit an examination of the status of visual memory through temporal manipulation for a copying task. Such manipulations include the amount of time for observing the stimulus and the period before responding. The Motor-Free Visual Perception Test, which assesses visual processing in diverse tasks without using a motor response, could be employed. A verbal cuing intervention could be applied in administering any of the visual perception assessments to note its effect on performance.

The essential strategy here is that a wide range of perceptual processing skills ought to be assessed in order to interpret cognitive skill deficits. These assessments, given the overlapping information they measure, should converge on an understanding of the source of the "sequencing" or "visual memory" disorder in terms of patterns of subskills and also provide an understanding of the child's retained strengths or functional skills.

It must be further recognized that perceptual diagnosis is characteristically taxonomic and hierarchical. The perceptual testing procedures mentioned above that were prescribed to answer questions on the parameters of a cognitive deficit would require an analysis themselves in terms of such a taxonomy. A determination of the level of any disordered processing function is a primary goal of neuropsychological assessments. This determination is paramount for eventual remediation. Accordingly, various levels of processing have been examined in the administration of the stipulated assessments. Even the encoding function of sensory attending, a Level 1 process (see Table 1), has, for example, been requisite for apprehending the examiner's instructions for any of the measures suggested. Integrative functions proposed in Level 2 of the taxonomic model are explored by the Motor-Free Visual Perception Test as pattern discrimination and pattern matching and by the Benton Visual Retention Test as copying. Benton copying tasks can also be a medium for observing memorial functions stipulated in Level 2 using the response function of delayed pattern reproduction, which is assessed again by Knox's Cube Test in a tactual reproductive mode.

Functions proposed in Level 4, cognitive abstraction, of the taxonomic model are most appropriately evaluated in the context of academic applications. In the instance described here for explanatory purposes in which visual sequencing and visual memory are suspected deficits, a number of response functions can be analyzed. Within a verbal construct, for example, an assessment utilizing perhaps the Stanford Diagnostic Reading Test, the Woodcock Reading Mastery Test, and the Gilmore Oral Reading Test can determine whether assessed deficits significantly interfere with the act of reading. Specificity of interference can be ascertained in noting whether comprehension or problem-solving behavior, such as visual word-attack skill which is dependent on sequencing and memory, is affected.

Subsequent to information gleaned from a taxonomic perceptually oriented evaluation, remediation to be implemented by the regular classroom teacher, the special education tutor, or the parent can be designed. An attribute of the type of neuropsychological assessment addressed in this section is that the status of processing abilities essential for coping with academic tasks is revealed. Taking the instance presented, the question of the usefulness of visual sequencing and visual memory for learning activities can be discussed satisfactorily. For example, had it been ascertained that visual sequencing is enhanced by tactual cues, suggestions for remediation would involve the use of tactile materials. Had assessment determined that short-term visual memory functions well with verbal cuing, an appropriate instructional strategy would involve learning to couple the performance of tasks dependent on visual memory with verbal mediation. The intimation is that with neuropsychological assessment, there is an elucidation of specific functional components that often allows the remedial programmer to combine asset and deficit areas in an intermodal procedure so that an area identified to be inadequately developed will never be abandoned entirely.

An understanding of the interrelationship of various processing functions is further enhanced and is directive of remediation as the stipulated taxonomic model is utilized; that is, the awareness that certain performance responses positioned later in the model are dependent on those with earlier level designation is accomplished. Therefore, improvement of simpler processing will have an enhancing effect on and make an essential contribution to the quality of the more complex functions.

For example, comprehension in reading, a Level 4 response function, will be increased as improvement of memory for visual word form combinations, functions of Levels 2 and 3, is established. Reading instruction strategies can themselves be determined by evaluation of perceptual abilities in order that a particular constellation of processing functions, ascertained through individual assessment, can be served by a selected methodology, for example, tactile materials with naming strategy activities to be assigned at expanded temporal intervals.

REFERENCES

Acredolo, L. P. The familiarity factor in spatial research. In R. Cohen (Ed.), *New directions for child development: Children's conceptions of spatial relationships*. San Francisco: Jossey-Bass, 1982.

Acredolo, L. P., & Hake, J. L. Infant perception. In B. Wolman (Ed.), *Handbook of developmental psychology*. Englewood Cliffs, N.J.: Prentice-Hall, 1982.

Aiken, L. S., & Williams, T. M. Development of multiple dimension use in form classification. *Child Development*, 1975, *46*, 123–132.

Appelle, S. Perception and discrimination as a function of stimulus orientation: The oblique effect in man and animals. *Psychological Bulletin*, 1972, *78,*, 266–278.

Aschkenasy, J. R., & Odom, R. D. Classification and perceptual development: Exploring issues about integrality and differential sensitivity. *Journal of Experimental Child Psychology*, 1982, *34*, 435–448.

Aslin, R. N. Development of binocular fixation in human infants. *Journal of Experimental Child Psychology*, 1977, *23*, 133–150.

Attneave, F. Some informational aspects of visual perception. *Psychological Review*, 1954, *61*, 183–193.

Attneave, F. Symmetry, information, and memory for patterns. *American Journal of Psychology*, 1955, *68*, 209–222.

Attneave, F. Physical determinants of the judged complexity of shapes. *Journal of Experimental Psychology*, 1957, *53*, 221–227.

Banks, M. S. The development of visual accommodation during early infancy. *Child Development*, 1980, *51*, 646–666.

Beck, J. Effect of orientation and of shape similarity on perceptual grouping. *Perception & Psychophysics*, 1966, *1*, 300–302.

Belmont, I. Perceptual organization and minimal brain dysfunctions. In H. E. Rie & E. D. Rie (Eds.), *Handbook of minimal brain dysfunction: A critical view*. New York: Wiley, 1980.

Bigler, E. D., & Ehrfurth, J. W. The continued inappropriate singular use of the Bender Visual Motor Gestalt Test. *Professional Psychology*, 1981, *12*, 562–569.

Boder, E. Developmental dyslexia: A diagnostic approach based on three atypical reading-spelling patterns. *Developmental Medicine and Child Neurology*, 1973, *15*, 663–687.

Bornstein, M. H., Ferdinandsen, K., & Gross, C. G. Perception of symmetry in infancy. *Developmental Psychology*, 1981, *17*, 82–86.

Brown, D. R., & Owens, D. H. The metrics of visual form: Methodological dispepsin. *Psychological Bulletin*, 1967, *68*, 243–259.

Chipman, S. F. & Mendelson, M. J. The development of sensitivity to visual structure. *Journal of Experimental Child Psychology*, 1975, *20*, 411–429.

Chipman, S. F., & Mendelson, M. J. Influence of six types of visual structure on complexity judgments in children and adults. *Journal of Experimental Psychology: Human Perception and Performance*, 1979, 5, 365–378.

Cohen, R. The role of activity in the construction of spatial representations. In R. Cohen (Ed.), *New directions for child development: Children's conception of spatial relationships.* San Francisco: Jossey-Bass, 1982.

Colarusso, R. P., & Hammill, D. D. *Motor-free visual perception test.* Novato, Calif.: Academic Therapy, 1972.

Corballis, M. C. & Zalik, M. C. Why do children confuse mirror-image obliques? *Journal of Experimental Child Psychology*, 1977, 24, 516–523.

Durant, W. *The story of philosophy.* New York: Simon & Schuster, 1959.

Essock, E. A. The oblique effect of stimulus identification considered with respect to two classes of oblique effects. *Perception*, 1980, 9, 37–46.

Fantz, R. L. Pattern vision in young infants. *Psychological Record*, 1958, 8, 43–49.

Fantz, R. L. Pattern vision in newborn infants. *Science*, 1963, 140, 296–297.

Fantz, R. L., & Miranda, S. B. Newborn infant attention to form of contour. *Child Development*, 1975, 46, 224–228.

Fisher, C. B., Ferdinandsen, K., & Bornstein, M. H. The role of symmetry in infant form discrimination. *Child Development*, 1981, 52, 457–462.

Fletcher, J. M. Linguistic factors in reading acquisition: Evidence for developmental changes. In F. J. Pirozzolo & M. C. Wittrock (Eds.), *Neuropsychological and cognitive processes in reading.* New York: Academic Press, 1980.

Fletcher, J. M., & Satz, P. Developmental changes in the neuropsychological correlates of reading achievement: A six-year longitudinal follow-up. *Journal of Clinical Neuropsychology*, 1980, 2, 23–37.

Forgus, R. H., & Melamed, L. E. *Perception: A cognitive-stage approach.* New York: McGraw-Hill, 1976.

Frostig, M. *Developmental test of visual perception.* Palo Alto, Calif.: Consulting Psychologists Press, 1963.

Garner, W. R. *The processing of information and structure.* Potomac, Md.: Erlbaum, 1974.

Geyer, L. H. *A two-channel theory of short-term visual storage.* (Doctoral dissertation, SUNY at Buffalo, Buffalo, N.Y., 1970). (University Microfilms, No. 71–7165).

Gibson, E. J. *Principles of perceptual learning and development.* Englewood Cliffs, N.J.: Prentice-Hall, 1969.

Gibson, E. J., & Levin, H. *The psychology of reading.* Cambridge: The M.I.T. Press, 1975.

Gibson, E. J., Owsley, C. J., & Johnston, J. Perception of invariants by five-month-old infants: Differentiation of two types of motion. *Developmental Psychology*, 1978, 14, 407–415.

Gibson, E. J., Owsley, C. J., Walker, A., & Megaw-Nyce, J. Development of the perception of invariants: Substance and shape. *Perception*, 1979, 8, 609–619.

Gibson, E. J., & Walk, R. The "visual cliff." *Scientific American*, 1960, 202, 64–71.

Gibson, J. J. *The ecological approach to visual perception.* Boston: Houghton Mifflin, 1979.

Golden, C. J. The Luria-Nebraska children's battery: Theory and formulation. In G. W. Hynd & J. E. Obrzut (Eds.), *Neuropsychological assessment and the school-age child.* New York: Grune & Stratton, 1981.

Harris, P. L., Le Tendre, J. B., & Bishop, A. The young child's discrimination of obliques. *Perception*, 1974, 3, 261–265.

Hartlage, L. C. & Telzrow, C. F. The neuropsychological basis of educational intervention. *Journal of Learning Disabilties*, 1983, 16, 521–528.

Hayes-Roth, F. Mediating the so-called immediate processes of perception. *Behavioral and Brain Sciences*, 1980, 3, 386–387.

90 LAWRENCE E. MELAMED AND ESTHER C. MELAMED

Helmholtz, H. *Treatise on physiological optics.* J. P. S. Southall (Ed.), translated from the 3rd German edition. New York: Optical Society of America, 1924. (Reprinted by Dover, 1962.)

Hochberg, J. Sensation and perception. In E. Hearst (Ed.), *The first century of experimental psychology.* Hillside, N.J.: Erlbaum, 1979.

Hochberg, J. Levels of perceptual organization. In M. Kubovy & J. R. Pomerantz (Eds.), *Perceptual organization.* Hillside, N.J.: Erlbaum, 1981.

Jones, R. K., & Pick, A. D. On the nature of information in behalf of direct perception. *Behavioral and Brain Sciences,* 1980, *3,* 388–389.

Kavale, K., & Mattson, D. One jumped off the balance beam: Meta-analysis of perceptual-motor training. *Journal of Learning Disabilities,* 1983, *16,* 165–173.

Kemler, D. G., & Smith, L. B. Accessing similarity and dimensional relations: Effects of integrality and separability on the discovery of complex concepts. *Journal of Experimental Psychology: General,* 1979, *108,* 133–150.

Koffka, K. *Principles of gestalt psychology.* New York, Harcourt Brace, 1935.

Koffka, K. *The growth of the mind.* New York: The Humanities Press, 1951.

Kosslyn, S. M., Pick, H. L., & Fariello, G. R. Cognitive maps in children and men. *Child Development,* 1974, *45,* 707–716.

Kuennapas, T., & Janson, A. J. Multidimensional similarity of letters. *Perceptual and Motor Skills,* 1969, *28,* 3–12.

Landau, B., Gleitman, H., & Spelke, E. Spatial knowledge and geometric representation in a child blind from birth. *Science,* 1981, *213,* 1275–1277.

Larsen, S. C., & Hammill, D. D. The relationship of selected visual-perceptual abilities to school learning. *Journal of Special Education,* 1975, *9,* 281–291.

Laughery, K. R. Computer simulation of short-term memory: A component decay model. In G. T. Bower & J. T. Spence (Eds.), *The psychology of learning and motivation: Advances in research and theory* (Vol. VI). New York: Academic Press, 1971.

Luria, A. R. *Higher cortical functions in man.* New York: Basic Books, 1966.

Lyon, R., Stewart, N., & Freedman, D. Neuropsychological characteristics of empirically derived subgroups of learning disabled readers. *Journal of Clinical Neruopsychology,* 1982, *4,* 343–365.

Maisel, E. B., & Karmel, B. Z. Contour density and pattern configuration in visual perferences of infants. *Infant Behavior and Development,* 1978, *1,* 127–140.

Marr, D., & Nishihara, H. K. Visual information processing: Artificial intelligence and the sensorium of sight. *Technology Review,* 1978, *81,* 1–23.

Mattis, S., French, J. H., & Rapin, I. Dyslexia in children and young adults: Three independent neuropsychological syndromes. *Developmental Medicine and Child Neurology,* 1975, *17,* 150–163.

Miccinati, J. Teach reading disabled students to perceive distinctive features in words. *Journal of Learning Disabilities,* 1981, *14,* 140–142.

Pastore, N. *Selective history of theories of visual perception: 1650–1950.* New York: Oxford University Press, 1971.

Pick, H. L., & Rieser, J. J. Children's cognitive mapping. In M. Potegal (Ed.), *Spatial abilities: Development and physiological foundations.* New York: Academic Press, 1982.

Pomerantz, J. R. Perceptual organization in information processing. In M. Kubovy & J. R. Pomerantz (Eds.), *Perceptual Organization.* Hilldale, N.J.: Erlbaum, 1981.

Pomerantz, J. R., & Kubovy, M. Perceptual organization: An overview. In M. Kubovy & J. R. Pomerantz (Eds.), *Perceptual organization.* Hilldale, N.J.: Erlbaum, 1981.

Reed, E. S., & Jones, R. K. James Gibson's ecological revolution in psychology. *Philosophy of the Social Sciences,* 1979, *9,* 189–204.

Rock, I. *An introduction to perception.* New York: Macmillan, 1975.

Rock, I. Difficulties with a direct theory of perception. *Behavioral and Brain Sciences*, 1980, 3, 398–399.

Rock, I., Hill, A. L., & Fineman, M. Speed constancy as a function of size constancy. *Perception & Psychophysics*, 1968, 4, 37–40.

Rourke, B. P. Central processing deficiencies in children: Toward a developmental neuropsychological model. *Journal of Clinical Neuropsychology*, 1982, 4, 1–18.

Rourke, B. P., Bakker, D. J., Fisk, J. L., & Strang, J. D. *Child neuropsychology: An introduction to theory, research, and clinical practice*. New York: Guilford Press, 1983.

Rudel, R. G. The oblique mystique: A slant on the development of spatial coordinates. In M. Potegal (Ed.), *Spatial abilities: Development and physiological foundations*. New York: Academic Press, 1982.

Ruff, H. A. The development of perception and recognition of objects. *Child Development*, 1980, 51, 981–992.

Ruff, H. A. Effect of object movement on infants' detection of object structure. *Developmental Psychology*, 1982, 18, 462–472.

Rugle, L., & Melamed, L. E. Perceptual processing abilities and school achievement in young children: Longitudinal findings with a construct valid perceptual processing instrument. Submitted for publication, 1985.

Satz, P., & Morris, R. Learning disability subtypes: A review. In F. J. Pirozzolo & M. C. Wittrock (Eds.), *Neuropsychological and cognitive processes in reading*. New York: Academic Press, 1981.

Schwartz, M., & Day, R. H. Visual shape perception in early infancy. *Monograph of the Society for Research in Child Development*, 1979, 44, (No. 182).

Selz, M. Halstead–Reitan neuropsychological test batteries for children. In G. W. Hynd & J. E. Obrzut (Eds.), *Neuropsychological assessment and the school-age child: Issues and procedures*. New York: Grune & Stratton, 1981.

Shannon, C. E., & Weaver, W. *The mathematical theory of communication*. Urbana: The University of Illinois Press, 1949.

Smith, L. B. Development and the continuum of dimensional separability. *Perception & Psychophysics*, 1980, 28, 164–172.

Smith, L. B., & Kilroy, M. C. A continuum of dimensional separability. *Perception & Psychophysics*, 1979, 25, 285–291.

Stork, D. G., & Levinson, J. Z. Receptive fields and the optimal stimulus. *Science*, 1982, 216, 204–205.

Ullman, S. Against direct perception. *Behavioral and Brain Sciences*, 1980, 3, 373–415.

Uttal, W. R. *A taxonomy of visual processes*. Hillsdale, N.J.: Erlbaum, 1981.

Walk, R. D. Depth perception and experience. In R. D. Walk & H. L. Pick (Eds.), *Perception and experience*. New York: Plenum Press, 1978.

Walk, R. D. Depth perception and a laughing heaven. In A. Pick (Ed.), *Perception and its development: A tribute to Eleanor J. Gibson*. Hillsdale, N.J.: Erlbaum, 1979.

Walker, A. S., Owsley, C. J., Megaw-Nyce, J., & Gibson, E. J. Detection of elasticity as an invariant property of objects by young infants. *Perception*, 1980, 9, 713–718.

Weber, G. Y. Visual disabilities—Their identification and relationship with academic achievement. *Journal of Learning Disabilities*, 1980, 13, 13–19.

West, R. L., & Odom, R. D. Effects of perceptual training on the salience of information in a recall problem. *Child Development*, 1979, 50, 1261–1264.

Wohlwill, J. F. *The study of behavioral development*. New York: Academic Press, 1973.

Yonas, A., Pettersen, L., & Grandrud, C. E. Infant's sensitivity to familiar size as information for distance. *Child Development*, 1982, 53, 1285–1290.

Zusne, L. *Visual perception of form*. New York: Academic Press, 1970.

CHAPTER 5

Temperament and the Development of Self-Regulation

MARY K. ROTHBART and MICHAEL I. POSNER

INTRODUCTION

Although infants enter the world with a set of inborn reflexes for reacting to external stimuli, they cannot be seen as passive machines responding only to external input; inborn programs of self-regulation modulate responsivity from the earliest days. With development, additional forms of regulation under voluntary control also become available to the child. Adult studies have developed criteria allowing us to separate more reflexive automatic activity from more voluntary regulatory control. Two central developmental problems involve identifying the biological timetable for development of regulatory mechanisms and the means whereby individual regulation comes under the influence of learning. In order to relate the basic biological characteristics of the infant to the acquisition of culture, it is necessary to explore development from both biological and psychological viewpoints.

At any given age, individuals differ in their reflexive (automatic) responses and in their capacity for self-regulation. These basic patterns of reflex and regulation are what we mean by *temperament* (Rothbart & Derryberry, 1981). Individual differences in temperament may be studied at different levels, each with its own principles and literature. In this chapter, we examine self-regulation at three levels. The first level concerns

MARY K. ROTHBART and MICHAEL I. POSNER • Department of Psychology, University of Oregon, Eugene, Oregon 97403. The writing of this chapter was supported in part by NIMH Grant SRO1MH26674 to the first author and an NIH Senior NRSA Fellowship to the second author.

internal psychological operations involved in self-regulation (intrapsychic level). The second considers neural systems that may subserve intrapsychic self-regulation (physiological level). The third concerns the interaction between individual self-regulation and that provided by the environment (behavioral level).

To pursue the goal of understanding regulation, it is necessary to develop a framework that allows us to relate biological and psychological studies. Our framework is adapted from adult studies of information processing and modified to incorporate a developmental perspective. We view regulation in terms of the interaction among several separate information-processing subsystem—arousal, activation, and effort (McGuinness & Pribram, 1980)—although we do not define these systems in precisely McGuinness and Pribram's terms.

We begin this chapter by reviewing traditional approaches to temperament and self-regulation. Next, we introduce the framework by considering systems of arousal, activation, and effort as they arise in studies of adult information processing. In the third section we trace the developmental sequence of these subsystems. Finally we seek to draw some implications for both clinical and basic research.

MODELS OF TEMPERAMENTAL SELF-REGULATION

Self-regulation has been a traditional concern of students of adult temperament (Eysenck, 1967, 1976, 1981; Gray, 1971, 1982; Zuckerman, 1979, 1983). In Eysenck's model, one of three major temperamental dimensions is introversion-extroversion. On this dimension, introverts are seen to possess more arousable ascending reticular activation systems than extroverts, resulting for the introvert in higher levels of cortical arousal for any given level of environmental stimulation. In Eysenck's view an "optimal level" of cortical arousal exists such that moderate arousal levels will be experienced as pleasurable and approached and low or high levels of arousal experienced as negative and avoided. Since introverts are seen as being more arousable, they are expected to reach their optimal level at lower levels of stimulation. Thus introverts would be more likely than extroverts to attempt to avoid novel or intense stimulation whereas extroverts would more often seek it. Eysenck's theory combines cortical arousability and self-regulation within a single dimension.

Jeffrey Gray (1971, 1982) has revised Eysenck's theory by emphasizing the effects of two limbic-centered emotional systems. The first of these is the "behavioral inhibition system," including septal-hippocampal structures. Responding to signals of punishment, nonreward, and novelty, this system inhibits motor behavior, activates the cortex, and directs attention. A second system involving the medial forebrain bundle is seen as sensitive to signals of reward and nonpunishment and facilitates approach. These two forms of regulation are described as impulsivity (approach) and anxiety (behavioral inhibition). In Gray's view, a balance weighted toward impulsivity is seen as extroverted; a balance toward anxiety is viewed as introverted; when both systems are highly reactive, the individual is seen as neurotic.

A similar theory that differs from Gray's chiefly in terms of the physiological structures to which it is related has been put forward by Zuckerman (1979, 1983). He proposes that "sensation seeking," that is, approach of novel and highly stimulating situations, is the result of a balance between reward–approach and punishment–avoidance systems. Zuckerman identifies three major reward systems, involving dopamine, norepinephrine, and the opioid peptides, and a punishment system involving serotonin. He also relates self–regulation to individual differences in monoamine oxidase and gonadal hormone levels.

Traditionally, dimensions of self-regulation have not played an important role in models of infant temperament. Thomas, Chess, Birch, Hertzig, and Korn (1963), Buss and Plomin (1975), and Goldsmith and Campos (1982), for example, all focus exclusively upon the behavioral aspects of temperament. Thomas *et al.* (1963; Thomas & Chess, 1977) have attempted to consider temperament as behavioral style, arguing that temperament is a nonmotivational construct. Nevertheless, the temperamental construct of approach-avoidance (positive affect and approach versus negative affect and avoidance in reaction to novelty) of Thomas *et al.* appears to assess fear, a self-regulative and motivational characteristic (Izard, 1977).

In our view (Rothbart & Derryberry, 1981), self-regulation is an essential aspect of temperament at all ages. It allows us to consider important links between adult and infant models of temperament, between temperament and attention (Posner & Rothbart, 1981), and between intrapsychic and physiological levels of analysis. Knowledge at each of these levels can serve to illuminate our understanding of the others. In the next section, we begin by discussing self-regulation at the adult level.

FRAMEWORK FOR SELF-REGULATION

Study of self-regulation in adults generally has been pursued under the rubric of "attention" (McGuinness & Pribram, 1980; Posner & Rothbart, 1981). In studies of human performance, attention has been used both to account for the fact that not all stimuli have equal influence on the subject's subjective experience and behavior and also for the fact that adults can exercise voluntary control over some aspects of their internal processes, but not all (Posner, 1982). In this sense, the ability of attentional mechanisms to guide the selection of stimuli and the production of responses represents the fundamental idea of self-control within an information-processing model.

In the study of attention it has been traditional to distinguish between two general systems: one *intensive*, the other *selective* (Kahneman, 1973). The first term deals with the system controlling a general level of energy and the second with the operations involved in selecting which information will be effective in actual processing at any given time. The intensive aspect of attention refers to processes involved in varying our level of arousal from deep sleep, at one extreme, to alert waking at the other. The contrast between the two refers not only to the coherence and variety of behavior shown by the organism in the waking state, but also to its relative sensitivity to environmental signals.

AROUSAL

Arousal can be thought of as a single dimension of cortical activity, but it also is possible to distinguish between the arousal level of different systems. For example, high sensitivity to external events is called alertness and can be distinguished from preparation of quick motor actions (called activation by McGuinness & Pribram [1980]). Some investigators (Routtenberg, 1971) have proposed that sensory and motor arousal can be seen as two mutually exclusive states. However, this view does not seem entirely justified. In many psychological tasks, one is aroused both to receive and to respond to information (Posner, 1978), although it is possible to put emphasis on changes in the sensory or the motor system.

It seems useful to preserve the term *arousal* for general improvements in efficiency of processing signals and allow for the possibility that there can be dissociations between central and autonomic arousal, between left and right hemisphere arousal, and between arousal of other internal systems (Derryberry & Rothbart, 1984).

ACTIVATION

Because information-processing models are concerned with internal systems such as those underlying language processing, spatial orienting, and emotion, merely distinguishing sensory and motor levels of activation is not sufficient to describe the activity states that prepare the organism for processing information. We use the term *activation* to refer to placing an internal representation of information (code) into an active state. Activation can come from two sources. It may be internally controlled from some central system or it may occur in response to an external stimulus event. Consider the presentation of a visual word. The presentation activates visual letter and word detectors, phonological codes of the word name, and semantic and evaluative meanings of the stimulus. The human memory system is thought to be a large semantic network of ideas that can be activated by appropriate input. According to many views this activation can take place either with attention, in the sense of mental effort as described below, or it may occur automatically without attention. If the latter, it is likely to bias the information selected for effortful processing. It is a considerable regulatory problem to control the flow of activation to keep a coherent goal-directed pattern of behavior and avoid interruption from parallel streams of activated pathways that might disrupt the pattern.

The concepts of arousal and activation can easily be confused at the intrapsychic level. As we view it, the former term is reserved for more general shifts of state affecting processing of broad classes of events (e.g., arousal of the motor system), whereas the latter refers to quite specific information such as activating a program to say a single word. In the extreme, the two concepts seem separate, even at the purely psychological level, but when one considers a subject's preparation for a visual event, it is difficult to know whether to consider this accomplished by a somewhat limited arousal process or by activation of quite general pathways. Indeed, unless the concepts are tied more rigorously to behavioral or physiological operations, it is hard to know how to make such a choice.

Experimental psychologists frequently attempt to set up a model task in order to study arousal and pathway activation (Posner, 1978). One method for studying arousal has been to introduce a warning signal prior to the occurrence of a sensory event. Ideally, the warning signal provides no specific information, but allows the subject to prepare maximal efficiency for processing the upcoming event and preparing a response. If only a small number of stimuli are used, the subject also can selectively activate pathways dealing with specific characteristics of the expected stimulus event. If, however, a large number of stimuli are possible, particularly with equal or nearly equal likelihood, the subject can make only a general preparation. In many situations this general preparation produces a marked change in the nervous system, including widespread blocking of the alpha rhythm and a distinct negative drift of the EEG (contingent negative variation). These represent a combination of facilitatory and inhibitory processes (Kahneman, 1973).

The model task described previously is used to trace the time course of these facilitations and inhibitions (Posner, 1978). Consider the effect of a warning signal on performance. It can best be understood with respect to a hypothetical build-up of pathway activation about the imperative stimulus (for example, a word). The build-up occurs in real time over several hundreds of milliseconds and involves activation of the stored codes of the word. In cases where the word is left on until the subject responds, the build-up of information eventually asymptotes. In such situations, the warning signal appears to affect mainly the time when subjects can respond, rather than the rate of activation of the internal pathway. We know this because the subject responds rapidly following a warning signal but with increased error. This result is consistent with a constant rate of build-up of information regardless of the level of arousal, but lowered criterion for responding to that information when arousal is increased. This results in faster but less accurate responding.

The same general theory predicts rather different results when the stimulus is presented only briefly. If arousal affects the time when the subject can respond and the stimulus is removed, it clearly is possible for a faster response to be based on a higher quality of sensory information. If the response is delayed, the activation produced by the stimulus may decrease, thus resulting in lower accuracy for slow responding. This constellation of results (fast reaction time and fewer errors) was reported by Fuster (1958). He presented monkeys with brief visual signals and varied their alertness by electrical stimulation of the reticular formation prior to the signal. These results have been replicated with human subjects when alertness is varied by a warning signal followed by a brief word or letter (Posner, 1975).

According to the theory of alertness outlined above, a warning signal improves reaction time, but it does not affect the build-up of pathway activation in the sensory memory system. One way to separate the build-up of information about a stimulus from the time to develop a response to it is to present a stimulus (for example, a word) followed after a short interval by a second stimulus (e.g., a second word). Suppose the task is to respond "same" if the words are identical, and otherwise "different." Performance on the second word improves, that is, both reaction time and errors in making the match decline regularly, as the time by which the first word precedes the second is increased from 0 to 300 msec. This improvement in reaction time and error contrasts markedly with changes due to presenting a warning signal alone. The time course of the improvement of handling the second word provides an indirect means of observing the process of pathway activation produced by the first word. When subjects are alerted prior to the presentation of the first word, they respond more rapidly than when they had not been alerted, but the extent of improvement in reaction time due to the specific information about the first word is completely unaffected by the warning.

This result is confirmation of the view that the rate of pathway activation can be unaffected by the level of arousal. It also suggests that the mechanisms that vary the level of arousal are independent of the mechanism that improves performance due to specific information about the first word. The effect of the first word is due to pathway activation. The specificity of this pathway is shown by the finding that the extent of improvement is greater the more the second word resembles the first. Here we have behavioral evidence that arousal induced by the warning and pathway activation make independent (additive) contributions to the speed of processing (Posner, 1978).

It is obvious that there are differences in the degree to which one is affected by the operations of arousal and pathway activation. For example, it has been shown (Kraut, 1976) that children usually show a reduction in performance if a warning signal is repeated over and over again in an experiment. Adults, however, usually do not show such a reduction in performance. Careful work by Kraut has suggested that the warning signal has two effects. One of them is an alerting effect; the other is activation of a specific pathway corresponding to the physical form of the signal. The alerting effect undergoes habituation due to repetition over trials. The pathway activation effect does not seem to undergo such an effect of repetition. Children are much more affected by the alerting aspects of the stimulus than they are by the pathway activation effects. Thus, repeating the stimulus reduces its alerting quality and harms their performance. Adults, on the other hand, are not as affected by alertness, presumably because their level of arousal is not so highly affected by time in the experiment or because stronger pathway activation effects overcome the reduced alerting effects.

EFFORT

A third aspect of attention has been called effort. It is most closely related to the subjective feeling of conscious experience with which we all are familiar. Of course, both arousal and activation are also necessary aspects for conscious experience, but neither of them is necessarily associated with the contents of consciousness, as is effort. When we refer to the act of attending to an idea, we are concerend with the selection of that idea by the processing system responsible for effort. The system giving rise to effort is apparently one of limited capacity, since effort directed toward any idea or task necessarily reduces it in any other direction

(Posner, 1978). The term *orienting of attention* refers to mental acts necessary to direct effort toward some content. Attention can be oriented either by some external signal that tends to draw it exogenously, or by some internal plan.

Chronometric studies of the type discussed previously have begun to provide some knowledge of the coordination of the regulatory mechanisms of arousal, pathway activation, and effort. There is evidence that arousal can be produced automatically without the intercession of systems involved in effort (Dawson & Schell, 1982). Thus, a word previously paired with shock presented to the unattended ear in a dichotic listening task produces an autonomic response even though the subject was unable to express any knowledge about that word. Similarly, split-brain subjects show arousal to warning signals (Gazzaniga & Hillyard, 1973) presented to the right hemisphere that do not reach systems responsible for verbal output.

The warning signal effects described previously suggest that arousal does not affect pathway activation. The question of how the level of arousal influences the efficiency of performance without affecting the way in which information builds up in the nervous system has been investigated via chronometric experiments. Consider the distinction between the activation of different pathways corresponding to the identification of words and the ability of subjects to output the activations produced by those pathways. The output processes appear to require the subjects to make a connection between the activated code and some nonhabitual response system. We do not habitually make arbitrary responses with keys to words. Thus words do not produce an automatic keypress; that requires the system responsible for effortful processing. Arousal makes this system more readily available, thus usually allowing more efficient information processing (Posner, 1978). This account of the effect of arousal on performance suggests that it modulates the balance between automatic or unconscious pathway activation processes and the higher level systems controlling effortful processes.

At low states of arousal or when the subject's active attention is directed toward another stimulus or memorial location, activation may take place without effort. On the other hand, it is possible for activation to take place through the exertion of effort. For example, when the subject thinks of a word or idea, it is activated as a result of the effort directed to it. Once a concept is activated, either through the occurrence of a sensory stimulus or by effort, it remains active for a brief period of time. During this time, it is more available for reactivation than if it had not been active previously. Thus, the threshold for sensory stimuli once activated is reduced, and it is likely that the thought processes will return to some formerly activated concept.

Effort allows a method of regulating complex activation patterns. Suppose many concepts are active at one particular moment. Effort directed toward any one of those concepts reduces the amount of available effort for handling other concepts. Since activation dies away with time, sustained effort on any concept reduces the likelihood that other activated concepts will affect thought processes or behavior. Thus effort becomes a regulatory mechanism, preventing some activation patterns from being expressed in the behavior or thought processes of the organism.

Although we have only briefly introduced a few of the basic concepts involved in intrapsychic regulation (see Posner, 1978, for a more detailed review), it should be possible to see that there is considerable opportunity for differences among ages and individuals in the way in which the elements of self-regulation interact. Highly overlearned concepts will show rapid and efficient activation. People obviously will differ in the degree of learning and thus the activation characteristics of various pathways. Differences in degree of learning would not necessarily be seen as temperamental variables, but individual differences in effort and arousal are likely to influence the degree of overlearning an individual is likely to achieve (Tucker & Williamson, 1984). The ease with which different sensory and motor systems can be aroused also will be a source of differences. Since arousal level affects the balance between automatic and effortful processes, it is easy to see how differences here can produce the tendency toward impulsivity or reflectivity that are postulated by developmental theories (see page 95). The study of regulatory systems at the intrapsychic level by methods of mental chronometry provides a way of assessing the regulatory characteristics of a person. However, a major advantage to the analysis of regulation in terms of arousal, activation, and effort is the possibility of establishing links to neural systems involved.

Neurological Systems

How do the known mechanisms of regulation within the nervous system relate to the intrapsychic mechanisms we have been discussing? Neuropsychological studies with patients provide the opportunity to determine if some of the intrapsychic mechanisms discussed above become dissociated in cases of brain injury. It is well known that damage to the reticular system can produce an organism difficult to arouse with marked slowing of behavior (Magoun, 1958). There also is good evidence for viewing arousal and pathway activation as resting upon independent mechanisms. For example, Gazzaniga and Hillyard (1973) have shown that the contingent negative variation induced by the presentation of a warning signal to one hemisphere of a split-brain patient spreads to the other hemisphere. This contrasts with information concerning identification of a stimulus (such as a letter) that is generally not available to the opposite hemisphere. Thus split-brain research provides additional support for the hypothesis that arousal induced by a warning signal involves a sub-cortical mechanism, whereas selection based on pathway activation related to the identification of a stimulus involves cortical processes.

When the physiological evidence for independent mechanisms is combined with the information-processing account (see page 100), the sense of independence between pathway activation and arousal is enlarged. The physiological evidence suggests a separation of location within the brain (subcortical in the case of arousal and cortical in the case of pathway activation). The psychological evidence adds to this an independence of function. Psychological studies suggest arousal chiefly operates not on the sensitivity of encoding information but on an effort system, while pathway activation changes the sensitivity of input pathways to stimuli.

In recent years the subcortical mechanisms mediating the arousal systems have been elaborated and more has become known about the various transmitter pathways involving sensory and motor systems. It seems clear that mechanisms exist to exert phasic and tonic influences at every level of information processing. Moreover, it also has been well established that deficits in neurotransmitter activity can provide specific deficits in aspects of information processing. For example, a deficit in dopamine found in Parkinson's disease leads to a difficulty in the initiation of motor activity that seems specific to that domain (Marsden, 1982). Patients who show severe slowing in motor behavior may show little or no general loss in alertness or ability to direct attention toward a sensory or memorial stimulus (Rafal, Posner, Walker, & Friedrich, 1984). These neuropsychological findings fit with the projection of dopamine pathways chiefly to anterior and motor systems and less to the sensory and associative areas of the cortex.

The anatomical distribution of norepinephrine and serotonin includes both sensory and motor systems and may act as an amplifier or facilitator of inhibitory inputs (Foote, Ashton-Jones, & Bloom, 1980). However, clear neuropsychological evidence of the effects of these transmitters on information processing such as that from the study of Parkinson's disease on dopamine is lacking. We are beginning to have some idea of how the midbrain systems regulate activation at the cortical level, but more specific models for intensive study will be needed.

According to the ideas outlined in the previous section, cognitive processes may be examined in terms of many parallel pathways, each capable of high-level semantic analysis and each operating with considerable independence, although with facilitatory and possibly inhibitory connections serving to regulate their activity. Work on split-brain patients, subjects with lateralized brain injury, and normal subjects has supported this view in the case of cognitive processes controlled by each hemisphere (Gazzaniga, 1970). Of course, an entire hemisphere represents a very gross neural system, but the ability to isolate the hemispheres surgically, the relative isolation of their blood supplies producing unilateral effects of stroke, and the capability of presenting sensory information to normal individuals that is processed initially by one hemisphere all have provided methodologies that allow investigation of how isolated neural systems may support cognition.

The results of these investigations have suggested that each hemisphere is capable of independent interpretation of complex input and that the analysis may differ between the two. The exact characterization of these two forms of interpretation is disputed, but roughly the right hemisphere appears to be more global, holistic, and analogical, whereas the left is more analytic, sequential, and verbal. Irrespective of the content of their cognition, it appears that the two systems maintain separate complex parallel analysis of input and contribute their habitual output which must be coordinated by later systems internal to each hemisphere. There is evidence that the dominance of one system over another may differ in development with the right hemisphere maturing somewhat earlier (Tucker, in press) and that it differs among individuals as well. In addition there is reason to suppose that fluctuations in input, strategy, or internal cycles shift the dominance of these systems within an individual in a dynamic way (Levy, Heller, Banich, & Burton, 1983). In the normal person there rarely is evidence of conflict between these separate processing systems. This may in part be because of strong reciprocal inhibitory connections that provide regulation between the two systems. Much of this regulation may come from the development of more anterior systems.

If the disconnected cerebral hemispheres are viewed as separate neural systems performing cognitive functions, it then becomes necessary to find a model of how they are regulated and coordinated in integrated performance. At the intrapsychic level the systems serving such high-level effortful regulation are correlated with the experience we call awareness or consciousness. When attention in the form of effort is brought to bear on any sensory or stored information, we have the subjective experience of being aware of that information. Chronometric experiments have demonstrated that such awareness can be time locked to the occurrence of signals and that it is accompanied by a widespread reduction in the efficiency of other processing (Posner, 1978).

From a neuropsychological viewpoint, the frontal lobes seem to exercise strong inhibitory control over more posterior systems (Tucker, in press). The posterior areas of the brain appear to handle most of the problems of representation, whereas the regulatory functions seem to be more anterior. Lesions of the frontal lobes produce a lack of coherence to behavior so that the patient behaves in socially inappropriate ways. According to Luria (1966), this regulatory function is different between the two sides of the brain, with lesions of the left frontal areas producing a loss of planning and goal-directed behavior and right lesions a reduction of appropriate social and emotional responses. These inhibitory and regulatory characteristics of frontal areas suggest that they play a basic role in the effort function outlined in the previous section.

One situation in which it has been possible to link specific brain injury effects to awareness has been in the case of unilateral parietal lesions. It has been known for many years that such lesions may lead to an inability to attend or process information that is on the side of space contralateral to the lesion (Weinstein & Freidland, 1977). Studies using patients with unilateral parietal lesions have shown that when attention is cued to the side ipsilateral to the lesion or even to fixation, targets that normally could be perceived efficiently either may be greatly reduced in efficiency or missed altogether (Posner, Walker, Friedrich, & Rafael, 1984). However, if given sufficient time to shift attention to a location opposite the lesion, patients seem to do well. This set of findings suggests that the probability a stimulus will be attended to consciously is reduced by parietal damage, but that the effort system must lie elsewhere, since the damaged side can be processed efficiently if cued. Although the data to date do not provide an explicit account of how effortful effects are produced, we are starting to develop paradigms that may provide more knowledge of its neural basis.

It seems likely that the course of development and the basis of individual differences in personality will rest on these three basic regulatory mechanisms. We turn now to a review of studies of the early development of humans and animals in an effort to examine issues of continuity and discontinuity in the attainment of self-regulation. Most of this literature deals with the behavioral and physiological levels of analysis. For this reason it has often proved difficult to achieve a consensus on the links between the development of physiological regulatory systems and their behavioral expression. We believe that the use of intrapsychic concepts such as activation and effort will help in the eventual achievement of stronger connections between neural mechanisms and behavior.

ONTOGENY OF SELF-REGULATION

We view the development of temperament as involving the addition of increasing regulatory control (effort) over initial patterns of reactivity (activation) (Derryberry & Rothbart, 1984; Rothbart & Derryberry, 1981).

In this section we describe the way in which built-in involuntary regulatory behaviors of the infant serve to guide caregiver regulation. We then identify likely transition periods in the development of self-regulation, that is, periods when children appear to demonstrate forms of regulation not previously present.

By making use of animal data on behavioral shifts and concurrent development of neurochemical regulatory systems and brain structures, we also suggest that developmental changes in brain function may be taking place. As a model of a developing temperamental characteristic with strong self-regulative components, we consider the emotion of fear. We argue that the basic reactive components of fearfulness are present at birth, although they appear to be activated chiefly by intensive aspects of stimuli, and that this reactivity is increasingly regulated by the development of behavioral inhibition and effortful action during the early years of life. Learning increases the range of potential stimuli automatically activating fear, but maturation of effort systems increasingly regulates this activation.

This developmental analysis adds the possibility of an important additional source of temperamental variability, namely, the rate at which children's regulative capacities develop. Children's experience may differ greatly depending on the point in development when self-regulatory controls are added (Rothbart & Derryberry, 1981, 1982).

THE INITIAL STATE: THE NEWBORN PERIOD TO 2 MONTHS

Bridges's (1932) early descriptions of infant emotions have been the starting point of many discussions of the ontogeny of emotions; they have strongly influenced Sroufe's (1979) view of emotional development. Bridges describes the newborn as evidencing only "general excitement"; later emotions are differentiated from this initial state. At 3 months, distress and delight are differentiated; at 6 months, fear, disgust, and anger are added; at 12 months elation and affection; and so on. In Sroufe's (1979) view, infant distress to "early obligatory attention" is expected to differentiate into wariness in response to incongruity and, later, into conditioned fear. Neither Bridges nor Sroufe specify in detail the mechanisms involved in this differentiation.

Alternatively, Izard (1977; Izard & Beuchler, 1979) argues that discrete emotions emerge independently at that point in development when they will be adaptive for the infant. Once an emotion is part of an infant's repertoire, it may blend with other emotions to allow for many variations of expression and experience. In Izard's framework, neonatal distress is adaptive for maintaining caregiver proximity and interaction; fear, maturing in the last quarter of the first year of life, is adaptive in allowing for self-control and self-protection. In addition to distress, Izard argues that the following discrete emotions are present at birth: pleasure, disgust, startle, and interest.

The view of McGuire and Turkewitz (1979) lies between these two positions on the ontogeny of emotions. Their position, following Schneirla's theory (1972a, b), identifies two processes as operative during the early weeks of life, withdrawal (W) and approach (A). These are processes driven by the intensity of a stimulus. Withdrawal (W) processes are seen to generally involve the expenditure of energy, to be controlled by the sympathetic branch of the autonomic nervous sytem, and to involve heart rate acceleration and looking or turning away, limb flexions, and distress. These behaviors generally serve to orient the infant away from the source of stimulation, as an initial form of self-regulation. These W processes overlap to some extent with Sokolov's (1963) defensive reaction and with Gellhorn's (1968) description of sympathetically controlled "ergotrophic" reactions.

Tonic approach (A) processes in McGuire and Turkewitz' (1978) framework are seen as generally conserving of body energy and under parasympathetic control. Tonic A processes include motor quieting, heart rate deceleration, regular respiration and blood pressure. Phasic A processes are described as basic to food getting and include looking toward, turning toward, smiling, and limb extensions. These are similar to Gellhorn's (Gellhorn, 1968; Gellhorn & Loofbourrow, 1963) "trophotropic" reactions. A typical neonatal trophotropic state for Gellhorn would be that involved in feeding, when muscular relaxation and frequently sleep are elicited.

In Schneirla's system, A responses are expected to have lower stimulus intensity thresholds than W responses, and A- and W-response systems are seen as acting in opposition to one another. Turkewitz and his associates have attempted to test the prediction that A responses will predominate at lower intensity levels and W responses at higher intensity levels during early infancy. By comparing limb flexion (W responses) with extension (A responses) in newborns, they have found that more intense auditory (Turkewitz, Moreau, Birch, & Davis, 1971) and interroceptive (Turkewitz, Fleischer, Moreau, Birch, & Levy, 1966) stimuli are associated with flexion movements, and lower intensities with extension. Comparable results also were found for motor movements in response to visual stimuli (McGuire & Turkewitz, 1978). In addition, Turkewitz and co-workers found that intensity of stimuli appear to summate across the sensory modalities of audition and vision in influencing infants' looking toward or away from a visual stimulus (Lawson & Turkewitz, 1980; Lewkowicz & Turkewitz, 1981), whereas intensity-related habituation was found to generalize from the visual modality to the auditory modality for 3-week-old infants but not for adult subjects (Lewkowicz & Turkewitz, 1980).

These results suggest that a kind of basic emotional processing is being carried out in the newborn related to reward and punishment (McGuire & Turkewitz, 1979). Although Turkewitz and co-workers stress the importance of stimulus intensity effects only during early infancy, sensory pleasure in adults also appears to be related to stimulus intensity, with lower intensity levels leading to feelings of pleasure, and higher levels to displeasure (Cabanac, 1979).

The expression of infant hedonic tone described previously has clear physiological and behavioral effects on the caregiver. Frodi, Lamb, Leavitt, and Donovan (1978) presented parents of newborn infants with a video-tape of a smiling or crying infant. Parents reported greater feelings of distress in connection with the crying infant and greater feelings of happiness and attentiveness with the smiling infant. Parents' diastolic blood pressure and skin conductance increased for the tape of the crying infant, but did not for the smiling infant. In the view of Frodi *et al.*, the infant's crying creates an aversive stimulus which the parent attempts to terminate. From the earliest days of the infant, caregivers use the infant's distress reaction to guide their regulatory interventions. The majority of interventions are initially of a soothing variety, responding to infant distress by picking up and initiating quieting procedures (Bell & Ainsworth, 1972; Korner & Thoman, 1972).

Do infants differ in their thresholds for approach and withdrawal processes? If so, this would constitute one of the earliest demonstrations of individual differences in temperament. One approach to this question is to test for stability over time in infants' tendency to show distress, given a standardized stimulus presentation. Birns, Barten, and Bridger (1969) investigated the stability of the following laboratory measures from the newborn period to 1, 3, and 4 months of age: irritability, soothability, activity level, alertness, vigor of responding, sensitivity, tension, and level of maturity. Among the measures, evidence for interindividual stability was found across all three sessions for irritability, soothability, sensitivity, and tension. Stability of activity was found from 1 month onward. The work of Birns *et al.* (1969) suggests that distress and motor tension aspects of W responses, as well as recovery time to distress, vary at birth and may show some short-term stability.

We now consider later transitions in infant behavior that appear related to the development of self-regulation and possible changes in brain function that may be related to these behavioral transitions.

THE 2- TO 3-MONTH TRANSITION

The period of 2–3 months of life has been identified by Emde and his associates (Emde, Gaensbauer, & Harmon, 1976; Emde & Robinson,

1978) as the time of a major biobehavioral shift. They note the onset of social smiling, a decrease in fussiness, increased ease of establishing habituation and maintaining avoidance learning and operant learning, increases in quiet sleep, and decreases in activation of transitory reflexes. Emde and Robinson describe the child as becoming more sensitive to exogenous stimulation during this period. This change may come about in part through increased resolution of the visual perceptual apparatus (Olson & Sherman, 1983); it also may be related to maturational changes in control mechanisms.

Whereas distress reactions showed some stability across the early months in the study by Birns et al., alertness did not. In addition, Lipton, Steinschneider, and Richmond (1961, 1966) examined cardiac reactivity to an air puff for infants during the newborn period and again at 2½ and at 5 months. No stability of individual differences was found between the newborn testing and 2½ months, but stability was found from 2½ to 5 months. Steinschneider (1973) suggests that this may be due to maturation of cardiac control mechanisms.

Graham, Strock, and Ziegler (1981) have provided the most recent review of the maturation of cardiac control, noting that noradrenergic excitatory effects (heart rate acceleration) are dominant immediately postnatally in human infants, with deceleration observed most clearly only after 2–3 months of age. Graham et al. (1981) note that in developing rats, early motor excitatory effects become increasingly regulated through cholinergic mechanisms by about 15–20 days of age. They suggest that the onset of strong heart rate decelerations in orienting of human infants also may be evidence of increasing cholinergic control of heart rate. In addition to heart rate deceleration, orienting reactions include motor quieting and negative shifts in EEG, indexing increased receptivity to the stimulus. These effects are similar to those observed in adult reactions to a warning signal.

Emotionality at birth thus may be seen to involve chiefly activation of gross W and A responses, including distress and a kind of vegetative pleasure. Withdrawal response would then constitute the first component of the emotion of fear. At 2–3 months, motor quieting and response preparation aspects of orienting are added. To the extent that this parasympathetic reaction opposes the sympathetic heart rate acceleration response associated with distress (Gellhorn, 1968; Porges, 1976), these maturational changes in orienting may result in an overall decrease in distress to overstimulation at this age, possibly corresponding to Benjamin's (1965) active "stimulus barrier." Benjamin argues that increased sensitivity in infants of 3 to 4 weeks of age continues until 8 to 10 weeks, making the infant highly vulnerable to distress, as in bouts of crying and fussiness. By 8 to 10 weeks, however, a "stimulus barrier" is established, allowing the maturing cortex to exercise increased inhibitory control.

Although at first it may seem unlikely that the 2- to 3-month changes are adding anything to the distress and withdrawal we already have identified as part of the fear reaction, the orienting reaction provides a period of appraisal that often precedes an overt fear response in older children and adults (Zegans & Zegans, 1972). At 2–3 months, we also note some differentiation of arousal. As reflected in heart rate (Porges, 1976), this includes initial heart rate acceleration, followed by a heart rate deceleration. During the deceleratory period, response preparation takes place. Later, in development of the arousal that is part of a reaction to a warning signal, this period may be extended over time for an event that requires choice and action. Porges (1976) also notes that when the infant is unable to enact a response and stimulation continues further, additional heart rate acceleration (correlated with effort) is likely to result. This reaction may be seen as an unconditioned form of fear. Heart rate acceleration also occurs when adult subjects engage in effortful problem solving (McGuinness and Pribram, 1980).

Development of Central Neurotransmitter Systems. We have mentioned the delayed onset of cholinergic regulation of behavioral activation in juvenile rats. In these animal studies, developmental behavior change is related to changes in levels and metabolism of neuroregulators. This research indicates that the earliest maturing systems in the rat brain are catecholaminergic, related to early high and increasing levels of motor activity, Norepinephrine concentrations show their greatest increases at 7–8 days of age, and neocortical innervations demonstrate adult levels of uptake by 9 days of age (Pradhan & Pradhan, 1980). Dextroamphetamine, an adrenergic stimulant, increases rats' activity level at 10 days of age (Pradhan & Pradhan, 1980). The subsequent development of motor inhibition and lowered activity levels have been related to development of serotonergic and cholinergic mechanisms. Serotonin antagonists do not increase activity level until 15 days of age (Mabry & Campbell, 1974), and cholinergic antagonists do not do so until 15–20 days (Pradhan & Pradhan, 1980). Evidence also has been put forward for an early motor excitatory (Phelps, Koranyi, & Tamasy, 1982; Schmidt, Bjorklund, Lindvall, & Loren, 1982) and a later-developing motor inhibitory (Heffner, Heller, Miller, Kotake, & Seiden, 1983; Shaywitz, Yager, & Klopper, 1976) dopaminergic effect in rats. The inhibitory effect is associated with the ventral tegmental area–prefrontal cortex pathway, rather than the substantia nigra–caudate–putamen dopamine pathway.

We cannot make direct translations from these findings to human development, but results in this rapidly advancing field suggest that different types of neurophysiological regulatory processes develop over time and are related to important changes in behavior. Motor inhibitory neuroregulatory processes also may have differential effects depending on whether the response is reflexive or voluntary (Williams, Hamilton, & Carlton, 1975). This animal model strongly suggests that biologically based components of control are added as the organism matures, an argument we wish to make concerning human development.

Infant–Caregiver Interaction. At 2–3 months, the extent of expressive communication from infant to caregiver is remarkable. Analyses of infants and their mothers filmed interacting with one another allow us to study effects of these expressive behaviors on maternal regulation more closely.

In a report from one of Stern's (1974) videotaped interactions of mother–infant play, he describes a 3-month-old becoming excited while looking at the mother. The child begins to smile, vocalize, and show signs of increasing motor activity. Stern continues:

> As the intensity of his state increased, he begins to show signs of displeasure, momentary sobering, and a fleeting grimace, interspersed with smiling. The intensity of arousal continue to build until he suddenly averts gaze sharply . . . while his level of "excitement" clearly declines. He then returns his gaze, bursting into a smile, and the level of arousal and affect build again. He again averts gaze, and so on. The infant gives the clear impression of modulating his states of arousal and affect within certain limits by regulating the amount of perceptual input. (pp. 208–209)

The mother is not inactive during these periods. When the infant looks away, she also is likely to look away and to decrease the intensity of her stimulation toward the child. She also may increase the infant's level of excitement by smiling, vocalizing, leaning forward, and touching the child (Brazelton, Koslowski, & Main, 1974; Stern, 1974). Brazelton and Stern were impressed by the smoothness of this dyadic interaction, which they found lacking in the infant's interactions with objects at this age. These observations have led investigators to conclude that young infants use smiles, gaze aversions, and other gestures intentionally to produce responses from the parent (Stern, 1977; Trevarthen, 1978).

Available evidence does suggest that mothers are sensitive to information being conveyed by the infant's behavior (Gottman & Ringland, 1981; Kaye, 1979), affecting both their subsequent behavior and their verbal interpretation of these events. In Gottman and Ringland's (1981) analysis, however, evidence for effects of the mother's state on the infant were not found for the youngest infants. Although infant behavior added predictability to mother's subsequent behavior beyond what would have been predicted from what the mother previously did, the mother's behavior did not increase predictability for the infant's subsequent behavior. Thus, although the mother appears to be "taking account" of the infant's state in her action, the infant is not "taking account" of the mother's. Only for the oldest infant studied did the converse also appear to be true; hence the ascription of intentional communication to very young infants does not appear warranted.

How then might we characterize the regulation taking place within the mother–infant dyad? The infant's patterns of reactivity and self-regulation appear to serve as signals to the mother and guide her actions (Brazelton et al., 1974; Emde et al., 1976; Emde & Robinson, 1978). At the same time, the mother's culture influences to some extent the kinds of states she attempts to achieve in the infant (Caudill & Weinstein, 1969). In infants studied in our country, when the mother wants to play and the child's attention is unfocused, the mother presents auditory and visual stimulation at the midline until the child is oriented toward her face (Als, Tronick, & Brazelton, 1980). When the child averts gaze, the mother appears to take this as a sign that the stimulation level is too high and she attempts to quiet the child by decreasing the intensity of her stimulation or beginning soothing procedures. Some parents may not heed these cues, however, leading to overstimulation of the infant (Brazelton et al., 1974).

THE 7- TO 9-MONTH TRANSITION: SENSITIVITY TO SIGNS OF PUNISHMENT; DEVELOPMENT OF THE BEHAVIORAL INHIBITION SYSTEM

The 7- to 9-month period appears to mark an important increase in self-regulation. Most of the research literature suggests that fear of strangers, fear of the visual cliff, and separation anxiety develop during this period (Emde et al., 1976). Two major elements of fear appear to be added at approximately this time. One is an increasing sensitivity to signs of punishment leading to behavioral distress, as in the infant's distress at the sight of a person in a white coat (Sroufe, 1979). An additional component of the fear response is *behavioral inhibition*, that is, the inhibition of approach responses. Schaffer (1974) has called this element wariness, but because the term wariness has been used with widely divergent meanings in the literature (see Bronson & Pankey, 1977; Schaffer, 1974; Sroufe, 1979; for three quite different uses of the term), and since inhibition allows us to consider some of the functional elements of Gray's (1982) "behavioral inhibition system," we will call the element inhibition.

Schaffer (1974) has observed that although infants of 5 months demonstrate via their looking patterns that they distinguish between novel and familiar objects, they reach equally quickly toward both novel and unfamiliar objects. At 8 months, however, they show greater hesitancy in grasping the novel toy. Similarly, at 5 months, infants indicate through their decelerating heart rate responses that they discriminate between being placed over the deep versus the shallow side of the visual cliff. At 9 months, however, they show distress and accelerating heart rate responses when placed above the deep side (Schwartz, Campos, & Baisel, 1973). Similar changes occur in infants' reactions to a stranger's approach across the period 5 to 9 months (Campos, Emde, & Gaensbauer, 1975). It appears that both behavioral inhibition and sensitivity to signals of punishment are increasing greatly during this period.

We may now review the components of fear carried over from previous developmental periods. These include the capacity for distress previously elicited by overstimulation; this distress now appears to be triggered by both unconditioned (novelty) and conditioned fear stimuli (the doctor's needle). The components also include orienting to novelty; a discrepancy- or novelty-checking apparatus appears to be in place before 7 months since it influences differential visual orienting to novel versus familiar stimuli. Now, however, novelty also demonstrates influences on developing approach responses via behavioral inhibition. This represents a major transition toward self-control as opposed to other-regulation. However, it also heralds a period when the caregiver serves an especially important function in providing security for the child. Fear reactions appear to be peremptory; something must be done to alleviate the distress before the infant will be able to explore the environment and objects in it, and the caregiver's presence serves this function (Bowlby, 1969). The period during which security remains a critical issue for the young child will last up until approximately 3 years of age (Bowlby, 1969).

We may now consider possible individual differences in the components of fear. Infants could differ in their degree of distress to a given level of novelty; they also could differ in the strength of their approach response and the extent to which their approach responses are inhibited. They could differ in the self-soothing techniques available to them, for example, gaze aversions, looking away, thumb-sucking, and so forth. For infants who are easily distressed, we would expect security to become more of an issue than for others. For infants who either are not easily distressed or are adept at soothing themselves, security will be less of an issue. Infants with stronger behavioral control and an accessible effort system may be able to stop, look, and decide on an appropriate action even though they are distressed. For children who are less sensitive to signs of punishment and with less well-developed behavioral inhibition, control will be a problem, especially if their approach responses are strong. These children may be described as impulsive or hyperactive (Douglas, 1980).

In Gray's (1982) system, central noradrenergic systems are important in both distress reactions and behavioral inhibition; serotonergic systems also may be important in eliciting behavioral inhibition in response to signals of punishment. As mentioned earlier, inhibiting effects of serotonergic systems in rats are not seen during the first weeks of life. Whether the effects of developing serotonergic systems are to some extent concurrent with the development of sensitivity to signals of punishment in humans is not yet determined. Hippocampal structures important in behavioral inhibition (Gray, 1982) develop over the early years of life (Douglas, 1975; Douglas, Packouz, & Douglas, 1972). However, behavioral components of Gray's (1982) "stop; check carefully" system appear to be at least somewhat developed by 9 months; the "check carefully" part of the system appears to be present even earlier. This regulation occurs at the sensorimotor level. Verbal control of these capacities will be added later, and we consider development of this control in the next section.

THE 18 MONTHS TO 4-YEAR TRANSITION: VERBAL SELF-REGULATION

Soviet research and theory identify the preschool years as importantly involved in the development of inhibition. In this connection, Pavlov (1961) discussed two major levels at which human behavior is regulated. The first, called the first signal system, is seen to function at the level of unconditioned reflexes and conditioned responses. The second level of control, found only in humans, employs the symbolic capacities of language and is called the second signal system. According to Luria (1961), the second system assumes control over the first, but does not replace it.

At the level of the first signal system, inhibition involves built-in reflexes, for example, orienting, and inhibition built up in repetition of nonreinforced stimuli or during passive avoidance conditioning. This latter form is called internal inhibition and it is seen to function in habituation, passive avoidance, and spontaneous alternation. According to Luria (1961), this capacity for internal inhibition provides an underlying mechanism for the development of verbal self-control. We (Reed, Pien, & Rothbart, 1984) have found a positive relation between a measure of internal inhibition (spontaneous alternation) and two measures of verbally regulated behavioral inhibition (a pinball game and simon-says) in children aged 40–49 months. This cluster appeared to be independent of age, although all measures in it showed strong age effects. Krakow and Johnson (1981), using different measures of voluntary inhibition with younger children (age 18–30 months), also have found an inhibitory cluster and large age effects. They find moderate levels of stability of inhibitory self-control across this 12-month period. Taken together, these studies indicate that there are increases in verbal self-regulation across 18–30 months (Krakow & Johnson, 1981) and across 40–49 months of age (Reed *et al.*, 1984). Our study also indicates increases in internal inhibition occurring relatively late in development.

Two brain structures possibly related to these developments require considerable time to mature. Rats with hippocampal lesions show deficits in passive avoidance, reversal shifts, extinction, and spontaneous alternation, as well as other measures. Douglas (1975) and Kimble (1968) have pointed out the relation between these behaviors and internal inhibition. Juvenile rats show increases of these behaviors at approximately 35 days, at a time of proliferation of cells in the hippocampal dentate gyrus (Altman, Brunner, & Bayer, 1973). Douglas *et al.* (1972) suggest that similar changes in the human may occur at about 4 years of age. Lesions of the prefrontal cortex also are associated with decreased performance on tasks seen as involving internal inhibition (Rosenkilde, 1979), and these prefrontal structures also demonstrate extended postnatal maturation (Rose, 1980). Luria (1973) suggests that maturation of the prefrontal cortex may occur as late as 5–7 years of age.

Most psychosurgical procedures interrupt major connections between the frontal lobe and limbic-subcortical structures (Nauta, 1973). In studies of effects of prefrontal damage, there have been observations of dissociations between an intact ability to describe the requirements of a task and subjects' inability to control their behavior in accordance with this analysis (Rosenkilde, 1979). Gray (1982) suggests that the prefrontal cortex may be a route whereby verbally coded descriptions of threats can contact the behavioral inhibition system. Thus the source of threat (e.g., a deadline) and the program necessary to subvert the threat (a set of rules to follow) may both be verbally coded, and constitute a new level of self-regulation; one that may correspond to the effects of the Pavlovian second signal system. Gray (1982) suggests that these types of fears may be resistant to pharmacotherapy but responsive to prefrontal or cingulate lesions (Laatinen & Vilkki, 1972). Dopaminergic projections appear to be important in the functioning of the prefrontal cortex in connection with anxiety (Gray, 1982), and Tucker (Tucker, 1984; Tucker & Williamson, 1984) has argued that left-hemisphere dopaminergic effects are implicated in human anxiety states.

What are possible connections between fear and the kind of verbally regulated self-control described in this section? Both fear and self-control make use of a behavioral inhibition system, just as fear and frustration reactions both include a component of behavioral inhibition (Gray, 1982). Verbal controls over inhibitory behavior may develop at about the same time as verbal controls over fear, but they need not. More research will be needed to address this question.

We may now return to studies of fear that involve the behavioral inhibition system. Garcia-Coll, Kagan, and Resnick (1984) have observed the behavior of 21-month-old infants in response to unfamiliar stimuli in the laboratory, noting their tendency to become inhibited (accompanied with distress) or uninhibited. Individual differences in inhibition showed moderate stability from 21 to 31 months of age.

Although involuntary inhibition related to fear may be associated with the voluntary self-control evidenced in preschool-aged children, this link has not yet been explored empirically. We would expect it to operate via increasing prefrontal control as suggested by the previous discussion (see also page 104). In any case, we expect that this period of developing language and verbal controls over behavior will allow for increasing sources of both fear and self-regulation, and that children will increasingly respond appropriately to situations in which control is needed. Children who lag behind in these maturational developments may demonstrate many fewer control strategies and create problems for parents and teachers.

LATER POSSIBLE TRANSITION PERIODS IN SELF-REGULATION

In addition to being instructed as to how they "should" feel in different situations (Hochschild, 1979), children also come to learn that external expressions of emotions should sometimes be suppressed or exaggerated. Saarni (1979) has studied the "display rule" knowledge of children from ages 6 to 10 years. She has found that with increasing age, children come to know more rules of display and these rules are more complex than those of younger children. Saarni (1982) also found that children above the age of 6 were more likely to employ an emotion-suppressive display rule in their social behavior. These rules likely have strong influences on the expression of emotions in children. Cognitive understanding of possible dissociations between feeling and action and related intentional dissimulation (Selman, 1980) also are probably important changes taking place at this time in the socialization of emotions.

Other important developments in reactivity and self-regulation may take place during adolescence, although more research is needed in this area. In his research on adults, Zuckerman (1979, 1983) and his associates have found relationships between levels of gonadal hormones (testosterone and estrogen) and a scale of sensation-seeking disinhibition. The disinhibition scale includes items describing the need to seek release in uninhibited social activities. Large prepubertal increases in gonadal hormones thus may be related to changes in approach and self-regulation. Changes in levels of gonadal hormones also may be related to changes in emotionality. Evidence for heightened emotionally during the early years of adolescence has been found in connection with increased nervous habits (Macfarlane, Allen, & Honzik, 1954), nervous tension (Davidson & Gottlieb, 1955), mood swings (Macfarlane et al., 1954), irritability (Macfarlane et al., 1954), quarrelsomeness (Gesell, Ilg, & Ames, 1956), and emotional outbursts (Gesell et al., 1956). Whereas depression is rare in younger children, depressive symptoms are fairly common in adolescence (Feinstein, 1975).

Changes during aging may constitute another self-regulative transition. In older subjects' performance on reaction time tasks, their responses tend to be slower than those of younger subjects. In situations when more necessary pathway activation will accrue during this period, their responses also are likely to be more accurate; in situations where necessary pathway activation is completed more rapidly, they may be less accurate, suggesting a slowing of arousal-related processes. This slowing of response may be related to the characteristics of cautiousness in aging individuals (Botwinick, 1959).

Studies of neurotransmitter changes in the aging rat brain also suggest that developmental regulative changes may be taking place (Timiras, Segall, & Walker, 1979). With some regional variability, serotonin concentrations were found to increase with advancing age. Norepinephrine levels showed a general decline and dopamine levels a marked decline. In humans, significant declines in norepinephrine have been reported with aging, and loss of cells in the locus ceruleus has been estimated at approximately 40% by the ninth decade of life (Blazar, 1982). Marked increases in plasma monoamine oxidase (MAO) with aging have also been found in platelets, plasma, and the human brain (Blazer, 1982).

CONCLUSIONS AND APPLICATIONS

There have been two major themes of this chapter. The first has attempted to identify components of self-regulation at behavioral, intrapsychic, and neuropsychological levels. The second has sought connections between these three levels of analysis. At the behavioral level, the early life of the child demonstrates changes that can be charted by the observation of behavior. These changes appear to reflect maturation of internal systems providing increasing degrees of self-regulation. There are suggestions that shifts in observed behavior may be related to the development of neural systems as studied in animal models. Although there is evidence of important normative shifts during the developmental process, there also appear to be underlying tendencies in reactivity and regulation that characterize the behavior of individuals. These relatively stable individual differences represent what we assume to be the basic temperamental characteristics of the person.

It is difficult to relate behavioral evidence obtained in systematic observation of children directly to the animal work on neural maturation because of obvious differences between species. Animal models become increasingly problematic as the child develops language and other skills intrinsic to the human being. It also is difficult to relate the temperamental characteristics of self-regulation demonstrated in the approach and avoidance patterns of young children to the subtle patterns of internal control in the interactions of adults with their physical and social environment. What is needed is a level of analysis appropriate to human beings that deals with intrapsychic systems serving to control overt behavior. This intermediate level of analysis is provided, at least to some degree, by the concepts of arousal, activation, and effort discussed in this chapter.

It should be obvious from reading this chapter that the connections between the three levels we outline for the development of self-regulation have not at this point been made securely. However, the direction of current thinking within each level that suggests a basis for making the needed connections has been discussed. The advantages in making such connections are considerable. There are many experimental paradigms in the study of adult arousal, activation, and effort that provide bases for observing systematic differences among individuals in the ability to execute elementary mental operations (Posner & McLeod, 1982). Thus far these paradigms have been applied mainly to intellectual performance (Carroll & Maxwell, 1979), but they also have much to offer in the study of basic aspects of temperament. The problem in doing so is to determine which operations are basic and which merely reflect the ability to perform in some experimental procedure. The developmental perspective provides one basis for suggesting components developing early in life and appearing fundamental in learning the cultural routines of society. These are the aspects of personality most likely to be grounded in the biology of the organism.

An understanding of the components involved in reactivity and self-regulation could be of use in aiding the clinician to conceptualize the problems of emotional and cognitive pathologies. Consider the problem of attention deficit disorder. The definition included in the *Diagnostic and Statistical Manual of Mental Disorders* (DSM, III, APA, 1980) involves

118   MARY K. ROTHBART AND MICHAEL I. POSNER

a gross characterization of the behavior patterns of the child, with little
regard to a theory of attention. Work on this disorder (Douglas, 1980;
Kinsbourne, 1984), however, has identified component processes such as
the rate of increase and maintenance of arousal and the effortful employment of self-control over state that may be functioning abnormally.
The framework proposed here additionally suggests that arousability and
effort will be related to each other.

One successful model of this approach appears to be the facility with
which attention can be employed in dealing with stimuli. The speed and
lability of attentional orienting is a basic component of adult information
processing that can be measured across experimental conditions (Keele
& Hawkins, 1982). In addition, differences in the probability, speed, and
maintenance of orienting appear to be important and easily observed
variables in the overt behavior of children (Rothbart & Derryberry, 1981).
We also know something about the neural systems that control overt and
covert shifts of attention from work with normal adults and patients (Posner & Rothbart, 1981; Posner, Cohen, & Rafal, 1982; Posner, 1982). We look
forward to future development of this model as a means of providing
links across levels of analysis and across the life span of the individual.

Acknowledgments

We appreciate Douglas Derryberry's helpful comments on an earlier
version of this chapter.

REFERENCES

Als, H., Tronick, E., & Brazelton, T. B. Stages of early behavioral organization: The study of
    a sighted infant and a blind infant in interaction with their mothers. In T. P. Field (Ed.),
    High-risk infants and children: Adult and peer interactions. New York: Academic Press,
    1980.
Altman, J., Brunner, R. L., & Bayer, S. A. The hippocampus and behavioral maturation. *Be-
    havioral Biology,* 1973, *8,* 557–596.
American Psychiatric Association. *Diagnostic and statistical manual of mental disorders* (3rd
    ed.). Washington, D. C.: Author, 1980.
Bell, S. M., & Ainsworth, M. D. S. Infant crying and maternal responsiveness. *Child Devel-
    opment,* 1972, *43,* 1171–1190.
Benjamin, J. Developmental biology and psychoanalysis. In N. Greenfield & W. Lewis (Eds.),
    Psychoanalysis and current biological thought. Madison: University of Wisconsin Press,
    1965.
Birns, B., Barten, S., & Bridger, W. Individual differences in temperamental characteristics
    of infants. *Transactions of the New York Academy of Sciences,* 1969, *31,* 1071–1082.
Blazer, D. G. *Depression in late life.* St. Louis: Mosby, 1982.

Botwinick, J. Drives, expectancies, and emotions. In J. E. Birren (Ed.), *Handbook of aging and the individual.* Chicago: University of Chicago Press, 1959.

Bowlby, J. *Attachment and loss, Vol. 1. Attachment.* New York: Basic Books, 1969.

Brazelton, T. B., Koslowski, B., & Main, M. The origins of reciprocity: The early mother–infant interaction. In M. Lewis & L. A. Rosenblum (Eds.), *The effect of the infant on its caregiver.* New York: Wiley, 1974.

Bridges, K. M. B. Emotional development in early infancy. *Child Development,* 1932, *3,* 324–341.

Bronson, G., & Pankey, W. On the distinction between fear and wariness. *Child Development,* 1977, *48,* 1167–1183.

Buss, A. H., & Plomin, R. *A temperament theory of personality.* New York: Wiley, 1975.

Cabanac, M. Sensory pleasure. *Quarterly Review of Biology,* 1979, *54,* 1–24.

Campos, J., Emde, R., & Gaensbauer, T. Cardiac and behavioral interrelationships in the reactions of infants to strangers. *Developmental Psychology,* 1975, *11,* 587–601.

Carroll, J. B., & Maxwell, S. E. Individual differences in cognitive abilities. *Annual Review of Psychology,* 1979, *30,* 603–640.

Caudill, W., & Weinstein, H. Maternal care and infant behavior in Japan and America. *Psychiatry,* 1969, *32,* 12–43.

Coll, C. G., Kagan, J., & Resnick, J. S. Behavioral inhibition in young children. *Child Development,* 1984, *55,* 1005–1019.

Davidson, H. L., & Gottlieb, L. S. The emotional maturity of pre- and postmenarcheal girls. *Journal of Genetic Psychology,* 1955, *86,* 261–266.

Dawson, M. E., & Schell, A. M. Electrodermal responses to attended and nonattended significant stimuli during dichotic listening. *Journal of Experimental Psychology: Human Perception and Performance,* 1982, *8,* 315–324.

Derryberry, D., & Rothbart, M. Emotion, attention and temperament. In C. E. Izard, J. Kagan, & R. Zajonc (Eds.), *Emotion, cognition and behavior.* Cambridge, England: Cambridge University Press, 1984.

Douglas, R. J. The development of hippocampal function: Implications for theory and for therapy. In R. L. Isaacson & K. H. Pribram (Eds.), *The hippocampus, Vol. 2. Neurophysiology and behavior.* New York: Plenum Press, 1975.

Douglas, R. J., Packouz, K., & Douglas, D. The development of inhibition in man. *Proceedings: American Psychological Association,* 1972, *7,* 121–122.

Douglas, V. I. Treatment and training approaches to hyperactivity: Establishing internal or external control. In C. K. Whalen & B. Henker (Eds.), *Hyperactive children.* New York: Academic Press, 1980.

Emde, R. N., Gaensbauer, R. J., & Harmon, R. J. Emotional expression in infancy. *Psychological Issues,* 1976, Monograph 37.

Emde, R. N., & Robinson, J. The first two months: Recent research in developmental psychobiology and the changing view of the newborn. In J. Noshpitz & J. Call (Eds.), *American handbook of child psychiatry.* New York: Basic Books, 1978.

Eysenck, H. J. *The biological basis of personality.* Springfield, Ill.: Charles C Thomas, 1967.

Eysenck, H. J. (Ed.). *The measurement of personality.* Baltimore, Md.: University Park Press, 1976.

Eysenck, H. J. (Ed.). *A model for personality.* New York: Springer Verlag, 1981.

Feinstein, S. C. Adolescent depression. In E. J. Anthony & T. Beredek (Eds.), *Depression and human existence.* Boston: Little, Brown, 1975.

Foote, S. L., Ashton-Jones, G., & Bloom, R. E. Impulse activity of locus ceruleus neurons in awake rats and squirrel monkeys is a function of sensory stimulation and arousal. *Proceedings of the National Academy of Sciences,* 1980, *77,* 3033–3037.

Frodi, A. M., Lamb, M. E., Leavitt, L. A., & Donovan, W. L. Fathers' and mothers' responses to infant smiles and cries. *Infant Behavior and Development*, 1978, *1*, 187–198.

Fuster, J. M. Effects of stimulation of brain stem on tachistoscopic perception. *Science*, 1958, *127*, 150–151.

Gazzaniga, M. S. *The bisected brain.* New York: Appleton, 1970.

Gazzaniga, M. S., & Hillyard, S. A. Attentional mechanisms following brain bisection. In T. S. Kornblum (Ed.), *Attention and performance* (Vol. IV). New York: Academic Press, 1973.

Gellhorn, E. Attempt at synthesis: Contribution to a theory of emotion. In E. Gellhorn (Ed.), *Biological foundations of emotion.* Glenview, Ill.: Scott, Foresman, 1968.

Gellhorn, E., & Loofbourrow, G. N. *Emotions and emotional disorders.* New York: Hoeber, 1963.

Gesell, A., Ilg, F. L., & Ames, L. B. *Youth: The years from ten to sixteen.* New York: Harper & Row, 1956.

Goldsmith, H. H., & Campos, J. J. Toward a theory of infant temperament. In R. N. Emde & R. J. Harmon (Eds.), *The development of attachment and affiliative systems.* New York: Plenum Press, 1982.

Gottman, J. M., & Ringland, J. T. The analysis of dominance and bidirectionality in social development. *Child Development*, 1981, *52*, 393–412.

Graham, F. K., Strock, B. D., & Ziegler, B. L. Excitatory and inhibitory influences on reflex responsiveness. In W. A. Collins (Ed.), *Aspects of the development of competence.* Hillsdale, N.J.: Erlbaum, 1981.

Gray, J. A. *The psychology of fear and stress.* New York: McGraw-Hill, 1971.

Gray, J. A. *The neuropsychology of anxiety.* London: Oxford University Press, 1982.

Heffner, T. G., Heller, A., Miller, F. E., Kotake, C., & Seiden, L. S. Locomotor hyperactivity in neonatal rats following electrolytic lesions of mesocortical dopamine neurons. *Developmental Brain Research*, 1983, *285*, 29–38.

Hochschild, A. K. Emotion work, feeling rules, and social structure. *American Journal of Sociology*, 1979, *85*, 551–575.

Izard, C. E. *Human emotions.* New York: Plenum Press, 1977.

Izard, C. E., & Buechler, S. Emotion expressions and personality integration in infancy. In C. E. Izard (Ed.), *Emotions in personality and psychopathology.* New York: Plenum Press, 1979.

Kahneman, D. *Attention and effort.* Englewood, N.J.: Prentice-Hall, 1973.

Kaye, K. Thickening thin data: The maternal role in developing communication and language. In M. Bullowa (Ed.), *Before speech: The beginning of interpersonal communication.* Cambridge, England: Cambridge University Press, 1979.

Keele, S. W., & Hawkins, H. H. Explorations of individual differences relevant to high level skill. *Journal of Motor Behavior*, 1982, *14*, 3–23.

Kimble, D. P. Hippocampus and internal inhibition. *Psychological Bulletin*, 1968, *70*, 285–295.

Kinsbourne, M. Toward a model for the attention deficit disorder. *Minnesota Symposium on Child Psychology*, 1984, *16*, 137–166.

Korner, A. F., & Thoman, E. B. The relative efficacy of contact and vestibular-proprioceptive stimulation in soothing neonates. *Child Development*, 1972, *43*, 443–453.

Krakow, J. B., & Johnson, K. L. *The emergence and consolidation of self-control processes from 18 to 30 months of age.* Paper presented at the meeting of the Society for Research in Child Development, Boston, April 1981.

Kraut, A. G. Effects of familiarization on alertness and encoding in children. *Developmental Psychology*, 1976, *12*, 491–496.

Laatinen, L. V., & Vilkki, J. Stereotaxic central anterior cingulotomy in some psychological disorders. In E. Hitchcock, L. Laatinen, & K. Vaernet (Eds.), *Psychosurgery*. Springfield, Ill.: Charles C. Thomas, 1972.

Lawson, K. R., & Turkewitz, G. Intersensory function in newborns: Effect of sound in visual performance. *Child Development*, 1980, *51*, 1295–1298.

Levy, J., Heller, W., Banich, M. T., & Burton, L. A. Are variations among right-handed individuals in perceptual asymmetries caused by arousal differences between hemispheres? *Journal of Experimental Psychology: Human Perception and Performance*, 1983, *9*, 329–359.

Lewkowicz, D. J., & Turkewitz, G., Cross-modal equivalence in early infancy: Auditory-visual intensity matching. *Developmental Psychology*, 1980, *16*, 597–607.

Lewkowicz, D. J., & Turkewitz, G. Intersensory interaction in newborns: Modification of visual preferences following exposure to sound. *Child Development*, 1981, *52*, 827–832.

Lipton, E. L., Steinschneider, A., & Richmond, J. B. Autonomic function in the neonate: Individual differences in cardiac reactivity. *Psychosomatic Medicine*, 1961, *23*, 472–484.

Lipton, E. L., Steinschneider, A., & Richmond, J. B. Autonomic function in the neonate: VII. Maturational changes in cardiac control. *Child Development*, 1966, *37*, 1–16.

Luria, A. R. *The role of speech in the regulation of normal and abnormal behavior*. New York: Liveright, 1961.

Luria, A. R. *Higher cortical functions in man*. New York: Basic Books, 1966.

Luria, A. R. *The working brain: An introduction to neuropsychology*. New York: Basic Books, 1973.

Mabry, P., & Campbell, B. A. Ontogeny of serotonergic inhibition of behavioral arousal in the rat. *Journal of Comparative and Physiological Psychology*, 1974, *86*, 193–206.

Macfarlane, J., Allen, L., & Honzik, M. P. *A developmental study of the behavior problems of normal children between twenty-one months and fourteen years*. Berkeley: University of California Press, 1954.

Magoun, H. W. *The waking brain*. Springfield, Ill.: Charles C Thomas, 1958.

Marsden, C. D. The mysterious motor function of the basal ganglia: The Robert Wartenberg Lecture. *Neurology*, 1982, *32*, 514–539.

McGuinness, D., & Pribram, K. The neuropsychology of attention: Emotional and motivational controls. In M. C. Wittrock (Ed.), *The brain and psychology*. Los Angeles: University of California Press, 1980.

McGuire, I., & Turkewitz, G. Visually elicited finger movements in infants. *Child Development*, 1978, *49*, 362–370.

McGuire, I., & Turkewitz, G. Approach-withdrawal theory and the study of infant development. In M. Bortner (Ed.), *Cognitive growth and development*. New York: Brunner/ Mazel, 1979.

Nauta, W. J. H. Connections of the frontal lobe with the limbic system. In L. V. Laatinen & R. E. Livingston (Eds.), *Surgical approaches in psychiatry*. Baltimore: University Park Press, 1973.

Olson, G. M., & Sherman, T. Attention, learning and memory in infants. In M. Haith & J. Campos (Eds.), *Manual of child psychology, Vol. 2. Infancy and the biology of development*. New York: Wiley, 1983.

Pavlov, I. P. *The essential works of Pavlov*. New York: Bantam Books, 1961.

Phelps, C. P., Koranyi, L., & Tamasy, V. Brain catecholamine concentration during the first week of development of rats. *Developmental Neuroscience*, 1982, *5*, 503–507.

Porges, S. W. Peripheral and neurochemical parallels of psychopathology: A psychophysiological model relating autonomic imbalance to hyperactivity, psychopathy, and autism. In H. W. Reese (Ed.), *Advances in child development and behavior*. New York: Academic Press, 1976.

Posner, M. I. Psychobiology of attention. In M. S. Gazzaniga & C. Blakemore (Eds.), Handbook of psychobiology. New York: Academic Press, 1975.

Posner, M. I. Chronometric explorations of mind. Hillsdale, N.J.: Erlbaum, 1978.

Posner, M. I. Cumulative development of attentional mechanisms. American Psychologist, 1982, 37, 168–179.

Posner, M. I., Cohen, Y., & Rafal, R. Neural systems control of spatial orienting. Proceedings of the Royal Society (London), Series B, 1982, 298, 187–190.

Posner, M. I., & McLeod, P. Information processing models: In search of elementary operations. Annual Review of Psychology, 1982, 33, 477–517.

Posner, M. I., & Rothbart, M. K. The development of attentional mechanisms. In J. Flowers (Ed.), Nebraska symposium on motivation (Vol. 28). Lincoln: University of Nebraska Press, 1981.

Posner, M. I., Walker, J., Friedrich, F., & Rafal, R. O. Effects of parietal lobe injury on covert orienting of visual attention. Journal of Neuroscience, 1984, 4, 1863–1874.

Pradhan, S. N., & Pradhan, S. Development of central neurotransmitter systems of ontogeny of behavior. In H. Parvez (Ed.), Biogenic amines in development. New York: Elsevier North-Holland, 1980.

Rafal, R. D., Posner, M. I., Walker, J. A., & Friedrich, F. Cognition and the basal ganglia: Separating mental and motor components of performance in Parkinson's disease. Brain, 1984, 107, 1083–1094.

Reed, M. A., Pien, D. P., & Rothbart, M. K. Inhibitory self-control in preschool children. Merrill-Palmer Quarterly, 1984, 30, 131–147.

Rose, D. Some functional correlates of the maturation of neural systems. In D. Caplan (Ed.), Biological studies of mental processes. Cambridge: Massachusetts Institute of Technology Press, 1980.

Rosenkilde, C. E. Functional heterogeneity of the prefrontal cortex in the monkey: A review. Behavioral and Neural Biology, 1979, 25, 301–345.

Rothbart, M. K., & Derryberry, D. Development of individual differences in temperament. In M. E. Lamb & A. L. Brown (Eds.), Advances in developmental psychology (Vol. 1). Hillsdale, N.J.: Erlbaum, 1981.

Rothbart, M. K., & Derryberry, D. Theoretical issues in temperament. In M. Lewis & L. T. Taft (Eds.), Developmental disabilities: Theory, assessment and intervention. New York: S. P. Medical and Scientific, 1982.

Routtenberg, A. Stimulus processing and response execution: A neurobehavioral theory. Physiology and Behavior, 1971, 6, 589–596.

Saarni, C. Children's understanding of display rules for expressive behavior. Developmental Psychology, 1979, 15, 424–429.

Saarni, C. Social and affective functions of nonverbal behavior: Developmental concerns. In R. Feldman (Ed.), Development of nonverbal behavior. New York: Springer Verlag, 1982.

Schaffer, H. R. Cognitive components of the infant's response to strangeness. In M. Lewis & L. A. Rosenblum (Eds.), The origins of fear. New York: Wiley, 1974.

Schmidt, R. H., Bjorklund, A., Lindvall, O., & Loren, I. Prefrontal cortex: Dense dopaminergic input in the newborn rat. Developmental Brain Research, 1982, 5, 222–228.

Schneirla, T. C. An evolutionary and developmental theory of biphasic processes underlying approach and withdrawal (1959). In L. R. Aronson, E. Tobach, D. S. Lehrman, & J. Rosenblatt (Eds.), Selected writings of T. C. Schneirla. San Francisco: Freeman, 1972.(a)

Schneirla, T. C. Aspects of stimulation and organization in approach-withdrawal processes underlying vertebrate behavior development (1965). In L. R. Aronson, E. Tobach, D. S. Lehrman, & J. Rosenblatt (Eds.), Selected writings of T. C. Schneirla. San Francisco: Freeman, 1972.(b)

Schwartz, A., Campos, J., & Baisel, E. The visual cliff: Cardiac and behavioral correlates on the deep and shallow sides at five and nine months of age. *Journal of Experimental Child Psychology*, 1973, *15*, 85–99.

Selman, R. *The growth of interpersonal understanding*. New York: Academic Press, 1980.

Shaywitz, R. A., Yager, R. D., & Klopper, J. H. Selective brain dopamine depletion in developing rats: An experimental model of minimal brain dysfunction. *Science*, 1976, *191*, 305–308.

Sokolov, E. N. *Perception and the conditioned reflex*. New York: Macmillan, 1963.

Sroufe, L. A. Socioemotional development. In J. Osofsky (Ed.), *Handbook of infant development*. New York: Wiley, 1979.

Steinschneider, A. Determinants of an infant's cardiac response to stimulation. In D. N. Walcher & D. L. Peters (Eds.), *The development of self-regulatory mechanisms*. New York: Academic Press, 1973.

Stern, D. Mother and infant at play: The dyadic interaction involving facial, vocal and gaze behaviors. In M. Lewis & L. Rosenblum (Eds.), *The effect of the infant on its caregiver*. New York: Wiley, 1974.

Stern, D. N. *The first relationship*. Cambridge, Mass.: Harvard University Press, 1977.

Thomas, A., & Chess, S. *Temperament and development*. New York: Brunner/Mazel, 1977.

Thomas, A., Chess, S., Birch, H. G., Hertzig, M. E., & Korn, S. *Behavioral individuality in early childhood*. New York: New York Universities Press, 1963.

Timiras, P. S., Segall, P. E., & Walker, R. F. Physiological aging in the central nervous system: Perspectives on "interventive" gerontology. In A. Dietz (Ed.), *Aging—Its chemistry*. Washington, D.C.: American Association for Clinical Chemistry, 1979.

Trevarthen, C. Modes of perceiving and modes of acting. In H. L. Pick & E. Saltzman (Eds.), *Modes of perceiving and processing information*. Hillsdale, N.J.: Erlbaum, 1978.

Tucker, D. M. Neural control of emotional communication. In P. Blanck,R. Buck, & R. Rosenthal (Eds.), *Nonverbal communication in the clinical context*. New York: Oxford University Press, in press.

Tucker, D. M., & Williamson, P. A. Asymmetric neural control systems in human self-regulation. *Psychological Review*, 1984, *91*, 185–215.

Turkewitz, G., Fleischer, S., Moreau, T., Birch, H., & Levy, L. Relationship between feeding condition and organization of flexor-extensor movements in the human neonate. *Journal of Comparative and Physiological Psychology*, 1966, *61*, 461–463.

Turkewitz, G., Moreau, T., Birch, H., & Davis, L. Relationship among responses in the human newborn: The non-association and non-equivalence among different indicators of responsiveness. *Psychophysiology*, 1971, *7*, 233–247.

Weinstein, E. A., & Friedland, R. P. *Hemi inattention and hemispheric specialization*. New York: Raven Press, 1977.

Williams, J. M., Hamilton, L. W., & Carlton, P. L. Ontogenetic dissociation of two classes of habituation. *Journal of Comparative and Physiological Psychology*, 1975, *89*, 733–737.

Zegans, S., & Zegans, L. S. Fear of strangers in children and the orienting reaction. *Behavioral Science*, 1972, *17*, 407–419.

Zuckerman, M. *Sensation seeking: Beyond the optimal level of arousal*. Hillsdale, N.J.: Erlbaum, 1979.

Zuckerman, M. A biological theory of sensation seeking. In M. Zuckerman (Ed.), *Biological bases of sensation seeking, impulsivity and anxiety*. New York: Erlbaum, 1983.

CHAPTER 6

Individual Differences in General Cognitive Ability

PHILIP A. VERNON

In the time that has elapsed since Spearman (1904, 1927) first proposed a g or general intelligence factor to account for the positive correlations he observed among diverse tests of mental ability, a great deal of research has been conducted in an attempt to "prove" or "disprove" the validity of this construct. Today, there is probably a considerably greater consensus that "general intelligence" and "general cognitive ability" are viable constructs, and that individual differences in performance on tests of reasoning, problem solving, and many other kinds of mental ability are to a large part attributable to differences in general cognitive ability. Of more concern, now, are questions regarding the *nature* and *structure* of general intelligence: given that there is such a construct, what underlying cognitive and neurophysiological processes and mechanisms does it comprise?

THREE STAGES OF INTELLIGENCE THEORIES

Sternberg and Powell (1982) have proposed a three-stage model of the evolution of theories of intelligence from Spearman to the present day. Their model is patterned after the classic "thesis-antithesis-synthesis" framework, and may be described briefly as follows. At the first stage, the essentially monistic theory of Spearman was countered by a pluralistic

PHILIP A. VERNON • Department of Psychology, University of Western Ontario, London, Ontario N6A 5C2, Canada.

theory best exemplified by Thomson (1939). Rather than attributing the
positive relationships between different tests to an underlying common
source of variance, Thomson argued that the correlations could be explained just as well in terms of a large number of "bonds," a common
or shared *subset* of which two or more related tests might draw on.

Competition between these Stage 1 theories led to an unstable synthesis at Stage 2. Synthesis was achieved by accepting that it is possible
to explain individual differences in intelligence in terms of both monistic
and pluralistic sources of variance. The instability resulted from two fur-
ther-competing conceptions of how such a synthesis could best be accomplished. On one side, a hierarchical model retained a single g-like
factor as the largest source of individual differences, but also included a
number of lower order major and minor group factors to account for the
relationship between some kinds of tests (e.g., verbal-educational) and
the differences between these and other kinds of tests (e.g., practical-
mechanical). At a lower level still, specific factors were included in this
model to reflect the fact that all tests contain a lesser or greater amount
of task-specific variance, which, by definition, is shared with no other
tests (Burt, 1940; Vernon, 1950). In contrast, Thurstone's (1938) nonhierarchical theory described individual differences in test performance in
terms of seven or eight primary mental abilities (verbal, perceptual speed,
number, rote memory, word fluency, space or visualization, inductive and
deductive reasoning), whereas Guilford's (1967) structure-of-intellect theory posited as many as 120 independent factors. Another example of the
hierarchical-nonhierarchical conflict is found in the comparison of Jensen's (1968, 1970) hierarchical Level I-Level II theory with Das's (1972, 1973a,
b) nonhierarchical model of simultaneous-successive processing (see
Vernon, 1981a).

Sternberg and Powell (1982) describe the Stage 3 resolution of the
Stage 2 hierarchical-nonhierarchical competition in terms of Guttman's
(1954, 1965) radex theory. In this theory, tests of the same general kind
(e.g., numerical) may be ordered on a hierarchical scale from simple to
complex, whereas tests of the same level of complexity may be arranged
nonhierarchically according to the particular type of ability they measure.
Individual differences in test performance, then, may be described *simultaneously* in terms of both hierarchical and nonhierarchical systems.
An alternative synthesis of the conflicting Stage 2 theories relates to the
finding that Thurstone's primary mental abilities are *not* independent,
but are correlated, and can themselves be factor analyzed to yield a g-
like factor that accounts for the largest part of the variance and a number
of group factors (e.g., Eysenck, 1939, who performed such an analysis on
Thurstone's own data). In addition, it is arguable that Guilford's 120 fac-

tors are not dissimilar to the specific factors at the lowest level of Vernon's (1950) hierarchical model.

Sternberg and Powell (1982) extend their model to encompass not only the correlational theories of intelligence that have been mentioned here but also more experimentally oriented approaches. Thus, they contrast the monistic Gestalt concept of insight (Kohler, 1927; Wertheimer, 1945) with Thorndike's (1926) pluralistic theory of stimulus–response bonds at Stage 1, and executive-based, hierarchical models of information processing (e.g., Brown, 1978) versus nonhierarchical models that do not distinguish executive from nonexecutive processes (e.g., Chi, Glaser, & Rees, 1982) at Stage 2. The Stage 3 synthesis of these conflicting theories has yet to be achieved, but Sternberg and Powell suggest that Sternberg's (1981) description of an integrated information-processing system is a good close-approximation to the kind of joint monistic-pluralistic/hierarchical-nonhierarchical model that would be characteristic of Stage 3 in their evolutionary scheme.

The question naturally arises, what happens after Stage 3? There is no immediately obvious conflict generated by a theory that apparently has combined all the best features and discarded all the worst features of its predecessors. According to Sternberg and Powell, however, tension does exist. The conflict results from the recognition that the Stage 3 theory cannot provide a complete explanation of the phenomena it was designed to explain and that, by its very nature as the ultimate, logical synthesis of all previous theories, the possibility of further evolution is eliminated. Rather than a Stage 4, then, Sternberg and Powell suggest that the most attractive and potentially most fruitful next step is either to try to find new subapproaches to dealing with questions that the theory cannot answer, or, alternatively, to seek a completely new approach to the study of intelligence; that is, to return to Stage 1.

RETURNING TO STAGE 1

The purpose of this preamble has been to provide a short summary of the background and current status of research on intelligence within the context of a framework that also indicates the general sort of direction for future theories to take. At this point, discussion will focus on two alternative approaches to the study of individual differences in intelligence which, in some respects at least, qualify as returns to Stage 1 theorizing. In the first approach, the relationship between the speed with which persons can execute a number of basic cognitive processes and their performance on tests of mental ability is the primary subject of investigation (Hunt, 1976; Jensen, 1979a, b, 1980, 1982a, b; Nettelbeck & Lally, 1976a, b; Spiegel & Bryant, 1978; Vernon, 1981b, 1983a, b; Vernon & Jensen, 1984). In the second, the study of evoked potentials and related neurophysiological measurements is seen as a potentially rich source of information about the nature of intelligence (Eysenck & Barrett, 1984; A. E. Hendrickson, 1982; D. E. Hendrickson, 1982; Hendrickson & Hendrickson, 1980; Schafer, 1982). Both of these approaches start with the assumption that traditional theories and ways of studying intelligence have developed as far as they can—Stage 3 has been reached—and each perceives the next step in intelligence research as encompassing a reassessment of earlier studies and an integration of some of their findings with the results of recent work in cognition and neuropsychology.

MENTAL SPEED AND INTELLIGENCE

A considerable amount of research has been conducted in the last few years examining the relationship between intelligence and speed of cognitive information-processing. Ironically, although research of this nature is often considered to be a "new" approach to the study of intelligence, its roots actually can be traced back more than a century to Sir Francis Galton. Not only was Galton the first to describe individual differences in intelligence in terms of differences in *general* cognitive ability, he also proposed that mental ability could be measured by means of a variety of tests of simple sensory-motor processes, including tests of reaction time.

Jensen (1982a) has provided a chronology of research on reaction time, in which he notes the failure of Galton and his followers to establish any relationship between measures of mental ability and reaction time (e.g., Cattell, 1890; Wissler, 1901). At the same time, Binet and Simon (1905) developed a truly practical test of intelligence, which required no laboratory equipment or apparatus for its administration, and, with a few exceptions (Lemmon, 1927; Peak & Boring, 1926), studies of the relationship between reaction time and intelligence were discontinued until the 1960s (Roth, 1964). Since then, a growing concern for a more cognitive approach to the study of intelligence has led to a greatly renewed interest in reaction time research, some of the major findings of which will now be described.

Speed of Decision-Making. Jensen (1979a, b, 1980, 1982a, b) has conducted extensive research on reaction times and their relationship with intelligence. In the great majority of his work, he has used equipment which is depicted in Figure 1. This is the subjects' response console. A central "home" button is surrounded by eight other buttons, each of which

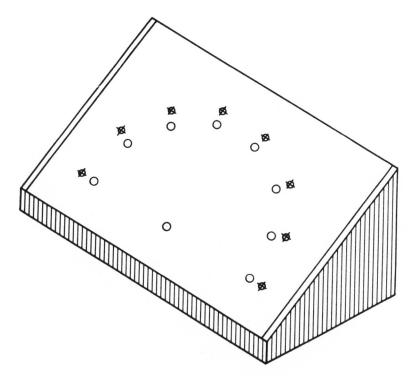

FIGURE 1. Reaction time apparatus.

has a light above it. When a subject presses down the home button, a "beep" that serves as a warning preparatory signal is heard. Within a random interval of from 1 to 4 sec after this signal, one of the eight lights goes on and the subject's task is to move from the home button to press the button below this light as quickly as possible. The subject's *reaction time* (RT) is measured as the time between the light going on and the subject's moving from the home button. The time it takes the subject to move from the home button and press the appropriate response button is measured separately as *movement time* (MT). Reaction time and MT are measured in milliseconds by two electronic timers connected to the response console. On each trial, they are recorded either by an experimenter or may be stored on tape or disk in a microcomputer.

Three different flat panels can be placed over the face of the subjects' response console, to expose either 1, 2, 4, or 8 light–button combinations, and to vary the number of choice-alternatives to which a subject must attend. Clearly, when only one light is exposed, no choice is involved.

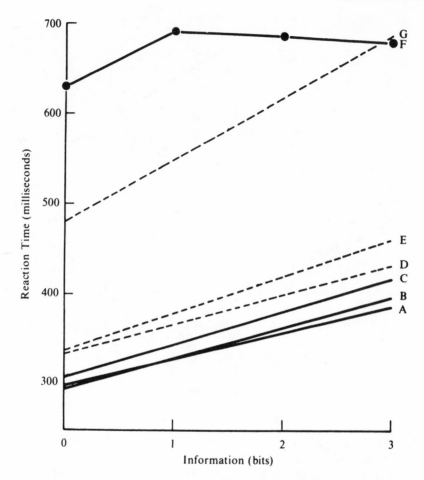

FIGURE 2. Reaction time as a function of *bits* in seven different groups: (A) university students (*n* = 155); (B) 9th-grade girls (*n* = 39); (C) 6th graders in a high-SES, high-IQ school (*n* = 50); (D) and (E) white (*n* = 119) and black (*n* = 99), respectively, male vocational college freshmen; (F) severely retarded young adults (*n* = 60); and (G) mildly retarded young adults (*n* = 46).

On each trial, the subject merely has to attend to the task at hand and no decision-making is required. One light, then, corresponds to 0 *bits* of decision-making information processing that the subject has to make and serves as a baseline against which the subject's performance under the other conditions can be compared. Two lights correspond to 1 *bit* of information, 4 lights to 2 *bits*, and 8 lights to 3 *bits* (since a *bit* is a $\log_2$ of the number of lights exposed). Typically, subjects have been given 15 trials under each condition.

The RT results of a number of different groups, varying in age and intelligence and all tested on this apparatus, are presented in Figure 2. It can be seen, first, that in all groups, with the exception of the severely retarded (line F), RTs increase linearly as a function of the number of *bits* involved in each condition. This finding was first reported by Hick (1952) and has proved to be highly stable. It has become known as Hick's law and is so robust a phenomenon that it appears not only within averaged group data but, with only a very few exceptions, within each individual (Jensen, 1982b).

The second feature of interest in Figure 2 relates to the intercepts and slopes of the lines of the different groups. University students and high-IQ children (lines A, B, and C) respond faster even at 0 *bits* (the intercept) than vocational college students of somewhat lower average mental ability (lines D and E). All of these groups, moreover, show intercepts and slopes that are distinctly different from those of mildly and severely retarded samples (lines F and G). Vernon and Jensen (1984) report the only instance in which groups that differed in average level of mental ability did not differ in RTs on this apparatus. It may be noted that these groups did differ considerably on several other RT tests (discussed later), so the finding of no difference on this equipment is something of an anomaly.

Within each of the samples in Figure 2, correlations between RTs and measures of intelligence have typically been quite low (averaging about − .30) but consistently in the "right" direction. That is, higher intelligence has always been found to be associated with faster RTs. Jensen (1982b) has described a number of reasons why the size of the obtained correlations is probably a considerable underestimate of the actual degree of association between RTs and intelligence, the most salient being that all of the samples studied have been quite restricted in range of intelligence and that RTs have low day-to-day stability (test-retest) coefficients. Generally, RT correlations with intelligence increase as a function of the number of *bits* in the different experimental conditions.

In addition to RTs, subjects' *intraindividual variability* of RTs (intra-*SD*) appears to be an important source of individual differences in mental ability. In fact, intra-*SD*s have generally been found to have higher correlations with intelligence test scores than have RTs and to account for a larger part of the difference between groups of different levels of mental ability (Jensen, 1982b; Vernon, 1981b, 1983b). Like RTs, intra-*SD*s have a very low stability coefficient, which accounts, in part, for the relatively small size of the correlations that have been obtained between them and intelligence. Jensen (1982b) reports that the average intra-*SD*/intelligence correlation is − .35, and suggests that the true figure might be − .70 or larger if corrections for instability and restriction of range were applied.

132   PHILIP A. VERNON

These issues notwithstanding—they actually can be satisfactorily resolved only when a large, heterogeneous sample is tested and reliable
estimates of the stability coefficients are obtained—Jensen's work has
established a highly consistent relationship between RTs, intra-*SDs*, and
measures of intelligence among a number of diverse groups. It is important
to stress the *simplicity* of the RT test with which these results were obtained. Performance on this test involves virtually no prior learning or
what ordinarily would be thought of as "mental ability," yet it is correlated
with highly complex tests of reasoning and problem-solving. Clearly, then,
some part of the individual differences in performance on these latter
kinds of tests (or intelligence tests, generally) is attributable to differences
in how quickly persons can process information that is relatively independent of any acquired knowledge or skills.

Inspection Time and Intelligence. Other tests that require no, or very
minimal, prior learning and that certainly share no surface content in
common with standard tests of intelligence, yet are correlated with them,
are referred to as tests of *inspection time* or IT (Brand, 1979, 1981, 1982;
Lally & Nettelbeck, 1977, 1980; Nettelbeck & Lally, 1976a, 1976b; Vickers,
Nettelbeck, & Willson, 1972). Typically, these tests have required subjects
to discriminate between the lengths of two lines presented for very short
durations by means of a tachistoscope. The shortest exposure duration
at which a subject can state successfully whether the long line appeared
on the left or on the right, on 95% of the trials, is the measure of IT. Each
exposure of the two lines is followed immediately by a backward mask,
so the test is actually a measure of how quickly subjects can encode
incoming information into short-term memory.

Brand (1982) has presented a comprehensive summary of studies of
the relationship between IT and tests of intelligence, and the results are
impressive: the median correlation in five studies is − .80. Unfortunately,
many of the studies were conducted with very small samples, although
a correlation of − .80 was obtained by Lally and Nettelbeck (1977) with a
sample of *n* = 48. Even this is a small sample; however, the correlation
is significant beyond the .001 level. Of more concern, perhaps, is the fact
that most of the studies have involved overly heterogeneous samples with
respect to IQ (although Brand [1982] suggests that the corrected correlations might drop only to about − .70) and typically have included a
number of mentally retarded subjects. Brand discounts this latter issue
as a factor influencing the magnitude of the relationship, although correlations between IT and intelligence among samples of above average
mental ability have been small or nonsignificant (Anderson, 1977; Deary,
1980; Grieve, 1979; Lally & Nettelbeck, 1977; Vernon, 1983a).

Nevertheless, speed of encoding or IT does appear to be a powerful discriminator between subjects of low and average or above average intelligence, and, as is the case with Jensen's RT test, the task does not involve any complex mental activities remotely similar to those demanded by intelligence tests. Rather, it measures the speed with which persons can perform a very basic cognitive process. Attention will now be given to research that has studied persons' speed of execution of other cognitive processes.

Speed of Short-Term Memory Processing. Sternberg (1966, 1969) developed a recognition test that allowed him to describe the processes involved in scanning information in short-term memory (STM). In this test, subjects are first presented with a string of digits, usually one to seven digits in length, which they are instructed to rehearse for later recall or recognition. Then, a single "probe" digit is presented, and the subjects' task is to indicate as quickly as they can whether or not the probe was a member of the original string of digits. Digit strings are presented randomly with respect to their length and whether they require a "yes" or "no" response. By comparing subjects' reaction times under the varying conditions, Sternberg described this task as involving serial and exhaustive processing of the digits in STM.

A number of researchers have compared the RTs and slopes of RTs as a function of the number of digits in each string obtained by groups of different levels of mental ability. Dugas and Kellas (1974) and Harris and Fleer (1974) found that mentally retarded subjects had significantly slower RTs on this test than subjects of average intelligence. McCauley, Dugas, Kellas, and DeVellis (1976) and Keating and Bobbitt (1978) reported similar significant RT and slope differences between average and high IQ samples. Keating and Bobbitt (1978) also reported a significant digit-string size by ability level interaction, indicating that RTs were increasingly correlated with mental ability as a function of increasing task complexity.

Snow, Marshalek, and Lohman (1976) regressed factor scores obtained from a large battery of tests of mental ability on RTs and slopes of RTs in the Sternberg test, and reported multiple Rs between .33 and .56. These Rs are undoubtedly underestimates, since they were obtained from a restricted sample of Stanford University students. Vernon (1983a) reported a multiple R in the same range as those—$R = .425$—obtained from the regression of full-scale Wechsler Adult Intelligence scale (WAIS) IQs on the parameters of the STM scanning test. Again, the sample was homogeneous with respect to IQ; when this correlation is corrected for restriction of range, it rises to .627.

I recently have begun testing subjects with a somewhat different test of STM processing, based on a test first described by Clark and Chase (1972). It is a sentence verification test in which subjects first are presented with a short statement of the form "A before B" or "A after B," and variations of these, including negative statements. After a variable time interval (see below), a test stimulus of the form "AB" or "BA" is presented and the subjects' task is to indicate as quickly as possible whether this stimulus conforms to the previous statement.

This test allows speed of STM processing to be measured in a different mode than the Sternberg task. Rather than involving the *scanning* of information in STM, the most successful strategy to the sentence verification test seems to involve "translating" or recoding the initial statement into the format of the to-be-presented stimulus. That is, the subject reads "B not after A" and recodes this as "BA." When the test stimulus is presented, the subject can make a direct comparison between it and the recoded statement and decide whether or not the two match. Not only is this a different process from that involved in the Sternberg test, it is one that is amenable to experimental manipulation by varying the time interval between the presentation of the statement and the test stimulus. To the extent that speed of processing on this test (in this case, speed of recoding the initial statement) is correlated with intelligence, it can be predicted that a higher correlation between RTs and IQ scores will be found when a short compared with a long interval is provided. Insufficient data are available to test this prediction at present, although other research (Baddeley, 1968) has reported a correlation of .59 between performance on a version of this test and British Army verbal intelligence test scores, establishing another link between speed of STM processing and mental ability.

Speed of Retrieval of Information from Long-Term Memory. Posner (1969; Posner, Boies, Eichelman, & Taylor, 1969) developed a measure of the speed with which persons can retrieve information from long-term memory (LTM). His test involves highly overlearned stimuli—letters of the alphabet—in which subjects are required to make discriminative judgments about pairs of letters that are either *physically* the same or different (e.g., AA or AB) or *semantically* the same or different (e.g., AA or Aa). Responses to the first type of stimuli (AB) require only recognition processes, whereas responses to the second type (Aa) also involve accessing semantic codes that are stored in LTM. The difference in RTs to the two types of stimuli, then, provides a measure of how quickly subjects can access and retrieve information from LTM.

Hunt (1976) reported the first study in which performance on this test was related to mental ability. He compared the RTs of university students who obtained high or low verbal scores on the Scholastic Aptitude Test. High-verbal subjects responded faster than low-verbals both on semantic and physical judgments, although the difference was larger and only reached significance under the semantic condition. Keating and Bobbitt (1978) also reported a significant condition by mental ability interaction, using the same test with children.

Goldberg, Schwartz, and Stewart (1977) used a modification of the Posner test, presenting low- and high-verbal-IQ subjects with pairs of *words* that were same or different either physically, homophonically, or taxonomically. High-verbal subjects responded markedly and significantly faster than low-verbals in both the homophone and taxonomic conditions. They also responded faster in the physical condition, but the difference was only marginally significant (*p* < .06). Importantly, there was no difference between high- and low-verbals in the number of errors they made, indicating that the information required to make same–different judgments was equally available to both groups. Rather, the differences between the groups were differences in speed of *accessing* and *retrieving* the information from LTM.

In a further modification of this test, Vernon (1983a) and Vernon and Jensen (1984) presented university and vocational college students with pairs of words that were the same or different either physically or that were synonyms or antonyms of one another. As was expected, RTs for both groups were longer to synonyms and antonyms than to physically same or different word pairs. University students performed significantly faster than the vocational college students, who were of lower average mental ability, under both conditions, although the difference between the groups was more pronounced on the synonyms/antonyms test requiring LTM retrieval.

Multiple Correlations between Speed of Processing and Mental Ability. Thus far, the studies described have investigated the relationship between speed of execution of one or another cognitive process—decision-making, encoding, STM processing, or LTM retrieval—and performance on tests of mental ability. In each case, a significant relationship has been found. The next step would be to see whether a *combination* of these processes would correlate still more highly with intelligence, and three studies have investigated this possibility.

The first, by Keating and Bobbitt (1978), regressed Raven matrices scores on three RT measures—decision-making (choice RT minus simple RT), STM processing (slope of RT as a function of digit-string length in the Sternberg test) and LTM retrieval (semantic minus physical RTs in the Posner test)—in a sample of 60 children at three grade levels, 3, 7, and 11. The multiple *R*s obtained in each grade were .59, .57, and .60, respectively, indicating that a fairly substantial proportion of the variance in mental ability is attributable to different, combined measures of speed of processing.

Vernon (1983a) tested 100 university students of above-average intelligence (mean full-scale WAIS IQ = 122) with a battery of RT tests
measuring simple and choice RT, encoding, STM processing, LTM retrieval, and tests designed to measure STM storage-processing trade-off.
The first four of these have been described previously, the last one was
essentially a combination of the Sternberg STM and the modified Posner
LTM tests. Subjects were first presented with a string of from one to seven
digits. Then, a pair of words was presented to which subjects responded
"same" or "different." Finally, a probe digit was presented and subjects
now indicated whether or not the probe was a member of the initial
string of digits. The test thus required subjects to retrieve information
from LTM (when the words were synonyms or antonyms) while simultaneously rehearsing the digits for the subsequent STM test.

This study reported a multiple R of .464, obtained from the regression
of WAIS IQ on RTs and intra-SDs on the several speed-of-processing tests.
Corrected for restriction of range in IQ, this correlation rose to .688. In
separate analyses, RTs and intra-SDs were found to be approximately
equally highly correlated with IQ, whereas tests measuring storage-processing trade-off consistently correlated higher with the WAIS than did
the other RT tests. Although parts of the WAIS are timed and subjects
were given higher scores if they performed these subtests within certain
time limits, it was shown that this did not contribute to the correlation
between the WAIS and RTs.

Vernon and Jensen (1984) administered the same or shortened versions of the same speed-of-processing tests to a sample of 106 male vocational college students (with the exception that speed of encoding was
not measured). The test of mental ability in this study was the Armed
Services Vocational Aptitude Battery (ASVAB), a group-administered test
containing 10 subtests. Replicating Vernon (1983a), they reported a near-
identical multiple R of .465, when ASVAB factor scores were regressed on
RTs and intra-SDs. Also replicated was the finding that storage-processing
trade-off made the greatest contribution to this correlation. In fact, the
relationship between the relative complexity of the various speed-of-processing tests (objectively assessed by the magnitude of their mean RTs)
and the degree to which they correlated with mental ability was even
more pronounced in this study: a correlation of .98 was found between
mean RTs on each of the tests and their zero-order correlation with ASVAB
factor scores. Vernon and Jensen (1984, p. 416) concluded:

> Clearly, the more complex the processing required by the different cognitive
> (RT) tests, the stronger is their relationship with the general ability factor of
> the ASVAB.

This was further borne out in two sets of group differences that were investigated. First, within the vocational college sample, whites $(n = 50)$ and blacks $(n = 56)$ differed significantly on both the ASVAB and the speed-of-processing tests. On average, whites obtained higher ASVAB scores, shorter RTs, and smaller intra-SDs. In a discriminant analysis, storage-processing trade-off made the largest contribution to the difference between these groups. Second, comparisons were made between the RTs and intra-SDs of the vocational college sample and the university sample tested by Vernon (1983a). Large and significant differences were found on all tests with the exception of simple and choice RT. Overall, in a discriminant analysis, a combination of RTs and intra-SDs correctly classified 91% of the subjects into their respective groups, with a multiple R between RTs, SDs, and group membership of .75. Again, the more complex the processing required by the different tests, the greater was their discriminatory power: correlations between mean RTs to each of the tests and the difference in RTs between the groups (in standard deviation units) were .876 for university students and .924 for vocational college students.

Summary and Theoretical Considerations. There is now a considerable body of evidence to support the hypothesis that individual differences in general intelligence are to a fairly substantial degree a function of differences in speed of execution of a number of cognitive processes. Jensen (1982a) and Vernon (1983b) have proposed what might be described as a first step toward a theoretical explanation of this phenomenon, and the formulations they have suggested will now be addressed.

The basis of the theory regarding the relationship between speed of processing and intelligence, as it now stands, is found in a number of well-established principles of cognitive psychology. First it is assumed that the distinction between a short-term or working-memory system and a long-term or storage-memory system is a valid one. This may or may not imply a structural difference—the distinction is primarily a conceptual one; however, certain well-known properties of the human information-processing system both support the distinction and form the basis of the RT-IQ theory to be described here.

Consider the task of being told an unfamiliar telephone number and having to retain it in memory for the time it takes to pick up a telephone and dial the number. Since the number contains only seven digits and a short time interval is involved, most people can accomplish this task rather easily, although retention would be impeded in the absence of continuous rehearsal of the digits. Suppose now, however, that a long-distance number, including an unfamiliar three-digit area code in addition to the other seven digits, was involved. Some people could no doubt accomplish this, but in the absence of any mnemonic strategy or "chunking" of the digits (e.g., into groups containing three-, three-, and four-digit numbers), the majority would at best find it difficult and most likely would be unable to recall all the digits in their correct order even after a short period of time.

This simple example illustrates two fundamental properties of the human working-memory system. First, it is a *limited capacity system* that can successfully hold up to about seven discrete units (or *chunks*) of information, but typically is unable to hold more than this in the absence of any recoding strategy (Miller, 1956). Second, without continued rehearsal, the limited amount of new information that can be accommodated is subject to very rapid decay or loss. In lay terms, unless the digits of the telephone number are repeated over and over, they will be forgotten quickly.

A third property of working-memory can be illustrated by imagining the result of being distracted—that is, having to perform some other mental task—while trying to rehearse the telephone number. Depending on the complexity of the distractor task and its similarity to the to-be-recalled digits, it is highly probable that retention of the number will be impeded (Posner & Konick, 1966; Watkins, Watkins, Craik, & Mazuryk, 1973). Working memory can only hold so much information and process this and other information at the same time. When its storage-processing capacity is reached, there is a trade-off between the two, which may result either in a failure to perform the later (distractor) task or a failure to retain the original information (in this example, the telephone number) or, conceivably, both.

These three properties of the working-memory system—limited capacity, rapid decay or loss in the absence of rehearsal, and a storage-processing trade-off—are partly responsible for the conceptual distinction between short-term and long-term memory, which, so far as is known, does not suffer from any of these limitations. The properties also provide one explanation as to why speed of processing is related to intelligence. Intelligence test items come in many varieties: matrices, vocabulary, block design, arithmetic, analogies, to name just a few; yet, despite their obvious surface or content differences, all involve, to a lesser or greater extent, a common set of cognitive processes that must be executed for their successful solution. Specifically, all require information to be encoded, all involve storage and processing of information in STM, and all require information to be retrieved from LTM. Possibly, they all may involve other shared underlying processes, but these either remain to be identified or their speed of execution has not yet been investigated as a correlate of intelligence.

Given the limiting properties of working-memory, even a relatively simple problem may involve sufficient storage, processing, and retrieval of information for the system's capacity or threshold to be reached. One way to manage despite the limitations, however, is to perform the requisite processes quickly. Rapid recoding of incoming information into a small number of chunks may prevent the information from exceeding working-memory's limited storage capacity. It also reduces the amount of information to be stored, thereby allowing a greater amount of processing to be carried out simultaneously. The more quickly the information can be processed, the less likely is earlier encoded information to decay or become inaccessible. At each step, the quicker the several operations are executed, the greater is the probability that the problem will be solved successfully. This, then, may account for the observed relationship between speed of processing and mental ability.

It is important to point out that this theoretical model does not address questions regarding the nature of the specific task-related processes involved in any particular kind of problem. Sternberg (1977, 1979, 1980), for example, has identified such processes as inference, mapping, application, justification, encoding, and responding as components that must be carried out during analogies and other related problem-solving tasks. Analysis and identification of such component processes are extremely important endeavors, but these components are, in a sense, contained within the sorts of processes that are the subject of the present discussion. Inference and mapping, for example, make up a part of the total amount of STM processing and LTM retrieval required by an analogy test. Further discussion of the sorts of component processes that Sternberg has described will not be given here, but not because such processes are unimportant. Rather, whereas a number of Sternberg's components (particularly metacomponents) are involved in a variety of different types of tasks or problems, the processes of encoding, STM processing, and LTM retrieval are probably involved in *all* types of intellectual activity, and their speed of execution may thus come closer to being identified with general cognitive ability.

A BIOLOGICAL BASIS OF INTELLIGENCE

Perhaps the most important result cited in the previous sections was the finding of the extremely close correspondence between the relative complexity of various tests of speed of processing and the degree to which these tests correlated with mental ability (Vernon & Jensen, 1984). Intuitively, this result seems reasonable, since it is to be expected that the more complex RT tests require a larger number of cognitive operations to be executed, thus more nearly approximating the processes performed while solving a reasoning problem or engaging in some other intellectual activity. Attention will now be given to recent neuropsychological research that has attempted to find a physiological basis for the relationship between speed of complex information-processing and intelligence.

Neural Adaptability and Intelligence. Schafer and Marcus (1973) and Schafer (1979, 1982) have reported significant relationships between measures of *neural adaptability* and intelligence. *Neural adaptability* is defined as

> the tendency of normal humans to produce cortical EPs (sensory evoked potentials) with large amplitude to unexpected or attended inputs and small amplitude to inputs whose nature or timing the person foreknows. (Schafer, 1982, p. 184)

Operationally, it is measured by comparing persons' visual or auditory EPs obtained under three conditions of stimulus presentation. In the first, the stimuli (light flashes or auditory clicks) are presented at regular 2-sec intervals; this is referred to as *periodic stimulation*. Second, in a *self-stimulation* condition, each subject controls the rate of the stimulus presentation by pressing a hand-held microswitch. The clicks in this condition are tape-recorded and subsequently played back to the subjects in the third, *automatic* or *random*, condition. Typically, 50 clicks are presented in each condition from which the subjects' averaged evoked potentials are obtained. (The reader is referred to Schafer [1982] for details of the specific nature of the intensity of the stimuli and method of measuring and recording EEGs.)

The arithmetical average of integrated amplitude values for the periodic (P), self-stimulation (S), and automatic (A) conditions (i.e., [P + S + A]/3) is used as a reference average amplitude measure against which the averaged EPs in each condition are compared. Thus, three amplitude ratios (periodic/average, self/average, and automatic/average) provide measures of neural adaptability, while an overall single neural adaptability index (NA) is computed as NA = ([A − S]/average) + 50. The constant of 50 is added simply to make all NA values positive.

Schafer and Marcus (1973) did not directly measure the intelligence or IQ of their subjects. Rather, they compared the neural adaptability measures obtained by three groups of subjects: low IQ Down's syndrome retardates; average IQ hospital technicians; and high IQ doctoral scientists. Significant differences between these groups were observed, although as Eysenck and Barrett (1984) have pointed out, this study suffers from a number of methodological weaknesses that attenuate the reliability of the results. Schafer (1982) modified the procedure to correct these flaws, and the results of this study will be described in some detail.

Schafer (1982) tested 109 normal and 52 mentally retarded subjects. A subsample of 74 of the normal subjects had a mean WAIS IQ of 118 (range 98 to 135), whereas the mean IQ of the retardates (measured by the Binet and Leiter International Performance Scale) was 37, ranging from 18 to 68. Auditory EPs were obtained from all the subjects, and the several measures of neural adaptability described above were computed.

The results demonstrate a close relationship between neural adaptability and intelligence. Under the self-stimulation condition, normal subjects gave a significantly (24%) smaller than average EP, whereas retardates showed no significant differences between their self-stimulation and average amplitudes. Under the automatic (random) condition, both normals and retardates gave significantly larger than average EPs, but the effect was significantly more pronounced for the normals (25% larger for normals compared with 14% for retardates). Thus, both of these indices of neural adaptability—habituation to expected stimuli in the self-stimulation condition, and orientation or attention to unexpected stimuli in the random condition—were related to level of intelligence. Higher IQ subjects *reduced* the amplitude of their cortical responses to expected stimuli and *increased* their EPs to unexpected stimuli to a significantly greater extent than lower IQ subjects.

Each of the neural adaptability measures also was found to be correlated significantly with IQ within the sample of normal subjects (n = 79). The three EP ratios—periodic/average, self/average, and automatic/average—correlated .40, .44, and .65, respectively, with full-scale WAIS IQ, and .30, .52, and .59, respectively, with Peabody Picture Vocabulary Test (PPVT) IQs (the latter obtained from 55 subjects). The single neural adaptability score correlated .66 with WAIS IQs and .60 with PPVT. Corrected for restriction of range in IQ, this correlation with the WAIS rises to .82, which is certainly a substantial figure.

Jensen, Schafer, and Crinella (1981) obtained neural adaptability scores and measures of mental ability from 54 severely retarded adults (mean IQ = 39). They also measured the subjects' speed of decision-making, employing the apparatus depicted in Figure 1. (This sample's RTs are shown as line F in Figure 2.) First factor scores from the psychometric tests (labeled a g factor) correlated .31 with the NA index and − .54 with a composite RT + MT measure from the RT test. Neural adaptability and the RT + MT composite correlated only − .33 with one another, and when g factor scores were regressed on them, the shrunken multiple R was .64. This was larger than the average correlation among the psychometric tests (r = .59), indicating that the RT, MT, and NA variables in combination showed about the same degree of relationship with general intelligence as did individual tests of mental ability.

Schafer (1982) adopts an evolutionary model to account for the relationship between neural adaptability and intelligence. Note that neural adaptability is manifested in two distinct types of cortical response: first, responses are inhibited when foreknown or expected stimuli are presented. This is interpreted as an efficient use of limited neural energy and functions, allowing a greater expenditure on other mental operations. Second, cortical responses are heightened to unexpected stimuli, indicating a strong orientation toward stimuli that in an evolutionary sense might have represented threatening or potentially dangerous situations. Schafer suggests, then, that a brain that could deal efficiently with both types of stimuli would be expected to demonstrate higher behavioral intelligence, and that neural adaptability might well be the biological basis of intelligence.

Biochemical Processes and Intelligence. An alternative theory of the underlying physiological basis of intelligence has been proposed by Hendrickson and Hendrickson (1980) (see also Eysenck & Barrett, 1984; A. E. Hendrickson, 1982; D. E. Hendrickson, 1982). The essence of their theory is that the fundamental purpose of neurons is to respond appropriately to incoming information, which they believe to be represented as a series of *pulses* forming a *pulse train*, and subsequently to send on an appropriate "message" to other neurons, which will in turn respond in a like manner. The Hendricksons have provided very detailed descriptions of what it means for a neuron to "respond appropriately"—this actually being the basis both of recognition memory and new learning—and a summary of their theory follows.

When a pulse arrives at a synapse, synaptic vesicles discharge acetylcholine which opens up channels between the synaptic cleft and the postsynaptic density (PSD), and sodium ions pass through the channels into the PSD chamber. Within the PSD chamber, it is hypothesized that there exists a special form of RNA, called *engram RNA* (eRNA), which is, in fact, the biological basis of memory. Like other forms of RNA, eRNA is a macromolecule made up of four nucleotides—guanine, cytosine, adenine, and uracil—arranged in an arbitrary sequence. Engram RNA is distinguished from other forms of RNA by its considerably smaller size: in humans it is hypothesized to be only some 21 bases long (i.e., about 150 angstroms in length).

Engram RNA is attached to a substrate by means of hydrogen bonds (H-bonds). As the positive-charged sodium enters the PSD, it weakens the H-bonds and causes some of the eRNA bases to detach from their substrate. Not all the bases are detached, because only part of the eRNA strand is exposed, the rest being covered by a shieldlike structure. As some of the eRNA bases are detached, however, the entire eRNA molecule begins to move out from under its shield, ready for exposure to the next influx of sodium.

Meanwhile, the sodium that initially entered the PSD chamber has been removed by a sodium pump that returns it to the synaptic cleft. More sodium can enter the PSD only when the next nerve pulse arrives at the synapse. This, in turn, will be a function of the strength and nature of the original sensory stimulus: different stimuli produce a train of pulses with very distinct patterns. When the next pulse does arrive, more sodium ions enter the PSD, and more of the eRNA strand may become detached from its substrate. The eRNA will become completely detached, however, only when there is a perfect match between the sequence of its bases and the continually rising and falling concentration of sodium in the PSD (unless an "error" occurs: see p. 000). The sodium concentration, in turn, is determined entirely by the pattern of the pulse train and the intervals between pulses, which, finally, are themselves a direct function of the original stimulus. If the eRNA strand is detached completely, then this is equivalent to its having "recognized" the stimulus that produced the particular pattern of pulses that led to its detachment. This "molecular recognition" is, the Hendricksons believe, the basis for the retrieval of memory.

Learning of new information is hypothesized to occur in a similar manner. New information implies a novel sensory stimulus and a pulse train that will be unrecognized by previously formed eRNA molecules. Briefly, it is hypothesized that the novel pulse train triggers the release of diphosphate nucleotides (precursors of RNA) which are then attached to one another by a hypothesized "learning enzyme" (which may be polynucleotide phosphorylene, or PNP) to form a new eRNA strand. This strand is then attached to an empty substrate and is ready to perform like other eRNA: that is, to scan subsequent incoming pulse trains to see if they match its sequence of bases. Each time a novel sensory stimulus causes the production of a new eRNA strand, learning is said to have occurred. Finally, a neuron can itself send out a pulse train in response to incoming pulses resulting in the release of PNP in another neuron and the formation of a *chain* of interconnected eRNA. Such a chain, whereby successive neurons respond to secondary pulse trains generated by neurons that may be a number of steps removed from the initial stimulus, is the basis of all complex mental activity, or intellectual behavior.

As a single eRNA strand is in the process of being detached from its substrate, two types of errors can occur. First, if sodium ions are pumped out of the PSD too quickly, some of the eRNA H-bonds may not detach when they should. This will result in a *recognition failure*, whereby an incoming pulse train will fail to elicit stimulus recognition even though there is a matching eRNA molecule. This also will result in the breakdown of the pulse chain that should have been initiated, since the first neuron will be unable to send out its secondary pulse train. Conversely, if sodium ions are not pumped out of the PSD quickly enough, sodium concentration will remain higher than it should, an eRNA strand may become completely detached, and a pulse train or stimulus will be "recognized" when it should not have been. This is referred to as *misrecognition* or *irrelevant recognition*.

These two types of recognition errors, or the probability of their occurrence, are the biological basis of individual differences in intelligence in the Hendricksons' theory. Persons are held to differ in the probability (R) that a pulse train will be correctly recognized by a single eRNA molecule. It is assumed that each synapse (within a given person) has the same value of R, so a pulse chain containing N independent pulse trains has a probability of success of $R.^N$ From another perspective, the average length of a pulse chain that can be executed successfully is $1/(1 - R)$. Very small differences in the value of R produce very large differences in the number of pulse trains that are likely to be executed successfully. Two individuals with R values of .9900 and .9999, for example, could be expected to successfully execute pulse chains containing 100 and 10,000 trains, respectively. The Hendericksons assume that the average human pulse train occurs in about 230 msec. In the language of engineering, the first person, with $R = .9900$, thus has an expected mean time before failure (MTBF) of 23 sec, whereas the second person's MTBF is 2300 sec, or slightly more than 38 min.

Faced with a simple problem, that is, one that involves a small pulse chain consisting of only a few steps, performance differences between these individuals would be minimal. For example, if the problem required 10 steps, the first person would have a .904 probability of success compared with .999 for the second person. On the other hand, if a problem required 1000 steps (corresponding to about 4 min of mental activity), the first person has only a .00004 probability of success, whereas the second has .904. Clearly, more complex types of problems do require more time for their solution, and, as can be seen, small differences in R values could account for large individual differences in performance capability.

Drawing on the results of studies by Fox and O'Brien (1965), Vaughan (1969), and Creutzfeldt, Rosina, Ito, and Probst (1969), the Hendricksons interpret the waveform of averaged EPs as representing a "picture" of the individual pulse trains that were triggered by the experimental stimuli (e.g., clicks or light flashes). Evoked potential waveforms, therefore, are hypothesized to be capable of providing measures of R values: persons' probability of pulse train recognition. Individuals with high R values (or low error probabilities) should show EP waveforms that maintain large-amplitude spikes for longer periods of time (poststimulus) than individuals with low R values. The waveforms of the latter—representing pulse trains containing a lot of "noise" or error—should become smoother over the same period of time. A. E. Hendrickson (1982) confirmed these hypotheses with a series of simulated, computer-generated pulse trains, with varying amounts of error added in.

The Hendricksons then derived two parameters of EPs to reflect the relatively more complex waveform associated with high R values. First, by imagining the waveform to be a piece of string, which could be stretched out into a straight line, they reasoned that at a standard period of time after a stimulus, the waveform of a more intelligent (higher R) person would be longer than that of a less intelligent person. The length of the contour perimeter of the waveform (called the "string measure"), then, would be expected to be correlated with intelligence test scores. In addition, intraindividual variability also should be predictive of intelligence: higher IQ persons showing *smaller* variance.

D. E. Hendrickson (1982) tested 219 adolescents (mean age = 15.6 years), collecting WAIS IQ scores and auditory EP data. The correlations between the string and variance measures with full-scale IQ were + .72 and − .72, respectively. A composite score, computed by subtracting the string score from the variance (both measures had very similar means and standard deviations), correlated − .83 with IQ. In addition, there was a definite trend for the EP parameters to be most highly correlated with the most g-loaded subtests of the WAIS. Correlations with the similarities, vocabulary, information, and arithmetic subtests, for example, were considerably greater than those with digit symbol. Eysenck and Barrett (1984) report a factor analysis of the Hendricksons' data, including the 11 WAIS subtests and the composite EP score, which led to one general factor on which EP loaded .77.

SUMMARY AND CONCLUSIONS

Three theoretical models involving speed of cognitive processing, neural adaptability, and neuronal biochemistry have been described as examples of current approaches to the investigation of the nature of general intelligence. In this final section, an attempt will be made to combine aspects of the three and derive a unified model that may account for individual differences in mental ability.

First, although the Hendricksons' theory has been conceived in elaborate detail and is certainly intriguing, it does not, as yet, rest on very solid ground. That is, insufficient experimental research has been conducted to test the validity of many of their propositions. In addition, the correlations they have reported between EP measures and IQ scores can be explained quite well by Schafer's neural adaptability theory. In D. E. Hendrickson's (1982) study, stimulus presentations during EEG recordings were pseudorandom (intervals between stimuli ranged from 1 to 8 sec, but each subject received the same random sequence), and thus correspond fairly closely to Schafer's automatic or random condition. As a result, subjects of higher intelligence would be expected to show heightened cortical responses, which would in turn be reflected by more complex waveforms, as the Hendricksons observed.

There is no real competition between the speed-of-processing and neural adaptability approaches. On the one hand, the speed with which basic cognitive processes are executed is hypothesized to allow the most efficient use of the limited processing and storage capacity of working-memory. If such processes as encoding, processing, and retrieval are not carried out quickly, there is a higher probability that the system will become "overloaded" and unable to perform whatever task it is engaged in. On the other hand, faster processing also implies that a greater *amount* of processing can be carried out in a given period of time, and this increased cortical activity might be expected to manifest itself across a wide variety of situations: even, for example, in response to a stimulus as simple as a click or a flash of light. In addition, Schafer describes neural adaptability as indicative of an efficient use of neural energy: conserving it when an expected or foreknown stimulus occurs and expending it more vigorously in response to unexpected stimuli. The important feature of each of these manifestations is that they imply an efficient cognitive processing system. This is also, of course, the basis of the speed-of-processing model.

Drawing on these approaches, then, individual differences in mental ability can be thought of as being a function of what appears to be a rather general factor of neural efficiency. At one level, neural efficiency allows information to be processed quickly, preventing an overload of the limited capacity of working-memory. At another level, the factor is expressed as neural adaptability, again relating to an efficient use of limited neural resources. At still a third level, neural efficiency will at some time undoubtedly be identified with some sort of neuronal biochemical processes, perhaps along the lines of what the Hendricksons have proposed.

In conclusion, the notion of neural efficiency and the three manifestations of it which have been described here represent a synthesis of some traditional ideas about the nature of intelligence with more recent findings in cognitive psychology and neuropsychology. Such a synthesis may not be what Sternberg and Powell (1982) had in mind when they discussed the most promising new directions for theories of intelligence, but as the various results cited in this chapter demonstrate, a fairly substantial amount of the variance in intelligence can be attributed to the factor of neural efficiency. Although it is true that the nature of general cognitive ability, or intelligence, still remains something of a mystery, the synthesis that has been achieved between the approaches described here would seem to afford a very fruitful means for further explorations of that mystery.

REFERENCES

Anderson, M. *Mental speed and individual differences in intelligence.* Final honours thesis, University of Edinburgh, 1977.

Baddeley, A. D. A 3-min reasoning test based on grammatical transformation. *Psychonomic Science,* 1968, *10,* 341–342.

Binet, A., & Simon, T. Methodes nouvelles pour le diagnostic du niveau intellectual des anormaux. *L'Année Psychologique,* 1905, *11,* 191–244.

Brand, C. R. The quick and the educable. *Bulletin of the British Psychological Society,* 1979, *32,* 386–389.

Brand, C. R. General intelligence and mental speed: Their relationship and development. In M. P. Friedman, J. P. Das, & N. O'Connor (Eds.), *Intelligence and learning.* New York: Plenum Press, 1981.

Brand, C. R. Intelligence and "inspection time." In H. J. Eysenck (Ed.), *A model for intelligence.* Berlin: Springer Verlag, 1982.

Brown, A. L. Knowing when, where, and how to remember: A problem of metacognition. In R. Glaser (Ed.), *Advances in instructional psychology* (Vol. 1). Hillsdale, N.J.: Erlbaum, 1978.

Burt, C. *The factors of the mind.* London: University of London Press, 1940.

Cattell, J. McK. Mental tests and measurements. *Mind,* 1890, *15,* 373–380.

Chi, M. T. H., Glaser, R., & Rees, E. Expertise in problem solving. In R. J. Sternberg (Ed.), *Advances in the psychology of human intelligence* (Vol. 1). Hillsdale, N.J.: Erlbaum, 1982.

Clark, H. H., & Chase, W. G. On the process of comparing sentences against pictures. *Cognitive Psychology,* 1972, *3,* 472–517.

Creutzfeldt, O. D., Rosina, A., Ito, M., & Probst, W. Visual evoked response of single cells and of the EEG in primary visual area of the cat. *Journal of Neurophysiology,* 1969, *32,* 127–139.

Das, J. P. Patterns of cognitive ability in nonretarded and retarded children. *American Journal of Mental Deficiency,* 1972, *77,* 6–12.

Das, J. P. Structure of cognitive abilities: Evidence for simultaneous and successive processing. *Journal of Educational Psychology,* 1973, *65,* 103–108.(a)

Das, J. P. Cultural deprivation and cognitive competence. In N. R. Ellis (Ed.), *International review of research in mental retardation* (Vol. 6). New York: Academic Press, 1973.(b)

Deary, I. J. *How general is the mental speed factor in "general" intelligence? An attempt to extend inspection time to the auditory modality.* Bachelor of Science (Medical Science) honours thesis, University of Edinburgh, 1980.

Dugas, J. L., & Kellas, G. Encoding and retrieval processes in normal children and retarded adolescents. *Journal of Experimental Child Psychology,* 1974, *17,* 177–185.

Eysenck, H. J. Primary mental abilities. *British Journal of Educational Psychology,* 1939, *9,* 270–275.

Eysenck, H. J., & Barrett, P. Psychophysiology and the measurement of intelligence. In C. R. Reynolds & V. Willson (Eds.), *Methodological and statistical advances in the study of individual differences.* New York: Plenum Press, 1984.

Fox, S. S., & O'Brien, J. H. Duplication of evoked potential waveform by curve of probability of firing of a single cell. *Science,* 1965, *147,* 838.

Goldberg, R. A., Schwartz, S., & Stewart, M. Individual differences in cognitive processes. *Journal of Educational Psychology,* 1977, *69,* 9–14.

Grieve, R. *Inspection time and intelligence.* Final honours thesis, University of Edinburgh, 1979.

Guilford, J. P. *The nature of human intelligence.* New York: McGraw-Hill, 1967.

Guttman, L. A new approach to factor analysis: The radex. In P. F. Lazarsfeld (Ed.), *Mathematical thinking in the social sciences.* Glencoe, Ill.: Free Press, 1954.

Guttman, L. A faceted definition of intelligence. In R. R. Eiferman (Ed.), *Scripta Hierosolymitana* (Vol. 14). Jerusalem, Israel: Magnes Press, 1965.

Harris, G. J., & Fleer, R. E. High speed memory scanning in mental retardates: Evidence for a central processing deficit. *Journal of Experimental Child Psychology,* 1974, *17,* 452–459.

Hendrickson, A. E. The biological basis of intelligence. Part 1: Theory. In H. J. Eysenck (Ed.), *A model for intelligence.* Berlin: Springer Verlag, 1982.

Hendrickson, D. E. The biological basis of intelligence. Part 2: Measurement. In H. J. Eysenck (Ed.), *A model for intelligence.* Berlin: Springer Verlag, 1982.

Hendrickson, D. E., & Hendrickson, A. E. The biological basis of individual differences in intelligence. *Personality and Individual Differences,* 1980, *1,* 3–33.

Hick, W. On the rate of gain of information. *Quarterly Journal of Experimental Psychology,* 1952, *4,* 11–26.

Hunt, E. Varieties of cognitive power. In L. B. Resnick (Ed.), *The nature of intelligence.* Hillsdale, N.J.: Erlbaum, 1976.

Jensen, A. R. Patterns of mental ability and socioeconomic status. *Proceedings of the National Academy of Science,* 1968, *60,* 1330–1337.

Jensen, A. R. Hierarchical theories of mental ability. In B. Dockrell (Ed.), *On intelligence.* Toronto: Ontario Institute for Studies in Education, 1970.

Jensen, A. R. g: Outmoded theory or unconquered frontier? *Creative Science & Technology,* 1979, *2,* 16–29.(a)

Jensen, A. R. Reaction time and intelligence. Address presented at the NATO conference on intelligence and learning, York University, York, England, 1979.(b)

Jensen, A. R. Chronometric analysis of intelligence. *Journal of Social and Biological Structures,* 1980, *3,* 103–122.

Jensen, A. R. Reaction time and psychometric g. In H. J. Eysenck (Ed.), *A model for intelligence.* Berlin: Springer Verlag, 1982.(a)

Jensen, A. R. The chronometry of intelligence. In R. J. Sternberg (Ed.), *Recent advances in research on intelligence.* Hillsdale, N.J.: Erlbaum, 1982.(b)

Jensen, A. R., Schafer, E. W. P., & Crinella, F. M. Reaction time, evoked brain potentials, and psychometric g in the severely retarded. *Intelligence,* 1981, *5,* 179–197.

Keating, D. P., & Bobbitt, B. Individual and developmental differences in cognitive processing components of mental ability. *Child Development,* 1978, *49,* 155–169.

Kohler, W. *The mentality of apes.* New York: Harcourt, Brace, 1927.

Lally, M., & Nettelbeck, T. Intelligence, reaction time, and inspection time. *American Journal of Mental Deficiency,* 1977, *82,* 273–281.

Lally, M., & Nettelbeck, T. Intelligence, inspection time and response strategy. *American Journal of Mental Deficiency,* 1980, *84,* 553–560.

Lemmon, V. W. The relation of reaction time to measures of intelligence, memory, and learning. *Archives of Psychology*, 1927, *15*, 5–38.

McCauley, C., Dugas, J., Kellas, G., & DeVellis, R. F. Effects of serial rehearsal training on memory search. *Journal of Educational Psychology*, 1976, *68*, 474–481.

Miller, G. A. The magical number seven, plus or minus two: Some limits on our capacity for processing information. *Psychological Review*, 1956, *63*, 81–97.

Nettelbeck, T. & Lally, M. Inspection time and measured intelligence. *British Journal of Psychology*, 1976, *67*, 17–22.(a)

Nettelbeck, T. & Lally, M. Age, intelligence, and inspection time. *American Journal of Mental Deficiency*, 1976, *83*, 398–401.(b)

Peak, H., & Boring, E. G. The factor of speed in intelligence. *Journal of Experimental Psychology*, 1926, *9*, 71–94.

Posner, M. I. Abstraction and the process of recognition. In G. H. Bower & J. T. Spence (Eds.), *The psychology of learning and motivation* (Vol. 3). New York: Academic Press, 1969.

Posner, M., Boies, S., Eichelman, W., & Taylor, R. Retention of visual and name codes of single letters. *Journal of Experimental Psychology*, 1969, *81*, 10–15.

Posner, M. I., & Konick, A. F. On the role of interference in short-term retention. *Journal of Experimental Psychology*, 1966, *72*, 221–231.

Roth, E. Die Geschwindigkeit der Verarbeitung von Information und ihr Zusammenhang mit Intelligenz. *Zeitschrift für Experimentelle und Angewandte Psychologie*, 1964, *11*, 616–622.

Schafer, E. W. P. Cognitive neural adaptability: A biological basis for individual differences in intelligence. *Psychophysiology*, 1979, *16*, 199.

Schafer, E. W. P. Neural adaptability: A biological determinant of behavioral intelligence. *International Journal of Neuroscience*, 1982, *17*, 183–191.

Schafer, E. W. P., & Marcus, M. M. Self-stimulation alters human sensory brain responses. *Science*, 1973, *181*, 175–177.

Snow, R. E., Marshalek, B., & Lohman, D. F. *Correlation of selected cognitive abilities and cognitive processing parameters: An exploratory study.* Technical Report 3, aptitude research project. School of Education, Stanford University, Palo Alto, California, 1976.

Spearman, C. "General intelligence:" Objectively determined and measured. *American Journal of Psychology*, 1904, *15*, 201–292.

Spearman, C. *The abilities of man.* New York: Macmillan, 1927.

Spiegel, M. R., & Bryant, N. D. Is speed of processing information related to intelligence and achievement? *Journal of Educational Psychology*, 1978, *70*, 904–910.

Sternberg, R. J. *Intelligence, information processing, and analogical reasoning: The componential analysis of human abilities.* Hillsdale, N.J.: Erlbaum, 1977.

Sternberg, R. J. The nature of mental abilities. *American Psychologist*, 1979, *34*, 214–230.

Sternberg, R. J. Sketch of a componential subtheory of human intelligence. *The Behavioral and Brain Sciences*, 1980, *3*, 573–614.

Sternberg, R. J. The evolution of theories of intelligence. *Intelligence*, 1981, *5*, 209–230.

Sternberg, R. J., & Powell, J. S. Theories of intelligence. In R. J. Sternberg (Ed.), *Handbook of human intelligence*. Cambridge, England: Cambridge University Press, 1982.

Sternberg, S. High-speed scanning in human memory. *Science*, 1966, *153*, 652–654.

Sternberg, S. Memory-scanning: Mental processes revealed by reaction-time experiments. *American Scientist*, 1969, *57*, 421–457.

Thomson, G. H. *The factorial analysis of human ability.* London: University of London Press, 1939.

Thorndike, E. L., Bregman, E. O., Cobb, M. V., & Woodyard, E. I. *The measurement of intelligence*. New York: Teachers College, 1926.

Thurstone, L. L. *Primary mental abilities*. Chicago: University of Chicago Press, 1938.

Vaughan, H. G. The relationship of brain activity to scalp recording of event-related potentials. In E. Donchin & D. B. Lindsley (Eds.), *Average evoked potentials*. NASA SP-191, Washington, D. C., 1969.

Vernon, P. A. Level I and Level II: A review. *Educational Psychologist*, 1981, *16*, 45–64.(a)

Vernon, P. A. Reaction time and intelligence in the mentally retarded. *Intelligence*, 1981, *5*, 345–355.(b)

Vernon, P. A. Speed of information processing and general intelligence. *Intelligence*, 1983, *7*, 53–70.(a)

Vernon, P. A. Recent findings on the nature of g. *Journal of Special Education*, 1983, *17*, 389–400.(b)

Vernon, P. A., & Jensen, A. R. Individual and group differences in intelligence and speed of information processing. *Personality and Individual Differences*, 1984, *5*, 411–423.

Vernon, P. E. *The structure of human abilities*. New York: Wiley, 1950.

Vickers, D., Nettelbeck, T., & Willson, R. J. Perceptual indices of performance: The measurement of "inspection time" and "noise" in the visual system. *Perception*, 1972, *1*, 263–295.

Watkins, M. J., Watkins, O. C., Craik, F. I. M., & Mazuryk, G. Effect of nonverbal distraction on short-term storage. *Journal of Experimental Psychology*, 1973, *99*, 226–230.

Wertheimer, M. *Productive thinking*. New York: Harper & Row, 1945.

Wissler, C. The correlation of mental and physical tests. *Psychological Review Monographs*, 1901, *3*, (6, Whole No. 16).

CHAPTER 7

Perspectives on Language Development

ELAINE Z. LASKY

The normal young child acquires a complex, multifaceted communication system in a relatively short period of time with apparent ease. The anatomical structure and physiological processes necessary for this acquisition have been subject to considerable discussion and research. *What* it is that the child acquires and *how* the child acquires it have been described, analyzed, and explained from a variety of positions. Jenkins (1969) suggests that one's definition of language determines *what* it is that is described and analyzed. If language is considered to be a set of words, then language acquisition begins with the child's production of the first word, and development is measured by the addition of more and more words. This view, which predominated for several decades, saw stages in development defined by the number of words a child understood or produced. Research emphasized counting words understood or used by representative groups of children under various conditions, for example, number of words at specified ages, mean number of words per utterance, or number of words comprehended. Language development was evaluated by counting and comparing the number and types of words used. Although many developmental charts retain this orientation, for example, norms of vocabulary levels from infancy through adulthood, the current view of language is much broader, more complex, and more encompassing.

ELAINE Z. LASKY • Department of Speech and Hearing, The Cleveland State University, Cleveland, Ohio 44115.

CURRENT APPROACH

The current approach in defining language and its acquisition has been outlined by Bruner (1978b). He emphasizes that this framework was initiated with Chomsky's (1965) model of language and language acquisition in which language is seen as a structured rule system containing specifiable universals. A child is "prewired" or has an innate predisposition to acquire syntactic or grammatic structures and the rules with which to combine them to generate an infinite number of novel utterances. A similar, orderly universal course of language acquisition is postulated for all children, with little room for individual differences except in rate of acquisition of the structures. Studies provided support by demonstrating similar patterns of combining words by children from various language communities (Brown, 1973). Early constructions are followed by acquisition of increasingly complex syntactical constructions and development is measured by observing these increasing complexities. Any child could be considered representative of this universal process, and variation due to individual, social, or cultural differences is minor or irrelevant (Nelson, 1981).

Modifications in this approach have been influenced by a series of critical observations concerning how a child conceptualizes and functions in the world (Bruner, 1978a). This viewpoint emphasizes that a child organizes the universe conceptually and makes systematic distinctions about actions, agents, and objects in acquiring linguistic labels (semantic knowledge). It recognizes that the child perceives and produces speech sound patterns in a specialized and systematic manner in acquiring phonologic knowledge. Further, the child attains prelinguistic knowledge of how to function (pragmatic knowledge); that is, various devices are used to signal what is wanted both before and certainly after the child is able to use language. Language, then, includes and must be described in terms of *phonology*, the sound system; *syntax*, the word-combining system; *semantics*, the word-meaning system; and *pragmatics*, the rules governing the functioning of language in context. Language development involves the acquisition of phonologic information to comprehend and produce phonetically consistent and meaningful forms, syntactic knowledge to order and generate novel utterances and relationships, semantic knowledge to code concepts, and pragmatic knowledge to use language for different purposes in different situations.

Similarly, studies of neural mechanisms underlying language have implicated hemispheric asymmetries in both children and adults, although little emphasis had been directed toward examining the nature of cortical mechanisms involved with these differences or toward identifying differential responses to aspects of the linguistic stimuli (Molfese, 1983). As with other human behaviors, language is complex and the neurophysiological underpinnings of language reflect this complexity. Specific neurologic structures appear to respond differentially to the phonologic, syntactic, semantic, and pragmatic components of language (Berndt, Caramazza, & Zurif, 1983; Segalowitz, 1983; Segalowitz & Bryden, 1983). Consideration of these components as separate entities and as combined in listening to and producing running speech and narratives is vital. Further, observations of specific areas or centers in the left or right cerebral hemispheres may reflect independent asymmetries, asymmetries related to an individual's mental state, the demands of the task, and the stimulus characteristics not only of verbal versus nonverbal stimuli but also those related to individual characteristics such as familiarity and word meaning (Segalowitz & Bryden, 1983; Valsiner, 1983).

To explain *how* the child acquires language, Bruner (1978b) underscores parent–child dialogue as the source for the child's learning of critical aspects of language. Variations in the way individual children approach and accomplish this task are acknowledged and analyzed (Nelson, 1981).

COMPREHENSION OF LANGUAGE/PRODUCTION OF LANGUAGE

Distinctions can be made between the processes of comprehension and production—separate processes using distinct strategies and relying on the integrity of various neurological structures. Comprehension is the process by which language is received through stimuli reaching the ears and eyes, interpreted via complex central neurological reception and association mechanisms and connections, and given meaning by the listener. It involves in addition to sensory reception any activity in processing or decoding components of the signal that results in the listener's understanding, interpretation, and assimilation of the message (Lasky & Katz, 1983). Production is the process by which the components of language are combined to generate a spoken message. It encompasses any activity involving encoding of the parameters of language to produce speech. It includes selecting what to say, how to say it, and the intricate neuromuscular feats necessary to coordinate and produce a fluent, articulate speech signal.

The neurological structures underlying the processes of comprehension and production have traditionally been localized to two separate regions of the perisylvian cortex of the dominant (usually left) hemisphere (Mateer, 1983). Considerable evidence for a strong neurological overlap and functional interdependence has been drawn from cortical stimulation studies, blood flow studies, and studies of patients following brain damage (Mateer, 1983). Following electrical stimulation mapping, Ojemann (1983) hypothesizes a particular site in the cortex, areas in the perisylvian cortex, that has implications for both perception (discrimination) of speech sounds and motor aspects of speech, an area of cortex common to both language production and understanding. Ojemann (1983) further indicates the ventral lateral nucleus of the thalamus may also show areas of overlap for mechanisms of motor control and perception of language and which seem to be correlated with specific cortical language tasks.

GROUP DATA AND INDIVIDUAL DIFFERENCES

Over the years, data have been gleaned through diary studies, naturalistic observations of individual children over time, informal observations of children's verbal and nonverbal interactions in groups of two or three, and formal experiments in which data were usually collected by an adult observing or interacting with one child at a time under controlled conditions. The data generally have been combined to propose models and explanations of normal language acquisition.

Only recently has attention been given to reporting individual variations in aspects of language acquisition. Differences have been described along a series of continua contrasting a predominance of word use to predominance of phrase use, predominance in use of object referents to a more social expressiveness, use of nominal forms to predominate use of pronomial forms (Nelson, 1981). Individual variation is now a critical aspect in neurolinguistic studies where differences occur due to individual variation in task performance, brain morphology, developmental experience that affects aspects of language functioning, and possibly even organization of the brain (Segalowitz & Bryden, 1983).

LANGUAGE DEVELOPMENT

DEVELOPMENT OF PHONOLOGY

Phonology, the sound system of language, is considered in terms of segmental and suprasegmental features. The segmental features are the dimensions distinguishing one phoneme from another; that is, features characterizing each consonant or vowel. Consonant phonemes are constrictions or stops in the air flow from the vocal tract which set up vibrations in the air that are transmitted as acoustical patterns to the listener and interpreted as speech sounds. Classification traditionally incorporates features of *manner* of articulation, *place* of articulation, and presence or absence of *voicing* (i.e., whether or not the consonant is accompanied by vibration of the vocal folds [*t* vs. *d*]). Manner of articulation describes modification of the airstream by structures in the vocal tract, that is, tongue, teeth, or lips. Stoppage of air, build-up of pressure, then quick release describes plosive consonants, such as [b], [p]. Forcing the airstream through a narrowed opening produces the fricatives, such as [v], [f]. Following a plosive immediately with a fricative produces affricatives, such as [d ž] as in *jewel*. Directing the airstream through the nasal passages produces the nasals, such as [m], [n].

The place the airstream is stopped in the vocal tract designates *place* of articulation: bilabial, labiodental, linguadental, lingua alveolar (ridge behind upper teeth), and linguaveolar (palate). Vowels are produced as the oral cavity is altered in size and shape. These modifications enhance patterns of frequencies in the acoustic wave which are then interpreted as specific vowel sounds.

Distinctive features distinguish one phoneme from others. Each phoneme is characterized by the presence (+) or absence (−) of each of a small set of articulatory (and hence, acoustic) features. For example, [b] includes the features +voice, +plosive, +bilabial, while [p] includes −voice, +plosive, +bilabial. These two phonemes differ by one feature: ± voicing.

Suprasegmental features are superimposed on the segmental features: rate, intonation patterns, pitch, and loudness. These suprasegmental features provide information regarding the topic of conversation, the emotions or attitudes of the speaker, intentions of the speaker, and so forth.

These points are critical in studying speech perception in infants and young children. The stimuli in these studies are usually consonant–vowel (CV) syllables differentiated by one or more distinctive features. Four different methodological approaches are used: high amplitude sucking (HAS), heart rate (HR), visual reinforced infant speech discrimination (VRISD), and auditory-evoked response (AER).

High amplitude sucking procedures (Eilers & Oller, 1983; Eimas, 1974) record the amount and amplitude of sucking by infants on a nonnutritive nipple while the infant is presented with a repeating speech syllable (e.g., /sa, sa, sa. . ./). The presentation of the speech stimulus is contingent on the number and amplitude of the infant's sucking relative to the infant's base line sucking. The more HAS by the infant, the more syllables presented, up to about one per second. Initially, the HAS typically increases and is interpreted as interest by the infant. It reaches asymptote and then begins to decline. At a defined level of decline, the infant is assumed to be less interested in the stimulus and, as seen by the fewer sucks, to have habituated. The experimental group then is presented with a new stimulus (e.g., /za, za, za. . ./), while the control group continues to receive the original. A significant increase in HAS in the experimental group indicates discrimination of the different speech stimulus. Discrimination is inferred by increases in HAS reflecting increased interest in the new stimulus. This procedure has been most useful with 1- to 4-month-olds and has been used with infants as young as 24 to 48 hours.

In the heart rate (HR) procedure (Eilers & Oller, 1983; Moffit, 1971), HR is recorded via polygraph while blocks of CV stimuli are presented. Infant HR generally decelerates with the onset of each block and returns to baseline between blocks during prehabituation. Heart rate deceleration is considered as an index of the orienting reflex in the infant. After several blocks are presented and deceleration is no longer observed, suggesting less interest in the repeating stimulus, a new stimulus is presented to the experimental group. Discrimination of the CV is inferred if deceleration is observed in response to the new stimulus in contrast to no HR deceleration by controls receiving an unchanged CV stimulus. The HR procedure generally is used with infants of 1 to 6 months of age, but theoretically could be used more extensively.

Visually reinforced infant speech discrimination (VRISD) (Eilers & Oller, 1983; Eilers, Wilson, & Moore, 1976) involves repeating a speech background stimulus (S_B), for example, /ba/. At a specified time, and for a fixed time, a contrasting speech stimulus (S_A) is presented, for example, /pa/. If the infant acknowledges this S_A by turning toward the sound source, a visual reinforcement of activation and lighting of a toy occurs at the sound source. During testing, infants are entertained with visually interesting but quiet toys at midline. Head turns during S_B, incorrect trials, and head turns during S_A, correct trials, make up the discrimination score. The procedure can be used with infants from 6 months to 18 months.

Procedures have been used less frequently and, to some extent, less successfully as infants approach 2 years of age. Generally, a syllabic stimulus is presented that requires selection of a picture or object (Eilers & Oller, 1983). Stimuli may be real words from the child's vocabulary (e.g., *pea, bee*), paired nonsense syllables associated with objects (e.g., *ris, wis*), or combination of real and nonsense words.

Eilers and Oller (1983) summarize results from various laboratories using these methodologies with naturally produced CVs and electronically produced or synthesized CVs. Infants have the neurological mechanisms for speech sound discrimination and their experience with speech sounds affects their discrimination abilities. For example, infants alter their HAS in response to voicing contrasts in synthetic CV /ba-pa/ and /da-ta/ and in naturally produced /ba-pa/. They also alter their HAS in discriminating place contrast in synthetic /ba-ga/, /dae-gae/, /ra-la/ and natural /sa-za/.

Discrimination also is seen between vowel contrasts /i-a/, /pa-pi/, /ta-ti/. Very young infants, then, demonstrate the neurolinguistic capacities to make fine discriminations between similar speech syllables.

Eilers and Oller (1983) further report learning, or improvement in discrimination, with experience and age; experience with listening improved performance. They also note adaptation by infants with exposure to specific patterns in their language environment. Six- to 9-month-old Spanish-learning babies were significantly better able to discriminate the specific Spanish /ba-pa/ voicing contrast than were English-learning babies (Eilers, Gavin, & Wilson, 1979). Six-month-old infants were able to transfer learnings and discriminate between vowels [a] and [i] produced by male talkers, female talkers, or child talkers (Kuhl, 1979). Hillenbrand (1983) suggests infants can be trained to focus on critical acoustic dimensions of phonemes and ignore nonrelevant dimensions; infants responded differently to CVs containing plosives than to CVs containing nasals.

The implications of these studies are that neonates and young infants have neurolinguistic structures to perceive speech sounds and make relatively fine discriminations among phonetic segments. Six-month-old infants can categorize contrasts, disregard variations in talker and pitch contours, and organize speech sounds at the abstract level of phonetic feature.

Further data on infant speech perception come from observing symmetrical and asymmetrical hemispheric responses through electrophysiologic recordings of the brain's auditory-evoked response (AER) to auditory stimuli. Summarizing numerous studies, Molfese, Molfese, and Parsons (1983) suggest that different perceptually important cues for speech perception seem to be subserved by different regions of the brain. The cues are processed by a number of different mechanisms that develop at different rates. The developmental pattern and underlying neural mechanism for speech-related perception may differ with the specific information according to Molfese (1983). He indicates contrasts due to place of articulation involve left-hemispheric processing whereas voicing contrasts involve left- and right-hemispheric processing. Place contrasts were seen in infants less than 30 hours of age whereas right-hemispheric voicing contrasts were not observed before infants were 2 months old. Some cues, then, are represented bilaterally and some are lateralized to one cortical region. Molfese and Molfese (1983) argue that how these processes interact is not known at this time, but language perception appears to utilize multidimensional and complex hemispheric processing even for relatively simple discrimination. They urge that "language perception should not be studied solely as a left or right hemisphere task, but should be studied for bilateral contributions" (p. 87).

In the development of *production* of phonology, infant vocalizations demonstrate increasing phonologic similarity to meaningful adult speech. Oller (1977) presents evidence indicating a clear relationship between phonetic structures in babbling and those in meaningful speech. He describes stages in phonetic control which are reviewed here briefly.

Through the first month, the infant produces numerous vowel-like vocalizations (no consonants and without full vocalic resonance). At 2 to 3 months, a vocalized back of the mouth closure is added producing vocalizations heard as "gooing" sounds. The repertoire increases during the fourth to sixth month with the addition of fully resonant vocalization which sometimes includes a bilabial fricative (a raspberry). Manipulation of pitch is seen with the addition of yells. A beginning babble reflects a slowness in the infant's movements from open sounds to closed sounds. Seven to 10 months brings reduplicated babbling, the *mamamama* and *babababa*, which parents may perceive as first words since they sound more like speech than previous vocalizations. Suprasegmental features of sharply rising then falling intonation are increasingly used to differentiate meaning (Menyuk, 1971). New segments are added to the reduplicated babbling during months 11 and 12. A variegated babbling appears with varied consecutive syllables and varied stress patterns. Oller (1977) emphasizes this systematic introduction of more and more speechlike characteristics into the infant's vocalizations. Many developmental changes reflect maturational changes in physical size, proportional relationships of the infant's vocal mechanism, postural changes, and changes in increasing neuromuscular control of the speech mechanism (Menyuk, 1971). Evidence concerning regional maturation of the brain relates development of babbling, mimicry, and other components of language to myelinization of fiber tracts and intracortical axons (Lecours, 1975).

Babbling begins at about the same age in deaf children as in hearing children and is similar in form. The continuation of babbling, its frequency, and its closer approximations to the language in the environment, however, depend on factors related to the child's hearing, cognitive and motor abilities, and social interactions. Brain organization may be affected somewhat by these variables and may interrelate with directions of further language development. Certain subgroups of deaf individuals do not show hemispheric asymmetry (Ross, 1983). Some of the differences within individuals reported in studies reviewed by Ross seemed to reflect variation due to individual processing strategies, experience, and other variables related to age of onset of the hearing loss, verbal fluency, and fluency in sign language.

Data reporting individual differences in babbling patterns are limited.

Oller (1977) does report data on children with Down's syndrome. Their early babbling patterns are similar, but often do not advance to variegated babbling.

Numerous studies have reported age norms for the acquisition of consonant sounds. Some lack of agreement in the ages reported reflect differences in the criteria defining mastery; that is, was the sound produced correctly by 75% of the children studied or by 100%? Other differences are related to sampling of the positions of a sound in a word, accuracy in phonetic judgments, and socioeconomic and dialectical considerations (Edwards & Shriberg, 1983). Prather, Hedrick, and Kern (1975) report data indicating that pronunciation of many speech sounds is acquired during the first three years, but certain sounds—for example, fricatives such as [Θ] (as in *thin*) or [dž] (as in *judge*), and liquids such as [r]—may be difficult for some children up to school age.

Numerous variables interact and affect the child's perception and production of speech sounds. A clear picture is not yet available, but sufficient data have been presented to implicate individual sensory, motor, and cognitive variables, and social and cultural variables. Although early sound patterns are biologically determined, later patterns are more affected by these individual and social variables operating on the biological organism.

DEVELOPMENT OF PRAGMATICS

Development of pragmatics concerns development of the use of language in social contexts. Beginning with the earliest social interactions between infants and their parents or caregivers, a framework is built by which the child acquires the pragmatic knowledge of the functions and uses of language, as well as the syntactic structures and semantic content of the language.

Heard or spoken language is not a random group of words or phrases, but is related to the context in which it is spoken, what has happened previously and what might be expected to happen, and the intentions of the speaker—why, what, and how it is being said. The relationship between speaker and listener and their emotions and attitudes are conveyed and comprehended pragmatically. These aspects influence the words selected, the style of stating them and how they are interpreted. A child looking at a plate of cookies at a neighbor's house may state, "Those cookies sure look good." This really means, "I want one." "I'm allowed to have juice" as follow-up after getting a cookie is probably not intended as a statement of fact—and is likely not interpreted as such.

To understand the development of pragmatic ability, we begin with early parent–child interactions and dialogues and continue as these conversations change with the child's increasing linguistic competence. A parent's inferences and interpretations of the infant's early actions, vocalizations, and facial expressions serve to regulate interaction patterns of joint attention and joint action (Bruner, 1975). These early movements, cries, vocalizations, and eye contact are not intended as signals by the infant, but meaning often is read into them by the adult; they are responded to accordingly and stimulate mutual feedback. Earliest interactions are observed in the neonate as they respond to parent vocalizations by focusing on the parent's face, turning and attending to the parent, and by movements of arms and legs which appear to be synchronized to vocal patterns of the caregiver. Interactions of mutual gaze, posture sharing, and covocalization are common in the 3- to 4-month-old (Cole, 1982), but early patterns have been reported in the 3- to 4-week-old (Brazelton, Koslowski, & Main, 1974). These interactions appear to enable the infant to begin to interpret the mother's signals and facilitate the infant's development of intentional signaling of needs and desires. Bell and Ainsworth (1972) noted that patterns of crying behavior in individual infants were affected by caregivers who responded promptly and frequently as compared with caregivers who did not do so. By about age 3 months, infants with responsive caregivers began to cry less frequently, with less urgency, and use other types of vocalizations earlier than those infants with less responsive caregivers.

Bruner (1978a) traces developments leading from prelinguistic communication to language. He notes that between 4 and 6 months of age, infants learn to follow another's line of regard and begin a calling vocalization followed by a pause awaiting a response. The 8- to 12-month-old shows an increase in intentional behaviors and begins to use an exchange mode of interaction, that is, demanding an object, giving it back, demanding it again, giving it back, and on and on. Bruner suggests that pointing and reaching are more efficient and specific as signaling devices than crying; learning to use these new forms to achieve desires encourages learning of even more specific signals: words. Other "conversational" interchanges may be observed in the games and routines, such as "patty-cake," "peekaboo," and "so big," which have defined formats and are repetitive in movement and in vocalized intonation pattern.

Specific advances in intentional communicative behaviors include participation in routine games, requests for objects or assistance, rejection of objects or actions, and indicating or commenting (vocalizing) about an object (Chapman, 1981). The conversational volley of speech in response to speech emerges in the 16- to 18-month-old. These volleys or exchanges are child initiated or adult initiated and are frequently requests for information and answers or comments and acknowledgment. Caregivers generally respond to these early vocalizations by acknowledging the vocalization, repeating it, perhaps affirming it, expanding it, and putting it into a sentence frame and pointing out salient features, such as in, "Doggie. Yes, that's a doggie. See the doggie? What does the doggie say? ... The doggie says 'Bow-wow'."

Halliday (1975) provides a developmental sequence in the intentional communications observed with his son. In the 16- month to 3-year period, Halliday describes Nigel's functional use of language as *instrumental*, i.e., requests for objects or entertainment; *regulatory*, i.e., requests for actions, activities, permission, or assistance; *interactional*, i.e., greeting, seeking, routines, responses to look or where questions; *personal*, i.e., comments on an object, comments on disappearance of object, expression of feelings of interest, pleasure, surprise, complaint; *heuristic*, i.e., requests for information, imitating; and *imaginative*, i.e., pretend play, jingles. These last two occur later. The functions classify utterances or verbalizations by their intended effects on the listener.

Other schemes code each utterance as to its functions in relation to a previous utterance or subsequent utterance by another person or in terms of turn taking or keeping a conversation going. Still other analyses look at the child's awareness of the listener's perspective, of polite or more polite forms, or of increasingly mature forms to use in different conversations for different purposes.

Once the child begins the conversation game, advances are seen as the child's response immediately follows the adult's (in adult-initiated volleys) and increasingly tends to continue the topic of the parent's utterance (Chapman, 1981). Chapman further notes a decrease in utterances that do not add anything new to the topic, but an increase in topic expansions. A beginning is seen in the child's introduction of related topics.

The reciprocity of these interactions seems to be an absolutely critical element in the development of language in the child. Aspects of parental behaviors and demands are modified by aspects of the child's behaviors; modifications in the child's language-learning strategies are related to the communicative behaviors of parents and caregivers (Lasky & Klopp, 1982). Numerous studies have described the sociolinguistic environment of the infant and have outlined the very specific ways that language presented to the infant and very young child differs from that presented to older children and adults. Speech to 18- to 20-month-old children, compared with speech to 45-month-old children, is much slower, more redundant, and marked by pauses at sentence boundaries only (Broen, 1972). Caregivers present a clear, well-marked signal. False starts, meaningless repetitions, hesitancies, or normal nonfluencies that occur in adult-to-adult speech do not occur in speech to children (Broen, 1972). Sentences to 1½- to 2-year-olds are shorter, syntactically simpler, and utilize a smaller and more concrete vocabulary (Broen, 1972; Fraser & Roberts, 1975; Snow, 1977). Mothers and caregivers use language to point out salient features in the environment; they use heavy stress to point out the critical part of the sentence (e.g., "There's a *doggy.*" "Where's your *nose?*" "Let's find *Grandma.*") (Lasky & Klopp, 1982). Questions and comments may be used as linguistic markings and interpretations (e.g., as the child whimpers and hands a puzzle piece to mother, mother interprets, "Is that too hard? You want Mommy to do it?"). At times mothers ask a question and answer themselves as though to explain an action or event.

As children's language comprehension and production progresses, language presented to them changes along various dimensions: increased length of the caregiver's sentences, use of redundancy through imitation, expression, and maternal repetition, and nonverbal pointing accmpanying the decreased verbal messages (Lasky & Klopp, 1982; Lund & Duchan, 1983). Mother's references gradually are shifted from those just concerning the child, to topics relating to others in the immediate situation, and then to topics not present (Cross, 1977). Since caregivers talk about objects and events children conceptually understand, an increase in references to location and time occur after comprehension of these concepts is indicated (Snow, 1977).

These patterns hve been documented in studies of mothers, fathers, caregivers, adults with little experience with children, and 8-year-olds and 5-year-olds talking with young toddlers (Anderson & Johnson, 1974; Harkness, 1974; Snow, 1977). They all seem to present a clear, well-marked, redundant signal that is easy to follow within the context and the expected patterns set up. As a child gains linguistic competence, the language used by caregivers more and more closely resembles adult-to-older-child and adult-to-adult interchanges. The adult's expectations of the child's comprehension and production of language increase.

Three-year-olds demonstrate increasing abilities in using language in social interchanges—comversation or discourse. They recognize a need for turn taking, a responsibility for acknowledging an utterance of another, for making eye contact, and for not interrupting. Certainly, the precursors may have been in the peekaboo-type routine and early conversational volleys. Now, however, several interesting developments occur. Along with requests for action, 3½- to 5½-year-olds begin to give justification for asking and also ask about the listener's willingness to perform the action, for example, "okay?" (Garvey, 1975). There is an increasing tendency to recognize when comprehension is lacking and when request for clarification is made by asking for repetition or additional information (Garvey, 1977). This is still a beginning tendency as recognizing a lack of comprehension is a later-developing ability.

At about age 3, most children begin to use devices of cohesion—devices to hold the discourse together. They use pronouns appropriately to tie back to a previous noun (Bloom & Lahey, 1978). They use ellipses: "It's raining." "No, it is not [raining]." They use articles with appropriate specificity: *a* frog, then *the* frog. They begin to comprehend and produce deictic forms, forms that vary with listener–speaker relationships or with place relationships, such as my/your, here/there, this/that, come/go, bring/take. To use deixis, the child must take the perspective of the listener and perceive aspects of the situation such as time and space. Time referents in deixis, such as yesterday, today, and tomorrow, are later developments, used by children around age 4 or 5 (Umiker-Sebeok, 1979).

Abilities to recognize a separation of speaker/hearer and take the perspective of the speaker increase and the child becomes more skilled in making and using presuppositions that take into account what information a speaker and listener share and what information is new—what information a listener must be told. Children of 2 and under generally show little recognition of the information the listener has or needs. They code or refer to the action or the new and salient information they perceive, for example, in holding up and referring to a newly broken toy airplane a child may likely say "broken" rather than the label, "airplane." Upon hearing a car drive in, the child may likely query, "Daddy?" Between 3 and 4, children learn to make judgments about a listener's need. Maratsos (1973) found children provided more information in describing toys to persons they believed were blind than to those they understood could see. Shatz and Gelman (1978) found 4-year-olds used a simpler content and form when they were talking to 2-year-olds than to peers or adults. They seemed to assume the 2-year-olds were less competent communicators than they, the 4-year-olds!

Comprehension of polite forms or indirect requests, such as "Can you close the door?" (meaning "Close the door") are generally understood as intended by children as young as 2 to 3 years. However, their comprehension strategies may be more context based than linguistically based. In producing polite forms, 4-year-old children proceed from direct to indirect forms, recognize indirect forms as more polite, and use intonation and the word "please" to indicate politeness (Bates, 1976).

Children of this age use different intonation patterns, word forms, and sentences with parents than with teachers, with friends and peers than with younger children, and with siblings than with classmates. They learn how to start a conversation and end one, how to maintain control of the floor as a speaker, how to avoid answering a question, and how to "fool around" with language. They develop humor and an understanding of why something is incongruous, thus funny, or ambiguous, thus funny. Language is used to serve communication in a myriad of ways. The development of social interaction patterns, including pragmatic skills and those patterns related to emotional experience and attachment is immensely complex and has important implications for developing motives for communication (Trevarthen, 1983), language development, and cortical structures.

DEVELOPMENT OF SEMANTICS

Semantics refers to word meaning; development is described by acquisition of comprehension and production of words and underlying *semantic relations* of words as they are used and as they are combined in phrases and sentences. The focus of this section is the semantic meanings a child develops, variables that seem to influence that development, and some tentative explanations of what seems to be involved in a child's coding of semantic concepts.

First Words. Proper names provide the simplest instances for the child to associate a particular sound pattern with a particular person, object, or event. There is only one referent for the word, albeit there are perceptual changes in the referent due to distance, angle of regard, clothing, and so forth (deVilliers & deVilliers, 1978). An infant of 6 to 9 months recognizes familiar persons and objects in different orientations and contexts, thus setting the prerequisites for associating them with specific sound patterns or words. Earliest words comprehended and produced, then, are proper nouns referring to Daddy, Mommy, Grandma, and so on.

Common nouns present an increasingly more complex task. Concrete common nouns refer to classes of objects that resemble each other in varying degrees. To the class of chairs belongs the soft one in the living room, the small one in the playroom, the high one the baby is placed in, the shiny one in the kitchen, the great big one Grandpa sits in, the rocking one, and the little one dolly sits in. To learn common nouns, the child much categorize a set of characteristics. Early categories appear to be based on functional similarities, how the object is used, or on salient perceptual similarities, such as size, shape, texture, taste, or sound, for example, except for milk and pop, any cold, sweet drink is labeled "juice." Among the child's first 50 words are names of important persons, names of favorite toys (which often have a single referent for the child), foods, and drinks—objects with which he interacts.

The child's earliest verbs refer to changes in the objects they play with (e.g., fell, broke) or to their own actions (e.g., run, eat) (Nelson, 1973). They talk about what they are doing, are going to do, or what they want someone else to do—action events. Later they encode experiential states— see, want—to express what they *see* others doing or what they *want*. First words, then, refer to objects, events, or actions that are useful, interesting, and important.

Individual Differences. Nelson (1973) observed some differences in the age of acquisition of the first 50 words (ages ranged from 14 months to 24 months). Differences were also observed in types of words learned. For most children, termed referential children, more of the first 50 words acquired tend to be words that refer to or name objects. Other children, termed expressive children, acquired more words for interpersonal and social interactions (e.g., "hi," "bye-bye," "I want it," "stop it"). These patterns continued, and by age 2 the referential children had a larger vocabulary, were more concerned with naming and directing attention to objects than expressive children, but were not more advanced in other measures of language development. The expressive children tended to develop more pronouns and more words for regulating social interactions with others. The naming or nominal usage by the referential child contrasted to the pronoun or pronomial emphasis by the expressive child reflects very different semantic behaviors (Nelson, 1981). The pronomial "it" requires a less-defined lexicon. The child need only acquire general distinctions between the animate and inanimate and between people and things. To use an object name, the child must build up an appropriate concept, develop a specifically defined lexicon.

Another difference observed was the usage of single words and combinations of words to form novel utterances by referential children compared with greater use of whole phrases and social routines by expressive children, for example, "What do you want?" (Rebecca, 16 months, from Nelson, 1973). These whole phrases or gestalts were produced as giant words without pauses, with clear intonation patterns but with imprecise articulation.

In later analysis, the patterns were seen to continue (Nelson, 1976). By age 30 months, although mean length of utterance did not differ, vocabulary did and referential children expressed semantic relations with more of the form adjective plus noun whereas expressive children used more possessive plus noun constructions. Some relationships were noted between the children's style and style of their mother's speech: some mothers tended to point out names and properties of objects most often whereas other mothers tended to use language more to direct their children's interactions and behaviors.

Nelson (1981) suggests differences in language acquisition, then, can be related to the form and content of language, the learning context, and different individual characteristics of the child. These individual differences may reflect differences in neurobiological make-up. Bates (1979) relates individual differences to a three-factor theory of symbolic development. Two factors represent ends on a cognitive dimension: analytic at one end and gestalt or holistic on the other. The third factor is communicative intent. Bates relates the two cognitive factors to proposed differential hemispheric processing—the analytical with the left, the gestalt with the right. Asymmetrical development, then, may affect the language acquisition strategies used by the child. Nelson's (1981) descriptors divide children into two groups: the terms expressive, pragmatic, pronomial, and gestalt are all associated with more influence from right-hemisphere processing and are contasted with referential, mathetic, nominal, and analytic, associated with left-hemisphere processing. These are hypothesized constructs and await confirming data.

Development of Semantic Categories and Concepts. The first words children comprehend and produce and the types of errors they make in understanding and using words tell us something about the categories or concepts they are developing. The process of categorization in concept formation is critical to organize perceptions. It helps to reduce and make manageable the complexities in our world. Anglin (1977) emphasizes that categorization allows us to render the unfamiliar familiar, to go beyond the perceptually obvious to make inferences about objects, events, persons, and situations. Theoretical models have been proposed to explain critical attributes used by the child to form categories or concepts and associate them with linguistic concepts. Nelson (1973) has emphasized the functions of objects or events in the child's day-to-day encounters as the critical element. Clark (1973, 1975), however, suggests the child codes perceptually salient features. In both models, the child, at first, acquires some but not all features or facets of the category or concept. As the child gains in experience and maturity, category boundaries are more appropriately defined to match adult categories. Because the child may not have categorized all aspects of a concept, instances can be noted when the child overextends a word, uses a word to refer to a broader range of objects than usually denoted by the word. Examples include a child's use of "horsie" to describe horse, cow, and deer; use of "car" to refer to all vehicles; "baby" to refer to anything small—including a small picture of a woman labeled by the child as a "baby mommy." Underextensions occur as the child applies a term to a narrower range of objects than an adult category, such as in rejecting ketchup as food or rejecting lollipops as food, and one child even rejected cookies as food (Anglin,

1977). Observations of these uses and misuses of words enable the observer to infer attributes the child may be using to build categories. Although instances have been cited in the literature in which children have produced overextensions on the basis of function, in a series of experiments Anglin (1977) demonstrated that three factors seemed to be most relevant: perceptual similarity was the most likely element, followed distantly by contiguity, and more distantly by function. He also noted more overextensions and underextensions were made by the 2- to 4-year-olds than the 4- to 6-year-olds. Overextensions were more likely to be observed and reported by researchers in studies of production of language; underextensions were more likely to be seen in tasks involving comprehension of language.

The specific words the child comprehends and produces are those frequently supplied by caregivers. The level of the word used by a caregiver seems to have a rather practical basis. "Dog" is used rather than the more specific term "collie" or "terrier" or the more general term "animal." "Bird" is supplied to a young child rather than "cardinal" or "blue jay." "Money" is the level selected rather than "nickel" or "dime," yet "apple" is specifically labeled, as is "orange" or "banana," not named with the more general term, "fruit," or even the larger category name, "food." "Hat," "shirt," or "pants" are used, not "clothing." The level selected in the hierarchy of collie-dog-animal, Plymouth-car-vehicle, apple-fruit-food, daisy-flower-plant, and so on appears to depend on its usefulness as it affects how the child needs to interact and behave toward the object, event, or person.

As children acquire semantic concepts, they then acquire some but not all of the adult meaning of the concept (Chomsky, 1969; Clark, 1973). Through experience and maturity, more and deeper knowledge is assimilated. At first, then, the child does not have the full adult concept as a linguistic concept is applied. We also can observe that, at times, chidren do not know that they do not know. A message presented to the child will be comprehended. The meaning extracted by the child may *not* be the same meaning used by the speaker, however. One example reported by one of my students: Her 5-year-old daughter's class was asked, "Who knows what a scale is?" She volunteered that she knew—a scale is where her mommy measures her feet every morning. She knew that she knew what scale meant. The child's meaning and her teacher's (and the adult world's) meaning were not the same. Is it not possible and even probable that as children, adolescents, and even adults continue through the life span to acquire semantic concepts that some but not all of the meaning of a concept is gained? Thus, as we become more experienced and familiar, our knowledge of any concept becomes more defined and involved.

For example, *microprocessor* or *semantics* is comprehended or talked about at different levels depending on our experience with these concepts. In observing comprehension and production of a child's semantic concepts, we must be careful about inferring what a child actually knows. We need to verify what the child has coded and categorized to fit the semantic label used.

Relational Terms. Relational words, such as tall-short or fat-thin, add greater complexities for the first-language learner since meaning is dependent on reference to a standard, and a shifting standard at that. We can have big trucks and little trucks, big airplanes and little airplanes, which are bigger than big trucks. And the trucks the child plays with can be little trucks and big little trucks, but smaller than truck trucks. By the time children are ready for school, most have acquired at least partial meanings for spatial adjectives (bottom, round, beside), polar adjectives (such as big-little, more-less, tall-short), color adjectives, prepositions expressing location (e.g., away from, at), relative position (e.g., over, under, below, behind, in front), passage (e.g., through, across, past), temporal relations (e.g., before, after, from-to), words expressing other abstract relations (e.g., with, because), plus a myriad of other words with which to learn and communicate.

Underlying Semantic Notions. A different approach to analyzing semantic development is presented by Leonard (1976). He reviewed a number of approaches and studies of semantic analysis among which are those of Bloom, Lightbown, and Hood (1975), Brown (1973), Chomsky (1965), Gruber (1975), Fillmore (1968, 1971), Ingram (1971), and Schlesinger (1971a, b). Using aspects of these and his own model, Leonard presents strong arguments emphasizing that a child's single-word utterances and in those of two or more words reflect the child's underlying semantic notions or relations. These semantic notions or relations represent important universal and nonsyntactic or nongrammatical aspects in the child's general developmental processes. They represent children's interpretations of their relations to objects, actions, and events in their world. They appear to learn and encode relations that make objects disappear and recur, move, be possessed, have location, and so forth. A system is proposed to describe the child's cognitive structures as mapped through expressed semantic relations. The child's single-word utterances have a *designation* which Leonard (1976) states,

> ... represents that which is named, not present, reappears, requested, noticed, acted upon, located, etc. It usually serves as the named entity toward which the child's activity or attention is directed. (p. 67)

As utterances expand in length and complexity, they reflect the child's increasing experiences and knowledge of the world. A somewhat consistent set and order of acquisition of semantic relations has been reported by Leonard (1976) and other studies just cited.

The early semantic notions specified, with an example of each include nomination (exemplified by, "that box," "what that"), recurrence (exemplified by "more," "another"), notice ("here box," "hi Oscar"), nonexistence ("no," "this gone," "all gone"), and denial ("it won't fit," "didn't work"), rejection ("stop," "don't want"). The next types of notions heard include agent ("mommy down," "I go"), action ("turn," "close it"), and object ("ball," as in "throw ball"), with action and object terms usually seen before agent (Leonard, 1976). Semantic notions next to emerge include place ("on head," "in box"), possessor ("Morgan bowl," "here mine"), and attribution ("big bed," "new shoe"). The semantic notions of instrument ("*with* pencil") and experience and experiencer ("finger hurt," "mommy want pillow") begin to emerge while the child is still producing utterances averaging about two words.

These categorizations of semantic notions or semantic relations allow us to see a continuity in development as the child progresses from one to two to multiword utterances. They also allow a broader analysis of meaning applied by the child in comprehending and producing language. Also included in Leonard's specifications are terms for illocutionary force, function, cause and effect relations, and other relations which provide interesting detail in describing the child's acquisition of semantic meaning, but which go beyond the scope of this chapter.

Children go on to code relationships, experiences, values, and ideas. They develop words whose meanings are abstractions with no observable referent, words with multiple meanings such as homonyms, and words with identical (similar) meanings, or synonyms. They learn words that depend on the speaker's position in space (here-there, this-that) and words that change in time (yesterday-today-tomorrow, this month-last month). They learn words that are not to be interpreted literally—idioms and metaphors. And they learn to understand and make jokes, riddles, and puns. The process of semantic development is (hopefully) a never-ending one as adults continue to expand their semantic horizons in various and individualized degrees.

DEVELOPMENT OF SYNTAX

Syntax refers to the rules by which words are combined and ordered to form phrases and sentences. In discussing semantics we noted children combine words to represent relational concepts. Children also must acquire linguistic rules and structures for comprehending and producing grammatical forms of the language of their community. In learning a first language, the young child is not taught the rules of grammar explicitly as may be the case with formal learning of a second or third language. Rather, a child must extract rules by which words are combined and modified to generate novel utterances, an infinite number of novel utterances, which eventually have the form recognized as grammatical by the native speakers of the language.

About the time children begin to signal semantic relations in their utterances, they begin to combine words and to add morphemes to alter the form of a word. A *morpheme* is the smallest meaningful unit of speech. The word "pencil" represents one morpheme; the word "pencils" adds a second morpheme indicating more than one. Know = 1 morpheme, knowing = 2 morphemes, knowingly = 3 morphemes, and unknowingly = 4 morphemes. Each unit, each morpheme, modifies the form or meaning. Grammatical morphemes indicate time and person inflections on verbs, plural and possessive inflections on nouns, signify adverbs, negations, and so on.

Heavy emphasis has been on characterizing development of syntactic ability as an increasing number of morphemes per utterance and thus an increasing length of utterance (Brown, 1973). To describe syntactic development, however, we also need to examine the types of morphemes acquired, how two-word constructions expand to phrases and to simple and complex sentences, how question forms develop, and how negation develops.

Although there appear to be individual differences in the *rate* at which a child acquires the morphemes, the *order* of acquisition of 14 early-developing morphemes appears relatively uniform (Brown, 1973; deVilliers & deVilliers, 1973). The earliest morpheme observed is the *-ing* form added to present progressive English verbs, as in *jumping* and *walking*. As children from early on talk about the here and now and what they are doing, they include the *-ing*, but without the auxiliary verb. The sentence is frequently of the form, "I going," or "He eating."

The prepositions *in* and *on* are rather concrete, observable in play, and occur next in verbalizations. They are numbers two and three in the order of acquisition. The plural *-s* form on nouns is marked next, number four. Fifth in the order is the usage of irregular past tense in verbs such as *ate, ran, saw, fell,* and *broke.* These refer to frequently occurring events in the child's life, and according to Brown (1973), the irregular past seems to have higher perceptual salience than the regular past tense. The possessive *'s* ending as in "daddy's coat" or "mommy's chair," signaled earlier by the child by juxtaposing the two words, is added next.

The *be* copula is used as a main verb in sentence as, "This *is* ice cream" or She *was* good." In the uncontracted or uncontractible form, it is used earlier than in the contractible form. The uncontractible form, *is*, *was*, or *are*, is ranked as number seven.

Articles *a* and *the* are mastered early, appearing next in the order of acquisition of morphemes. *A* is unspecified and is used when the listener is not expected to know the specific referent, for example, "Do you have *a* pencil?" *The* is specific and is used when both speaker and listener are supposed to know the referent, for example, "Do you have *the* pencil?"

Ninth in order of acquisition is the regular past tense *-ed* or *-en* as in *jumped*, *walked*, and *broken*. A frequent occurrence at this point is for children to regularize the irregular forms they previously used correctly. We hear *goed, ated, runned,* and *sleeped* for a short time, until children return to the correct irregular past, *went, ate, ran,* and *slept.* This over-regularization is another example of overextension cited earlier.

Third-person regular and third-person irregular are the only inflected present tense forms in English (excluding copula and auxiliaries). The tenth acquired morpheme is frequently the *-s* on "she swim*s*," "he walk*s*." The eleventh is the irregular form, "he *has*," "she *goes*," "he *does*."

The auxiliary form of *to be,* necessary for accurate production of present progressive, includes *am* walking, *is* walking, *are* walking, *was* walking, and *were* walking. In this uncontractible form, it usually is acquired twelfth. As the child begins to contract the copula, it is used next in sentences like "I'm hot," "he's tired," at position thirteen. Last of the 14 morphemes is the contractible auxiliary as in "I'm walking," "he's going," "they're eating."

Correct use of these grammatical morphemes presumes the child distinguishes nouns from verbs, and apparently children do code objects or actions on the basis of grammatical cues of *a--, some--,* or *--ing* (deVilliers & deVilliers 1978). Children identified "*a* sib" as a tool, "sib-*ing*" as an action, and "*some* sib" as a substance (Brown, 1957). One hypothesis indicates that the more complex the decision or the more information needed to select the correct morpheme, the later the morpheme is acquired by a child. This is a parsimonious explanation and has, thus far, been confirmed in the literature.

The two-word phrases, by adding morphemes, expand to three and multiword phrases. These expansions can be described by examining briefly expansion of the noun phrase, the verb phrase, and conjoined and embedded sentences. A sentence (S) consists of a noun phrase (NP) and a verb phrase (VP). The NP may consist of a noun (N) only as, "Bill," in the sentence, "Bill presented." Expanding the NP, we might obtain, "The loudmouthed Bill, who is running for congress from the congressional district in which unemployment is the highest in the state, presented."

We have added an article, a modifier, a relative clause as an embedded sentence, and a further relative clause as an embedded sentence. Similarly we can expand the VP as well to "... presented a vicious, inflammatory speech that incited the audience to create a riot by overturning cars, looting, burning, and vandalizing property that belonged to the companies declaring bankruptcy under Chapter XI." This expanded VP now contains a NP containing modifers, a relative clause contining a VP complement, and so forth.

We now describe how our 1½- to 4-year-old child progresses to multiword constructions. We only briefly suggest evidence indicating the grammatical rules by which the child gets to the complex S as above.

Expansion of the NP occurs earliest by the addition of a generalized modifier, for example, "*a* coat," "*that* car," "*more* milk." Shortly, demonstratives and articles may be added separately and in addition to modifiers to get "*that big* dog." It is the NP in the VP that is usually expanded first, as in, "I want *that big dog.*"

The VP elaboration expands with addition of elements of the verbal, as -*ing*, then the auxiliary, and person and tense morphemes. Early verb phrase complements are "I'm gonna go," "I wanna see," "lemme see" (Lee, 1974). Use of the auxiliary, *have*, as in "I have ridden" is early (Chapman, 1981). When the child has a mean length of utterance (MLU) of 4.5 to 5.5, modals *can, will, would,* and *could* appear with increasing frequency (Chapman, 1981).

Negation appears early in development of syntax. First signified by intonation pattern, the 1½- to 2-year-old with an MLU of 1.0 to 1.9 begins to add *no* to negate whatever comes next: "no go," "no doctor," "no milk," "no go bye-bye." Later the negative can be *no, not, can't,* and *won't* and follows the subject or head NP: "I not fall," "Daddy can't go," "Bobby won't play." The *can't, don't,* and *won't* are considered single morphemes learned by the child not as contractions of *do* + *not, can* + *not,* or *will* + *not,* but rather as *don't, can't, won't* (Lee, 1974).

In English syntax, proper negative formation needs the auxiliary to which the negative is attached and the forms appear: "This isn't mine," "They didn't go." With modal development in the auxiliary, negative may be attached to the modal: "He wouldn't eat," "They shouldn't do that."

Yes/no questions develop in a similar pattern to negatives, first as rising intonation pattern: "Go bye-bye?" "See Grandma?" As with the negative, the auxiliary is needed in English for proper questions. When the auxiliary is added, the child begins to invert it with the head NP for an interrogative reversal: "Can I go?" "Is it big?" Rising intonation continues to be used.

Wh- questions are also similar in pattern, first indicated by intonation

LANGUAGE DEVELOPMENT   173

pattern. In the one- to three-word stage, the child adds *wh-* to any statement to make a *wh-* question: "What this?" "Where Daddy?" "When we
going home?" As the auxiliary is added, the child begins to invert the
auxiliary and the head NP properly to get: "Where is Daddy?" "When are
we going home?" These constructions are expected as the child has an
MLU of 3.0 to 3.49 and a predicted chronological age of 35 to 42 months
($\pm$ 1 SD = 28–45 months) (Chapman, 1981).

Complexity may be increased by adding conjunctions to conjoin two
or more sentences. They increase the syntactic complexity and also alter
the meaning or logical relation of the conjoined sentences. Conjunctions
increasing in difficulty include *and, or, nor, if–then, except,* and *until.*
Conjunctions are used to modify temporal relations *(while, when, then)*
causal relations *(because),* conditional *(if,–then),* or disjunctive *(but, although, except).* Complexity is further increased by embedding clauses
such as relative clauses, NP complements, and VP complements.

Acquisition of syntax is demonstrated by children as they acquire
more grammatical categories such as pronouns, adjectives, adverbs, conjunctions, and verbs; as they use more complex constructions of these
grammatical classes (i.e., pronouns increase in complexity from *it* or *me*
to *whomever,* or verbs increase from *run* to *could have been running);* and
the number of conjoined and embedded sentences increases.

Language presented in social settings and in the classroom, even in
the nursery or primary grades, contains complex syntactic constructions.
Semantic concepts are complex as well. Children need comprehension
strategies to decode these complex constructions. Development of comprehension strategies has received limited attention, but several principles
have been demonstrated. A major strategy children use appears to be
situational context. Nonlinguistic information, what is present in the environment and what is the expected relation between objects or actions,
seems to govern early strategies. In the one-word stage, children may
ignore longer statements made to them and pick out a familiar word to
comprehend the speech event (Benedict, 1979). Performance in comprehension tasks indicates young children interpret utterances to be consistent with their knowledge of the world (Lund & Duchan, 1983). It is
difficult for the young child to comprehend prepositional locatives without
relying on context (Lund & Duchan, 1983). Interpretation of a two-word
utterance depends on whether the context is familiar or one of the words
is familiar, whether it is perceptually salient or within the child's attention
at the moment.

Earliest interpretations of three-word, subject–verb–object (SVO)
sentences also are determined by the likelihood of the events (Lund &
Duchan, 1973). The next development is attention to word order. A se-

quence of noun-verb-noun is interpreted as agent-action–object (Bever, 1970). This works nicely with "the car bumped the truck"; a misinterpretation, however, is seen with "the truck was bumped by the car."

With multiple-clause sentences, sentences containing embedded clauses or conjoined sentences, a child's linguistic knowledge becomes more critical for comprehension. Some constructions use ellipses such as in "Mary is running and John is running" which becomes "Mary and John are running." This type of ellipsis appears to present little problem for 3- to 4-year-olds (Lund & Duchan, 1983). Deletions in sentences such as, "John went to the zoo and now Mary wants to do the same," or "Barbara drew an apple, Mary a cat, and Alice a boy," are more difficult for 4-year-olds, but performance becomes progressively better for 5- and 6-year-olds (Baumgardner & Lasky, 1978).

Although clear, consistent data have not been presented detailing development of comprehension of syntax, there are clear indications that as syntactical complexity increases, comprehension performance is negatively affected, both in speed and accuracy (Lasky, 1983; Lasky & Chapandy, 1976). Evidence also has been presented to implicate the obvious: semantic complexity of the terms in the construction interact with syntactic complexity.

DEVELOPMENT OF METALINGUISTIC SKILLS

As children develop language, they play with sounds and sound patterns, self-correct sound patterns or syntactic forms, and ask how to say certain things. They begin to make judgments about how another person talks or how funny a baby sounds; they may think about language and comment on it; they may recognize the ambiguity and incongruity in language that can lead to humor. Children become aware of language as an entity. They use language not only to communicate, but to think about language, perhaps talk about language, learn about language, and make judgments about language.

Although defined and invariant relationships among cognitive, perceptual, social, and linguistic development have not been described, there seems to be little question as to their interdependency. Early patterns in the preoperational period of cognitive development include development of word and sentence comprehension and a tendency to code and interpret the most salient and, at times, superficial properties (Hakes, 1980). As children develop decentering skills (abilities to look at and shift to different aspects of a situation at one time), they are in transition to the concrete operational period. It is at this time they begin to show metalinguistic skills. Metalinguistic skills include the ability to talk about language as an entity, to talk about what words mean, what sounds make up a word, what is a big word, what is a sentence, and so forth. Children can comprehend and produce verbal language with some degree of success, yet be totally unable to segment sounds in a word, separate gramatically correct from incorrect forms, or talk about style of communication.

As a child matures, different aspects of metalinguistic awareness evolve. Clark (1978) reviews developing metalinguistic behaviors, some seen in children as young as 2 years of age. Earliest behaviors are the spontaneous self-corrections in pronunciations, word forms, word order, or, with bilingual children, the selection of the language to use at a given time. Children begin, then, to ask questions about which is the right word or way to say something. They begin to reflect and make comments about the accent and pronunciation of others. One may hear a child comment about the baby who "talks funny."

Children gradually gain the ability to judge appropriateness of grammatical forms, polite forms, and style of a speaker. By 4½ years, normal children show a consistency in considering less direct forms as more polite, in recognizing certain intonation patterns as polite, and the word "please" as polite (Bates, 1976). Recent work with language-impaired 5½- to 6½-year-olds suggests greater than anticipated difficulties in performance and large individual differences. Prinz and Ferrier (1983) suggest that recognizing polite forms requires the ability to consider another person's point of view. There appear to be not only linguistic skills involved, but *social, perceptual,* and *cognitive skills* as well.

Asking children to judge syntactical statements as right or wrong (or good or silly), using different methodological approaches, has shown somewhat similar results. Younger children judged a sentence acceptable if it was understandable and if the meaning seemed true (deVilliers & deVilliers, 1978; Hakes, 1980). The children directed their attention to meaning only and did not focus on syntax (e.g., even in sentences as, "cake the eat" or "drink the chair"). Slightly more advanced children appeared to recognize the grammar as incorrect, but could not correct the model. Judging grammatical correctness is a later developing ability than producing or comprehending the syntactical constructions. Hakes suggests a pattern of changes in performance on metalinguistic tasks: early decisions appear to be based on meaning. If sentences were understood or interpreted, they were acceptable. Children do not appear to use criteria for these early decisions. Progress occurs as first one and then a set of criteria is used to make a decision on the acceptability or correctness of a model.

Clark (1978) presents a preliminary taxonomy of metalinguistic skills and their approximate order of acquisition reported from naturalistic observations and demonstrated in experimental studies. First indicated is the children's monitoring of their own utterances as seen by their spontaneous self-repairs, and practicing and playing with words, sounds, and sentences. These behaviors often are observed as early as 1½ to 2 years of age. Another example of this type of metalinguistic skill is the adjustments children make in their speech directed to younger children.

Next in the ordinal listing involves checking the effect or result of an utterance—has the listener understood it? Is a repair necessary? Is more information necessary? About this time, commenting on and correcting utterances of oneself and of others is observed. Related to these are the child's efforts to try out a word or description, decide on its effects, and add another, if necessary.

Deliberate attempts are initiated to learn and practice new sounds, words, and expressions. Role playing for voices and styles of other speakers are noted. Ability to make judgments as to the more appropriate grammatical forms or polite forms is demonstrated and now children *can* correct the form earlier judged to be "silly."

As children approach school age, most begin to be able to reflect on aspects of the utterance: they can identify linguistic units (phrases, words, syllables, sounds); provide definitions; explain rules relating to sentence form; and understand and repeat and begin to construct puns and riddles. The earliest verbal riddles seem to be homonymic (Sutton-Smith, 1976, as cited in Clark, 1978) as in:

Q. Why did the dog go out in the sun?
A. He wanted to be a hot dog.

The development of use of puns, jokes, and riddles shows large individual differences. These differences in comprehension and production seem related to more than just age, experience, and cognitive ability. Metalinguistic abilities are not necessarily related to the ability to use appropriate grammar. Speaking and understanding do not require the conscious reflection needed for metalinguistic skills. The learning of these skills is, for many, a task that continues through the school years. How these skills are coordinated at a neurolinguistic level is not defined at this time. Some data have been reported by Foldi, Cicone, and Gardner (1983) from studies of patients following neurological insult regarding their use of reference and literal/nonliteral meanings in comprehending jokes, puns, and metaphors. Patients with more anterior (Broca's area) damage use reference; they make reference to and comprehend reference about objects and events in their environment while those with posterior (Wernicke's area) damage have more difficulty with referencing cues. Right-hemisphere-damaged patients are more competent with literal meaning whereas they often have difficulty with the nonliteral meaning; that is, they miss the point of jokes and metaphors. Patients with damage to the dominant hemisphere and subsequent aphasia demonstrate amusement with jokes and metaphors.

The development of metalinguistic awareness is currently a very exciting and fruitful area of research. It is of special interest in this volume: if we are examining individual differences in language development, it is in the area of metalinguistic understanding and usage that the greatest differences are found. Gleitman and Gleitman (1979) argue that the phonological and syntactical differences among children and among adults are small and relatively subtle. Semantic differences are related to context—in many situations in our lives, the semantic usage observed is similar among adults and similar among children of like ages. Because of professional, motivational, and other factors, however, differences may be observed as the need for varying and complex semantic concepts arises. A similar characterization is proposed for pragmatics—the need for individuals to acquire and use pragmatic skills varies with the individual's professional and social activities. These components, then, may be seen on a continuum; phonology and syntax may be more automatic behaviors for much of the time, semantic and pragmatic behaviors probably are less automatic and may consume greater metalinguistic applications.

The behaviors generally subsumed under metalinguistic awareness, then, might be thought of as residing at an executive level, called on as needed for judgments, decisions, and consultations. Metalinguistic awareness might, then, be expected to show greatest individual variations.

CONCLUSION

A major intent of the review presented in this chapter has been to emphasize the incredible complexities of the task facing the first-language learner. A disorder in the acquisition of language may be observed in any one or all of the components of language discussed. What is indeed remarkable is that comprehension and production of language emerge in relatively similar sequences, regardless of great differences in individual ability, in cultural and social experiences, and in the content of the input received by the child.

Those differences that do appear to make the greatest differences may be seen among children with some neurological deficit (Menyuk, 1982). The types of disorders, the number and pattern of difficulties, and the severities observed are in direct relationship to the nature, site, and extent of neurological damage. These factors and most certainly age of the occurrence of the insult, affect the neurophysiological mechanism in various and, as yet, not fully specified ways.

Sources used to draw inferences about neurolinguistic mechanisms in the brain suggest that processing of the components of language must be observed and analyzed in order to fill in a more accurate picture of neurolinguistic functioning. The concern is not merely with right hemisphere versus left hemisphere, but with the centers within one or both hemispheres sensitive to one or more aspects of language. Language processing appears localized to discrete sections in the dominant hemisphere at cortical and thalamic levels. The perisylvian language cortex appears important in sequencing motor movements for speech and in discrimination of phonemes, that is, important in production and comprehension of language (Ojemann, 1983). Berndt et al. (1983) used brain-damaged subjects to demonstrate the neurological separability of individual components of a language system. Based on a review of research data, they conclude that the lexical-semantic component of language can be disrupted independently of phonological and syntactic processing mechanisms, and "... that a disruption in the lexical semantic system affects performance in both expressive (naming) and receptive (comprehension) modalities "(p. 13). In addition to acknowledging difficulties inherent in investigations based on symptoms resulting from neurological insult, they indicate a separation of linguistic function related to anterior versus posterior locations in the dominant hemisphere.

The perception of phonologically relevant cues was noted to be subserved by different brain mechanisms that develop at different rates. Some cues appear to have bilateral representation whereas others appear to be lateralized to one hemisphere (Molfese, 1983). Pragmatic skills seem to depend on each of the mechanisms indicated and, perhaps, others not yet implicated. Changes in neural mechanisms occur related to stimulation, experience, and learning (Valsiner, 1983).

Organization of the brain for language is currently being studied by various disciplines. A body of information is emerging that will provide insight regarding the complexities and interrelationships involved in the comprehension and production of phonologic, pragmatic, syntactic, and semantic components of language. Data should also become available describing variations indicating problems in processing and use of language.

REFERENCES

Anderson, E. S., & Johnson, C. E. *Modification in the speech of an eight year old as a reflection of age of listener.* Paper presented at SSRC Conference on Language Input and Acquisition, Boston, 1974.

Anglin, J. M. *Word, object, and conceptual development.* New York: Norton, 1977.

Baumgardner, M. J., & Lasky, E. Z. Acquisition of comprehension of the verb phrase anaphora construction. *Journal of Speech and Hearing Research,* 1978, *21*(1), 166–173.

Bates, E. *Language and context: The acquisition of pragmatics.* New York: Academic Press, 1976.

Bates, E. *The emergence of symbols.* New York: Academic Press, 1979.

Bell, S. M., & Ainsworth, M. D. S. Infant crying and maternal responsiveness. *Child Development,* 1971, *43*, 1171–1190.

Benedict, H. Early lexical development: Comprehension and production. *Journal of Child Language,* 1979, *6*, 183–200.

Berndt, R. S., Caramazzo, A., & Zurif, E. Syntax and semantics. In S. J. Segalowitz (Ed.), *Language functions and brain organization.* New York: Academic Press, 1983.

Bever, T. G. The cognitive basis for linguistic structures. In J. R. Hayes (Ed.), *In cognition and the development of language.* New York: Wiley, 1970.

Bloom, L., & Lahey, M. *Language development and language disorders.* New York: Wiley, 1978.

Bloom, L. M., Lightbown, P., & Hood, L. Structure and variation in child language. *Monographs of the Society for Research in Child Development,* 1975, *40*(2, Serial No. 160).

Brazelton, T., Koslowski, B., & Main, M. The origins of reciprocity: The early mother-infant interaction. In M. Lewis & L. Rosenbaum (Eds.), *The effect of the infant on its caregiver.* London: Wiley, 1974.

Broen, P. A. The verbal environment of the language learning child. *ASHA Monograph* (Vol. 17). Washington, D.C.: American Speech and Hearing Association, 1972.

Brown, R. Linguistic determinism and part of speech. *Journal of Abnormal Social Psychology,* 1957, *55*, 1–5.

Brown, R. *A first language: The early stages.* Cambridge: Harvard University Press, 1973.

Bruner, J. S. The onto-genesis of speech acts. *Journal of Child Language,* 1975, *2*, 1–19.

Bruner, J. S. On prelinguistic prerequisites of speech. In R. N. Campbell & P. T. Smith (Eds.), *Recent advances in the psychology of language.* New York: Plenum Press, 1978.(a)

Bruner, J. S. The role of dialogue in language acquisition. In A. Sinclair, R. Jarvell, & W. Levelt (Eds.), *The child's conception of language.* New York: Springer Verlag, 1978.(b)

Chapman, R. S. Exploring children's communicative intents. In J. F. Miller (Ed.), *Assessing language production in children: Experimental procedures.* Baltimore: University Park Press, 1981.

Chomsky, C. *The acquisition of syntax in children from five to ten.* Cambridge: M.I.T. Press, 1969.

Chomsky, N. *Aspects of the theory of syntax.* Cambridge: M.I.T. Press, 1965.

Clark, E. V. What's in a word? On the child's acquisition of semantics in his first language. In T. E. Moore (Ed.), *Cognitive development and the acquisition of language.* New York: Academic Press, 1973.

Clark, E. V. Knowledge, context and strategy in the acquisition of meaning. In D. P. Dato (Ed.), *Georgetown University round table on languages and linguistics.* Washington, D.C.: Georgetown University Press, 1975.

Clark, E. V. Awareness of language: Some evidence for what children say and do. In A. Sinclair, R. Jarvella, & W. Levelt (Eds.), *The child's conception of language.* New York: Springer Verlag, 1978.

Cole, P. R. *Language disorders in preschool children.* Englewood Cliffs, N.J.: Prentice-Hall, 1982.

Cross, T. G. Mothers' speech adjustments: The contribution of selected child listener variables. In C. E. Snow & C. A. Ferguson (Eds.), *Talking to children.* London: Cambridge University Press, 1977.

deVilliers, J. G., & deVilliers, P. A. A cross-sectional study of the acquisition of grammatical morphemes in child speech. *Journal of Psycholinguistic Research*, 1973, *2*, 267–278.

deVilliers, J. G., & de Villiers, P. A. *Language acquisition*. Cambridge: Harvard University Press, 1978.

Edwards, M. L., & Shriberg, L. D. *Phonology: Applications in communicative disorders*. San Diego, Calif.: College-Hill Press, 1983.

Eilers, R. E., Gavin, W. J., & Wilson, W. R. Linguistic experience and phonemic perception in infancy: A cross-linguistic study. *Child Development*, 1979, *50*, 14–18.

Eilers, R. E., & Oller, D. K. Speech perception in infancy and early childhood. In E. Z. Lasky & J. Katz (Eds.), *Central auditory processing disorders: Problems of speech, language, and learning*. Baltimore: University Park Press, 1983.

Eilers, R. E., Wilson, W. R., & Moore, J. M. Discrimination of synthetic prevoiced labial stops by infants and adults. *Journal of the Acoustical Society of America*, 1976, *60* (Suppl. 1), S91A.

Eimas, P. Linguistic processing of speech by young infants. In R. Schiefelbusch & L. Lloyd (Eds.), *Language perspectives: Acquisition, retardation, and intervention*. Baltimore: University Park Press, 1974.

Fillmore, C. J. The case for case. In E. Bach & R. T. Harms (Eds.), *Universals of linguistic theory*. New York: Holt, Rinehart & Winston, 1968.

Fillmore, C. J. Some problems for case grammar. *Georgetown University Monograms in Language and Linguistics*, 1971, *24*, 35–56.

Foldi, N. S., Cicone, M., & Gardner, H. Pragmatic aspects of communication in brain-damaged patients. In S. J. Segalowitz (Ed.), *Language function and brain organization*. New York: Academic Press, 1983.

Fraser, C., & Roberts, N. Mother's speech to children of four different ages. *Journal of Psycholinguistic Research*, 1975, *4*, 9–16.

Garvey, C. Requests and responses in children's speech. *Journal of Child Language*, 1975, *2*, 41–63.

Garvey, C. The contingent query. In M. Lewis & L. Rosenblum (Eds.), *Interaction, conversation and the development of language*. New York: Wiley, 1977.

Gleitman, H., & Gleitman, L. Language use and language judgement. In C. Fillmore, D. Kempler, & W. S-Y Wang, (Eds.), *Individual differences in language ability and language behavior*. New York: Academic Press, 1979.

Gruber, J. Topicalization revisited. *Foundations of Language*, 1975, *13*, 57–72.

Hakes, D. *The development of metalinguistic abilities in children*. New York: Springer Verlag, 1980.

Halliday, M. A. K. *Learning how to mean: Explorations in the development of language*. New York: Elsevier-North Holland, 1975.

Harkness, S. *Aspects of social environment and first language acquisition in rural Africa*. Paper presented at SSRC Conference on Language Input and Acquisition, Boston, 1974.

Hillenbrand, J. Perceptual organization of speech sounds by infants. *Journal of Speech and Hearing Research*, 1983, *26*, 268–282.

Ingram, D. Phonological rules in young children. *Papers and Reports on Child Language Development*, 1971, *3*, 31–49.

Jenkins, J. J. The acquisition of language. In D. A. Goslin (Ed.), *Handbook of socialization theory and research*. Chicago: Rand McNally & Co., 1969.

Kuhl, P. Speech perception in early infancy: Perceptual constancy for spectrally dissimilar vowel categories. *Journal of the Acoustical Society of America*, 1979, *66*, 1668–1679.

Lasky, E. Parameters affecting auditory processing. In E. Z. Lasky & J. Katz (Eds.), *Central auditory processing disorders: Problems of speech, language, and learning*. Baltimore: University Park Press, 1983.

Lasky, E. Z., & Chapandy, A. Factors affecting language comprehension. *Language, Speech, and Hearing Services in Schools*, 1976, 7, 159–168.

Lasky, E. Z., & Katz, J. *Central auditory processing disorders: Problems of speech, language, and learning*. Baltimore: University Park Press, 1983.

Lasky, E. Z., & Klopp, K. Parent-child interactions in normal and language-disordered children. *Journal of Speech and Hearing Disorders*, 1982, 47, 7–18.

Lecours, A. R. Mylogenetic correlates of the development of speech and language. In E. H. Lenneberg & E. Lenneberg (Eds.), *Foundations of language development: A multidisciplinary approach*. New York: Academic Press, 1975.

Lee, L. *Developmental sentence analysis*. Evanston, Ill.: Northwestern University Press, 1974.

Leonard, L. *Meaning in child language. Issues in the study of early semantic development.* New York: Grune & Stratton, 1976.

Lund, N. J., & Duchan, J. F. *Assessing children's language in naturalistic contexts.* Englewood Cliffs, N.J.: Prentice-Hall, 1983.

Maratsos, M. Nonegocentric communicative abilities in preschool children. *Child Development*, 1973, 44, 697–700.

Mateer, C. A. Motor and perceptual functions of the left hemisphere and their interaction. In S. J. Segalowitz (Ed.), *Language functions and brain organization*. New York: Academic Press, 1983.

Menyuk, P. *The acquisition and development of language*. Englewood Cliffs, N.J.: Prentice-Hall, 1971.

Menyuk, P. Language development. In C. Kopp & J. B. Krakow (Eds.), *Child development in a social context*. Reading, Mass.: Addison-Wesley, 1982.

Moffitt, A. R. Consonant cue perception by twenty- to twenty-four-week-old infants. *Child Development*, 1971, 42(3), 717–731.

Molfese, D. L. Neural mechanisms underlying the processing of speech information in infants and adults: Suggestions of differences in development and structure from electrophysiologic research. In U. Kirk (Ed.), *Neuropsychology of language, reading, and spelling*. New York: Academic Press, 1983.

Molfese, D. L., & Molfese, V. J. Development of symmetrical and asymmetrical hemispheric responses to speech sounds: Electrophysiologic correlates. In E. Z. Lasky & J. Katz (Eds.), *Central auditory processing disorders: Problems of speech, language, and learning*. Baltimore: University Park Press, 1983.

Molfese, D. L., Molfese, V. J., & Parsons, C. Hemisphere processing of phonologic information. In S. J. Segalowitz (Ed.), *Language functions and brain organization*. New York: Academic Press, 1983.

Nelson, K. Structure and strategy in learning to talk. *Monographs of the Society for Research in Child Development*, 1973, 38 (Serial No. 149, Nos. 1–2, I, II).

Nelson, K. Some attributes of adjectives used by young children. *Cognition*, 1976, 4, 13–30.

Nelson, K. Individual differences in language development: Implications for development of language. *Developmental Psychology*, 1981, 17, 170–186.

Ojemann, G. A. Interrelationships in the brain organization of language related behaviors: Evidence from electrical stimulation mapping. In U. Kirk (Ed.), *Neuropsychology of language, reading, and spelling*. New York: Academic Press, 1983.

Oller, D. K. *Infant vocalization and the development of speech*. Paper presented at Milwaukee Conference on Early Intervention with Infants and Young Children, University Of Wisconsin, 1977.

Prather, E. M., Hedrick, D. L., & Kern, C. A. Functions of consonant assimilation and reduplication in early word productions of mentally retarded children. *Journal of Speech and Hearing Disorders*, 1975, 40, 179–191.

182 ELAINE Z. LASKY

184

Prinz, P. M., & Ferrier, L. J. "Can you give me that one?" The comprehension, production and judgment of directives in language impaired children. *Journal of Speech and Hearing Disorders*, 1983, 48, 44–54.

Ross, P. Cerebral specialization in deaf individuals. In S. J. Segalowitz (Ed.), *Language functions and brain organization*. New York: Academic Press, 1983.

Schlesinger, I. Learning grammar: From pivot to realization rule. In R. Huxley & E. Ingram (Eds.), *Language acquisition: Models and methods*. New York: Academic Press, 1971.(a)

Schlesinger, I. Production of utterances and language acquisition. In D. Slobin (Ed.), *The ontogenesis of grammar*. New York: Academic Press, 1971.(b)

Segalowitz, S. J. Language as a mental organ or a mental complex. In S. J. Segalowitz (Ed.), *Language functions and brain organization*. New York: Academic Press, 1983.

Segalowitz, S. J., & Bryden, M. P. Individual differences in hemisphere representation of language. In S. J. Segalowitz (Ed.), *Language functions and brain organization*. New York: Academic Press, 1983.

Shatz, M., & Gelman, R. Beyond syntax: The influence of conversational constraints on speech modification. In C. Snow & C. Ferguson (Eds.), *Talking to children, language input and acquisition*. New York: Cambridge University Press, 1978.

Snow, C. E. Mother's speech research: From input to interaction. In C. E. Snow & C. A. Ferguson (Eds.), *Talking to children*. London: Cambridge University Press, 1977.

Trevarthen, C. Development of the cerebral mechanisms for language. In U. Kirk (Ed.), *Neuropsychology of language, reading, and spelling*. New York: Academic Press, 1983.

Umiker-Sebeok, D. Preschool children's interconversational narratives. *Journal of Child Language*, 1979, 6, 91–109.

Valsiner, J. Hemispheric specialization and integration in child development. In S. J. Segalowitz (Ed.), *Language functions and brain organization*. New York: Academic Press, 1983.

CHAPTER 8

The Neuropsychology of Learning Disabilities

FRANCIS J. PIROZZOLO and WALTER HARRELL

WHAT IS A LEARNING DISABILITY?

The term *learning disability* was created so that a categorical mechanism could be established by which monies would be made available to provide remedial services for those students who did not qualify for such services under the traditional categories of exceptionality. It probably was never intended to refer to a homogeneous and internally consistent diagnostic entity. The literature on learning disabilities contains innumerable discussions concerning whether learning disabilities exist, and if so, how they are defined and what constitutes an adequate diagnosis. At the heart of these debates, one finds disparate theoretical orientations of various professional groups. The current theories of learning disabilities and the controversies related to its diagnosis, definition, etiology, and remediation have existed in one form or another for almost a century.

Much of the terminology used to describe learning-disabled children is derived from the work done in neuropsychology and behavioral neurology during the 19th and early 20th centuries with brain-injured adults. During this time, postmortem findings were correlated with postinjury behavioral observations, and these clinicopathological correlations provided evidence for the localization of behavioral functions to circumscribed regions of the brain. Most of this "map making," as it was referred to, was done on the basis of observations of patients who had lost the

FRANCIS J. PIROZZOLO and WALTER HARRELL • Department of Neurology, Baylor College of Medicine, Houston, Texas 77030.

ability to speak, to understand the spoken word, or to carry out other higher mental functions.

By the mid-1960s, there were over 38 terms used to describe children who had trouble in school, but did not warrant inclusion into established categories of mental deficits (Clements, 1966). Despite the abundance of diagnostic and descriptive terminology, there was little progress in understanding these disorders. The field was criticized for the apparent circularity that existed because of the practice of classifying children as "brain injured" based solely on behavioral characteristics and without so-called "hard" neurologic findings (e.g., sensory or motor impairments such as visual field defects, paraplegias, etc.).

Several studies have suggested that current definitions of learning disabilities preclude accurate and reliable identification of such students and therefore hinder research (Epps, McGue, Ysseldyke, 1982; Ysseldyke, Algozzine, & Epps, 1982). Definitional ambiguities make diagnostic findings particularly sensitive to financial, political, and practical considerations (Sabatino, 1983). Recently, there have been numerous attempts to classify children into subcategories on the basis of common distinguishing attributes. In a sense, this completes the cycle from descriptions of the specific deficits based on assumed brain behavior relationships in the 19th and early 20th centuries to generic global descriptions aimed at providing services to a larger group of children in the 1960s and 1970s, back to a search for more precise referents.

PATHOPHYSIOLOGY OF LEARNING DISABILITIES

The pathophysiology of learning disabilities is not presently understood, although there have been several anatomical case reports in the literature that have provided some insight into possible pathophysiological processes involved. The first autopsy report was published by Drake (1968). He performed postmortem examination on a 12-year-old boy who had died as a result of a cerebellar hemorrhage. Previous neuropsychological examinations were unremarkable except for unexplained dizzy spells and "blackouts." The child had achieved most age-appropriate developmental milestones, was of average intellect, but experienced difficulty in reading, writing, and calculations. His medical background was significant for enuresis, asthma, and hyperactivity. He experienced concomitant emotional problems that aggravated his impaired condition and often resulted in behavioral outbursts. He expired in his sleep as a result of a massive hemorrhage involving the inferior vermis of the cerebellum and extending into subarachnoid and ventricular spaces. Gross examination of the cytoarchitectonic structure of the cerebral hemispheres revealed atypically wide and disconnected gyral patterns in both parietal lobes. In addition, there was significant callosal atrophy. Microscopic examination revealed spindle-shaped and ectopic neurons in the white matter, abnormally thick cortex with columnar lamination, and an apparent cerebellar angioma (capillary telangiectasis) which resulted in the hemorrhage.

It is interesting to speculate on the relationship between these findings and the subject's learning difficulties. The compromised cortical regions are well within the areas known to be involved in reading (as inferred from studies of alexia). However, Drake (1968) did not speculate on this point.

More recently, a cytoarchitectonic study was carried out on a left-handed 20-year-old dyslexic male who died as a result of a construction accident (Galaburda & Eidelberg, 1982; Galaburda & Kemper, 1979). This patient had a seizure disorder and evidence of EEG abnormalities in a sleep study. Dichotic-listening testing revealed strong lateralized language processing in the left cerebral hemisphere despite left-handedness. He showed evidence of delayed onset of speech and had difficulties in reading and writing. He was observed to be "clumsy" and had a positive history of familial left-handedness and reading retardation. He died of multiple internal injuries and there was no evidence of trauma or gross abnormalities to the brain at the time of autopsy. Serial sections of the brain were examined and normal hemispheric asymmetry was noted, with the possible exception of the left planum temporale, which was equivalent in length to the right planum temporale. The corpus callosum, ventricular system, and subcortical structures appeared normal. Several abnormalities were observed on microscopic examination. Polymicrogyria in the posterior parts of Heschl's gyrus and the planum temporale were noted. There was evidence of undifferentiated and fused molecular areas in this region. Dysplasia was seen in the auditory cortex and in the cingulate and anterior insular areas. Finally, abnormally large neurons were found in all layers of the cortex and in the white matter. The aforementioned abnormalities were confined to the left hemisphere; the right hemisphere was free of anomalous findings in both gross and microscopic examinations. The only bilateral deficits appeared to be in disruptive thalamic pathways (Eidelberg & Galaburda, 1982).

Clinicopathological correlations are difficult to draw for a number of reasons, and this particular case is complicated further by the fact that the patient suffered from a seizure disorder. Nevertheless, the majority of the cortical and subcortical abnormalities described by Galaburda and

Eidelberg (1982) were in regions known to be crucial to reading comprehension and may be offered as a possible explanation for this individual's
symptoms of developmental dyslexia.

BIOCHEMICAL THEORIES OF LEARNING DISABILITIES

There are numerous theories that suggest that the symptom complex
of attentional deficits, hyperactivity, and learning disorders result from
biochemical abnormalities in the brain. Wender (1971, 1975a, b) proposed
that these children have enzymatic deficits that affect monoamine metabolism. Specifically, he suggested that they have impaired noradrenergic
function that fails to keep the dopaminergic system at normal levels. Evidence of this hypothesis is seen in the ameliorative effect of drugs that
act directly on the bioamines in children. However, the literature in this
area is equivocal for a number of reasons. There is evidence that these
drugs exert their effects on numerous biochemical systems (Rapaport,
Buchsbaum, Zahn, Weingartner, Ludlow, & Mikkelsen, 1978). Also, behavioral modification techniques in conjunction with medications have
only questionable clinical efficacy (Wender and Wender, 1976). Finally,
the "paradoxical effect" is not paradoxical in that these agents are known
to increase attention in normals (Ludlow, Rapoport, Cardano, & Mikkelsen,
1978).

Other biochemical theories have been offered as well. Many investigators believe that the serotonergic system is primarily responsible for
hyperkinetic behavior. Greenberg and Coleman (1976) reported low blood
serotonin levels in hyperkinetic brain-damaged children. Similar findings
were reported by Brase and Loh (1975), who were able to demonstrate a
relationship between blood serotonin levels and clinical symptomatology.
It should be noted that blood levels do not necessarily correspond with
levels in brain tissue (Coleman, Hart, Randall, Lee, Hijada, & Bratenahl,
1977).

More recently the GABAergic system has been investigated for its
involvement in learning disabilities. It has been argued that cholinergic
and aminergic interaction, or specifically, systems involving gamma-ami-
nobutyric acid (GABA) and acetylcholine (ACh) are dysfunctional in a portion of learning-disabled children (Silbergeld, 1977). Goldberg and Silbergeld (1978) suggest that among other dysfunctions there could be
decreased cholinergic or GABAergic functioning in dyslexics. This is partially supported by the results of investigations that demonstrated improved reading ability after administration of nootropic compounds (Wilshire, Atkins, & Manfield, 1979).

HEMISPHERIC ASYMMETRIES IN LEARNING DISABILITIES

Hemispheric asymmetries and the lateralization of sensory, motor, language, and other cognitive functions have been examined critically in the literature for years. The two sides of the brain have developed specialized functions, and differences in hemispheric function have been noted in several species (LeMay, 1977; Nottebohm, 1980; Yeni-Komshian, Isenberg, & Goldberg, 1975). Whitaker and Ojemann (1977) suggest that the differences are due to cortical rather than subcortical structures. The most extensively studied asymmetry of cerebral anatomy is that of the relative enlargement of the left planum temporale, which is believed to be specialized for language function (Geschwind & Levitsky, 1968; Wada, Clarke & Hamm, 1975; Witelson & Pallie, 1973). Blood flow and computerized tomographic studies demonstrate clear morphological differences, and this asymmetry may provide a favorable anatomical substrate for language (Ingvar & Philipson, 1977; LeMay, 1976; Risberg, Halsey, Wills, & Wilson, 1975).

Two recent studies utilizing computerized tomograms on dyslexic brains provided support for the "reverse cerebral dominance" hypothesis in dyslexia. Hier, LeMay, Rosenberger, and Perlo (1978) found that almost half their subjects demonstrated a reversal of the typical cerebral asymmetry. None of the dyslexics had evidence of brain damage. Rosenberger and Hier (1980) found that 42% of the children in their study who had verbal learning deficits demonstrated wider right than left parieto-occipital regions. In addition, there was evidence that depressed verbal IQ scores were related to increased size in this area.

Results such as these are not completely compelling and numerous questions remain. There are asymmetrical aspects to all internal organs and many areas of the body. Almost one fourth of "normal" brains do not demonstrate this asymmetry, and a very small percentage shows a reversal of this tendency (Lansdell, 1980). Rather than being a causal determinant for learning disabilities, this may be a risk factor.

Indirect evidence of deviant neurological organization is seen in a host of studies employing dichotic-listening techniques in an attempt to explore the relationship between language lateralization of the brain and reading and learning ability. There has been a wide variety of findings and therefore a clear picture has not emerged (Pirozzolo, Rayner, Hansch, & Hynd, 1981). However, some research has compared normal readers with retarded readers (Bakker, 1980; Obrzut, 1979; Witelson & Rabinovitch, 1972; Zurif & Carson, 1970), and it has been suggested that incomplete cerebral dominance or left hemisphere dysfunction of speech is the norm among dyslexic populations. Several researchers have observed significant right-ear superiority in older dyslexic subjects, and they attribute their findings to a lack of functional cerebral development (Leong, 1976; McKeever & Van Deventer, 1975; Yeni-Komshian, Isenberg, & Goldberg 1975). Their studies have been controversial and the reader is referred to Hynd and Cohen (1983) for a complete review of the recent literature.

Perceptual and perceptual motor asymmetries in dyslexic populations have been examined by employing the tachistoscopic visual half-field techniques. This line of research examines cerebral dominance by the presentation of verbal or nonverbal stimuli to either the right or left visual field. Children with learning disorders and reading difficulties often do not show the right visual field–left hemisphere advantage (Marcel, Katz, & Smith, 1974; Pirozzolo, 1979; Pirozzolo & Rayner, 1979; Pirozzolo et al., 1981; Hynd, Obrzut, Weed, & Hynd, 1979). Taken together with the dichotic-listening studies, there appears to be evidence that dyslexic and learning-disabled children have less hemispheric specialization for language, and that deficits or inefficient linguistic processing exist. Whether this is attributable to subtle disorders of left hemisphere function, to bilateral representation of spatial or verbal abilities that interfere with the normal development of hemispheric specialization for language, or to anomalous right-hemispheric representation of language function is not known.

ELECTROPHYSIOLOGICAL CORRELATES OF LEARNING DISABILITIES

There is evidence to suggest that learning-disabled children differ from normal children with respect to electrophysiological activity during cognitive tasks. Such findings have been derived from several different types of studies, including EEG correlates of learning disabilities, power spectrum analysis, brain electrical activity mapping, and event-related potentials. Although abnormal findings are not in themselves pathognomonic, the deficits in learning-disabled children are consistent with what is known about brain structure–function relationships and higher cognitive tasks.

Electroencephalographic investigations with learning-disabled children have been done for almost 40 years. Many researchers have described EEG abnormalities in these children (Ayers & Torres, 1967; Hughes, 1971; Hughes, Leander & Ketchum, 1949; Hughes & Park, 1968; Kennard, Rabinovitch, & Wexler, 1952; Muehl, Knott, & Benton, 1965; Webb & Lawson, 1956). Typical findings are a slowing at the posterior occipital leads, focal sharp waves, and 14 - 6 per second positive spike patterns during sleep. Unfortunately, a positive correlation between the degree of reading disability and EEG abnormalities has not been established (Muehl et al., 1965), and higher frequencies of abnormalities have been reported in borderline rather than severely learning-disabled children (Hughes, 1971).

As the technology has become more sophisticated, new techniques have been employed. Among them is power spectrum analysis, a quantitative method of analyzing various frequency domains simultaneously. This neurometric approach has uncovered specific EEG deviations in learning-disabled children. Common in these studies is the finding of increased power in the theta and delta ranges, particularly at the parieto-occipital and temporal derivations (Ahn, Prichep, John, Baird, Trepetin, & Kaye, 1980).

Similarly, procedures have been developed for brain electrical activity mapping (BEAM). Duffy, Denckla, Bartels, and Sandini (1980) developed this procedure that allows computer generation of topographic EEG images to elucidate regional dynamics of electrical activity at rest and during mental processing. They found increased mean alpha and to a lesser extent theta activity, with hemispheric differences over medial frontal, temporal, and occipital regions. The finding of increased alpha activity, which has been shown in other studies as well (Fuller, 1977), is indicative of underactivation of the underlying cortical structures. A clinical classification scheme was derived from the BEAM technique with impressive results (Duffy et al., 1980). As topographical distribution and quantitative analysis techniques become more sophisticated, the clinical diagnostic utility undoubtedly will improve.

Event-related potentials (ERP) have been utilized as an electrophysiological index of brain function in the learning-disabled subject. This method of analysis permits examination of discrete epochs of brain activity following specifiable sensory, motor, or cognitive events. Most of the studies with learning-disabled children have focused on stimulus-evoked potentials. Connors' (1971) studies of flash-evoked responses in several groups of learning-disabled children found that significant amplitude differences existed at the P3 electrode for the N200 wave VI between "good" and "poor" readers within a learning-disabled population. Essential agreement can be found in a study conducted by Preston, Guthrie, and Childs (1974). Evidence of asynchronous hemispheric activity was suggested by Ross, Childers, and Perry (1973). They found phase reversal of the right occipital electrode relative to the posterior midline in 20 of 30 learning-disabled children. These findings, coupled with those of Preston, Guthrie, Kirsch, Gertman, and Childs (1977), suggest that ERP differentiation between groups can be made, especially in posterior left parietal occipital regions.

There are few studies of examined ERPs reflecting cognitive events in dyslexic children. Fenelon (1978) found decreased contingent negative variation wave-form amplitude in the reading-disabled compared with normal readers during simultaneous visual and auditory presentation. This was evident more clearly over the left parietal region, but did not reach statistical significance. Musso and Harter (1978) found delayed latencies for the P300 component at both the vertex and O2 in reading-disabled children. Further, the children whose disability was attributable to visual problems demonstrated greater latencies than when compared with those with auditory problems. Finally, increased amplitude differentiation at O2 in task-relevant conditions was seen relative to normal children in the visual dyslexics. The authors suggest that these findings reflect enhanced attention in compensating for slowing in sensory-neural information processing in this group.

Taken together, the EEG findings, especially those employing ERPs, BEAMs or power spectrum analysis, indicate that localized wave-form aberrations in the left parietal occipital cortex may reflect a compromise in this region in learning-disabled children. These new techniques will allow more flexible and complex experimental designs and provide increased understanding of electrocortical manifestations of complex cognitive deficits in learning-disabled children.

PERCEPTUAL AND INFORMATION PROCESSING

The ability to perceive sensory input and organize it in some meaningful fashion is critical for learning. The role of perception in learning disabilities has been investigated extensively for decades. Remedial strategies based on assumptions of compromised auditory and visual perception have been developed, although with mixed results (Bruinincks, 1970; Smith, 1971). This section will examine some of the literature that offers support for perceptual and information-processing deficits as an etiology of learning disabilities.

AUDITORY PROCESSING

It is known that auditory processing in learning involves discriminating sounds and sorting them into meaningful units, sequencing them so that they are in proper order, remembering them, and then responding appropriately (Rosner, 1973). Although deficits at any level can result in difficulties in learning, there have been relatively few studies conducted that examine auditory information processing in learning-disabled children.

In 1966, McReynolds studied aphasic children and compared them with non-brain-damaged children in the ability to discriminate sounds, particularly when sounds were embedded in nonsense syllables. It was determined that aphasic children exhibit impairment relative to the non-brain-damaged group and that a deterioration in performance occurred as the task increased in difficulty. Similarly, Grassi (1970) found that normal adolescents performed better than the behavior-disorder group who in turn performed better than brain-injured adolescents in their vigilance for auditory stimuli. Dykman, Ackerman, Clements, and Peters (1971) compared a group of learning-disabled (LD) children and a minimally cerebral-damaged (MCD) group on discriminating auditory stimuli. The MCD children performed less well than the LD children in discriminating tones and following instructions. In addition, they did not appear to profit from task practice. Finally, Rourke and Czudner (1972) compared normal and brain-injured children on vigilance tasks and found an age-by-disability interaction. The brain-injured children's performance was comparable to their normal counterparts on attentiveness to auditory stimuli; however, the young brain injured were less vigilant.

Selected studies have compared normal children with LD students on a variety of auditory-processing tasks (Bryan, 1972; Connors, Kramer, & Guerra, 1969). The study by Connors et al. (1969) examined short-term memory and auditory synthesis by the ability to remember numbers presented in a dichotic-listening task and the ability to identify the correct word that had been presented incompletely. The performance of the LD group was comparable to that of normal children on short-term memory tasks, but they did less well on the synthesis tasks. The authors concluded that the ability to synthesize sounds was of critical importance. Bryan (1972) compared normal and LD subjects' visual and auditory processing by presenting two lists of words to be learned, one by tape recorder and another by slide projector. The results indicated that normal children outperformed LD children in both modalities and that performance for both groups was superior in the visual modality.

There are numerous factors that affect performance on cognitive tasks. Specifically, the age of the child, complexity of the task, the type of task, response demands, and interactions all affect performance. It is known that attention deficits are common in LD children and this alone could explain some of the reported results. Also, language proficiency may play an important role. Wood (1971) found that verbal skills are correlated with sound perception and that lexical ability affects responses to auditory tasks. It could be that studies of auditory processing reported here comparing normal with LD children were not effective since they obscure salient features concerning how processing occurs in these children. Clearly more work in this area is needed before definitive statements can be made regarding the role of auditory processing in the etiology of learning disabilities.

VISUAL PERCEPTION

The idea that an inability to perceive visual symbols adequately could cause learning deficits was originally proposed by Orton (1928, 1937). This hypothesis was extended greatly by numerous others who investigated a variety of perceptual-motor dysfunctions. It was generally assumed that perceptual development is a forerunner of conceptual development and that motor development precedes and is necessary for perceptual development. The underlying assumption was that deficits in these abilities reflect brain injury, although a gradual de-emphasis on etiology and an increasing trend toward diagnosis and remediation of the non-brain-injured is seen in their work. Many early remedial approaches (which are still popular today) were derived from this work.

Among the major contributors to psychoeducational assessment and remediation of spoken language disorders were Osgood (1953) and Wepman (1958). They attempted to account for the projection of receptor and muscle events to the brain, the integration and organization of neuronal inputs and outputs, and finally the nature of the representation of language. Wepman and others developed models to account for memory, modality of transmission, and external feedback in spoken language. These conceptualizations of spoken language were employed by Kirk, McCarthy, and Kirk (1968) to develop the Illinois Test of Psycholinguistic Abilities (ITPA), a test still in use today.

Support for visual perception and information processing as a cause of learning disabilities can be seen in recent studies. Lyle and Goyen embarked on a series of studies (Lyle, 1969; Lyle & Goyen, 1968, 1975) that showed that children under 8 years of age tend to have deficits in perceptual tasks, children over 8 tend to have deficits in verbal tasks, and younger children tend to overlook critical details of stimulus materials and are slower in response time. Guthrie and Goldberg (1972) found that retarded readers did not perform as well on visual memory tasks as did their normal reader counterparts, although they did do as well on the ITPA. Doehring (1960) showed that aphasics did worse on short-term visual memory than did groups of deaf and normal children. Further support for the visual perceptual deficit can be seen in the work of Poppen, Stark, Eisenson, Forrest, and Wertheim (1969), Czudner and Rourke (1970), Dykman et al. (1971), and Jansky and deHirsch (1972).

It should be stated that there is a considerable body of resarch that refutes this position, and in general there are assumptions made about the measures employed in previous work that appear to be unwarranted. For example, after conducting a series of experiments with disabled readers, Vellutino and co-workers (Vellutino, Steger, & Kandel, 1972; Vellutino, Steger, Kaman, & Desetto, 1975) found that the performance of poor readers was similar to that of normal readers in copying simple geometric designs, and although the disabled readers often were able to copy stimulus words, they could not pronounce them. Later Vellutino (1978) suggested that the perceptual deficits demonstrated in LD populations could be explained best by linguistic intrusion errors or deficient verbal processing. Findings suggesting that reading difficulties might reflect linguistic characteristics rather than visual properties also were made by Fischer, Lieberman, and Schankweiler (1978). Commonly used tests thought to reflect perceptual and perceptual-motor skills (Frostig and ITPA) had been found not to reflect perceptive skills, but rather language abilities, and that visual perception and visual-motor dysfunction might not be an important contributor to reading ability (Burns & Watson, 1973; Nielson & Binge, 1969).

INTERSENSORY PROCESSING DEFICITS

Some researchers have avoided intermodal perception deficits as an explanation of learning disabilities. Birch and colleagues were among the first to argue that the deficits of LD children were not a result of auditory or visual perception deficits, but rather impaired intersensory integration. They investigated audiovisual integration and important trends were noted (Birch & Belmont, 1964, 1965; Birch & Lefford, 1963). Retarded readers demonstrated more difficulty on the experimental tasks, but auditory-visual integration correlated with reading ability only for the first- and second-grade readers. This developmental trend suggests that cross-modal integration is important in the early stages of learning to read.

Sterritt and Rudnick (1966) argued that the Birch studies (1963, 1964, 1965) were evaluating intramodal transfer, specifically the translation of visual-temporal to visual-spatial rather than the auditory to visual cross-modal processing as discussed. They further argued that the measures used were highly correlated with IQ, which had not been controlled adequately. In their study, they found that IQ could account for 50% of the variance and that auditory to visual cross-modal translation could account for 23% of the variance. They conclude that the ability to translate auditory-temporal information into visual-spatial information was of critical importance, and that auditory pattern perception ability was the primary function related to reading. In a follow-up developmental study (Rudnick, Sterritt, & Flax, 1967), evidence of a developmental trend was found. On the basis of the findings, it was concluded that visual perception declined in importance with age, whereas auditory and cross-modal perception ability became important predictors of reading ability. As with the previous study, IQ could account for a significant proportion (30%) of the variance.

Other studies have provided equivocal or contradictory evidence of cross-modal integration deficits in LD children. Blank, Weider, and Bridger (1968) found that retarded readers were impaired on intramodal tasks. These children appeared unable to convert temporally distributed stimuli into spatially distributed tasks. The retarded readers were significantly deficient in their abilities to verbalize the patterns of temporally presented lights. Finally, Senf and his colleagues (Senf, 1969; Senf & Fesback, 1970; Senf & Freunal, 1971) found that the performance of LD children was similar to normal children in cross-modal integration, but was inferior to normal children in intramodal and sequencing tasks. In addition, the LD children did not show evidence of improvement with age as did the controls.

There are several alternative explanations that potentially could elucidate the observed results in these studies. Deficits in symbolic mediation could explain some of the results. The level of abstraction of the tasks required for the subjects determines success or failure, which suggests that ability to succeed is correlated with intelligence. Also, deficits in cross-modal processing could be attributable to impaired processing in a single modality. Evidence for this is seen in the Senf and Freunal (1971) finding that the reading-disabled groups were inferior at discrimination and coding or recall of visual material and that there was evidence of strong auditory preference.

EYE MOVEMENTS AND READING DISABILITIES

It is a well-established fact that the behavior of the eye is an accurate reflection of the integrity of the central nervous system. The appearance and movement of the eye tells much about the brain. A careful examination of the eye can determine not only visual acuity, but the status of the retina, optic pathways, extraocular muscles and the cranial nerves that innervate them, deep brain structures, and higher cortical functioning. Assessment of saccadic eye movements during perceptual and cognitive tasks provides useful data in determining the operating characteristics of the brain (Rayner, 1978).

Saccadic latency, saccadic accuracy, fixation duration, fixation frequency, and fixation density are of specific interest to neuropsychologists. The complex neural network responsible for generating saccades, although involving subcortical mechanisms, is thought to be influenced by visual-spatial, cognitive operations. Consider the rich feedback mechanism needed for successful scanning: computations are made regarding the location of an object in space, a ballistic flight of the eyes is launched to that visual space, visual feedback is analyzed toward the end of the saccade, and corrections to the motor program are calculated. Each step of the process leading to a series of corrected saccades and fixations is necessary for successful visual scanning and reading. The sensitivity of eye movement to cognitive processes is well-documented. Patients with dementia have compromised saccadic latency and accuracy (Hutton, Johnson, Shapiro, & Pirozzolo, 1979; Pirozzolo, 1978; Pirozzolo & Hansch, 1981; Pirozzolo & Rayner, 1978b), and aberrant eye movement as a possible etiology of reading disabilities has been the focus of much research (Zangwill & Blakemore, 1972).

Early studies regarding abnormal eye movements as a causal factor in dyslexia were unable to show a clear relationship. When text difficulty is controlled for, there appears to be no difference in the pattern of eye movements between most dyslexic and normal children (Pirozzolo, 1979). In addition, eye movement training has been unsuccessful in remediating reading disabilities. This suggests that patterns of eye movements in most readers reflect linguistic demands placed on the reader. Other research suggests that some dyslexics have deficits in fundamental oculomotor function, which is suggestive of underlying pathophysiology. It is known that reading can be disrupted by lesions in the central nervous system that interfere with normal performance of the ocular motor system. Some dyslexics have difficulty with return sweeps (Pirozzolo, 1979; Pirozzolo & Rayner, 1978a; Zangwill & Blakemore, 1972) and in locating the targets of the next saccade and making an accurate, rapid eye movement to that location. The evidence suggests that these findings actually may reflect a faulty visual-spatial control mechanism that guides the eye rather than a disturbance in the ocular motor mechanism itself. As more research is conducted, a consensus among professionals regarding the nature of dyslexia and the role of eye movement is emerging. There may be several basic types of deficiencies that can result in reading disability, for example, visual-spatial perceptual disorders, auditory-linguistic disorders, ocular-motor disorders, sequencing disorders, and general language disorders

(Boder, 1973; Mattis, 1981; Pirozzolo, 1982). Because of the complexity of the cognitive demands for reading, fully articulated causal mechanisms are not likely to be understood in the near future. Nevertheless, assessment of eye movements in perceptual and language processes will contribute to this effort.

SUMMARY

Any group of LD children is likely to be heterogeneous to the point that no single statement regarding their deficits or the etiology of such deficits will be adequate. The recent learning disabilities' literature has begun to reflect this orientation, due in part to increased elucidation of "subtypes" of learning disabilities. This idea had its neuropsychological beginnings in the work of Joseph Wepman, and later Marcel Kinsbourne, Elena Boder, and, more recently, Steven Mattis. These researchers have established the great variability in the learning-disabled population and have demonstrated that "subtypes" may exist. Trends in the neurosciences have suggested that discrete physiological subtypes also may exist. In the future, multidisciplinary studies involving the basic sciences and employing new methodologies such as positron emission tomography and nuclear magnetic resonance should be combined with traditional neuropathological and neuropsychological methods and improved neuropsychological measurement techniques in order to better understand the deficits that cause unexpected learning failure.

REFERENCES

Ahn, H., Prichep, L., John, E. R., Baird, H., Trepetin, M., & Kaye, H. Developmental equations reflect brain dysfunction. *Science*, 1980, *210*, 1259–1262.
Ayers, F. W., & Torres, F. The incidence of EEG abnormalities in a dyslexic and a control group. *Journal of Clinical Psychology*, 1967, *23*, 334–336.
Bakker, D. J. Cerebral lateralization and reading proficiency. In Y. Lebrun & O. Zangwill (Eds.), *Lateralization of language in the child*. The Hague, Netherlands: Lisse, Swets, and Zetlinger, 1980. (From the symposium held in St. Ode, Belgium.)
Birch, H., & Belmont, L. Auditory-visual integration in normal and retarded readers. *American Journal of Orthopsychiatry*, 1964, *34*, 852–361.
Birch, H., & Belmont, L. Auditory-visual integration, intelligence, and reading ability in schoolchildren. *Perceptual and Motor Skills*, 1965, *20*, 295–305.
Birch, H. G., & Lefford, A. Intersensory development in children. *Monographs of the Society for Research on Child Development.*, 1963, *28*.
Blank, M., Weider, S., & Bridger, W. Verbal deficiencies in abstract thinking in early reading retardation. *American Journal of Orthopsychiatry*, 1968, *38*, 823–834.

Boder, E. Developmental dyslexia: A diagnostic approach based on three atypical reading-spelling patterns. *Developmental Medicine and Child Neurology*, 1973, *15*, 663–687.

Brase, D. A., & Loh, H. M. Possible role of 5-hydroxytryptamine in minimal brain dysfunction. *Life Sciences*, 1975, *16*(7), 1005–1015.

Bruinincks, R. Teaching word recognition to disadvantaged boys. *Journal of Learning Disabilities*, 1970, *3*, 28–35.

Bryan, T. The effect of forced medication upon short-term memory of children with learning disabilities. *Journal of Learning Disabilities*, 1972, *5*, 605–609.

Burns, G. W., & Watson, B. L. Factor analyses of the revised ITPA with underachieving children. *Journal of Learning Disabilities*, 1973, *6*, 371–376.

Clements, S. D. *Minimal brain dysfunction in children—Terminology and identification.* NINBD Monograph No. 3, Washington, D.C.: U.S. Public Health Service, 1966.

Coleman, M., Hart, P. N., Randall, J., Lee, J., Hijada, D., & Bratenahl, C. G. Serotonin levels in the blood and central nervous system of a patient with sudanophilic leukodystrophy. *Neuropädiatrie*, 1977, *8*,(4), 459–466.

Connors, C. K. Cortical visual evoked response in children with learning disorders. *Psychophysiology*, 1971, *7*, 418–428.

Connors, C. K., Kramer, K., & Guerra, F. Auditory synthesis and dichotic listening in children with learning disabilities. *Journal of Special Education*, 1969, *3*, 163–170.

Czudner, G., & Rourke, B. P. Simple reaction time in brain damaged and normal children under regular and irregular preparatory internal conditions. *Perceptual and Motor Skills*, 1970, *31*, 767–773.

Doehring, D. Visual spatial memory in aphasic children. *Journal of Speech and Hearing Research*, 1960, *3*, 138–149.

Drake, W. E. Clinical and pathological findings in a child with a developmental learning disability. *Journal of Learning Disabilities*, 1968, *1*, 486–502.

Duffy, F. H., Denckla, M. B., Bartels, P. H., & Sandini, G. Dyslexia: Regional differences in brain electrical activity by topographic mapping. *Annals of Neurology*, 1980, *7*, 412–420.

Dykman, R. A., Ackerman, P. T., Clements, S. D., & Peters, J. E. Specific learning disabilities: An attentional deficit syndrome. In H. R. Myklebust (Ed.), *Progress in learning disabilities* (Vol. 2). New York: Grune & Stratton, 1971.

Eidelberg, D. S., & Galaburda, A. M. Symmetry and asymmetry of the human posterior thalamus: I. Cytoarchitectonic analysis in normal persons. *Archives of Neurology*, 1982, *34*, 325–332.

Epps, S., McGue, M., & Ysseldyke, J. E. Interjudge agreement in classifying students as learning disabled. *Psychology in the Schools*, 1982, *19*, 209–220.

Fenelon, B. Hemispheric effects of stimulus sequence and side of stimulation on slow potentials in children with reading problems. In D. A. Otto (Ed.), *Multidisciplinary perspectives in event-related brain potential research.* Washington, D.C.: Government Printing Office, 1978.

Fischer, W. F., Lieberman, I. V., & Schankweiler, D. Reading reversals and developmental dyslexia: A further study. *Cortex*, 1978, *14*, 496–510.

Fuller, P. W. Computer estimated alpha attenuation during problem solving in children with learning disabilities. *Electroencephalography and Clinical Neurophysiology*, 1977, *42*, 149–156.

Galaburda, A. M., & Eidelberg, D. Symmetry and asymmetry in the human posterior thalamus: II. Thalamic lesions in a case of developmental dyslexia. *Archives of Neurology*, 1982, *39*, 333–336.

Galaburda, A. M., & Kemper, T. Cytoarchitectonic abnormalities in developmental dyslexia. A case study. *Annals of Neurology*, 1979, *6*, 94–100.

198   FRANCIS J. PIROZZOLO AND WALTER HARRELL

Geschwind, N., & Levitsky, W. Human brain: Left-right asymmetries in temporal speech region. *Science*, 1968, *161*, 186–188.

Goldberg, A. M., & Silbergeld, E. K. Animal models of hyperactivity. In I. Hanin & E. Usdin (Eds.), *Animal models in psychiatry and neurology*. New York: Pergamon, 1978.

Grassi, J. Auditory vigilance performance in brain damaged, behavior disorders, and normal children. *Journal of Learning Disabilities*, 1970, *3*, 302–304.

Greenberg, A. S., & Coleman, M. Depressed 5-hydroxyindole levels associated with hyperactive and aggressive behavior: Relationship to drug response. *Archives of General Psychiatry*, 1976, *33*(3), 331–336.

Guthrie, J. T., & Goldberg, H. K. Visual sequential memory in reading disability. *Journal of Learning Disabilities*, 1972, *5*, 41–46.

Hier, D. B., LeMay, M., Rosenberger, P. B., & Perlo, V. P. Developmental dyslexia: Evidence for a subgroup with a reversal of cerebral asymmetry. *Archives of Neurology*, 1978, *35*, 90–92.

Hughes, J. R. Electroencephalography and learning disabilities. In H. R. Myklebust (Ed.), *Progress in learning disabilities*. New York: Grune & Stratton, 1971.

Hughes, J. R., Leander, R., & Ketchum, G. Electroencephalographic study of specific reading disabilities. *Electroencephalography and Clinical Neurophysiology*, 1949, *1*, 377–378.

Hughes, J. R., & Park, G. E. The EEG in dyslexia. In P. Kellaway & I. Peterson (Eds.), *Clinical electroencephalography of children*. Stockholm: Almquist and Wiksell, 1968.

Hutton, J. T., Johnston, L., Shapiro, I., & Pirozzolo, F. J. Oculomotor programming disturbances in the dementia syndrome. *Perceptual and Motor Skills*, 1979, *49*, 312–314.

Hynd, G., & Cohen, M. *Dyslexia*. New York: Grune & Stratton, 1983.

Hynd, G. W., Obrzut, J. E., Weed, W., & Hynd, C. R. Development of cerebral dominance: Dichotic listening asymmetry in normal and learning disabled children. *Journal of Experimental Child Psychology*, 1979, *28*, 445–454.

Ingvar, D. H., & Philipson, L. Distribution of cerebral blood flow in the dominant hemisphere during motor ideation and motor performance. *Annals of Neurology*, 1977, *2*(3), 230–237.

Jansky, J. J., & deHirsch, K. *Preventing reading failure: Prediction, diagnosis, and intervention*. New York: Harper & Row, 1972.

Kennard, M. A., Rabinovitch, R., & Wexler, D. The abnormal electroencephalogram as related to reading disability in children with disorders of behavior. *Canadian Medical Association Journal*, 1952, *67*, 330–333.

Kirk, S. A., McCarthy, J. J., & Kirk, W. D. *Examiner's manual: Illinois Test of Psycholinguistic Abilities* (Rev. ed.). Urbana, Ill.: University of Illinois Press, 1968.

Lansdell, H. Theories of brain mechanisms in minimal brain dysfunctions. In H. E. Rie & E. D. Rie (Eds.), *Handbook of minimal brain dysfunctions: A critical view*. New York: Wiley, 1980.

LeMay, M. Morphological cerebral asymmetries of modern man, fossil man and non-human primate. *Annals of the New York Academy of Sciences*, 1976, *280*, 389–366.

LeMay, M. Asymmetries of the skull and handedness. *Journal of Neurological Sciences*, 1977, *32*, 243–253.

Leong, C. K. Lateralization in severely disabled readers in relation to functional cerebral development and synthesis of information. In R. M. Knights & D. J. Bakker (Eds.), *Neuropsychology of learning disorders: Theoretical approaches*. Baltimore: University Park Press, 1976.

Ludlow, C. L., Rapoport, J. L., Cardano, C. B., & Mikkelson, E. J. Differential effects of dextroamphetamine on language performance in hyperactive and normal boys. In R. M. Knights & D. J. Bakker (Eds.), *Rehabilitation, treatment and management of learning disorders*. Baltimore: University Park Press, 1978.

Lyle, J. G. Reading retardation and reversal tendency: A factorial study. *Child Development,* 1969, *40,* 833–843.

Lyle, J. G., & Goyen, J. Visual recognition, developmental lag and strephosymbolus in reading retardation. *Journal of Abnormal Psychology,* 1968, *73,* 25–29.

Lyle, J. G., & Goyen, J. Effects of speed of exposure and difficulty of discrimination on visual recognition of retarded readers. *Journal of Abnormal Psychology,* 1975, *8,* 613–616.

Marcel, T., Katz, K., & Smith, M. Laterality and reading proficiency. *Neuropsychology,* 1974, *12,* 131–139.

Mattis, S. Dyslexia syndromes in children: Toward the development of syndrome-specific treatment programs. In F. J. Pirozzolo & M. C. Wittrock (Eds.), *Neuropsychological and cognitive processes in reading.* New York: Academic Press, 1981.

McKeever, W. F., & Van Deventer, A. D. Dyslexic adolescents: Evidence of impaired visual and auditory language processing. *Cortex,* 1975, *11,* 361–378.

McReynolds, L. V. Operant conditioning for investigating speech sound discrimination in aphasic children. *Journal of Speech and Hearing Research,* 1966, *9,* 519–528.

Muehl, S., Knott, J. R., & Benton, A. L. EEG abnormality and psychological test performance in reading disability. *Cortex,* 1965, *1,* 434–440.

Musso, M. R., & Harter, M. R. Contingent negative variation, evoked potential, and psycho-physical measures of selective attention in children with learning disabilities. In D. A. Otto (Ed.), *Multisensory perspectives in event-related brain potential research.* Washington, D.C.: Government Printing Office, 1978.

Nielson, H., & Binge, K. Visuoperceptual and visuomotor performance of children with reading disabilities. *Scandinavian Journal of Psychology,* 1969, *10,* 225–237.

Nottebohm, F. (1980) Brain pathways for vocal learning in birds: A review of the first ten years. *Progress in Psychobiology and Physiological Psychology,* 1980, *19,* 85–124.

Obrzut, J. E. Dichotic listening and bisensory memory skills in qualitatively diverse dyslexic readers. *Journal of Learning Disabilities,* 1979, *12,* 304–314.

Orton, S. T. Specific reading disability—strephosymbolus. *Journal of the American Medical Association,* 1928, *10,* 1095–1099.

Orton, S. T. *Reading, writing, and speech problems in children.* New York: Norton, 1937.

Osgood, C. *Method and theory in experimental psychology.* New York: Oxford University Press, 1953.

Pirozzolo, F. J. Slow saccades. *Archives of Neurology,* 1978, *35,* 618.

Pirozzolo, F. J. *The neuropsychology of developmental reading disorders.* New York: Praeger, 1979.

Pirozzolo, F. J. Eye movements and reading disabilities. In K. Rayner (Ed.), *Eye movements in reading: Perceptual and language processes.* New York: Academic Press, 1982.

Pirozzolo, F. J., & Hansch, E. C. The neurobiology of developmental reading disorders. In R. N. Malatesha & P. G. Aaron (Eds.), *Neuropsychological and neurolinguistic aspects of reading disorders.* New York: Academic Press, 1981.

Pirozzolo, F. J., & Rayner, K. Disorders of oculomotor scanning and graphic orientation in Developmental Gerstmann Syndrome. *Brain and Language,* 1978, *5,* 119–126.(a)

Pirozzolo, F. J., & Rayner, K. The neural control of eye movements in acquired and developmental reading disorders. In H. Whitaker & H. A. Whitaker (Eds.), *Studies in neurolinguistics,* (Vol. 4). New York: Academic Press, 1978. (b)

Pirozzolo, F. J., & Rayner, K. Cerebral organization and reading disability. *Neuropsychologia,* 1979, *17,* 485–489.

Pirozzolo, F. J., Rayner, K., Hansch, E., & Hynd, G. The measurement of cerebral hemispheric asymmetries in children with developmental reading disability. In J. Hellige (Ed.), *Cerebral hemispheric asymmetry: Theory, method, and application.* New York: Praeger, 1981.

Poppen, R. J., Stark, J., Eisenson, T., Forrest, T., and Wertheim, G. Visual sequencing performance of aphasic children. *Journal of Speech and Hearing Research*, 1969, *12*, 288–300.

Preston, M. S., Guthrie, J. T., & Childs, B. Visual evoked responses (VERs) in normal and disabled readers. *Psychophysiology*, 1974, *11*, 452–457.

Preston, M. S., Guthrie, J. T., Kirsch, J. T., Gertman, D., & Childs, B. VERS in normal and disabled adult readers. *Psychophysiology*, 1977, *14*, 8–14.

Rapoport, J. L., Buchsbaum, M. S., Zahn, T. P., Weingartner, H., Ludlow, C., & Mikklesen, E. J. Dextroamphetamine: Cognitive and behavioral effects in normal prepuberal boys. *Science*, 1978, *199*, (4328), 560–563.

Rayner, K. Eye movements in reading and information processing. *Psychological Bulletin*, 1978, *85*, 618–660.

Risberg, J., Halsey, J. H., Wills, E. L., & Wilson, E. M. A hemispheric specialization in normal man studied by bilateral measurements of the regional cerebral blood flow: A study with the 133-3a inhalation technique. *Brain*, 1975, *98*(3), 511–524.

Rosenberger, P. B., & Hier, D. B. Cerebral asymmetry and verbal intellectual deficits. *Annals of Neurology*, 1980, *8*, 300–304.

Rosner, J. Language arts and arithmetic achievement and specifically related perceptual skills. *American Educational Research Journal*, 1973, *10*, 59–68.

Ross, J. J., Childers, D. G., & Perry, N. W. The natural history and electrophysiological characteristics of familial language dysfunction. In P. Satz & J. J. Ross (Eds.), *The disabled learner; Early intervention and treatment*. Rotterdam: University of Rotterdam Press, 1973.

Rourke, B. P., & Czudner, G. Age difference in auditory reaction time of brain damaged and normal children under regular and irregular preparatory internal conditions. *Journal of Experimental Child Psychology*, 1972, *14*, 527–539.

Rudnick, M., Sterritt, G. M., & Flax, M. Auditory and visual rhythm perception and rearing ability. *Child Development*, 1967, *37*, 581–587.

Sabatino, D. A. The house that Jack built. *Journal of Learning Disabilities*, 1983, *16*, 26–27.

Senf, G. M. Development of immediate memory for bisensory stimuli in normal children and children with learning disabilities. *Developmental Psychology*, 1969, *6*, 28.

Senf, G. M.,& Fesback, S. Development of bisensory memory in culturally deprived dyslexic and normal readers. *Journal of Educational Psychology*, 1970, *61*, 461–470.

Senf, G. M., & Freunal, P. C. Memory and attention factors in specific learning disabilities. *Journal of Learning Disabilities*, 1971, *4*, 94–106.

Silbergeld, E. K. Neuropharmacology of hyperkinesis. In W. B. Essman & L. Vasselli (Eds.), *Current developments in psychopharmacology*. New York: Spectrum, 1977.

Smith, C. M. The relationship of reading method and reading achievement to ITPA sensory modalities. *Journal of Special Education*, 1971, *5*, 143–149.

Steritt, G. M., & Rudnick, M. Auditory and visual rhythm perception in relation to reading ability in fourth grade boys. *Perceptual and Motor Skills*, 1966, *22*, 859–864.

Vellutino, F. F. Toward an understanding of dyslexia: Psychological factors in specific reading disabilities. In A. L. Benton & D. Pearl (Eds.), *Dyslexia: An appraisal of current knowledge*. New York: Oxford University Press, 1978.

Vellutino, F. F., Steger, J. A., Kaman, M., & Desetto, L. Visual form perception in deficient and normal readers. *Cortex*, 1975, *11*, 22–30.

Vellutino, F. F., Steger, J. A., & Kandel, G. Reading disability: An investigation of the perceptual deficit hypothesis. *Cortex*, 1972, *8*, 106–118.

Wada, J. A., Clarke, R., & Hamm, A. Cerebral hemispheric asymmetry in humans: Cortical speech zones in 100 adults and 100 infant brains. *Archives of Neurology*, 1975, *32*, 239–246.

Webb, E. M., & Lawson, L. The EEG in severe speech and reading disabilities of childhood. *Electroencephalography and Clinical Neurophysiology,* 1956, *8,* 168.

Wender, P. H. *Minimal brain dysfunction in children.* New York: Wiley, 1971.

Wender, P. H. A possible monoaminergic basis for minimal brain dysfunction. *Psychopharmacology Bulletin,* 1975, *11*(3), 36–37. (a)

Wender, P. H. The minimal brain dysfunction syndrome. *Annual Review of Medicine,* 1975, *26,* 45–62.(b)

Wender, P. H., & Wender, E. H. Minimal brain dysfunction myth. *American Journal of Diseases of Children,* 1976, *130* (8), 900–902.

Wepman, J. *Test of auditory discrimination.* Chicago: Language Research, 1958.

Whitaker, H. A., & Ojemann, G. A. Graded localization from electrical stimulation mapping of left cerebral cortex. *Nature,* 1977, *270* (5632), 50–51.

Wilshire, C., Atkins, G., & Manfield, P. Piracetam as an aid to learning in dyslexia. *Psychopharmacology,* 1979, *65,* 107–109.

Witelson, S. F., & Pallie, W. Left hemisphere specialization for language in the newborn: Neuroanatomical evidence of asymmetry. *Brain,* 1973, *96,* 641–646.

Witelson, S. F., & Rabinovitch, M. S. Hemispheric speech lateralization in children with auditory-linguistic deficits. *Cortex,* 1972, *8,* 412–426.

Wood, N. E. Auditory perception in children. Social and rehabilitation service research grant (RD-2574-S). Los Angeles: University of Southern California, 1971.

Yeni-Komshian, G., Isenberg, D., & Goldberg, H. Cerebral dominance and reading disability: Left visual field deficit in poor readers. *Neuropsychologia,* 1975, *13,* 83–94.

Ysseldyke, J. E., Algozzine, B., & Epps, S. *A logical and empirical analysis of current practices in classifying students as handicapped* (Research Report No. 92). Minneapolis: University of Minnesota Institute for Learning Disabilities, 1982.

Zangwill, O., & Blakemore, C. Dyslexia: Reversal of eye movements during reading. *Neuropsychologia,* 1972, *10,* 371–373.

Zurif, E. B., & Carson, G. Dyslexia in relation to cerebral dominance and temporal analysis. *Neuropsychologia,* 1970, *8,* 351–361.

CHAPTER 9

Neuropsychological Bases of Psychopathological Disorders

CHARLES J. GOLDEN and ROBERT F. SAWICKI

The purpose of this chapter is to review findings that suggest a relationship between various forms of psychopathology and an underlying brain impairment. The postulated brain impairment has been sought in biochemical abnormalities, structural differences, and dynamic metabolic differences. For clinicians the possible overlap between behavioral disorders and brain dysfunction, what has been called "organic brain syndrome," has presented both troublesome diagnostic issues as well as difficulties in determining intervention strategies. This chapter will focus on the empirically identified relationships between the schizophrenic syndromes, the affective disorders, and brain impairment. After reviewing such research, we will then consider the manner in which these findings may be related to developmental hypotheses.

THE SCHIZOPHRENIC SYNDROMES

DIAGNOSTIC ISSUES

It is customary to start discussions of schizophrenia with mention of Kraeplin and Bleuler and indicate their focus on *thought disorder* as central to any discussion of the schizophrenic disorders. In discussing schizophrenia in this chapter, the traditional concept of thought disorder

CHARLES J. GOLDEN • Department of Psychology, University of Nebraska Medical Center, Omaha, Nebraska 68105. ROBERT F. SAWICKI • Lake Erie Institute of Rehabilitation, Erie, Pennsylvania 16507.

will be reviewed in terms of a broader definition of a cognitive disorder that appears to have its basis in brain dysfunction. The initial review will focus on the relation between symptoms defined for the schizophrenic syndromes by the *Diagnostic and Statistical Manual of Mental Disorders* (3rd ed.) (DSM-III) (American Psychiatric Association, 1980) and brain impairment. The DSM-III identifies delusional thinking, hallucinatory sensory perceptions, incoherence, and loosening of goal-directed speech among the observable symptoms of schizophrenia. In addition, one expects to see evidence of a deterioration from a previous level of functioning and continuous signs of the illness for at least six months. It is of interest that according to the DSM-III criteria, attribution of any of these symptoms to an identified brain impairment suggests that one is not observing a schizophrenic disorder. Although this is an obvious attempt to avoid labeling neurologically impaired persons as schizophrenic, it does not deal with the issue that symptoms constituting a schizophrenia may themselves be representative of a particular type of brain dysfunction.

Before reviewing the DSM-III symptom list in the context of brain impairment, we must amplify the description of schizophrenia as a syndrome. The Gerard research paradigm (Gerard & Mattsson, 1963) assumes that the specific diagnostic category of schizophrenia covers a variety of disorders that may have diverse etiologies, but overtly share common manifestations. Investigations employing this model seek commonalities in biology and behavior that transcend etiologies and peripheral symptoms in order to identify pathognomonic markers that may be used diagnostically. From the point of view of this paradigm, brain impairment may be contiguous with, associated with, or the cause of the schizophrenic disorder. From a more psychodynamic view, Bellak (1979) describes schizophrenia as a final common pathway for any number of disorders that share disturbance in ego functioning as the central symptom.

BRAIN IMPAIRMENT AND DSM-III CRITERIA

The symptomatology listed in the DSM-III diagnostic criteria may be reorganized into the following superordinate categories: cognitive/perceptual disturbances (delusions), language and language-related disturbances (circumstantiality, looseness of association, etc.), sensory disturbances (hallucinations), and praxic disturbance (behavioral disorganization). Individually, and in combinations, these disturbances may be related to a wide variety of brain-related diseases.

These symptoms also may be viewed in terms of an underlying dimension, that is, a disturbance in the executive functions of the brain: what Luria (1980) termed *tertiary functions.* Holzman (1978) supports a similar conceptualization of findings related to schizophrenia in a review of research which reinterprets the cognitive disturbance of schizophrenia as a disinhibition syndrome. He points out that when the language of schizophrenics is observed, several inferences may be made about both the language and the underlying thought processes of schizophrenics. (a) The rules of thought as expressed by language remain. A thought disorder may be identified despite the preservation of overall cognitive structures. (b) Thought disorders may be described as rate phenomena; that is, the disturbance is not constantly present across contexts. (c) Thought disorder is not unique to the schizophrenic syndromes. Cognitive slippage may occur among a variety of individuals including, under certain circumstances, persons with no diagnosable disorder. From this observation, Holzman infers that the extreme thought disturbance observed in schizophrenics may be placed on a continuum with normal thinking.

Holzman cites several sources of support for such a view. In a study of schizophrenics and their first-degree relatives, 65 to 80% of schizophrenic persons and 45% of their first-degree relatives show a disturbance in smooth visual pursuit (Holzman, Proctor, Levy, Yasillo, Meltzer, & Hurt, 1974). This and subsequent studies observed the relationship in performance by such persons for both smooth pursuit movements (those which are observed when a subject visually tracks a moving object, e.g., a pendulum) and saccadic eye movements (the quick eye movements a subject would use to move visual focus from one object to another). In this series of studies, the saccadic eye movements showed no impairment for the samples in which smooth pursuit was impaired (Holzman, 1978; Holzman, Proctor, & Hughes, 1973; Shagass, Amadeo, & Overton, 1974). This may be due to the inability of subjects to inhibit rapid saccadic motions during the smooth pursuit task.

The performance of schizophrenic persons could be improved by superimposing a vivid, attentional cue on the pursuit object (Holzman, 1978), suggesting that a basic difficulty involves the schizophrenics' inability to spontaneously maintain functional levels of attention. Additional investigations also indicate that providing external feedback serves to limit pathological behavioral displays. Holzman and Rousey (1971) note that schizophrenic communication shows markedly more aggressive, hostile, and sexual themes during periods when they are not monitoring their speech in comparison to times when they are able to monitor their language. The inference drawn from this series of research suggests that what one observes in the schizophrenic disorders is a disinhibition syndrome that affects a range of behaviors (Holzman, 1978). In such a model, cognitive impairment becomes one of many examples of such disinhibition.

The model described by Holzman is strongly reminiscent of the effects of frontal damage described by Luria (1980). Specifically, Luria states that

> the plan of action that is selected quickly loses its regulating function on behavior as a whole and is replaced by perseveration of one particular link of the motor act or by the influence of some connection established during the patient's past experience. (Adams & Victor, 1981, p. 303)

Luria's model has been criticized for lack of empirical support in terms of both neuropsychological and physiological evidence (Adams & Victor, 1981); however, such criticisms were unprepared for recent findings that appear to support Luria's postulates regarding frontal area functioning and the inferences that suggest that brain dysfunction is an underlying component of schizophrenia.

NEUROPSYCHOLOGICAL INVESTIGATIONS OF THE SCHIZOPHRENIC SYNDROMES

PROBLEMS IN INVESTIGATIONS OF BRAIN IMPAIRMENT AND SCHIZOPHRENIA

Before reviewing several studies that describe a relationship between schizophrenic disorders and a pattern of neuropsychological deficits, some of the limitations to such investigations will be identified.

Diagnostic Issues. The unreliability of psychiatric diagnosis is a basic issue that is raised constantly in the criticism of any study involving behaviorally disturbed subjects. When the study also involves the analysis of brain impairment, the degree to which samples have been neurologically screened and the form which that screening has taken become equally important issues. Lack of diagnostic controls is a basic fault in studies that seem to assume that schizophrenia and brain impairment are mutually exclusive and therefore do not neurologically screen members of the schizophrenic sample. Thus studies must be read carefully for the definition of the criteria by which diagnoses were made. In studies that focus on demonstrations of brain impairment, the neurological and neuropsychological screening devices need to be described and applied equally to all components of the subject population.

Malec (1978) cites the omission of separate hit rates for neurologically defined subjects and schizophrenic subjects as an error that undermines the interpretability of findings. Newlin (1983) extends this argument to include the need to publish differential accuracy rates for the separate neurophychological tests employed in order to interpret findings meaningfully, since one may *not* assume that all tests identified as "neuropsychological" evaluate the same behavioral functions and lead to the same interpretation.

Sampling Issues. The method of subject selection for studies considering the relationship of brain impairment and schizophrenia provides the greatest threat to internal validity. Several common mediating factors may enter such selection, when not directly considered by the investigator: (a) duration of illness (chronic vs. acute) between groups; (b) length of institutionalization; (c) type and extent of involvement in treatment; and (d) type and dosage of psychoactive medication. To these, Newlin (1983) adds the effects of age and premorbid intellectual level. Intellectual level raises an especially critical issue for the interpretation of the results of an investigation when subjects are matched by intellectual performance (e.g., Wechsler Adult Intelligence Scale [WAIS] IQ). As has been pointed out by Heaton and Crowley (1981), the WAIS is itself sensitive to brain impairment and such matching may obscure differences when groups are later compared on neuropsychological variables. However, since one may observe significant relationships between intellectual performance and certain neuropsychological tests (Wiens & Matarazzo, 1977), the use of premorbid estimates can only be reiterated as a way to remove the effects of differential cognitive abilities in such studies.

APPLICATIONS OF NEUROPSYCHOLOGICAL INSTRUMENTS WITH SCHIZOPHRENICS

The basic question that is present when psychometric instruments are applied to schizophrenic populations is whether the cognitive impairment evident in the schizophrenic will obscure findings to the point that no pattern of performance will emerge that is identifiable as consistent with brain dysfunction. Wiens and Matarazzo (1977) restate this to ask: At what intensity of emotional disturbance will neuropsychological performance be affected?

To respond to this issue, schizophrenic samples have been compared with neurologically impaired samples using several procedures. Two general results have been observed: (a) impairment in functioning of the anterior area of the dominant hemisphere (e.g., Flor-Henry, 1976; Flor-Henry & Yeudall, 1979; Flor-Henry, Fromm-Auch, & Schopflocher, 1983) and (b) bilateral anterior dysfunction (e.g., Alpert & Martz, 1977; Taylor & Abrams, 1983). Some of the discrepancy among findings has been explained in terms of the assessment procedures used; that is, when single tests are used, one is more likely to identify anterior, dominant dysfunction, whereas test batteries tend to produce results more consistent with bilateral anterior dysfunction (Taylor & Abrams, 1983). As an alternative to both sets of results, Scarone, Gambini, and Pieri (1983) suggest that in chronic patients, the observed frontal deficits are manifestations of a more basic temporolimbic disturbance. A defect of the corpus callosum also has been postulated as a basis of the disorder (Rosenthal & Bigelow, 1972). In order to place these findings in a context, several assessment instruments as well as test batteries will be reviewed.

Wechsler Adult Intelligence Scale. Two types of studies that describe a relationship between WAIS performance and schizophrenia may be found in the literature: those which observe deficit patterns and those which review classification accuracy after such deficit patterns have been translated into classification rules. DeWolfe, Barrell, Becker, and Spaner (1971) contrasted a group of schizophrenics with a sample of bilaterally, brain-damaged patients and found a specific pattern of Comprehension deficit in both younger and older schizophrenics. The older group also is reported to show a specific impairment in Picture Completion, whereas Block Design remained relatively spared. This pattern of findings was refined and implemented as a set of identification rules (De Wolfe, 1971). Using 50 chronic schizophrenics and 50 diffusely brain-impaired subjects, an overall accuracy rate of 75% was identified, with a hit rate of 72% for schizophrenics and 78% for neurologically impaired subjects. A replication study (Watson, 1972) of these rules produced mixed results. A sample of 40 chronic schizophrenics and 40 organic brain syndrome patients produced a hit rate of 74%, with 73% for schizophrenics and 75% for the mixed organic brain syndrome group, whereas another sample with 50 subjects in each group did not improve classification beyond chance. A further refinement of these rules by Golden (1977) optimized the hit rate. Lower classification rates were identified by Chelune, Heaton, Lehman, and Robinson (1979) when either WAIS level of performance or WAIS deficit pattern scores were used. From such investigations, one may infer that the WAIS subscale pattern alone is of questionable utility in discriminating brain-impaired persons from schizophrenic persons.

If one attends to which subscales appear relatively spared and which show decrements, a pattern begins to emerge among studies. Beginning with the investigation by Dewolfe *et al.* (1971), low scores for the Comprehension subtest in relation to the scores for performance measures were observed. Such deficits must be seen in the greater context of more general decrements in the verbal subscales of the WAIS for schizophrenics. When Flor-Henry (1976) reviewed his findings which indicated lower verbal IQ among schizophrenics when compared with affective disorders, he found that Vocabulary and Digit Span were major contributors to the significant differences between groups. Similar findings were noted by Abrams, Redfield, and Taylor (1981), who demonstrated that the full-scale IQ of schizophrenics was significantly lower when compared with two other psychotic groups. Follow-up analysis indicated that impaired Comprehension, Similarities, and Vocabulary scores ($p < .01$) among the schizophrenics accounted for the majority of the difference among groups. Approaching the same issue from another direction, Gruzelier, Mednick, and Schulsinger (1979) compared 140 boys and girls between the ages of 10 and 13, who were at risk for schizophrenia (at least one parent had been diagnosed as schizophrenic) with matched control children. Their results indicated that the "at risk" children had significantly lower verbal IQs.

Thus, although performance patterns from the WAIS do not appear sufficient to discriminate schizophrenic subjects from brain-impaired subjects, a pattern of deficits for schizophrenic subjects does recur for WAIS IQ scores and their underlying subscales.

Halstead–Reitan Neuropsychological Battery. Like the literature on the WAIS, studies employing the Halstead–Reitan Neuropsychological Battery (HRNB) also focus on attempts either to identify classification rules or patterns of impairment; however, in the case of the HRNB, attempts to provide classification rules predominate. Heaton, Baade, and Johnson (1978) reviewed studies published prior to 1975 and reported two discrepant findings: the accuracy rate for modified versions of the HRNB was 75%, when discerning nonschizophrenic psychiatric patients from brain-impaired subjects; in contrast, discriminating chronic schizophrenics from brain-impaired subjects was only slightly beyond chance, 54%. Similar findings were noted in an updated study by Heaton and Crowley (1978). These findings suggest that the difficulty in accurate discrimination may lie not in the test battery but in the meaning of the results. Several reviewers (Goldstein, 1978; Heaton *et al.*, 1978; Malec, 1978) interpret these results as a demonstration of an underlying cerebral deficit in schizophrenia. Such an inference is made due to the similarity in performance between schizophrenics and brain-damaged subjects, whereas accurate discrimination occurs between brain-damaged and nonschizophrenic psychiatric patients for the same tasks.

Improvement in classification accuracy was noted when multivariate statistical classification rules were combined with a standard set of HRNB measures. Golden (1977) reports an accuracy rate of 100% for psychiatric patients and 94% for neurologic patients consequent to a discriminant function analysis. This study was used to generate optimal cutoff scores when the HRNB is used to identify brain damage in a psychiatric population. Due to their being generated on an acute sample and the application of classification analysis to the same sample from which the rules were generated, cross validation is necessary before the generalizable accuracy of these rules may be stated.

Another study that reports an improved accuracy for the HRNB is that of Donnelly, Weinberger, Waldman, and Wyatt (1980). These investigators attempted to predict the presence of computed tomography (CT) ventricular abnormality (Weinberger, Torrey, Neophytides, & Wyatt, 1979) from HRNB performance for a group of 15 chronic schizophrenics. Unlike many of the earlier studies, Donnelly et al. (1980) demonstrated a hit rate of 80%, suggesting both a direction for future investigations as well as the potential of the HRNB. This study also reiterates the relationship between subgroups of schizophrenics and demonstrable brain damage.

Looking at this relationship from another point of view, Flor-Henry (1983a; Flor-Henry et al., 1983) describes an elaborate study that analyzed the performance of 172 psychiatric patients and 193 matched controls for 30 neuropsychological tests, which included not only the HRNB and the WAIS, but also Raven's Matrices, Oral Word Fluency, Memory for Designs, Purdue Pegboard, L.J. Tactile Recognition, Written Word Fluency, and the Wisconsin Card Sorting test. Subjects represented both neurotic and psychotic depression, mania, and schizophrenia. Only right-handed, nonmedicated persons between ages 16 and 65, whose history indicated absence of neurological disease including seizures or head injury, were included. Analysis of the data included not only statistical discrimination procedures but also blind clinical interpretation of the protocols. Clinical ratings were performed according to methods described by Reitan (Reitan & Davison, 1974). Results were consistent with a dominant frontal impairment in both schizophrenia and mania. An unexpected finding of this study was an interaction between gender and dysfunction. The dominant anterior dysfunction for mania and schizophrenia was found only in males, whereas the nondominant impairment among depressive psychoses was identified only for females. Thus Flor-Henry (1983a), although identifying confirmation for his earlier work; also opens questions for future investigations.

One may summarize the studies with the HRNB to suggest that the basic issue is not how accurate the HRNB is in discriminating brain-impaired subjects from schizophrenics, but what kinds of deficits does the HRNB describe that are indicative to brain dysfunction among certain classes of schizophrenics.

Luria-Nebraska Neuropsychological Battery. The Luria-Nebraska Neuropsychological Battery (LNNB) is a set of standardized procedures (Golden, Hammeke, & Purisch, 1980) that capitalize on the tasks identified by Luria (1980) as discriminating between brain-impaired and unimpaired persons. Moreover, the pattern of deficits that appears among the various tasks is useful to identify the probable brain area whose damage underlies observed dysfunction. Validational investigation has demonstrated high accuracy rates, based on the results of discriminant analysis, for discerning the performance of neurologic from that of schizophrenic patients (88%) (Purisch, Golden, & Hammeke, 1978). A cross validation of this study yielded similar results. Moses and Golden (1980) applied the earlier Purisch *et al.* (1978) equation and accurately identified 87% of their sample. The subjects of the Moses and Golden study had been screened to include only those without positive neurological signs of brain damage in the schizophrenic sample.

The Pathognomonic scale showed best discrimination ability, whereas the Rhythm, Receptive Speech, Memory, and Intelligence scales did not discriminate schizophrenic subjects from neurologic subjects. The Pathognomonic scale is composed of items that are purported to be sensitive to acute brain impairment (Golden *et al.*, 1980). Neurologic subjects scored significantly higher on this scale.

Since neurologic subjects scored consistently higher on the LNNB scales when compared with this schizophrenic sample, which had longer durations of hospitalization, institutionalization cannot adequately explain the results. A further study by Lewis, Golden, Purisch, and Hammeke (1979) also found no significant effects on LNNB scores associated with length of hospitalization.

Luria-Nebraska Neuropsychological Battery performance also has been linked to CT scan findings. When Golden, Moses, Zelazowski, Graber, Zata, Horvath, and Berger (1980) investigated the relationship between ventricular enlargement and LNNB scaled scores, a multiple correlation of .72 was identified. Of the eight scales showing significant positive relationships with increased ventricular size, the Pathognomonic scale showed the highest correlation. The scales that failed to accurately discriminate subjects in the two earlier studies (Moses & Golden, 1980; Purisch *et al.*, 1978) were the four remaining scores. When optimized actuarial rules were used to classify protocols as predicting enlarged ventricular area, an accuracy rate of 85% was achieved (Golden *et al.*, 1980). Golden summarized these results and earlier findings to suggest that in young, chronic schizophrenics, LNNB scores are the result of actual brain damage rather than distractibility or institutionalization (Newlin, 1983).

A final classification study (Kane, Sweet, Golden, Parsons, & Moses, 1981) observed the ability of expert clinicians to rate blindly the LNNB and HRNB protocols of 23 mixed psychiatric subjects, including 18 schizophrenics, and 23 mixed neurologic subjects as brain impaired or unimpaired. The LNNB and HRNB demonstrated comparable results, with both batteries showing accuracy rates well above chance. Like the HRNB, the LNNB offers a way to observe performance suggestive of brain impairment among schizophrenics.

Throughout the preceding sections, several studies have been cited that indicate relationships between results of neuropsychological tests and more direct evidence of cerebral impairment. The following sections will review radiographic and electropotential studies that suggest structural and dynamic dysfunction in the brains of schizophrenics.

NEUROANATOMICAL MARKERS OF SCHIZOPHRENIA

PNEUMOENCEPHALOGRAM STUDIES

The *pneumoencephalogram* (PEG) is a radiographic technique used to picture the ventricular system. Air is injected into the ventricular system, then scanned by x-ray. Thus PEG is useful to demonstrate increases in ventricular size. An extensive review of PEG studies related to schizophrenia was recently published by Seidman (1983). Several consistent trends are evident in the studies described within this review.

1. Schizophrenics primarily demonstrate ventricular enlargement suggestive of diffuse subcortical atrophy rather than focal disease, which was more evident among mixed psychiatric patients, or marked cortical abnormalities, which are found among comparison neurologic controls (Haug, 1962).
2. The degree of intellectual and personality disintegration correlates positively with severity of ventricular enlargement (Asano, 1967; Haug, 1962; Huber, 1957; Lemke, 1936), as does overall adaptive impairment (Haug, 1962; Kiev, Chapman, Guthrie, & Wolff, 1962; Lonnum, 1966).
3. In comparison to autopsy data, PEG findings suggest that cerebral changes are a component of the schizophrenic process and a biological marker of the dementia noted in the disorder (Seidman, 1983).

COMPUTER-ASSISTED TRANSAXIAL TOMOGRAPHY

Like PEG, the CT scan provides a static image of cranial structures; however, unlike PEG, the CT scan offers the possibility of identifying specific areas of dysfunction by relatively more direct observation rather than inference alone. Thus, while PEG suggests cerebral atrophy, the CT scan indicates the likely basis of such atrophy. A limitation of such observation is the dynamic homeostasis that is maintained within the cranium between tissue and fluid; that is, sulci may increase in size from any portion of the brain atrophying without direct suggestion that it is the specific tissue surrounding that sulcus which has lost neuronal matter.

Computed tomography studies focusing on ventricular enlargement have produced findings that are supportive of earlier PEG results (Seidman, 1983). In addition to increased ventricular area, investigations have noted cortical atrophy (Golden, Graber, Coffman, Berg, Newlin, & Bloch, 1981; Rieder, Donnelly, Herdt, & Waldman, 1979), reversed cerebral asymmetry (Luchins, Weinberger, & Wyatt, 1982), and cerebellar atrophy (Weinberger, Torrey, & Wyatt, 1979). Seidman (1983) points out, however, that ventricular enlargement is by far the most common abnormality cited. He also indicates that the "prevalence" of this finding across studies appears to be a function of differences in measurement techniques, the definition of ventricular enlargement, differential sample characteristics (especially age, chronicity, and severity of illness), and specification of control groups.

As already stated, the finding of ventricular enlargement is only indicative of the probability of atrophy somewhere in the brain without specifying the actual cite of abnormality. Weinberger and Wyatt (1980) report several differences in brain structure that suggest possible areas of lesions. Chronic schizophrenics showed greater widths for the sylvian fissure ($p < .005$), the interhemispheric fissure ($p < .05$), and the mean width of the cortical sulci in general ($p < .01$) when compared with controls. The sylvian abnormality was the most common finding among the schizophrenic subjects. Weinberger and Wyatt note that their findings could not be explained by either demographic data or histories of alcohol abuse, electroconvulsive therapy (ECT), or length of illness. An unexpected finding in their study was a subgroup of 10 schizophrenics with atrophy of the anterior cerebellar vermis. The latter finding is consistent with other research that suggests interaction between the anterior cerebellar vermis and parts of the limbic system, which have been implicated in relation to schizophrenia (Snider, Maiti, & Snider, 1976). Although these differences appear to suggest specific areas of dysfunction among schizophrenics, no single area or pattern has been associated consistently with the schizophrenic disorder. Other investigators have identified density differences (atrophy) in the anterior dominant hemisphere (Golden et al., 1981). As reported earlier by Teuber (1972) and re-emphasized by Melnechuk (1980), it is unlikely that a single lesion will explain the schizophrenic disorder; the observable disorder may be more likely the expression of a pattern of brain disturbances.

Several studies have reported behavioral anomalies in association with CT findings. Luchins, Weinberger, and Wyatt (1979) observed that schizophrenics demonstrating reversed asymmetry (larger left than right frontal area and larger right than left occipital area) also demonstrated lower verbal than performance IQ when compared with those with normal asymmetry. Andreasen, Olsen, Dennert, and Smith (1982) observed that schizophrenics with enlarged ventricles showed more negative symptoms—that is, behavioral absences (e.g., flat affect, loss of motivation, anhedonia, etc.)—whereas those with smaller ventricles were more likely to show positive symptoms (e.g., active thought disorder, delusions, hallucinations, etc.). Seidman (1983) summarizes these findings and others to suggest that subgroups may be present among individuals in which schizophrenic symptoms are observed: (a) those without an observable brain structure abnormality; (b) those with enlarged ventricles and inferred cortical atrophy; and (c) those with atypical brain asymmetries. To these groups may be added individuals with dominant anterior atrophy and schizophrenics with atrophy of the anterior cerebellar vermis. Although such classifications may be useful to stimulate future investigations, they do not respond to the issue of the relationship between observed structural anomalies and schizophrenic behavior. The inconsistency among CT investigation results awaits standardization both in methods of CT interpretation as well as CT measurement before comparable results are truly produced across studies. A second issue is the need to include neuropsychological (behavioral) descriptions of the samples that are observed by the CT procedure, so that structural differences are not observed in a vacuum. With the development of more powerful, noninvasive techniques (i.e, nuclear magnetic resonance scanning), the need to provide more than just biologically interesting data becomes even more important.

Computed tomography-based studies also are limited by the fact that unless dynamic CT scanning is done, the CT, like the PEG produces a static picture of the brain, which may be missing differential metabolic activity in the brains of schizophrenics. The electroencephalogram (EEG), cerebral blood flow (CBF), and positron emission tomography (PET scan) techniques provide some methods of observing differential brain activity.

ELECTROENCEPHALOGRAM

The EEG is a record of amplified, constantly changing electrical potential taken from the scalp. Electrical potentials are assumed to originate in the cerebral cortex as slow postsynaptic potentials (Creuzfeldt, 1974). The pattern observed in the EEG frequencies is assumed to parallel changes in brain activation during various mental states. Alpha activity (average frequency) suggests a resting state, whereas theta (low frequency) is associated with drowsiness and beta activity (high frequency) indicates sensory or cognitive stimulation. A given brain area may be enhanced to produce a certain kind of frequency (e.g., left parietal beta activity is enhanced by reading during the EEG [Osborne & Gale, 1976]). The EEG pattern is observed for shifts that cannot be attributed to change in mental sets; for example, focal sharp waves, high-voltage spikes, or dysrhythmia (Buchsbaum, 1979).

Among schizophrenics the trend has been to identify greater beta activity in resting, off-medication individuals (Itil, Saletu, & Davis, 1972; Itil, Saletu, Davis, & Allen, 1974; Lifshitz & Gradijan, 1972; Rodin, Grisell, & Gottlieb, 1968). Children at risk for the disorder have shown a similar pattern (Itil, 1977; Itil, Saletu, Hsu, & Mednick, 1974). The latter finding suggests that the EEG pattern may preexist the observable disorder (Buchsbaum, 1979). In a careful study that attempted to deal with many of the criticisms of previous EEG research, Itil (1980) again found the pattern of increased background beta activity. Two aspects make this study important. First, a large sample was employed (100 schizophrenics and 100 matched normals) and diagnosis was clearly defined. Second, computer-assisted analysis was performed on the EEG results.

Ancillary findings to this study demonstrated that schizophrenics could be differentiated from the controls ($p < .005$) using a multiple discriminant analysis. In addition, the EEG differences in comparison to normal controls continued when schizophrenics were tested at weekly and at monthly intervals (Itil et al., 1972). Thus the EEG differences cannot be attributed to acute symptoms or hospitalization variables.

Although no specific pattern of EEG abnormality identifies schizophrenics (Seidman, 1983), when focal disturbance is observed, it is usually bilateral temporal slowing (Abenson, 1970; Fenton, Fenwick, Dollimore, Dunn, & Hirsch, 1980). Studies involving spectral analysis of EEG recordings also have noted a greater proportion of power in the beta activity of the left hemisphere in contrast to the right hemisphere for schizophrenics when compared with normal subjects (Flor-Henry, Koles, Bo-Lassen, & Yeudall, 1975). A left hemisphere discrepancy also was noted among individuals diagnosed as schizophrenic with no family history of schizophrenia (Hays, 1977). Thus, although not prevalent across all samples, the suggestion of a dominant hemisphere dysfunction also arises among EEG findings.

CEREBRAL BLOOD FLOW

Like the EEG, CBF techniques describe dynamic brain activity. This technique is based on the observed relationship between cerebral energy metabolism in a given area and increased blood flow to that area. As a given area is activated during a task, glucose and oxygen consumption increase, resulting in increased blood flow to the area. Two major methods of measurement exist. The first is an intra-arterial clearance technique (Lassen & Ingvar, 1972), in which a bolus incorporating a marked isotope (xenon 133) is injected into an internal carotid artery. Measurements are then taken to record the arrival of the marked material and its washout interval at various locations. A battery of 64 detectors is placed on one side of the head. Since only one side of the head is done at a time, this presents a limitation to the technique. The alternate method is to have a subject breathe oxygen in a room which also contains small amounts of xenon 133 gas. Again, a washout interval is recorded. Newer techniques allow for measurement from both hemispheres simultaneously.

In normal subjects, the results of such measurement indicate high neuronal activity in precentral regions with the subject apparently at rest (Ingvar, 1980), whereas postcentral regions show significantly lower activity. Ingvar (1980) suggests that such findings in normal subjects indicate that the resting conscious state is accompanied by inhibition of trivial sensory input, whereas cognitive activity reviews past action and prepares for future performance. Such an interpretation is supported by findings that indicate that such frontal activity disappears during general anesthesia and coma (Ingvar & Gadea Ciria, 1975); thus the noted frontal activity is not merely a rest artifact.

In contrast to normal subjects, one observes hypofrontal activity in schizophrenics at rest with hyperarousal in postcentral sensory and association areas (Ingvar, 1980). Such findings indicate that schizophrenics may be unable to inhibit trivial stimulation and are constantly bombarded by auditory, visual, and somatosensory stimuli that are ignored by normal subjects. Ingvar (1980) postulates that such unrelenting stimulation may lead to sensory overflow, heightened anxiety, and general disruption of planful activity. Ingvar's findings appear unrelated to age or neuroleptic treatment (Ingvar, 1976).

In a study comparing regional cerebral blood flow (rCBF) of chronic schizophrenics with that of volunteer, normal controls, Ariel, Golden, Berg, Quaife, Dirksen, Forsell, Wilson, and Graber (1983) found that schizophrenics not only demonstrated lower overall flows when compared with normal subjects, but also showed reduced anterior in comparison to posterior flow. These findings were unrelated to educational level, gender, or medication dosage.

POSITRON EMISSION TRANSAXIAL TOMOGRAPHY

Recent studies measuring local glucose metabolism by means of positron emission transaxial tomography (PETT) scan demonstrate findings consistent with earlier CBF investigations (Buchsbaum, Ingvar, Kessler, Waters, Cappelletti, van Kammen, King, Johnson, Manning, Flynn, Mann, Bunney, & Sokoloff, 1982; Farkas, Reivich, Alavi, Greenberg, Fowler, MacGregor, Christman, & Wolf, 1980). Behaviorally, increased perceptual dysfunction was positively related to postcentral blood flow and negatively related to frontal irrigation (Ingvar, 1980; Seidman, 1983). Negative symptoms were more correlated with decreased frontal flow (Ingvar, 1976, 1980; Seidman, 1983).

THE AFFECTIVE DISORDERS

The association between affective disturbances and brain impairment has been less intensely and articulately studied than similar considerations in relation to schizophrenia. Several reasons may be postulated for this difference in research focus. (a) Except when extreme or manic, depressive symptoms are much less attention arousing than schizophrenic symptoms; (b) many more individuals have had intimate experience with depression and may assume that episodes are a normal part of life, thus a relationship with brain dysfunction would be antithetical; (c) intuitively acceptable antecedent causes may be cited in many cases; (d) forms of depression appear reversable with psychotherapy and chemotherapy; and (e) the majority of research in affective disorders has focused on hormonal imbalance and pharmaceutical treatment issues.

In a partial review by Fromm-Auch (1983), the support for a relationship between affective disturbance and brain dysfunction is based on findings that indicate greater likelihood of affective (depressive) signs in both children (Shaffer, Bijur, & Chadwick, 1981) and adults (Ross & Rush, 1981) after right frontal injuries. Pathological weeping is more likely after anterior, nondominant injuries, whereas uncontrolled laughing is more evident with dominant hemisphere trauma (Fromm-Auch, 1983). A pattern of affective impairment, including mood lability, dysthymia, and overt depressive symptoms has been identified in concert with a nondominant focus for seizure activity (Flor-Henry, 1969). Ross and Rush (1981) postulate an "aprosodic" disorder for nondominant disturbance to parallel "aphasic" disturbances that are often associated with dominant hemisphere impairment. Aprosody refers to the inability to modulate behavior. Monotonic speech is a good example of such a disturbance. In the case of an affective disorder, aprosody would be expressed as the inability to modulate emotional response. The majority of investigations, however, have been performed to describe more general brain activity in relation to normal emotional expression. Inferences from these studies have then been used to describe the probable brain concomitants of a major affective disorder.

DIAGNOSTIC ISSUES

On review of Lishman's (1978) book or Jefferson and Marshall's (1981) text, one will note that depression may be a related or consequent condition of a multitude of brain-related pathological conditions. Although one may phenomenologically explain some of these associations as a common reaction to injury or serious disease, the existence of such findings muddies the possibility of describing a pattern of brain impairment that is intimately linked to depression and affective disturbance in general.

The DSM-III describes major depressive disorder as characterized by dysphoric mood, hypoactivity, loss of interest in usual activities; changes in eating, sleeping, or sexual habits; rumination over feelings of worthlessness or guilt, which may take on delusional magnitude; and delusions, hallucinations, or bizarre behavior may occur, although they will not dominate the clinical picture. *Manic episodes* are described as distinct periods during which an elevated, expansive, or irritable mood predominates. Delusional grandiosity may be present, as well as flight of ideas, motor restlessness, pressured speech, and distractibility.

A brief review of these characteristics suggests easily observable overlap between affective and schizophrenic disturbances. Such an observation is consistent with existing literature. Flor-Henry (1983a) states that a categorical, independent disease hypothesis is not supported when comparisons are made of persons with manic-depressive illness and others diagnosed as schizophrenic. Flor-Henry concludes that psychoses may be a better descriptive category with schizophrenia and affective disorder as dimensional representations of such a unitary category.

Flor-Henry bases such an interpretation on earlier findings that indicate an absence of a region of rarity between schizophrenic and manic-depressive disorders when an attempt was made to identify differentiating symptoms with a discriminant function analysis (Brockington, Kendall, & Wainwright, 1980; Brockington, Kendall, Wainwright, Hiller, & Walker, 1980; Kendall & Brockington, 1980). The research surrounding the symptomatology of the schizoaffective disorders lends further support for a probable underlying continuum rather than discrete categories of disorders (Cohen, Allen, Pollin, & Hurbec, 1972; Welner, Croughan, Fishman, & Robins, 1977; WHO, 1975).

The conclusions drawn from these additional findings serve to reiterate a point made earlier: affective and schizophrenic diagnoses may more aptly represent two dimensions rather than discrete pathological categories (Flor-Henry, 1983a). As an alternative, Jablensky (1981) suggests diagnostic categorization based on severity of the presenting symptoms, trends observable in the process of the disorder, and social adaptiveness. To these, Flor-Henry (1983a) adds the presence of bipolarity and gender and age of onset as interacting variables. In summary, these findings indicate that what have been considered traditional differences between affective and schizophrenic disorders may for the most part be the result of both conceptual limitations and research design artifacts. The differences between these psychopathological dimensions may be more aptly described as differences in end-state emphasis, which in terms of the relationship to underlying brain impairment may be a result of subtle differences in systems that are dysfunctional as well subtle differences in the way individual brains are premorbidly organized.

NEUROPSYCHOLOGICAL INVESTIGATIONS OF AFFECTIVE DISORDERS

Many of the threats that affect studies of schizophrenic samples also affect studies of persons who are affectively disturbed. In addition, Carpenter (1983) cites several other threats to the validity of studies focusing on mood disturbances.

1. Although schizoaffectives bear a close resemblance to persons classified as manic-depressive and may even represent a special case of manic-depressive disorder, their uncited inclusion confounds the meaning of derived results.
2. Affectively disordered persons will or will not look brain impaired depending on the heterogeneity of the neurologic comparison group that is employed: they will look less like brain-impaired subjects in comparison to groups composed generally of dominant hemisphere dysfunctions, but will look more like brain-impaired persons in samples generally composed of nondominant hemisphere disorders.
3. Similarly, the instruments selected will affect whether or not mood-disturbed subjects appear brain damaged: instruments sensitive to nondominant hemisphere functioning are more likely to pick up disordered performance than those representative of dominant hemisphere functioning.
4. Comparison samples that do not allow for a normal, nonbehaviorally disturbed group offer the probability of producing results that cannot be meaningfully interpreted: one will not be able to determine if group differences, should they occur, are the result of impairment in the affectively disturbed group or the comparison psychiatrically disturbed group.

WECHSLER ADULT INTELLIGENCE SCALE

The general trend in performance differences suggests that performance IQ will be lower than verbal IQ for affective disorders. Such findings have been documented for adults (Flor-Henry, 1983b), children (Brumback & Staton, 1980; Sackheim & Decina, 1983), and children at risk (Flor-Henry, 1983a). No particular pattern of subscale results, as has earlier been cited with schizophrenia, is evident. These findings, given Flor-Henry's (1983a) results, suggest a disorder that preexists the overt symptoms.

HALSTEAD-REITAN NEUROPSYCHOLOGICAL BATTERY

After reviewing the literature that reported HRNB patterns among affectively disordered persons, Carpenter (1983) concluded that the majority of melancholics who participated in the reviewed studies tended to produce results that were suggestive of mild brain impairment. Again, performance during nonverbal tasks was more likely to produce results similar to that of brain-damaged subjects. Notably, affectives were observed to show impaired performance for the Trails B and Trails A + B, Tactual Performance Test (TPT) Localization and Memory, and nonpreferred-hand finger oscillation (Flor-Henry & Yeudall, 1979). Such findings are consistent with earlier research that indicates that when a mixed group of depressives and a mixed group of neurologic patients are equated on ability, differences for neuropsychological tests sensitive to nondominant dysfunction disappear, whereas significant differential performance for Scale 2 (Depression) of the Minnesota Multiphasic Personality Inventory (MMPI) remains (Watson, Davis, & Gasser, 1978).

Findings with other instruments usually applied in neuropsychological investigations support the previously cited data. For example, Orme, Lee, and Smith (1964) found many false positives for depressives when verbal/nonverbal discrepancy scores, which were computed from the Mill Hill Vocabulary score minus the Raven's Colored Progressive Matrices score, were used to classify neurologic, schizophrenic, and melancholic patients as brain impaired. Silverstein and Meltzer (1983) compared the functioning of both affectives and schizophrenics for both the HRNB and LNNB. Their results indicate that the two batteries performed comparably.

In contrast to other studies but consistent with diagnostic issues raised earlier, Silverstein and Meltzer describe findings that do not demonstrate clear left anterior findings for schizophrenics and clear nondominant disturbance for affectives. Although the HRNB showed greater differentiation between diagnostic groups for performance usually associated with the right hemisphere (but not the left), affectively disturbed subjects showed a greater than expected left hemisphere dysfunction for this battery. Consistent with earlier findings, however, when anterior left dysfunction was observed, it was predominantly among schizophrenics for both batteries. The results of this study raise the point that reporting specific (lateralized) dysfunction between these two psychopathological dimensions may be premature. A similar interpretation is offered by Taylor and Abrams (1983), who report bilateral dysfunction among schizophrenics. Carpenter (1983) summarizes the majority of this research to indicate that although one may expect to find impaired performance for tasks usually associated with right hemisphere function, when dominant hemisphere tasks are included in the test protocol, deficits are also observed, although these ae usually milder than the nondominant hemisphere deficits.

NEUROANATOMICAL INDICATORS OF AFFECTIVE DISORDERS

COMPUTER-ASSISTED TRANSAXIAL TOMOGRAPHY

At present, the availability of CT studies with affectives is limited. There is some suggestion, however, that enlarged ventricles also are observed among affectively disturbed persons (Pearlson & Veroff, 1981; Scott, Golden, Ruedrich, & Bishop, 1984).

ELECTROENCEPHALOGRAM

The incidence of EEG abnormalities among affective disorders is greater than that found in a normal population (Kiloh, McComas, & Osselton, 1972). Some reports have indicated similar findings among manic-depressives (fast activity), as has been reported earlier for schizophrenics (Davis, 1939–1940). Such activity has been observed to diminish with clinical remission (Finley, 1944).

More contemporary investigations tend to support a finding of EEG abnormality in the right anterior area of the brain among subgroups of affectively disturbed subjects (Abrams & Taylor, 1979; Flor-Henry, 1969; von Knorring, 1983). Electroencephalogram findings suggest several dysfunctions that are more notable among affectives than normals.

When successive EEG trials are observed for normals, one finds a unimodal distribution for amplitude. The EEG's of mentally disturbed persons, however, tend to demonstrate a polymodal distribution (Goldstein, 1975, 1981; von Knorring & Goldstein, in press). The importance of such findings is that specific EEG abnormalities are not associated with particular diagnoses, but with symptoms (Perris, von Knorring, & Monakhov, 1979). Among depressed persons, significantly more polymodality is found in the right hemisphere than is observed among normal controls (von Knorring, 1983). Von Knorring (1983) reports polymodal occurrences in the right hemisphere to be related to symptoms like heightened anxiety and worrying over trifles, whereas such findings in the left hemisphere appear to be associated with sadness and pessimistic thoughts.

An additional finding of von Knorring's investigations suggests that whereas normals are able to activate various brain areas selectively during tasks that are usually associated with either right or left hemisphere processing, affectives are not. Affectively disturbed subjects are able to demonstrate relative activation of the left hemisphere during verbally laden tasks; however, they are not able to produce such selective activation during right hemisphere tasks (e.g., listening to music). Such findings suggest an underlying defect in areas that may subserve accurate conscious interpretation of nonverbal stimuli (e.g., emotional components of communication and feedback).

Quantifiable differences also have been documented for persons identified as dexamethasone suppressors in comparison to nonsuppressors for computer-assisted EEG analysis (Kruszewski, Goldstein, Swartzburg, & Krawciw, 1983). The dexamethasone suppression test (DST) has been used to identify persons with abnormal control of diurnal variations in cortisol levels. It has been estimated that 45 to 50% of persons categorized as endogenously depressed fail to suppress during the DST (Kruszewski et al., 1983). Kruszewski et al., for their sample of female nonsuppressors, report results indicating a hyperarousal (beta activity) of the right hemisphere. Although the direction for differences was similar for males, the small size of the sample may have affected identifying significant differences in their case. The noted hyperarousal appears to affect the efficiency of both integration of information as well as interhemispheric transfer. Such findings may account for the psychomotor slowing observed among depressed persons. The identified hyperarousal also may explain the overlap in early EEG findings with schizophrenics.

DISCUSSION

It is clear from these data that there exists at least a subgroup of schizophrenics who show significant indicators of brain damage. Such damage appears to be located most commonly in the anterior areas of the left hemisphere, but there also may be involvement of the anterior areas of the right hemisphere as well. In addition, such damage can occur in the presence or absence of damage to other areas of the brain. Those schizophrenics with this damage are more likely to be seen as chronic schizophrenics whose problems reflect more "negative" systems as previously discussed.

Affective disorders may be associated with damage more to the right anterior rather than left anterior areas, although the evidence for such a theory is much weaker at present than is the evidence for brain damage in schizophrenia. In addition, it is not clear which if any specific symptoms separate the brain–damaged from non-brain-damaged affectively disturbed individuals. As with the damage in schizophrenics, the dysfunction may occur in the context of more diffuse or other localized damage as well.

Relating these disorders to the development of the individual, however, provides some significant problems. As can be seen from the literature review, there have been no longitudinal studies that prove that a certain brain injury leads to these symptoms. Indeed, the clinical literature can be interpreted in much the opposite way: many individuals with localized frontal injuries, either left or right, do not develop schizophrenia or an affective disorder. Thus, we have a situation in which brain injury alone cannot be seen to be a cause of the disorder. We also have those cases of schizophrenic or affective disorders where there is no demonstrable brain damage. Although it is possible that such cases do have damage too subtle for us to identify with current techniques, we must conclude that brain damage is only one possible precursor to these disorders.

Another problem in establishing cause and effect is the argument that the emotional disorder causes brain damage rather than brain damage causing emotional disorders. This approach argues that the development of abnormal thinking patterns and learning itself leads to disuse or misuse of certain brain areas which then leads to the damage. This is not seen by the authors as a likely explanation, since from this theory we would expect that time since onset of the disorder would be correlated with degree and incidence of brain damage, a finding that has not been seen within numerous studies. Such a theory also is difficult to explain on a physiological level, since it is not clear why one form of thinking leads to damage whereas many others that are different from one another do not. Still, despite these objections, this hypothesis remains somewhat viable, mostly due to the incomplete state of our current knowledge. For the purposes of our discussion, though, this hypothesis will be treated as likely to be disproved as more data are collected.

Another important issue is to recognize the difference for our discussion of adult- and child-onset schizophrenia. It should be clear that any single neural mechanism should result in similar symptoms and development. Clearly, this is not the case with childhood and adult schizophrenia, where the age of onset varies considerably. Thus, it is likely that we are dealing with different mechanisms. Since the vast majority of studies have used adult-onset schizophrenics, we will begin with a discussion of that syndrome. It should be emphasized again that we are discussing only a subset of schizophrenics, and that explanations for other types may have to depend on research in areas other than neuropsychology.

ADULT-ONSET SCHIZOPHRENIA

The striking feature of adult-onset schizophrenia is that the individual is able to function more or less effectively until the onset of the disorder. In more chronic cases, which are the ones most likely to be brain injured, this is then followed by a generally unremitting increase in symptomatology and decrease in personal effectiveness. It would be tempting to argue that the individual in such a case was once normal neurologically, but developed brain damage at a certain age and from that point on showed the symptoms. This, however, does not agree with the histories of these patients. Rather than an abrupt onset, there is a gradual increase in symptoms until they reach the point where they are labeled as schizophrenic. When there is a clear history of injury to the brain, the injury may have happened six months before, at birth, six years earlier, or at any other time, if at all.

Thus, the idea of a temporally contiguous injury leading to the symptoms of schizophrenia is highly questionable. A much sounder formulation would be to look toward the development of the brain. Here, it can be seen that the prefrontal areas, which appear to be the focus of the injury in schizophrenia, are the last area of the brain to be developed, with EEG and CT changes in this area extending through adolescence. Behaviorally, the major functions of the frontal lobe also appear to become significant only in the adolescent years. These skills include long-term planning, self-evaluation, internalized control of behavior, ability to fully discriminate reality from fantasy, selective attention, ability to control and understand complex emotional behaviors, ability to inhibit impulsive behavior, and the complex integration and understanding of the physical, social, and psychological world. The more posterior areas of the frontal lobes also are heavily involved in the planning and regulation of motor behavior.

It is the symptoms of frontal lobe disorders that are seen so frequently in the schizophrenic. Such a model would assume that damage to this area occurs either through injury at some time prior to the onset of the symptoms or as the result of the failure of these areas of the brain to develop properly. However, it must be recognized that such an injury is not seen as sufficient in itself to cause schizophrenia, since not all in-

dividuals with such injuries become schizophrenic. Luria (1973) emphasizes the importance of also considering the environment when looking
at the patient's actual behavior. Thus, the brain injury is seen as a condition that predisposes an individual toward the development of schizophrenic behavior.

This degree of predisposition varies greatly from very mild in the
case of the slightest injury to very likely in greater injuries, although in
the case of the most severe injuries, which can involve the whole brain
as well, behavior may be so reduced as to preclude the ability to evaluate
these skills at all. The greater the degree of predisposition, the less demanding or dysfunctional the environment necessary to produce the
schizophrenic behavior.

A variety of aspects of the environment may be found to be related
to the likelihood of schizophrenia. First is complexity, the degree to which
the environment demands self-control and internalized analysis of events
rather than providing clear-cut discriminative stimuli and consequences.
This would include the double-bind environment, as well as generally
stressful environments (as perceived by the individual). Depending on
the degree of brain dysfunction and its exact nature, the degree of stress
or complexity that could be handled over time would be different. Frankly
schizophrenic symptoms would appear at the point in which the patient's
level of tolerance was exceeded.

The brain-injured patient also would be more prone to learning
schizophrenic behaviors. For example, in cases where the patient is unable
to make the necessary distinctions among environmental events, the patient may accept a simplistic or paranoid version of reality in order to
be able to make sense of the world. An inability to differentiate correctly
between internal speech and external instructions may lead to perceiving
internal speech as hallucinatory "voices," especially when the content is
unacceptable or the patient is under stress. Such an assumption again
would simplify the world for patients and enable them to handle some
forms of conflict. (It should be noted that such an interpretation would
suggest that long-term brain-injured patients would be more subject to
auditory hallucinations since that is the manner in which most people
represent internal speech. Other types of hallucinations would be seen
as more acute, severe disruptions of brain integrity, such as those caused
by acute drug ingestion.)

Thus, the end schizophrenic behavior would reflect a combination
of environmental and internal events. Neither would be sufficient by itself
except under the most extreme conditions; however, with severe damage,
a relatively benign environment could lead to the disorder, whereas individuals with relatively intact brains could become schizophrenic in a

severe environment. Conversely, an individual could withstand a significant brain injury or a poor environment if the other factor was satisfactorily strong.

The brain-injured schizophrenic can be distinguished neuropsychologically from the non-brain-injured schizophrenic through an analysis of their behavior between acute episodes. In these periods, where stress is low or controlled, the brain-dysfunctional patient will continue to show neuropsychological deficits, whereas the intact schizophrenic will display a normal neurological status. Testing between episodes has the advantage of insuring that neuropsychological symptoms are real and not due to anxiety or an external source, something which can be difficult to determine in the patient with a current acute exacerbation. We also would expect that although the brain injury itself would not increase with age (with the exception noted below), behavior would deteriorate as the patient exhausts his or her ability to handle stress.

Although the brain injury itself would not get worse with age (except in degenerative conditions), we would expect the aging schizophrenic to show more aging effects than the normal individual. This is because we resist aging effects by employing alternate pathways within the brain to accomplish tasks, as well as relying on our past learning. Because of their brain injury, schizophrenics are less well able to employ alternate pathways which may themselves be impaired, as well as having a poorer store of past learning. Thus, the behavioral appearance will be of more rapidly deteriorating behavior than need be seen by the degree of neurological impairment. In our brain-injured population of schizophrenics, we have seen a much sharper decline of behavioral skills than in normal individuals.

Again, it should be emphasized that not all schizophrenics become schizophrenic because of brain damage, nor do those with brain damage have damage that is always limited to the prefrontal areas of the brain. Damage may involve other areas, in which case there will be other historical and current symptoms consistent with that disorder, or there may be no damage at all, allowing the patient to return to neuropsychological normal during the nonacute phase of the disorder. It also should be emphasized that not all brain-injured schizophrenics will be identified by current methods of testing: as neuropsychological, neuroradiological, and EEG methods increase in accuracy, we are finding indications of brain dysfunction in patients previously identified as normal.

Another caution is that we are not clear about the mechanisms involved in this dysfunction. Damage can be biochemical, causing structural dysfunction because of the inability to function metabolically; damage can be structural, interfering with metabolic processes through the poor production of neurotransmitters and other substances because the producing structures are damaged; or developmental, the result of certain brain structures failing to develop on a metabolic or structural level without there being identifiable occurrence of damage. At present, there is no way to discriminate easily between these alternatives other than history.

EARLY-ONSET SCHIZOPHRENIA

It is not possible to account for early-onset schizophrenia by the same mechanisms, since we would not expect the effects to show up until late childhood at the earliest. In early cases, when there is brain dysfunction, it is likely that the dysfunction involves the more primitive areas of the brain, particularly what Luria (1973) calls the "first unit," which consists of the reticular activating system and related areas within the deeper structures of the brain. In the young infant and child, these areas serve many of the same functions as the frontal lobes, dealing with attention, concentration, arousal, emotional status, emotional lability, focusing, and general behavioral efficiency. As the person ages, these functions are generally inhibited by the cortex and replaced by the more sophisticated frontal mechanisms. (Inhibition of lower cortical centers is a major aspect of the function of the highest cortical areas.)

Control of these functions by Unit 1 is much more primitive and "built in," rather than learned, and generally less susceptible to learning and experience, especially in those cases where there is pathology. Injuries to these areas can lead to severe overstimulation and flooding of the brain with sensory impressions (high arousal/low attention) or to a cutoff of sensory impressions and a lack of contact with the outside world (low arousal/low attention) as well as to instability in mood. Either of these conditions, if extreme enough, can lead to inadequate learning and coping with reality, forcing the person to turn inward for stimulation or for defense against overwhelming and confusing impressions. This in turn can lead to the symptoms of early-onset schizophrenia or, if the disorder is significant enough to be apparent at an early age, to autism.

Thus, early-onset schizophrenia is seen primarily as a disorder of Unit 1, with the exact mechanisms possibly being varied. When there is dysfunction of Unit 1, other behavioral disorders will be seen that resemble disorders of the higher cortical centers because of the need of basic Unit 1 functions before these areas can develop properly. Thus, the presence of additional symptoms suggesting injuries in other areas must be evaluated cautiously as reflecting behavioral dysfunction rather than necessarily structural or biochemical dysfunction in the higher cortical areas.

In these disorders, the other areas may be injured, but this must be determined by CT scan or other direct assessment of brain status.

Because of this, Unit 1 dysfunctions can look like impairment of the brain as a whole. Thus, such individuals often look much more severe than their adult-onset counterparts since they do in fact represent a much different brain injury. As with the adult-onset disorders, severity can vary and the tolerance of the individual to complexity and stimuli can vary significantly. In the milder cases, environment can play a significant role in what symptoms, if any, are seen. In more severe cases, the environment has a less profound impact.

AFFECTIVE DISORDERS

Developmentally, the affective disorders are seen in much the same way as adult-onset schizophrenia, except that the injury is more localized to the right (nondominant) frontal lobe rather than the left (dominant) frontal lobe. For our purposes, the major role of the right anterior brain appears to be the analysis and regulation of emotional stimuli and states. Analysis of emotion requires an integration of many internal and external cues, and this integration appears to require the adequate function of the right anterior brain. In addition, the anterior right temporal lobe, which is closely interconnected with the subcortical structures of Unit 1 and the limbic system as well as with the anterior frontal areas of the brain, also appears important to the analysis of new nonverbal, nonpracticed patterns, skills important in recognizing and analyzing one's own emotional state as well as that of others. Moreover, the right frontal lobe appears to play an important role in the inhibition and regulation of the subcortical emotional system.

Disorders of these areas can lead to significant fluctuations in emotional level and lability, causing the symptoms of classic depressive or manic-depressive states. Such patients also have difficulty in simply recognizing emotional states on an intellectual level and in then inhibiting or regulating them as required in social interaction. In extreme cases, the patient's behavior is fully out of control, and mood determines cortical functioning rather than cortical functioning inhibiting, altering, and controlling mood states.

The onset of these disorders is generally later in life, as such emotional controls become more demanded by the environment. As long as such controls are not expected, the patient functions within "normal limits" except in the more extreme cases. Other milder problems show up as response to stress or in the face of conditions that further compromise the functioning of the right frontal areas. For example, many diseases of aging (e.g., Alzheimer's) may affect the right frontal lobe, causing disorders that have been labeled as "involutional depression." These disorders often occur in individuals with prior suggestive histories of mild dysfunction in these skills, but which were not severe enough to cause behavior labeled as an affective disorder. It also can show up in individuals with no previous problems, but the injury generally must be more severe in those cases. Similarly, highly stressful situations that demand control of stronger emotions or more tight control can be sufficient to highlight an otherwise mild problem. (In such cases, the disorder can be misdiagnosed as acute rather than chronic.)

Early-onset versions of this disorder share the symptomatology of the early-onset schizophrenias, as well as resembling adjustment disorders, and so are classified within these groups. Whereas cases of pure depression are diagnosed in children, they are generally related to environmental loss or frustration (reactive) rather than related to the functions described here. Thus, these disorders do not fall under the purview of this chapter.

Since injuries limited to the right frontal areas do not have the cognitive and planning components seen in left frontal injuries, they are not as readily recognized nor as easily diagnosed. Neuropsychological problems are seen generally on complex tests of pattern analysis, integration, and recognition, tests which are often missed by many normal individuals at average or below-average IQ levels. Deficits, when present, can be mild and demonstrable only through a pattern analysis. As a consequence, these disorders are often seen only as emotional problems or the function of psychodynamics, with the underlying brain dysfunction missed or ignored. When these deficits are present within the context of a larger brain injury, they are most likely to be seen. They also are more easily diagnosed when the symptoms follow a clear brain injury, such as head trauma or a tumor.

Again, we must emphasize that these ideas are speculative at best. The research in this area has been skimpy and difficult to interpret for many of the reasons discussed above. As research progresses in all areas, we should be better able to refine our ideas and adopt new, more precise formulations.

SUMMARY AND CONCLUSIONS

This chapter has reviewed representative research in the area of brain function and the development of the major psychiatric disorders. While the current evidence points to a brain function etiology in at least a significant subset of individuals with these disorders, the state of the art is at best primitive and our conclusions tentative. At present, the research on schizophrenia is clearer and more convincing, but there is slowly accumulating a literature on the affective disorders that we believe eventually will be equally strong.

From a theoretical perspective, our musings must be seen as even more tentative. There have been no long-term studies clearly relating brain injury at any age to later psychiatric disturbance except correlationally. Indeed, all the research at the moment is single-shot, correlational investigations rather than longitudinal studies that can support our etiological hypothesis. Even if the causation is assumed to be established, the mechanism involved remains questionable and debatable.

Despite these caveats, the area remains one of significant interest and excitement. Our research and clinical experience have convinced us that neuropsychological and neurological approaches present effective methods of investigating and understanding these disorders, eventually to lead to programs of treatment and, more importantly, prevention. Only future work will determine the accuracy of these assumptions, but it is likely that such work will be among the major contributions of the last 15 years of this century.

REFERENCES

Abenson, M. H. EEGs in chronic schizophrenia. *British Journal of Psychiatry*, 1970, *116*, 421–425.

Abrams, R., Redfield, J., & Taylor, M. A. Cognitive dysfunction in schizophrenia, affective disorder and organic brain disease. *British Journal of Psychiatry*, 1981, *139*, 190–194.

Abrams, R., & Taylor, M. A. Differential EEG patterns in affective disorders and schizophrenia. *Archives of General Psychiatry*, 1979, *36*, 1355–1358.

Adams, R. D., & Victor, M. *Principles of neurology*. New York: McGraw-Hill, 1981.

Alpert, M., & Martz, M. J. Cognitive views of schizophrenia in light of recent studies of brain asymmetry. In C. Shagass, S. Gershon, & A. J. Friedhoff (Eds.), *Psychopathology and brain dysfunction*. New York: Raven Press, 1977.

American Psychiatric Association. *Diagnostic and statistical manual of mental disorders* (3rd ed.). Washington, D.C.: Author, 1980.

Andreasen, N. C., Olsen, S. A., Dennert, J. W., & Smith, M. R. Ventricular enlargement in schizophrenia: Relationship to positive and negative symptoms. *American Journal of Psychiatry*, 1982, *139*, 297–302.

Ariel, R. N., Golden, C. J., Berg, R. A., Quaife, M. A., Dirksen, J. W., Forsell, T., Wilson, J., & Graber, B. Regional cerebral blood flow in schizophrenia with the 133-Xenon inhalation method. *Archives of General Psychiatry*, 1983, *40*, 258–263.

Asano, N. Pneumoencephalographic study of schizophrenia. In H. Mitsuda & O. Takasuki (Eds.), *Clinical genetics in psychiatry: Problems in nosological classification*. Tokyo: Igaku-Shion, 1967.

Bellak, L. Introduction: An idiosyncratic overview. In L. Bellak (Ed.), *Disorders of the schizophrenic syndrome.* New York: Basic Books, 1979.

Brockington, I. F., Kendall, R. E., & Wainwright, S. Depressed patients with schizophrenic or paranoid symptoms. *Psychology and Medicine,* 1980, *10,* 655–675.

Brockington, I. F., Kendall, R. E., Wainwright, S., Hiller, V. F., & Walker, J. The distinction between the affective psychoses and schizophrenia. *British Journal of Psychiatry,* 1979, *135,* 234–248.

Brumback, R. A., & Staton, R. D. Neuropsychological study of children during and after remission of endogenous depressive episodes. *Perceptual and Motor Skills,* 1980, *53,* 219–234.

Buchsbaum, M. S. Neurophysiological aspects of the schizophrenic syndrome. In L. Bellak (Ed.), *Disorders of the schizophrenic syndrome.* New York: Basic Books, 1979.

Buchsbaum, M. S., Ingvar, D. H., Kessler, R., Waters, R. N., Cappelletti, J., van Kammen, D. P., King, A. C., Johnson, J. L., Manning, R. G., Flynn, R. W., Mann, L. S., Bunney, W. E., & Sokoloff, L. Cerebral glucography with positron tomography: Use in normal subjects and in patients with schizophrenia. *Archives of General Psychiatry,* 1982, *39,* 251–259.

Carpenter, B. N. Neuropsychological examination of the affective disorders. In C. J. Golden, J. A. Moses, Jr., J. A. Coffman, W. R. Miller, & F. D. Strider (Eds.), *Clinical neuropsychology: Interface with neurologic and psychiatric disorders.* New York: Grune & Stratton, 1983.

Chelune, G. J., Heaton, R. K., Lehman, R. A., & Robinson, A. Level versus pattern of neuropsychological performance among schizophrenic and diffusely brain damaged patients. *Journal of Consulting and Clinical Psychology,* 1979, *47,* 155–163.

Cohen, S. M., Allen, M. G., Pollin, W., & Hurbec, Z. Relationship of schizo-affective psychosis to manic-depressive psychosis and schizophrenia. *Archives of General Psychiatry,* 1972, *26,* 539–545.

Creuzfeldt, O. (Ed.). The neuronal generation of the EEG. In A. Redmond (Ed.), *Handbook of EEG and neurophysiology.* Amsterdam: Elsevier, 1974.

Davis, P. A. Evaluation of the electroencephalogram of schizophrenic patients. *American Journal of Psychiatry,* 1939–1940, *96,* 851.

DeWolfe, A. S. Differentiation of schizophrenia and brain damage with the WAIS. *Journal of Clinical Psychology,* 1971, *27,* 209–211.

DeWolfe, A. S., Barrell, R. P., Becker, B. C., & Spaner, F. E. Intellectual deficit in chronic schizophrenia and brain damage. *Journal of Consulting and Clinical Psychology,* 1971, *36,* 197–204.

Donnelly, E. F., Weinberger, D. R., Waldman, I. N., & Wyatt, R. J. Cognitive impairment associated with morphological brain abnormalities on computed tomography in chronic schizophrenic patients. *Journal of Nervous and Mental Disorders,* 1980, *5,* 305–308.

Farkas, T., Reivich, M., Alavi, A., Greenberg, J. H., Fowler, J. S., MacGregor, R. R., Christman, D. R., & Wolf, A. P. ^{18}F-deoxy-2-fluoro-D-glucose and positron emission tomography in the study of psychiatric conditions. In J. V. Passonneau, R. A. Hawkins, W. D. Lust, & F. A. Welsh (Eds.), *Cerebral metabolism and neural function.* Baltimore: Williams & Wilkins, 1980.

Fenton, G. W., Fenwick, P. B. C., Dollimore, J., Dunn, T. L., & Hirsch, S. R. EEG spectral analysis in schizophrenia. *British Journal of Psychiatry,* 1980, *136,* 445–455.

Finley, K. H. On occurrence of rapid frequency potential changes in the human electroencephalogram. *American Journal of Psychiatry,* 1944, *101,* 194.

Flor-Henry, P. Psychosis and temporal lobe epilepsy—A controlled investigation. *Epilepsia,* 1969, *10,* 363–395.

Flor-Henry, P. Lateralized temporal limbic dysfunction and psychopathology. *Annals of the New York Academy of Science,* 1976, *280,* 777–795.

Flor-Henry, P. *Cerebral basis of psychopathology.* Boston: John Wright PSG, 1983.(a)

Flor-Henry, P. Neuropsychological studies in patients with psychiatric disorders. In K. M. Heilman & P. Satz (Eds.), *Neuropsychology of human emotion.* New York: Guilford Press, 1983.(b).

Flor-Henry, P., & Yeudall, L. T. Neuropsychological investigation of schizophrenia and manic-depressive psychoses. In J. Gruzelier & P. Flor-Henry, (Eds.), *Hemisphere asymmetries of function in psychopathology.* Amsterdam: Elsevier/North Holland Biomedical Press, 1979.

Flor-Henry, P., Fromm-Auch, D., & Schopflocher, D. Neuropsychological dimensions in psychopathology. In P. Flor-Henry & J. Gruzelier (Eds.), *Laterality and psychopathology.* Amsterdam: Elsevier/North Holland Biomedical Press, 1983.

Flor-Henry, P., Koles, Z. J., Bo-Lassen, P., & Yeudall, L. T. Studies of the functional psychoses: Power spectral EEG analysis. *Psychiatry and Clinical Psychology,* 1975, *3,* 87.

Fromm-Auch, D. Neuropsychological assessment of depressed patients before and after drug therapy: Clinical profile interpretation. In P. Flor-Henry & J. Gruzelier (Eds.), *Laterality and psychopathology.* Amsterdam: Elsevier, 1983.

Gerard, R. W., & Mattsson, N. B. The classification of schizophrenia. In J. A. Jaquez (Ed.), *The diagnostic process.* Ann Arbor: University of Michigan, 1963.

Golden, C. J. Validity of the Halstead–Reitan Neuropsychological Battery in a mixed psychiatric and brain injured population. *Journal of Consulting and Clinical Psychology,* 1977, *45,* 1043–1045.

Golden, C. J., Graber, B., Coffman, J., Berg, R. A., Newlin, D. B., & Bloch, S. Structural brain deficits in schizophrenia: Identification by computed tomographic scan density measurements. *Archives of General Psychiatry,* 1981, *38,* 1014–1017.

Golden, C. J., Hammeke, T. A., & Purisch, A. D. *The Luria—Nebraska Neuropsychological Battery manual.* Los Angeles: Western Psychological Services, 1980.

Golden, C. J., Moses, J. A., Zelazowski, R., Graber, B., Zata, L. M., Horvath, T. B., & Berger, P. A. Cerebral ventricular size and neuropsychological impairment in young, chronic schizophrenics: Measurement by the standardized Luria-Nebraska Neuropsychological Battery. *Archives of General Psychiatry,* 1980, *37,* 619–623.

Goldstein, G. Cognitive and perceptual differences between schizophrenics and organics. *Schizophrenia Bulletin,* 1978, *4,* 160–185.

Goldstein, L. Time domain analysis of the EEG: The integrative method. In G. Dolce & H. Kunkel (Eds.), *CEAN.* Berlin: Gustav Fischer, 1975.

Goldstein, L. Statistical organizational features of the computerized EEG under various behavioral states. *Advances in Biological Psychiatry,* 1981, *4,* 160–185.

Gruzelier, J., Mednick, S., & Schulsinger, F. Lateralized impairments in the WISC profiles of children at genetic risk for psychopathology. In J. Gruzelier & P. Flor-Henry (Eds.), *Hemisphere asymmetries of function in psychopathology.* Amsterdam: Elsevier/North Holland Biomedical Press, 1979.

Haug, J. O. Pneumoencephalographic studies in mental disease. *Acta Psychiatrica Scandinavica* (Supple.), 1962, *165,* 100–104.

Hays, P. Electroencephalographic variants and genetic predisposition to schizophrenia. *Journal of Neurology, Neurosurgery, and Psychiatry,* 1977, *40,* 753–755.

Heaton, R. K., Baade, L. E., & Johnson, K. L. Neuropsychological test results associated with psychiatric disorders in adults. *Psychological Bulletin,* 1978, *85,* 141–162.

Heaton, R. K., & Crowley, T. J. Effects of psychiatric disorders on neuropsychological test results. In S. B. Filskov & T. J. Boll (Eds.), *Handbook of clinical neuropsychology.* New York: Wiley, 1981.

Holzman, P. S. Cognitive impairment and cognitive stability: Towards a theory of thought disorder. In G. Serban (Ed.), *Cognitive defects in the development of mental illness.* New York: Brunner/Mazel, 1978.

Holzman, P. S., Proctor, L. R., & Hughes, D. W. Eye-tracking patterns in schizophrenia. *Science,* 1973, *181,* 179–181.

Holzman, P. S., Proctor, L. R., Levy, D. L., Yasillo, N. J., Meltzer, H. Y., & Hurt, S. W. Eye-tracking dysfunction in schizophrenic patients and their relatives. *Archives of General Psychiatry,* 1974, *31,* 143–151.

Holzman, P. S., & Rousey, C. Disinhibition of communicated thought: Generality and role of cognitive style. *Journal of Abnormal Psychology,* 1971, *77,* 263–274.

Huber, G. *Pneumoencephalographische und psychopathologische Bilder bei endogen Psychosen.* Berlin: Springer Verlag, 1957.

Ingvar, D. H. Functional landscapes of the dominant hemisphere. *Brain Research,* 1976, *107,* 181–197.

Ingvar, D. H. Abnormal distribution of cerebral activity in chronic schizophrenia: A neurophysiological interpretation. In C. Baxter & T. Melnechuk (Eds.), *Perspectives in schizophrenia research.* New York: Raven Press, 1980.

Ingvar, D. H., & Gadea Ciria, M. Assessment of severe damage to the brain by multiregional measurements of cerebral blood flow. In B. Jennett & F. Plum (Eds.), *Outcome of severe damage to the central nervous system.* Amsterdam: Elsevier, 1975.

Itil, T.M. Qualitative and quantitive EEG findings in schizophrenia. *Schizophrenia Bulletin,* 1977, *3,* 61–79.

Itil, T.M. Computer-analyzed electroencephalogram to predict the therapeutic outcome in schizophrenia. In C. F. Baxter & T. Melnechuk (Eds.), *Perspectives in schizophrenia research.* New York: Raven Press, 1980.

Itil, T. M., Saletu, B., & Davis, S. EEG findings in chronic schizophrenics based on digital computer period analysis and analog power spectra. *Biological Psychiatry,* 1972, *5,* 1–13.

Itil, T. M., Saletu, B., Davis, S., & Allen, M. Stability studies in schizophrenics and normals using computer-analyzed EEG. *Biological Psychiatry,* 1974, *8,* 321–325.

Itil, T. M., Saletu, B., Hsu, W., & Mednick, S. Computer EEG and auditory evoked potential investigations in children at high risk for schizophrenia. *American Journal of Psychiatry,* 1974, *131,* 892–900.

Jablensky, A. *Symptoms, patterns of course and predictors of outcome in the functional psychoses: Some nosological implications.* Presented at the Institute Mario Negri Symposium on Epidemiology and Psychopharmacology, Milan, Italy, 1981.

Jefferson, J. S., & Marshall, J. R. *Neuropsychiatric features of medical disorders.* New York: Plenum Press, 1981.

Kane, R. L., Sweet, J. J., Golden, C. J., Parsons, O. A., & Moses, J.A., Jr. Comparative diagnostic accuracy of the Halstead–Reitan and standardized Luria-Nebraska Neuropsychological batteries in a mixed psychiatric and brain damaged population. *Consulting and Clinical Psychology,* 1981, *49,* 484–485.

Kendall, R. E., & Brockington, I. F. The identification of disease entities and the relationship between schizophrenia and affective psychoses. *British Journal of Psychiatry,* 1980, *137,* 324–331.

Kiev, A., Chapman, L. F., Guthrie, T. C., & Wolff, H. G. The highest integrative functions and diffuse cerebral atrophy. *Neurology,* 1962, *12,* 385–393.

Kiloh, L. G., McComas, A. J., & Osselton, J. W. *Clinical electroencephalography* (3rd ed.). New York: Appleton-Century-Crofts, 1972.

Kruszewski, S., Goldstein, L., Swartzburg, M., & Krawciw, N. Computerized hemispheric

EEG, clinical and endocrinological data in depressed patients. In P. Flor-Henry & J. Gruzelier (Eds.), *Laterality and psychopathology*. Amsterdam: Elsevier, 1983.

Lassen, N. A., & Ingvar, D. H. Radioisotopic assessment of regional cerebral blood flow. *Progress in Nuclear Medicine*, 1972, *1*, 376–409.

Lemke, R. Untersuchungen über die social Prognose der Schizophrenie unter besonder Berücksichtigung des encephalographischen Befundes. *Archiv für Psychiatrie*, 1936, *104*, 89–136.

Lewis, G., Golden, C. J., Purisch, A., & Hammeke, T. The effects of chronicity of disorder and length of hospitalization on the standardized version of Luria's neuropsychological battery in a schizophrenic population. *Clinical Neuropsychology*, 1979, *1*, 13–18.

Lifshitz, K., & Gradijan, J. Relationships between measures of the coefficient of variation of the mean absolute EEG voltage and spectral intensities in schizophrenic and control subjects. *Biological Psychiatry*, 1972, *5*, 149–163.

Lishman, W. A. *Organic psychiatry: The psychological consequences of cerebral disorder*. Oxford: Blackwell Scientific, 1978.

Lonnum, A. *The clinical significance of central cerebral ventricular enlargement*. Oslo: Universitetsforlaget, 1966.

Luchins, D. J., Weinberger, D. R., & Wyatt, R. J. Schizophrenia: Evidence for a subgroup with reversed cerebral asymmetry. *Archives of General Psychiatry*, 1979, *36*, 1309–1311.

Luchins, D. J., Weinberger, D. R., & Wyatt, R. J. Schizophrenia and cerebral asymmetry detected by computed tomography. *American Journal of Psychiatry*, 1982, *139*, 753–757.

Luria, A. R. *The working brain*. New York: Basic Books, 1973.

Luria, A. R. *Higher cortical functions in man*. New York: Basic Books, 1980.

Malec, J. Neuropsychological assessment of schizophrenia versus brain damage: A review. *Journal of Nervous and Mental Disease*. 1978, *166*, 507–516.

Melnechuk, T. Discussion. In C. Baxter & T. Melnechuk (Eds.), *Perspectives in schizophrenia research*. New York: Raven Press, 1980.

Moses, J., & Golden, C. J. Discrimination between schizophrenic and brain-damaged patients with the Luria-Nebraska Neuropsychological Battery. *International Journal of Neuroscience*, 1980, *10*, 121–128.

Newlin, D. Assessing brain damage in schizophrenia. In C. J. Golden, J. A. Moses, Jr., J. A. Coffman, W. R. Miller, & F. D. Strider (Eds.), *Clinical neuropsychology: Interface with neurologic and psychiatric disorders*. New York: Grune & Stratton, 1983.

Orme, J. E., Lee, D., & Smith, M. R. Psychological assessments of brain damage and intellectual impairment in psychiatric patients. *British Journal of Social and Clinical Psychology*, 1964, *3*, 161–167.

Osborne, K., & Gale, A. Bilateral EEG differentiation of stimuli. *Biological Psychology*, 1976, *4*, 185–196.

Pearlson, G. D., & Veroff, A. E. Computerized tomographic scan changes in manic-depressive illness. *Lancet*, 1981, *1*, 470.

Perris, C., von Knorring, L., & Monakhov, K. Functional interhemispheric differences in affective disorders. In J. Obiols, C. Ballus, & E. Gonzales Monclus (Eds.), *Biological psychiatry today*. Amsterdam: Elsevier, 1979.

Purisch, A., Golden, C. J., & Hammeke, T. Discrimination of schizophrenic and brain-injured patients by a standardized version of Luria's neuropsychological tests. *Journal of Consulting and Clinical Psychology*, 1978, *46*, 1266–1273.

Reitan, R., & Davison, L. (Eds.). *Clinical neuropsychology: Current status and applications*. New York: Wiley, 1974.

Rieder, R. O., Donnelly, E. F., Herdt, J. R., & Waldman, I. N. Sulcal prominence in young chronic schizophrenic patients: CT scan findings associated with impairment on neuropsychological tests. *Psychiatry Research*, 1979, *1*, 1–8.

Rodin, E., Grisell, J., & Gottlieb, J. Some electrographic differences between chronic schizophrenic patients and normal subjects. In J. Wortis (Ed.), *Recent advances in biological psychiatry* (Vol. 10). New York: Plenum Press, 1968.

Rosenthal, R., & Bigelow, L. B. Quantitative brain measurements in chronic schizophrenia. *British Journal of Psychiatry*, 1972, *121*, 259–264.

Ross, E. D., & Rush, A. J. Diagnosis and neuroanatomical correlates of depression in brain-damaged patients. *Archives of General Psychiatry*, 1981, *38*, 1344–1354.

Sackheim, H. A., & Decina, P. Lateralized neuropsychological abnormalities in bipolar adults and in children of bipolar probands. In P. Flor-Henry & J. Gruzelier (Eds.), *Laterality and psychopathology*. Amsterdam: Elsevier, 1983.

Scarone, S., Gambini, O., & Pieri, E. Dominant hemisphere dysfunction in chronic schizophrenia: Schwartz test and short aphasia screening test. In P. Flor-Henry & J. Gruzelier (Eds.), *Laterality and psychopathology*. Amsterdam: Elsevier, 1983.

Scott, M. L., Golden, C. J., Ruedrich, S. L., & Bishop, R. J. Ventricular enlargement in major depression. *Psychiatry Research*, 1983, *8*, 91–93.

Seidman, L. J. Schizophrenia and brain dysfunction: An integration of recent neurodiagnostic findings. *Psychological Bulletin*, 1983, *94*, 195–238.

Shaffer, D., Bijur, P., & Chadwick, O. *Localized cortical injury and psychiatric symptoms in childhood*. Unpublished manuscript, 1981.

Shagass, C., Amadeo, M., & Overton, D. A. Eye-tracking performance in psychiatric patients. *Biological Psychiatry*, 1974, *9*, 245–260.

Silverstein, M. L., & Meltzer, H. Y. Neuropsychological dysfunction in the major psychoses: Relation to premorbid adjustment and social class. In P. Flor-Henry & J. Gruzelier (Eds.), *Laterality and psychopathology*. Amsterdam: Elsevier, 1983.

Snider, R. S., Maiti, A., & Snider, S. R. Cerebellar pathways to ventral midbrain and nigra. *Experimental Neurology*, 1976, *53*, 714–728.

Taylor, M., & Abrams, R. Cerebral hemisphere dysfunction in the major psychoses. In P. Flor-Henry & J. Gruzelier (Eds.), *Laterality and psychopathology*. Amsterdam: Elsevier, 1983.

Teuber, H. L. Effects of focal brain lesions. *Neuroscience Research Program Bulletin*, 1972, *10*, vii, 369–507.

von Knorring, L. Interhemispheric EEG differences in affective disorders. In P. Flor-Henry & J. Gruzelier (Eds.), *Laterality and psychopathology*. Amsterdam: Elsevier, 1983.

von Knorring, L., & Goldstein, L. Quantitative hemispheric EEG differences between healthy volunteers and depressed patients. *Research in Community Psychological & Psychiatric Behavior*, in press.

Watson, C. G. Cross-validation of the WAIS sign developed to separate brain damaged from schizophrenic patients. *Journal of Clinical Psychology*, 1972, *28*, 66–67.

Watson, C. G., Davis, W. E., & Gasser, B. The separation of organics from depressives with ability- and personality-based tests. *Journal of Clinical Psychology*, 1978, *34*, 393–397.

Weinberger, D. R., & Wyatt, R. J., Structural brain abnormalities in chronic schizophrenia: Computed tomography findings. In C. Baxter & T. Melnechuk (Eds.), *Perspectives in schizophrenia research*. New York: Raven Press, 1980.

Weinberger, D. R., Torrey, E. F., Neophytides, A. N., & Wyatt, R. J. Structural abnormalities in the cerebral cortex of chronic schizophrenic patients. *Archives of General Psychiatry*, 1979, *36*, 935–939.

Weinberger, D. R., Torrey, E. F., & Wyatt, R. J. Cerebellar atrophy in chronic schizophrenia. *Lancet*, 1979, *1* (8118), 718–719.

Welner, A., Croughan, J., Fishman, R., & Robins, E. The group of schizoaffective and related psychoses: A follow-up study. *Comprehensive Psychiatry*, 1977, *18*, 413–422.

Wiens, A.N., & Matarazzo, J.D. WAIS and MMPI correlates of the Halstead–Reitan neuropsychological battery in normal male subjects. *Journal of Nervous and Mental Disorders*, 1977, *164*, 112–121.

World Health Organization (WHO). *Schizophrenia: A multinational study.* Public Health Paper No. 63, Geneva, 1975.

CHAPTER 10

Sex Differences in Neuropsychological Function
A Vector Model

MARLIN L. LANGUIS and PAUL J. NAOUR

A PERSPECTIVE ON SEX DIFFERENCE

Contemporary concern for providing equality of opportunity for both women and men is not only appropriate, it is long overdue. Stereotyped and biased conceptions of the cognitive capacities of women restrict the access of females to many areas of personal, career, and professional development. Sex stereotyping also limits the range of opportunity for males in some areas, although these restrictions are not often emphasized. In the final analysis, both women and men profit from a wide range of opportunity.

How does research in sex difference relate to issues of sex equity? A major source of controversy in sex difference research is whether evidence of differences associated with gender may be used inappropriately to feed sex stereotyping. A model that focuses on differences of individual members of the female and male gender groups and the sex-related changes that may occur during development of the individual may be useful to defuse sex difference controversy.

In most of the literature on gender difference, human females and males typically are considered to be discrete groups; in reality no individual is totally female or male. It may be more appropriate to say that

MARLIN L. LANGUIS • Department of Educational Theory and Practice, Ohio State University, Columbus, Ohio 43210. PAUL J. NAOUR • Department of Special Education, Muskingum College, New Concord, Ohio 43762.

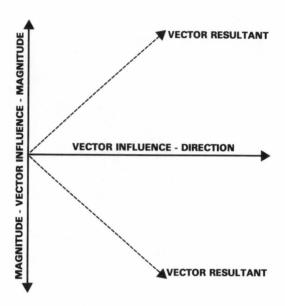

FIGURE 1. Generalized model of vector attributes.

each individual falls at some point along the feminine-masculine continuum when any of a number of crucial sex-related variables are considered.
The sex hormones estrogen and testosterone provide a good illustration
of a sex-related variable that influences neuropsychological function (as
we shall discuss in some detail later). Estrogen, the feminizing sex hormone, and testosterone, the masculinizing sex hormone, are present
during development in every individual whether that individual is female
or male. The relative proportion of estrogen to testosterone is higher in
females than in males and vice versa; but both are present and the levels
of the two sex hormones vary substantively within the members of the
same sex group. In addition, the level of the sex hormones fluctuates
dramatically at certain points in the individual's lifespan (particularly *in
utero* and during adolescence), and such fluctuation is associated with
developmentally sensitive periods (Languis, Sanders, & Tipps, 1980).

Therefore it is appropriate to view sex difference in terms of the individual member of the gender group in two important ways. First, the
position of the individual along the feminine-masculine continuum with
respect to key sex-related variables must be considered. Second, the magnitude of change in position of the individual at developmentally sensitive
periods along the female–male continuum for the key sex-related variables
must be recognized.

The vector model in mathematics provides a useful metaphor for conceptualizing human gender differences as we have just described them. In a simplified way, a vector is a quantity (e.g., a force) that has both direction and magnitude (an assigned value). Any change in a vector is the result of influences acting on it. The influences may originate internally or externally; however, the central concept is that identifiable influences are responsible for the origination of the vector quantity and for every subsequent change in vector values. Therefore, sex-related variables may be viewed as providing the vector attributes (direction and magnitude) for the individual's neuropsychological function in the area of gender differences. In addition to explaining average differences between female and male gender groups, the vector model of sex differences is adequate to deal with the range of individual differences observed within a gender group and with change in sex-related attributes of individuals or gender groups over time. In addition, the vector model provides a

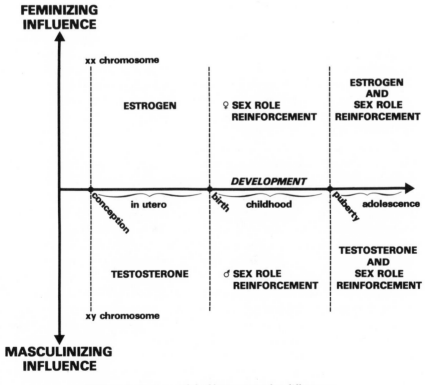

FIGURE 2. Vector model of human gender differences.

means of conceptualizing gender differences consistent with notions of individual differences in cognitive and learning style patterns in practice in the helping professions (Languis, 1981a,b, 1983b,c). The discussion that follows considers some of the key variables in the vector model of sex differences in neuropsychological function.

CRITICAL VARIABLES INFLUENCING EXPRESSION OF MALE-FEMALE GENDER ROLE BEHAVIOR

ANATOMY

There has been increasing interest in the gross anatomic description of sex differences in asymmetries of the right and left cerebral hemispheres. In addition, efforts have been made to link such asymmetries to functional, performance-related differences between the sexes (Bradshaw & Nettleton, 1983; Wittig & Petersen, 1979). Major problems that frequently confound empirical studies of sex differences include small investigative sample sizes and large intragroup variation which in turn restricts definitive statistical analysis. Bryden (1982) described the nature of reported anatomic differences between the sexes as suggestive and tentative. However, as knowledge of anatomical sex differences has increased, explaining their functional meaning has become relevant.

Male infants have been reported to have larger temporal planes in both left and right hemispheres than female infants (Wada, 1976). Witelson and Pallie (1973) suggested that at comparable ages female infants have greater asymmetry than males and display a left hemisphere advantage. Although Wada, Clarke, and Hamm (1975) reported a trend for a larger left planum temporale in adult males, they also reported that more male infants show right hemisphere asymmetry as compared with female infants. deLacoste-Utamsing and Holloway (1982) reported evidence for a female advantage in increased size of the corpus callosum. They examined 14 normal adult brains at autopsy. Nine male and five female brains were sectioned midsagittally precisely through the cerebral aqueduct. Even with the small sample size, the resulting cross section of the corpus callosum revealed statistically significant sexual dimorphism in the shape and size (relative to total brain weight) of the splenium. The splenium comprises roughly the posterior 20% of the corpus callosum. The female splenium was more bulbous and widened markedly with respect to the body of the callosum while the male counterpart was relatively continuous in width. The enlarged splenium suggests a greater number of fibers interconnecting homologous areas in the left and right hemispheres toward

SEX DIFFERENCES IN NEUROPSYCHOLOGICAL FUNCTION   241

the back of the brain. These data may suggest a greater capacity for females to utilize both hemispheres in a more integrated fashion. Perhaps less asymmetry can be attributed to the integration of hemisphere function, with bilateral representation of language processes and a weak right hemisphere spatial ability. The reports also suggest that males have a greater tendency to develop lateral specialization of cognitive function and therefore are more prone to functional disorders thought to be related to lateralization, such as stuttering, dyslexia, learning disorders, and autism (Bradshaw & Nettleton, 1983).

HORMONES

Description of sex differences in anatomic asymmetry has little meaning in isolation. However, when taken as an indicator of more meaningful functional differences, we begin to search for the underlying developmental causes. Obviously, the most important variable is the genetic difference between males (XY) and females (XX). Other than providing for genitalia, hormone variability is likely the most critical variable in the development of male-female functional anatomic differences, as well as diversity in cognitive processing characteristics and overt behavioral patterns. General patterns of behavior in all members of the species are very similar in that all persons ingest food, interact with the environment, possess language skills, and display aggression. However, in a quantitative sense, males ingest larger amounts of food and interact more actively with the environment, yet females have superior language ability and demonstrate significantly less overt physical aggression (Goy & McEwen, 1980).

The critical element impacting the variability in development has been suggested to be circulating androgens from the testes (Phoenix, Goy, Gerall, & Young, 1959). Phoenix et al. (1959) suggested that the circulating androgens are both morphogenetic and psychogenetic. Their organizational hypothesis suggests that both neural processes mediating sexual behavior and the reproductive organs innately tend toward the female pattern. However, androgens have the effect of enhancing male patterns of overt behavior and the male reproductive organs. In females, the critical element in the development of behavioral and physical characteristics seems to be the greatly reduced levels of androgens (Goy & McEwen, 1980). Thus the Y chromosome, the obvious marker for masculinity, modifies both female structural and functional characteristics via the androgen level. The literature on sex differences in behavior consistently documents the impact on the masculinizing gender role of the androgens. Likewise, females who have been androgenized prenatally assume some male gen-

der role behaviors (Ehrhardt & Baker, 1974). Most common in the data
are reports of behavior of females masculinized *in utero* by the impact
of the adrenogenital syndrome (congenital adrenal hyperplasia). Ehrhardt
and Baker (1974) report that these females demonstrate higher activity
levels, tomboyishness, a preference for male friends, and less interest in
dolls.

The significance of these data is that circulating androgens *in utero*
have tremendous impact on the developing fetus that results in behavioral
variability. It is important to suggest that the result is not necessarily an
either-or proposition, resulting in the development of a normal male,
feminized male, normal female, or masculinized female (Reinisch, Gandelman, & Spiegel, 1979). Obviously, the interaction of variables results
in the potential for a continuum of behavioral effects. The extreme cases
(e.g., adrenogenital syndrome) serve to illustrate the potential extreme
result (masculinized female). However, our hypothesis suggests that the
variability in levels of circulating androgens during *in utero* development
results in a behavioral continuum upon which males and females might
be placed. The literature consistently describes the following general fe-
male/male behavioral dichotomy:

Female	*Male*
Accommodating	Aggressive
Social	Exploratory
Verbal	Visual spatial
Compliant	Dominant

In addition, other research suggests that two female behavioral patterns
are innate: sexual attraction to men and a care-giving attachment to children, whereas the male has only the innate sexual attraction to the female
and must learn parenting behavior from the female (Goy & McEwen, 1980).
The list obviously can continue, but the point remains that the stereotypic
female/male behavioral dichotomy suggests very different behavioral patterns. The argument remains as to whether behaviors are biologically
controlled, culturally reinforced, or perhaps an interaction of the two
(Bradshaw & Nettleton, 1983). Clearly, a more productive model of sex
difference is needed to resolve compartmentalizing dichotomies.

PATTERNS AND DISORDERS IN LANGUAGE AND SPATIAL LEARNING

The tendency has been to oversimplify explanations of female/male
behavioral dichotomies using arguments based on the significant hormone differences in each gender group (Rogers, 1976). The hormone var-

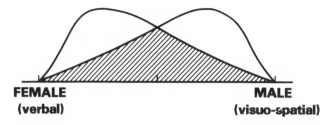

FEMALE　　　　　　　　　　　　　**MALE**
(verbal)　　　　　　　　　　　　**(visuo-spatial)**

FIGURE 3. Gender relationships in verbal and visuospatial abilities.

iable is only a portion of the picture, albeit a large part. Indirectly related to hormone variability is the development of higher cognitive abilities, such as language. The highly developed verbal ability of humans is a characteristic that makes our species unique from all others and that also has been demonstrated to be quite different between females and males (Bradshaw & Nettleton, 1983). Development of lateralization for language processes has been suggested to be a very different process between the sexes (McGee, 1979; McGlone, 1980; Witelson, 1976). Although there is a more defined pattern for each sex, a continuum of developmental patterns may be appropriate here, as in overt behavioral characteristics influenced by hormones. As suggested by the vector model of sex differences, individuals comprising the extremes on the continuum would be females on one end and males on the other, but the bulk of females and males may fall within a shared region. Such a concept may be represented by Figure 3.

In the following discussion we will contrast language ability with visuo-spatial ability and will deliberately utilize the simplistic female/male dichotomy in order to describe the extreme cases from the model shown in Figure 3. The early literature suggested that the differences noted in verbal behavior could be attributed to the male brain being more symmetrical (Buffery & Gray, 1972). However, little support has been documented for this hypothesis. McGlone (1980) reviewed data suggesting that the female brain is more symmetrically organized and the male brain more asymmetric for verbal and visuospatial functions. What developmental phenomena might be the source of the anatomic difference? More importantly, what functional characteristics are a result of the female/male differences and what makes their expression so different?

Once again the extreme case will provide insight into the underlying components of the female/male differences. Developmental learning disorders (dyslexia, stuttering, etc.) provide the extreme case. Developmental learning disorders may be described as a combination of characteristics:

inability to learn to read, poor auditory memory, poor spelling, and delays in language acquisition. Males are much more likely to have such disorders than females. Estimates range from 75% to 90% depending on the definition of the learning disorder. Research in the area has been especially fruitful over the last several years and may be useful in serving as a basis for drawing more subtle comparisons in lateral brain development and function between males and females.

Initially, rate of neural maturation was suggested as the potential source of differences in verbal and visuospatial skills (Waber, 1979). In the case of developmental learning disorders, excessive delay in left-hemispheric development was said to result in the disability. Generally, it was suggested that the overall delay in rate of maturation among males resulted in the increased likelihood for later development of lateral specialization than females. In addition, deLacoste-Utamsing and Holloway (1982) report that the splenium of the female corpus callosum is larger, supporting the notion that there is more similarity of function left to right due to greater capacity for interhemispheric communication. Differences in cognitive ability might then be a result of very different patterns of development in cortical organization. Bradshaw and Nettleton (1983) suggest that the first stages of language development occur during a time when the left hemisphere and then the right pass through a critical state of neural plasticity. The result is an expression of specialization in both hemispheres for language processes. Such a process will lead to a lack of development of visuospatial functions more commonly reserved for the right hemisphere. The more typical male pattern of delay in maturation would lead to greater lateral specialization of function reserving the right hemisphere for visuospatial specialization. However, in the extreme case, there is a much increased likelihood that males will suffer from developmental learning disorders related to the delay in language specialization. The literature describing these developmental differences is extensive and suggests strong support for the developmental hypothesis (Berlin & Languis, 1980; Harris, 1978; Kraft, 1985; Levy, 1976; Witelson, 1976). In a sociobiologic sense, the enhanced hemispheric lateral specialization in males may have developed to provide the development of spatial skills critical for survival in travel, hunting, and so forth. Similarly, female development for functional strength in language may have enhanced verbal capability to carry on oral transmission of family and culture.

Embedded within the variable of developmental delay are important dimensions: the timing and duration of delay. The timing and duration of the delay provide the potential for variability in expression of the development of right/left, symmetry/asymmetry, and verbal/visuospatial functioning. Recently, Geschwind and Behan (1982) have suggested a more inclusive hypothesis for the expression of developmental learning disorders. They propose that the level of testosterone, along with its timing and duration, is a critical factor. Their research suggests relationships among a cluster of characteristics common to individuals having developmental learning disorders. These characteristics include higher male incidence of learning disorders, higher rate of left-handedness in males generally, and in the left-handed male population a much higher incidence of immune system dysfunction (asthma, allergy, migraine, etc.) and abnormal development of left temporal cortex (Galaburda & Kemper, 1979). All of these factors can be explained by *in utero* levels of testosterone. Increased levels of testosterone *in utero* result in potential delay of development of the thymus gland, which influences immune regulation. Most importantly, testosterone controls neuronal migration to the cortex during fetal development. Increased levels may result in delays of cortical cellular lamination or pathologic lamination (Gallaburda & Kemper, 1979). Gallaburda and Kemper have described cortical abnormalities in brains of several males identified with developmental learning disabilities who have come to autopsy. Most importantly, the abnormalities are limited to the left inferior temporal-parietal region and left thalamus. Geschwind (1983) suggests that the increased incidence of left-handedness relates to the pathology of the left hemisphere, forcing right hemisphere dominance and left-handedness. Obviously, the cortical pathology in the left hemisphere language association region leads to the likelihood of developmental learning disorders. Geschwind and Behan (1982) suggest that males are more likely to manifest these characteristics because the fetal testes *in utero* produce testoterone at levels per unit body weight higher than during adolescence. Geschwind (1983) also is quick to point out that right hemisphere dominance in males and in non-right-handed populations leads to much higher visuospatial ability, superior skill in such areas as geometry and problem solving in mathematics, and a resulting overrepresentation in occupations such as architecture, engineering, and athletics. However, learning disabilities may be a result as well.

Sex difference in mathematical reasoning for high-ability students has been reported in a series of studies by Benbow and Stanley (1983). Mathematical reasoning was assessed by the mathematical portion of the College Board Scholastic Aptitude Test (SAT-M). Particularly at the levels of mathematical reasoning above 600 (maximum score possible = 800), the number of boys exceeded the number of girls by more than four to one. These data have elicited substantial controversy. Benbow and Stanley (1983) argue that hypothesized explanations of sex difference in mathematical reasoning may not be explained by differential formal training in mathematics, course taking, attitudes toward mathematics, or overall background. Moreover, they argue that the observed sex difference in SAT-M, particularly of the highest levels of performance above 700, is in place before students enter adolescence.

Parsimonious evaluation of the literature and data on sex difference in mathematics at this time do not permit an interpretation that the observed difference between females and males in mathematics is related directly to neurological factors. The neurological substrates of mathematical performance are not at all clear. For example, it is inappropriate to attempt to draw relationships between reports of dyscalculia in patients with neurological insult and the academic performance of highly talented individuals in mathematics. More precise definition of cognitive and neural substrates of mathematics is required before a neuropsychological interpretation of sex difference in mathematics is warranted. Nevertheless, neurodevelopmental substrates relating gender difference in mathematics may emerge eventually. It may be that existing neuropsychological and neurodevelopmental evidence of sex differences in verbal and spatial abilities may be related to components of performance in mathematics in ways that are not yet apparent. For example, Kraft (in press) assessed familial handedness in 155 boys and girls between the ages of 2 1/2 and 5 1/2 years. She assessed performance on dichotic presentation of digits and environmental sounds and on three Wechsler subscales (Vocabulary, Geometric Design, and Block Design). She found sex differences in lateral specialization and spatial ability favoring boys as young as 2 1/2 years of age. Kraft interpreted her data to suggest a transition in cortical organization from subcortical to cortical structures, including the corpus callosum, at about 4 years of age with developmental differences between boys and girls.

General female/male behavioral characteristics may be better understood in light of these data. The extreme case of high *in utero* levels of testosterone may lead to several subtle pathologies in brain structure and immune regulation. However, a continuum again may be suggested wherein levels of testosterone comprise the variable. As the delay in development of the left hemisphere in males continues, a higher degree of lateralization of function results. Seemingly, the greater the delay (levels of testosterone), the greater the likelihood for a dominant visuospatial function. The more within normal ranges levels of testosterone remain, the more likely normal male development may occur. For the female as well, circulating androgens at some level are part of the fetal environment, and variability of intensity may result in the development of lateralization of function according to the same continuum suggested earlier.

The literature tends to confound sex differences by describing statistical results in an oversimplified way. Research data on gender differ-

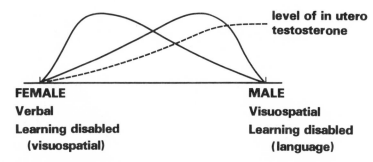

FEMALE
Verbal
Learning disabled
(visuospatial)

MALE
Visuospatial
Learning disabled
(language)

FIGURE 4. Developmental influences on gender variability in patterns of strength and weakness.

ence characteristically are treated statistically in two discrete groups—females or males. In the process, the continuum of variability has a tendency to be lost—as depicted in Figure 4. Obviously, some females have developmental learning disorders, are left-handed, and represent themselves in professions dependent on visuospatial dominance in cognitive ability. The continuum described above accounts for the extremes most generally observed in males and females, but also explains the normal variability between the sexes.

The differences between the sexes are significant, yet the variability in their expression in both sexes obviously prohibits describing the differences as examples of sexual dimorphism in the human species. Instead, we suggest that the general variability in functional lateralization has provided the species with unique survival characteristics that have been selected for biological and social relevance.

PHYLOGENETIC DEVELOPMENT OF SEX DIFFERENCES

The basis for many observed differences between males and females in behavior and cognitive processing lies in the bilateral nature of brain structures and lateral specialization of function of the hemispheres. Levy (1977a) argues that the functional asymmetry of the human brain is a biological adaptation and that variations in the degree of lateralization indicates the operation of distinctive selection processes. This variation, most dramatic between the sexes, occurred in a social context that functioned to enhance the fitness of the entire species. Lateral specialization of function nearly doubled the cognitive capability of the human species. In addition, the process by which one hemisphere predominates in cognitive activity may serve to enhance the survival capability of the species since it varies among members of the species and between the sexes. Members of the human species have been mutually dependent for their survival; thus such specialization of cognitive function among the members increased the overall fitness of the species.

Both culture and social structure are shaped by biological imperatives, whereas biological traits are altered through behavior patterns that are directly related to selective processes of survival and reproduction (Lumsden & Wilson, 1981). We suggest that development of lateral specialization of function in the human species resulted from an interaction among the biological imperative of survival, the development of a social structure, and biological traits that directed specific behavioral patterns among members of the species. These behavioral patterns differed among the members, especially between males and females, but served to enhance the survival capacity of the species as a whole. These behavioral characteristics, founded in biological imperative, were selected for and became a critical part of the human species. Primitive humans would have benefited from very specific differences between the sexes in behavioral ability. Visuospatial ability would enhance the need males fulfilled as hunter, whereas the species benefited from the female verbal ability to transmit culture. Female/male variability would benefit the species in areas such as parenting instinct, socialization, and lower need for activity (female), and high activity needs and aggressiveness (male). In contemporary society, the species advantage of sex difference in primitive cultures no longer holds. But contemporary culture is of very recent origin compared with the overall phylogeny of man. In dealing with sex differences in our contemporary culture, it is important to recall our biological heritage.

It appears that *Homo sapiens* is a reflection of the primitive selection process to adapt biologically to the needs of the species and the environment. Our unique behavioral synthesis is a reflection of the mechanism by which we accomplished the test of survival—lateral specialization of cognitive function between the sexes. However, the characteristics are expressed variably between males and females due to the mechanism by which it is accomplished. *In utero* levels of circulating androgens in both males and females has been suggested as the critical component in a variability of behavioral expression.

CONCLUSION

In conclusion, an appropriate understanding of sex differences in neuropsychological and cognitive function requires a model of individual difference that permits consideration of the dynamic interaction of a cluster of key variables. These variables comprise a broad profile adequate to explain the individual differences in characteristic cognitive and learning-style pattern (Languis, 1983b, 1984). Languis defined learning style as the consistent pattern of behavior and performance by which an individual approaches educational experiences. It is formed in the deep structure of neural organization and personality, which molds and is molded by human development variables and cultural influences of experience in the home, school, and society (Languis, 1981a,b). An individual's learning style is consistent with the general expectation that the individual brings to an experience and the strategies by which he or she constructs personal meaning from the experience.

Individuals develop and exhibit a learning style rather early in life. Structure, originally laid down through inheritance, is influenced prenatally, as we have seen. That with which one is born provides a predisposition toward a consistent learning pattern, but it is only the beginning. Development and change continue through the individual's encounters with the environment. Learning style therefore needs to be conceptualized in terms of deeply embedded structures within the individual. This definition of learning style suggests that we will not make lasting contributions to educational practice by diagnosing learning styles solely on the basis of self-report measures of students' preferences. The definition also suggests that learning style is a reflection of basic and deeply embedded structures that comprise individual differences.

As such the individual's learning style is rather stable but is not fixed. First, any individual's world view is broad enough to allow the individual to adapt somewhat to the conditions of a particular learning situation. There is some range of accommodation within each individual's learning style. But the nature of that adaptive range will vary among individuals. Moreover, the manner by which each individual adjusts will be unique to him or her. Therefore we need to look beyond surface features and behaviors to understand the learning processes individuals employ in adapting their learning styles to cope with educational tasks. Consideration of a vector model of gender difference may be useful in conceptualizing the necessary breadth and complexity of human sex differences and to provide directions for research, development, and application to practice in the helping professions.

REFERENCES

Benbow, C., & Stanley, J. Sex differences in mathematical reasoning: More facts. *Science,* 1983, *222,* 1029–1033.

Berlin, D., & Languis, M. L. Hemispheric brain function and sex differences in FDI and spatial measures. *Perceptual and Motor Skills,* 1980, *50,* 959–967.

Bradshaw, J. L., & Nettleton, N. C. *Human cerebral asymmetry*. New York: Prentice-Hall, 1983.

Bryden, M. P. *Laterality: Functional asymmetry in the intact brain*. New York: Academic Press, 1982.

Buffery, A. W., & Gray, J. A. Sex differences in the development of spatial and linguistic skills. In C. Ounsted & D. C. Taylor (Eds.), *Gender differences: Their ontogeny and significance*. London: Churchill Livingstone, 1972.

deLacoste-Utamsing, C., & Holloway, R. L. Sexual dimorphism in the human corpus callosum. *Science*, 1982, *216*, 1431–1432.

Ehrhardt, A. A., & Baker, S. W. Fetal androgens, human CNS differentiation and behavior sex differences. In R. C. Friedman, R. M. Richart, & R. L. Vande Wiele (Eds.), *Sex differences in behavior*. New York: Wiley, 1974.

Galaburda, A., & Kemper, T. Cytoarchitectonic abnormalities in developmental dyslexia: A case study. *Annals of Neurology*, 1979, *6*, 94–100.

Geschwind, N. *Associations of dominance with immune disease, migraine and other biological features*. Paper presented at the Conference on Biological Foundations of Cerebral Dominance, Harvard University School of Medicine, Boston, April 1983.

Geschwind, N., & Behan, P. Left-handedness: Association with immune disease, migraine, and developmental learning disorder. *Proceedings of the National Academy of Science*, 1982, *79* , 5097–5100.

Goy, R. W., & McEwen, B. S. *Sexual differentiation of the brain*. Cambridge, Mass.: M.I.T. Press, 1980.

Harris, L. J. Sex-differences in spatial ability: Possible environmental, genetic, and neurological factors. In M. Kinsbourne (Ed.), *Asymmetrical function of the brain*. Cambridge, England: Cambridge University Press, 1978.

Kraft, R. Lateral specialization and verbal/spatial ability in preschool children: Age, sex and familial handedness differences. *Neuropsychologia*, 22, 319–335.

Languis, M. L. *Learning style: A point of view for valuing young learners*. Paper presented at a conference of the National Association for the Education of Young Children, Detroit, November 1981.(a)

Languis, M. L. *Some considerations in an approach to cognitive and learning styles: Task force on learning styles and brain behavior*. National Association of Secondary School Principals, Reston, Va., 1981.(b)

Languis, M. L. *Cognititve dimensions of spatial learning with the personal computer*. Paper presented at a conference of the Ohio Academy of Science, Bowling Green, Ohio, May 1983.(a)

Languis, M. L. A model of learning style in professional development programs for physicians. In L. Curry (Ed.), *Learning style in continuing medical education*. Ottawa, Canada: Canadian Medical Association, 1983.(b)

Languis, M. L. *Neurocognitive substraits of learning style*. Proceedings of the 36th Annual Conference on Engineering in Medicine and Biology, Columbus, Ohio, September 1983.(c)

Languis, M. L., & Kraft, R. H. Neuroscience and educational practice: Asking better questions. In V. Rentel, S. Corson, & B. Dunn (Eds.), *Psychophysiological aspects of reading and learning*. New York: Grune & Stratton, 1985.

Languis, M. L., Naour, P. J., Martin, D. J., & Buffer, J. (Eds.). *Cognitive science: Contributions to educational practice*. Columbus, Ohio: Educational Resources Information Services, in press.

Languis, M. L., Sanders, T., & Tipps, S. *Brain and learning: Directions in early childhood education*. Washington, D.C.: National Association for the Education of Young Children, 1980.

Levy, J. A review of evidence for a genetic component in handedness. *Behavior Genetics*, 1976, *6*, 422–453.

Levy, J. The mammalian brain and the adaptive advantage of cerebral asymmetry. *Annals of the New York Academy of Sciences*, 1977, *229*, 264–272.(a)

Levy, J. The origins of lateral asymmetry. In S. R. Harnad, R. W. Doty, L. Goldstein, J. Jaynes, & G. Krauthamer (Eds.), *Lateralization in the nervous system*. New York: Academic Press, 1977.(b)

Lumsden, C. J., & Wilson, E. D. *Genes, mind and culture*. Cambridge, Mass.: Harvard University Press, 1981.

McGee, M. G. Human spatial abilities: Psychometric studies and environmental, genetic, hormonal, and neurological influences. *Psychological Bulletin*, 1979, *86*, 889–918.

McGlone, J. Sex differences in human brain asymmetry: A critical survey. *The Behavioral and Brain Sciences*, 1980, *3*, 215–263.

Naour, P. J., Languis, M. L., & Martin, D. J. *Electrophysiological evidence for a predominantly visuospatial processing style in learning disability students*. Paper presented at a conference of the American Educational Research Association, New Orleans, April 1984.

Phoenix, C. H., Goy, R. W., Gerall, A. A., & Young, W. C. Organizational action of prenatally administered testosterone propionate on the tissues mediating behavior in the female guinea pig. *Endrocrinology*, 1959, *65*, 369–382.

Reinisch, J. M., Gandelman, R., & Spiegel, F. S. Prenatal influences on cognitive abilities: Data from experimental animals and human and endocrine syndromes. In M. A. Wittig & A. C. Petersen (Eds.), *Sex-related differences in cognitive functioning*. New York: Academic Press, 1979.

Rogers, L. Male hormones and behaviour. In B. Lloyd & J. Archer (Eds.), *Exploring sex differences*. New York: Academic Press, 1976.

Waber, D. P. Cognitive abilities and sex-related variations in the maturation of cerebral cortical functions. In M. A. Wittig & A. C. Petersen (Eds.), *Sex-related differences in cognitive functioning*, New York: Academic Press, 1979.

Wada, J. A. Cerebral anatomical asymmetry in infant brains. In D. Kimura (Chair), *Sex differences in brain asymmetry*. Symposium presented at the 4th annual meeting of the International Neurological Society, Toronto, February 1976.

Wada, J. A., Clarke, R., & Hamm, A. Cerebral hemispheric asymmetry in humans. *Archives of Neurology*, 1975, *32*, 239–246.

Witelson, S. F. Sex and the single hemisphere: Specialization of the right hemisphere for spatial processing. *Science*, 1976, *193*, 425–427.

Witelson, S. F., & Pallie, W. Left hemisphere specialization for language in the newborn: Neuroanatomical evidence of asymmetry. *Brain*, 1973, *96*, 641–646.

Wittig, M. A., & Petersen, A. C. (Eds.). *Sex-related differences in congitive functioning*. New York: Academic Press, 1979.

CHAPTER 11

A Survey of Developmental Neurologic Conditions
Implications for Individual Neuropsychological Differences

PATRICIA L. HARTLAGE

INTRODUCTION

Other than those occasional delightful interlopers who are found to have benign developmental aberrations such as large heads of a familial nature or night terrors, and the farewell visits with the fortunate few who have recovered from acute neurological disorders like Reye's syndrome or CNS infections, the pediatric neurologist deals with the nervous system in disease and not in health. Yet, in surveying our larger experience with the nervous system in childhood involved in some disease state, one can still glean a great deal of information about the influences of the congenital endowment of the brain and the effects of events in the early development on behaviors observed later in life both in individuals considered within and outside of the limits of normal psychological function.

CONGENITAL INFLUENCES ON NEUROPSYCHOLOGICAL DIFFERENCES

GENETIC ENDOWMENT

All parents and grandparents delight in pointing out familial physical resemblances in new offspring, and most also identify, as the child grows

PATRICIA L. HARTLAGE • Division of Pediatric Neurology, Medical College of Georgia, Augusta, Georgia 30902.

and matures, personality and cognitive styles in the child resembling those of immediate ancestors, for obvious reasons finding it easier to recognize similar positive characteristics to one's own side of the family tree and negative traits common to the in-laws. The popular press periodically recounts reunions of identical twins and in recent years one set of identical triplets separated at birth and reunited in adult life. These accounts often emphasize remarkable similarities in the individuals, not only in physical appearance but also in career choice, leisure interests, and spouse characteristics. A few scientific studies of identical twins (Rose, Harris, Christian, & Nance, 1979) and of a comparison of fraternal and identical twins (Vandenberg, 1976) suggest a significant hereditary function in learning.

Jensen's papers on the population genetics of intelligence (Jensen 1969a,b) suggested heredity is the major determinant of intelligence and brought tremendous visibility to this issue, although inspiring more social protest than hard science. The most receptive audience for this concept included people working in the field of mental retardation who were seeking to understand why so many more boys than girls were retarded, and why there were so many families with several retarded male members. Lehrke (1972) hypothesized that several major genes related to intelligence were located on the X chromosome, which would help explain not only sex-linked recessive mental retardation, but also the greater variation in intelligence in males, with over representation of males at both ends of the intellectual scale. This hypothesis also is compatible with previous observations of sex-linked inheritance of spatial abilities (Stafford, 1961) and the increased incidence of mild mental retardation and lower verbal IQs in boys with X-linked muscular dystrophy (Liebowitz & Dubowitz, 1981). Recently, techniques actually have demonstrated fragility of the X chromosome in affected males and their mothers in some families with X-linked mental retardation (Turner, Till, & Daniel, 1978).

The autosomal chromosomes appear to carry so much genetic information that either excesses or deletions of all or even part of one of these chromosomes usually results in loss of the pregnancy or in multiple malformations and mental retardation in survivors. The former outcome probably is more frequent, since of the 0.5% of live-born infants who demonstrate chromosome abnormalities, half have abnormalities of the sex chromosome pair. Whereas the exact contribution of the X chromosome to cognitive traits cannot be inferred from its absence, since at least one must be present for a fetus to survive, other accidents of nature involving sex chromosomes have given some interesting insights into the genetics of neuropsychological functioning. The Y chromosome's primary function seems to be to organize development of a masculine phenotype and it does so even in the presence of more than one X chromosome. A second effect appears to be to influence the organism to develop at a slightly slower rate and this phenomenon is probably the key to the sex differences in cognition (Hutt, 1978; Ounsted & Taylor, 1972). A slower maturation rate of the nervous system allows greater phenotypic expression of the genotype, that is, of more desirable and more undesirable traits, lengthened periods of vulnerability to insult, and more time for the brain to develop specialized functions in discrete locations, a phenomenon that appears to encourage the development of spatial skills. Waber (1976) noted that in girls as well as in boys later physical maturation correlated with better development of spatial abilities.

In the absence of a Y chromosome the organism develops in a female pattern, for example in Turner's syndrome with sex chromosome genotype XO. Affected Turner's syndrome females, although sterile and requiring hormonal supplements for development of normal secondary sexual characteristics, usually are of normal intelligence, but consistently show selective space/form deficits (Money & Alexander, 1966; Schaffer, 1962; Waber, 1979), thus supporting the theories of Y chromosome effects on brain development. The presence of identical spatial deficits in girls with Turner's syndrome due to 45X/46XY mosaicism (Ebbin, Howell, & Wilson, 1980) must be explained, and the possible explanation may be inferred from the behavior of cells in culture from mosaic individuals where the XO cells grow much faster than the other cell lines (Barlow, 1973).

Studies of persons with other sex chromosome errors have yielded much less specific information about brain–behavior relationships. Both XYY and XXY genotypes have been associated with similar mild global intellectual dysfunction (Witkin, Sarnoff, Schulsinger, Bakkeström, Christiansen, Goodenough, Hirschhorn, Lundsteen, Owen, Philip, Rubin, & Stocking, 1976), and genotypes of XXX, XXXX, and so forth, usually result in global retardation of increasing degree in proportion to the number of superfluous X's (Barlow, 1973).

Some hereditary inborn errors of metabolism lead to devastating neurological results when the infant is exposed to normal diet. Strict dietary limitations can prevent damage in disorders like phenylketonuria and galactosemia, for which all newborns are now typically screened. More subtle inherited inborn predispositions to metabolic diseases affecting the brain also exist. A well-characterized neuropsychiatric disorder, the Wernicke–Korsakoff's syndrome, results from dietary thiamine deficiency in a small minority of alcoholics and other chronically malnourished persons. The predisposing factor appears to be an inherited inefficiency of the enzyme transketolase (E.C. 2.2.1.) which binds thiamine pyrophosphate (Blass & Gibson, 1977).

The inheritance of most manic-depressive psychosis is recognized
to be autosomal dominant with variable penetrance. A possible locus for
the gene has been suggested to exist on chromosome 6 (Weitkamp, Stancer, Persad, Flood, & Guttormsen, 1981). Similarly, Tourette's syndrome
of childhood-onset motor and verbal tics, which has no psychotic or intellectual concomitants but usually includes some element of attentional
deficit disorder, also follows a pattern of dominant transmission with
mixed penetrance.

The risk of schizophrenia to relatives of schizophrenic patients increases markedly with the degree of genetic relatedness, with an identical
twin of a schizophrenic three times as likely as a fraternal twin to develop
schizophrenia and 35 to 60 times as likely as an unrelated person in the
general population (Gottesman & Shields, 1982). The pattern of inheritance
of schizophrenia does not follow a simple Mendelian pattern, and a poly-
genic transmission may be present. These hereditary factors seem active
only in schizophrenia with onset after puberty and not in childhood psychosis.

DEVELOPMENTAL, STRUCTURAL, AND PHYSIOLOGICAL DIFFERENCES

Dyslexia probably is the prototype of specific neuropsychological
dysfunctions. In many cases it is a hereditary trait, but it may be an acquired dysfunction as well. One autopsy study of a dyslexic man described
both abnormal neuronal migration and reduction in size of the left planum
temporale (Galaburda & Kemper, 1979). Electrophysiological studies employing computer analyses of brain electrical activity at rest and during
behavioral testing and of evoked responses in the brain to various sensory
stimuli have been conducted. Electrophysiological profiles have been
found in dyslexic students that are distinctive from normals, arithmetic
underachievers, and from those underachieving in both reading and
arithmetic (John, Karmel, Corning, Easton, Brown, Ahn, John, Harmany,
Prichep, Toro, Gerson, Bartlett, Thatcher, Kaye, Valdes, & Schwartz, 1977),
and have been proposed to be of use diagnostically in dyslexia (Duffy,
Denckla, Bartels, Sandini, & Kiessling, 1980). Although the major electrophysiological differences in dyslexics appear to be in the left posterior
temporal parietal area, studies looking at electrical activity in all cortical
areas show abnormalities in a widely distributed brain system involved
in language, rather than a discrete focal lesion. Duffy, Denckla, Bartels,
and Sandini (1980) found four distinct regions of differences between
dyslexics and normals: the supplementary motor areas in both medial
frontal lobes, the left lateral frontal lobe, the left midtemporal area, and
the traditionally implicated left posterior temporoparietal area, correlating
well with cerebral blood flow studies that show activation of all of these

areas during oral or silent reading, as well as spontaneous speech. Other syndromes of cognitive dysfunction, such as Gerstmann's syndrome of finger agnosia, right–left disorientation, dysgraphia, and dyscalculia due to disorders of the dominant parietal lobe originally described in adult brain injury have been identified in genetic and perinatally acquired forms (Hermann & Norrie, 1958; Kinsbourne & Warrington, 1963).

Balancing these and other syndromes of specific dysfunction are the specific cognitive excellences, which also might have underlying structural or physiological correlates. One of the best documented of these groups, the mathematically gifted (Benbow & Stanley, 1983), shares with dyslexia being heavily male and having an increased incidence of left-handedness and autoimmune disorders (Kolata, 1983; Marx, 1982). Norman Geschwind had proposed for several years that testosterone in fetal life favors development of the right hemisphere, and predicted just such a mixture of impaired and enhanced abilities in the left-handed male. The sex differences in neuropsychology are covered more completely in Chapter 10, but require mention here since they illustrate another congenital structural or psychological phenomenon. Nowhere do these differences stand out so clearly as when one looks at how, rather than how well, males and females do things (Coltheart, Hull, & Slater, 1975; Thomas, Jamison, & Hummel, 1973). The numerous studies conducted on normal individuals exploring and defining sex differences have been an impetus to expanding the assessment of cognitive function beyond the psychometric approach to the strategies involved in problem solving and to examine individual differences in mental processes (Hunt, 1983).

INTRAUTERINE ENVIRONMENTAL INFLUENCES

Whereas the basic structures of the nervous system and of organ systems are formed early in fetal life, migration of neurons to their eventual intended locations continues throughout gestation, and the establishment and refinement of the connections between neurons continues well beyond the time of birth. Infections that can be acquired transplacentally will cause quite different effects on the developing organism depending on the time of exposure. Malformations of multiple organ systems result from infections in the first trimester, whereas damage that is more restricted to the developing brain is associated with infections occurring later in the pregnancy. The sequelae of intrauterine infection may be apparent at birth in a neurologically abnormal infant who has a small brain and head, or latently present in a normal-looking newborn who later in life is found to have some hearing impairment, social or behavioral problems, or learning disabilities (Kairam & DeVivo, 1981).

The most common intrauterine toxin is likely to be alcohol; heavy continuous exposure throughout the pregnancy results in the fetal alcohol syndrome characterized by multiple congenital anomalies and mental retardation. Examination of the brains in these infants reveals them to be small, with a markedly disordered pattern of neuronal migration. As an increasing number of drugs have been shown to have at least some potential for fetal damage (Arena, 1979; Jick, Holmes, Hunter, Madsen, & Stergachis, 1981), there is great concern about the effects of any drug used during pregnancy. Even drugs with good safety records in common use for morning sickness (Cordereo, Oakley, Greenberg, & James, 1981) are being taken off the market. Within recent years, a new field, behavioral teratology, has emerged to study birth defects of the mind, such as hyperactivity and mild intellectual deficits and again certain drugs are being implicated as having a causal relationship in such disorders (Kolata, 1978).

The chemical milieu *in utero*, with potential aberrant contributions from either maternal (Lipson, Beuhler, Bartley, Walsh, Yu, O'Halloran, & Webster, 1984; Yalom, Green, & Fisk, 1973) or fetal sources, appears to contribute to the development of behavioral patterns that may be lifelong. The excessive androgens produced because of enzymatic block in the adrenogenital syndrome cause both physical and behavioral virilization of infant girls, the latter persisting despite medical and surgical correction of the physical effects of the disorder (Ehrhardt & Meyer-Bahlburg, 1979). In the normal male infant, androgens produced *in utero* similarly contribute to the enhancement of male behavior characteristics and may play a role in sex differences in the prevalence of developmental language disorders and in qualitative differences in cognitive skills (e.g., considerable evidence indicates that women tend to perform somewhat better on verbal and men on spatial and mathematical measures [Maccoby & Jacklin, 1974]). Further evidence of the importance of androgens early in life to sex-specific cognitive traits is found in studies of adult men with normal 46 XY karyotypes who have idiopathic hypogonadotropic hypogonadism which was identified when normal pubescence failed to occur. These males of average intelligence have markedly impaired spatial ability in comparison to controls and to men who acquire hypogonadism after puberty (Hier & Crowley, 1982), and hormone replacement did not improve their spatial skills. In another study of younger children with hypogonadism, selected on the basis of a small penis being noted at birth, IQs approximated a normal distribution, but the entire curve was skewed with 75% of these youngsters having a Full-Scale IQ over 109. The major focus of this report was a caution about almost predicting adverse cognitive function in congenital syndromes. Although it is very difficult to resist the temptation to deduce other correlations from the study, it is notable that even in this more gifted group verbal reasoning ability was the highest and numeric reasoning the lowest (Money, Lehne, & Norman, 1983).

Mechanical disruption of normal brain growth is best exemplified by congenital hydrocephalus which may occur as an isolated anomaly or in conjunction with defects of neural tube closure. The earlier the onset of the obstruction, the more dilation of the ventricular system posteriorly and the more relative compression of the visual and perceptual systems of the brain. Defective ocular motility because of pressure effects further impedes input into these areas, and the resultant neuropsychological profile of the hydrocephalic child is well known to all developmental specialists, with the striking relative preservation of verbal abilities even when mental retardation is present (Dennis, Fitz, Haywood-Nash, Hendrick, Hoffman, Humphreys, Netley, & Sugar, 1981) and the frequently identified "cocktail party personality." One issue of special interest in regard to hydrocephalus is the relationship of the thickness of the remaining cortical mantle to predictions of eventual intellectual abilities in the hydrocephalic infant. With continuing surgical experience employing increasingly improved shunting techniques for hydrocephalus, neurosurgeons have ceased to be shocked at the normal intellectual function observed in children whose cortical mantle was measured in millimeters preoperatively. Even without surgical intervention normal function may be preserved. Professor John Lorber of the Spina Bifida Unit in Sheffield, England, in a paper entitled, "Is Your Brain Really Necessary?," reviewed over 600 neuroradiological studies on patients and noted that even in the 10% who were severely hydrocephalic, with ventricular expansion filling 95% of the cranium, over half of the group had IQs above 100 (Lewin, 1980). Another observation that questions traditional beliefs about the exclusive role of the cerebral cortex in behavior is the demonstration in a newborn twin with a severe birth defect involving absence of the entire cerebral cortex of associative learning in both the impaired and normal co-twin (Tuber, Berntson, Bachman, & Allen, 1980).

Although the cases described pertain to a few unique situations, they have applications for each and every live-born human in illustrating that by birth, environment already has influenced development and may have profound implications for future behavioral functioning. A survey addressing the "continuum of reproductive casualty" in the entire first grade in a normal public school found a relationship between academic performance and the number of minor congenital anomalies that reflect first-trimester adverse influences. The children with the highest number of minor anomalies were more likely to be in the 15% of children who were recommended to repeat first grade (Rosenberg & Weller, 1973). In a study of 81 hyperactive boys, the number of minor congenital anomalies cor-

related with severity of hyperactivity (Quinn & Rapoport, 1974), and in
the one published prospective study of 30 newborn male infants, similar
correlations were seen between minor anomalies noted at birth and hyperactive behaviors at age 3 (Waldrop, Bell, McLaughlin, & Halverson, 1978).

POSTNATAL INFLUENCES ON THE DEVELOPING BRAIN

The timing of a given neurological insult may be as important as the
nature of the insult in determining the results. The outcomes of perinatal
hypoxia and circulatory disturbances are profoundly different in the premature than in the term infant (Pape & Wigglesworth, 1979; Volpe & Pasternak, 1977). Beyond the perinatal period, although the plasticity of the
very young nervous system seems to allow better recovery from focal insults, younger children with diffuse injuries such as meningitis or Reye's
syndrome display poorer recovery of function than older children (Chelune & Edwards, 1981).

There is an increasing and appropriately concerned awareness of
the serious behavioral sequelae of so-called "minor head injuries" or con-
cussions (Rimel, Giordani, Barth, Boll, & Jane, 1981) in adults and one
wonders whether to presume a higher or lower level of concern for the
young child after such an event. The peak incidence of childhood trauma
is under 1 year of age, approximately half of these involving birth trauma.
This unfortunately coincides with the period of most rapid brain growth.
The compliance and smooth interior of the infant skull and the elastic
properties of the less-well-myelinated infant brain results in different types
of traumatic damage pathologically, with tears in the white matter the
predominant result of trauma up to 5 months of age, rather than the
contusions and hemorrhages seen later in life. Many clinical observations
suggest different sequelae of head trauma in early life. In the child less
than 5 years of age, trauma is more likely to result in seizures, especially
when the child is younger than 1 year of age at the time of injury. Yet,
the surgical loss of large portions of cortex has a much better prognosis
for recovery of function when the individual is less than 2 years of age.
It is a small wonder so many discordant ideas about children's prognoses
after brain injury exist, and it is certain one cannot extrapolate from adult
data relating computed tomography scan findings or length of coma as
equally valid prognostic indicators after head trauma to the childhood
population (McLaurin & McLennan, 1982). It is unusual to encounter individuals who have never experienced some sort of head trauma, and
injuries with brief losses of consciousness and apparent rapid recovery
are extremely common. The timing of these minor traumata, which are

almost a way of life for the active growing child, especially a boy, probably equals or exceeds the degree of injury in determining whether or not there will be some mild but persistent behavioral consequence.

Nutrition usually exerts its influence on brain growth and function only postnatally because of nature's extremely privileged arrangements for the fetus, especially in the first and second trimesters. However, in cases of prenatal growth retardation, the special vulnerability of the youngest brains to nutritional influences is emphasized. When a child's growth pattern already has been seriously impaired by the time of birth, subsequent development may be impaired as well. In a longitudinal study to school age of low-birth-weight infants in England, those of small size at full term fared less well developmentally than prematurely born infants of similar weight (Neligan, Kolvin, Scott, & Garside, 1976).

Severe malnutrition postnatally has its severest long-term behavioral consequences on the youngest infants, with permanent retardation in both physical and mental growth occurring in many, and impairments in coordination, concentration, and short-term memory in most. This period of nutritional vulnerability to irreversible dysfunction extends from the third trimester through the normal period of breast-feeding, a period when dendrites sprout from the neurons to form synaptic connections, failure of which is the common anatomic correlate of mental retardation of various causes.

The common association of nutritional and social deprivation confounds interpretation of the relative effects of each, but in the British study cited, the small-for-gestational-age infants actually were more socially advantaged, and studies of disadvantaged children in Central America suggest nutritional variables and behavioral competence that are independent of socioeconomic variables. Also, longitudinal follow-up of Korean infants adopted into privileged homes in the United States found that although those infants who had been malnourished at the time of adoption were of normal intelligence later in life, those who were not malnourished were above average in intelligence (Read & Felson, 1976). In highly developed countries one of the factors most contributing to the decreasing neurological morbidity of prematurity is the improvement in nutritional support for these babies at high risk.

There is a great deal of interest in the role of diet and hyperactivity, and more controversy than agreement exists on this issue, but the relationship between iron deficiency and behavior is well established. The behavioral characteristics of the iron-deficient infant or child are well-known to every pediatrician. These are irritable children, uncoordinated and poorly attentive to their surroundings, and remarkably responsive within days of initiation of iron therapy in terms of these behavioral aberrations, well before any hematological response is observed in their iron deficiency anemia (Oski & Honig, 1978).

BIOCHEMICAL INFLUENCES ON BEHAVIOR

There appear to be biochemical correlates of certain disorders of behavior. Paranoid schizophrenics have been reported to have elevations of norepinephrine in the cerebrospinal fluid (Lake, Sternberg, Van Kammen, Ballenger, Ziegler, Post, Kopin, & Bunney, 1980), lower activity in the blood of the enzyme involved in its degradation (Potkin, Cannon, Murphy, & Wyatt, 1978), and increased excretion of phenylethylamine (Potkin, Karoum, Chuang, Cannon-Spoor, Phillips, & Wyatt, 1979), an "endogenous amphetamine" that also has been noted to be excreted in the urine by normal people under stress (Paulos & Tessell, 1982). Low urine concentrations of the further metabolite of phenylethylamine, phenylacetic acid, has been proposed as a biochemical marker for depression (Gonzalez, 1983; Sabelli, Fawcett, Gusovsky, Javiad, Edwards, & Jeffries, 1983). A subgroup of autistic children have elevated blood serotonin levels and some of their symptoms respond to drugs that decrease brain serotonin (Geller, Ritvo, Freeman, & Yuwiler, 1982; Ritvo, Freeman, Geller, & Yuwiler, 1983). Numerous human and animal studies support the theory that hyperactive children may have depletion of dopamine (Golden, 1982). None of these biochemical correlations are consistent enough nor specific enough to threaten the livelihood of the diagnostic clinician.

There are individual differences in the rate of aging, both physically and mentally. The most common cause of dementia in middle and late life, Alzheimer's disease, is neuropathologically identical to changes that happen in any brain with extremely advanced age, but recently there has been identified a dysfunction of a specific pathway from the nucleus basalis of Meynert in the basal forebrain to various regions of the cerebral cortex. This pathway uses acetylcholine as its neurotransmitter (Whitehouse, Price, Struble, Clark, Coyle, & Delong, 1982).

The activation and function of various systems and pathways in the brain depend on chemical synapses. Neurotransmitters like acetylcholine, dopamine, norepinephrine, and serotonin are highly localized in specific populations of neurons. The deterioration of the dopaminergic pathway from the substantia nigra in the brain stem to the basal ganglia in Parkinson's disease has been well studied, and symptomatic treatment for those afflicted by replacement of the deficient neurotransmitter by oral administration of its precursor is well established, but other dopaminergic pathways also exist and project heavily to the limbic system. Norepinephrine-containing neurons in the brain stem have been identified to project to all brain regions. The neurons containing these two chemically related catecholamine transmitters, dopamine and norepinephrine, make up only a small fraction of all neurons in the human brain, and multi-synaptic pathways with multiple neurotransmitters are likely. However, these catecholamines were the first identified and are the best studied of the lot and there is some general agreement about the effects of various drugs prescribed to treat psychiatric illness on these systems (Moskowitz & Wurtman, 1975).

The psychotropic drugs exert their influence by preventing or facilitating access of the transmitter to its receptor site by influencing transmitter synthesis, storage, or release, or by influencing its degradation. Most of the biogenic amines have their greatest concentration of activity in the limbic system, and it is no surprise that the drugs acting on these amines influence an individual's affective and behavioral state.

Depletion or inactivation of norepinephrine induces somnolence and depression, whereas increasing or potentiating its action results in stimulation and has antidepressant effects. The major tranquilizers partially block the receptors of norepinephrine and dopamine, the latter blockade causing side effects similar to the symptoms of parkinsonism when these drugs are employed. There appears to be a direct correlation of the clinical potency of the major tranquilizers in controlling the symptoms of schizophrenia with their affinity to bind to a specific subgroup of dopamine receptors, the D_2 receptors (Gottesman & Shields, 1982). Amphetamines, in contrast, stimulate release or block re-uptake of dopamine and norepinephrine. Monoamine oxidase inhibitors used in the treatment of depression block their catabolism. The mechanism of action of many psychotropic drugs is poorly understood, and how lithium carbonate can smooth out both the highs and lows of manic-depressive illness remains a puzzle.

Hemispheric differences in neurotransmitter concentration are not unlikely given the different behavioral profiles of right and left brain injury. The depression associated with right hemisphere dysfunction (Weintraub & Mesulam, 1983) and the more selective impairments observed in depressed patients of neuropsychological parameters associated with right hemisphere function have suggested the possibility of potential benefits of antidepressant medications for both groups (Brumback, Staton, & Wilson, 1984) and should recapture the interest of neuropsychologists in affective disorders.

CONCLUSION

It is an essential human quality for each individual to be unique from any other member of the species. The footprinting of infants and fingerprinting of criminals for identification capitalizes on two of the more simple anatomic parameters that illustrate the uniqueness of all persons. Although each individual's behavior also appears to be unique, until recently it has been only on autopsy that one could actually see that each human brain, despite similarities to other human brains, has its own unique anatomic characteristics. Recent advances in neuroradiological imaging allow us to look safely and closely at the structure of the brain in life. Figures 1 through 3 demonstrate the detail that can be observed in the living brain with computerized axial tomography and nuclear magnetic resonance imaging.

For many years the electrical activity of the brain has been studied and correlated with various neurological functions and dysfunctions in both the waking and sleeping brain. Neurological surgeons have for some time employed electrical stimulation of the brain exposed at surgery in attempting to map out the location of various functions in an individual brain. As mentioned in the section on dyslexia, the application of computer technology to the analysis of brain rhythms recorded from standard

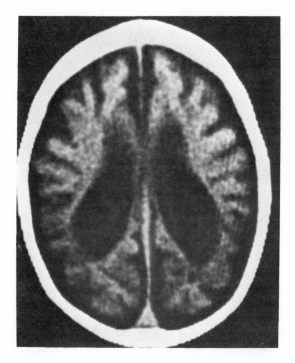

FIGURE 1. Computerized axial tomogram, horizontal section, of the brain showing severe atrophy and enlargement of the ventricles.

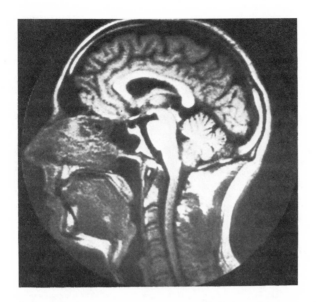

FIGURE 2. Nuclear magnetic resonance tomogram, sagittal view of intracranial contents.

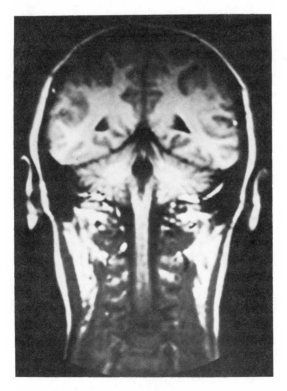

FIGURE 3. Nuclear magnetic resonance tomogram, coronal section of posterior portion of intracranial contents.

surface electrodes has provided noninvasive methods to study the electrical patterns of the brain, providing a look at both the normal and abnormal nervous system at rest and in the performance of various tests. A variety of techniques have been devised to measure regional cerebral blood flow, which correlates with brain activity in function as well as the integrity of brain vasculature, and most neuroscientists look to the latest of the neuroradiological tests in development, positron emission tomography, to have the highest yields of all in understanding basic brain–behavior relationships, since this technique can image metabolism of brain regions.

Historically, neurologists have learned about the normal functions of the brain only from the observation of the effects of specific dysfunctions. The neurodiagnostic techniques mentioned above were designed for the diagnosis and management of neurological disease, but the potential application of these technologies to the study of individual differences should inspire and encourage behavioral scientists to look to them to demonstrate profiles of specific cognitive behaviors and perhaps even to determine patterns that might be, in effect, the cognitive fingerprints of the individual. Advances in genetic techniques have potential applications not only for studying the inherited aspects of physical health, but also inherited aspects of human behavior. Finally, perhaps the most important behavioral insights will come from advances in biochemistry, since the observations of biochemical correlates of schizophrenia, autism, and depression have profound implications for the behavioral neuroscientist. Thus the future would seem destined to begin to close the gap between medical and surgical neuroscientists and behavioral neuroscientists because of the development of tools to study the brain which can be utilized productively by both groups and can form a common bond for classification, communication, and fruitful collaboration.

REFERENCES

Arena, J. M. Drug and chemical effects on mother and child. *Pediatric Annals*, 1979, *8*, 690–697.

Barlow, P. W. X-Chromosomes and human development. *Developmental Medicine and Child Neurology*, 1973, *5*, 205–207.

Benbow, C. P., & Stanley, J. C. Sex differences in mathematical reasoning ability: More facts. *Science*, 1983, *222*, 1029–1031.

Blass, J. P., & Gibson, G. E. Abnormality of a thiamine–requiring enzyme in patients with Wernicke–Korsakoff syndrome. *New England Journal of Medicine*, 1977, *297*, 1367–1370.

Brumback, R. A., Staton, R. D., & Wilson, H. Right cerebral hemispheric dysfunction. *Archives of Neurology*, 1984, *41*, 248–249.

Chelune, G. J., & Edwards, P. Early brain lesions: Ontogenetic environmental considerations. *Journal of Consulting and Clinical Psychology*, 1981, *49*, 777–790.

Coltheart, M., Hull, E., & Slater, D. Sex differences in imagery and reading. *Nature*, 1975, *253*, 438–440.

Cordero, J. F., Oakley, G. P., Greenberg, F., & James, L. M. Is Benedectin a teratogen? *Journal of the American Medical Association*, 1981, *245*, 2307–2310.

Dennis, M., Fitz, C. R., Haywood-Nash, D. C. F., Hendrick, E. B., Hoffman, H. J., Humphreys, R. P., Netley, C. T., & Sugar, J. The intelligence of hydrocephalic children. *Archives of Neurology*, 1981, *38*, 607–615.

Duffy, F. H., Denckla, M. B., Bartels, P. H., & Sandini, G. Dyslexia: Regional differences in brain electrical activity by topographic mapping. *Annals of Neurology*, 1980, *7*, 412–420.

Duffy, F. H., Denckla, M. B., Bartels, P. H., Sandini, G., & Kiessling, L. S. Dyslexia: Automated diagnosis by computerized classification of brain electrical activity. *Annals of Neurology*, 1980, *7*, 421–428.

Ebbin, A.J., Howell, V. V., & Wilson, M. G. Deficits in space-form perception in patients with sex chromosome mosaicism (45, X/46, XY). *Developmental Medicine and Child Neurology*, 1980, *22*, 352–361.

Ehrhardt, A. A., & Meyer-Bahlburg, H. F. L. Prenatal sex hormones and the developing brain: Effects on psychosexual differentiation and cognitive function. *Annual Review of Medicine*, 1979, *30*, 417–430.

Galaburda, A. M., & Kemper, T. L. Cytoarchitectonic abnormalities in developmental dyslexia: A case study. *Annals of Neurology*, 1979, *6*, 94–100.

Geller, E., Ritvo, E. R., Freeman, B. J., & Yuwiler, A. Preliminary observations on the effect of Fenfluramine on blood serotonin and symptoms in three autistic boys. *New England Journal of Medicine*, 1982, *307*, 165–169.

Golden, G. S. Neurobiological correlates of learning disabilities. *Annals of Neurology*, 1982, *12*, 409–418.

Gonzalez, E. R. A new biological marker for depression? *Journal of the American Medical Association*, 1983, *250*, 21.

Gottesman, I. I., & Shields, J. *Schizophrenia: The epigenetic puzzle*. Cambridge, England: Cambridge University Press, 1982.

Hermann, K., & Norrie, E. Is congenital word blindness a hereditary type of Gerstmann's syndrome? *Psychiatria Et Neurologia*, 1958, *136*, 59–73.

Hier, D. B., & Crowley, W. F., Jr. Spatial ability in androgen-deficient men. *New England Journal of Medicine*, 1982, *306*, 1202–1205.

Hunt, E. On the nature of intelligence. *Science*, 1983, *219*, 141–146.

Hutt, C. Biological bases of psychological sex differences. *American Journal of Disease of Children*, 1978, *132*, 170–177.

Jensen, A. R. How much can we boost IQ and scholastic achievement? *Harvard Educational Review*, 1969, *39*, 1–123.(a)

Jensen, A. R. Reducing the heredity-environment uncertainty: A reply. *Harvard Educational Review*, 1969, *39*, 449–483.(b)

Jick, H., Holmes, L. B., Hunter, J. R., Madsen, S., & Stergachis, A. First-trimester drug use and congenital disorders. *Journal of the American Medical Association*, 1981, *246*, 343–346.

John, E. R., Karmel, B. Z., Corning, W. C., Easton, P., Brown, D., Ahn, H., John, M., Harmany, T., Prichep, L., Toro, A., Gerson, I., Bartlett, F., Thatcher, R., Kaye, H., Valdes, P., & Schwartz, E. Neurometrics. *Science*, 1977, *196*, 1393–1410.

Kairam, R., & DeVivo, D. C. Neurologic manifestations of congenital infection. *Clinics in Perinatology*, 1981, *8*, 445–465.

Kinsbourne, M., & Warrington, E. K. The developmental Gerstmann syndrome. *Archives of Neurology*, 1963, *8*, 490–501.

Kolata, G.B. Behavioral teratology: Birth defects of the mind. *Science*, 1978, *202*, 732–734.

Kolata, G.B. Math genius may have a hormonal basis. *Science* 1983, *222*, 1312.

Lake, C. R., Sternberg, D. E., Van Kammen, D. P., Ballenger, J. C., Ziegler, M. G., Post, R. M., Kopin, I. J., & Bunney, W. E. Schizophrenia: Elevated cerebrospinal fluid norepinephrine. *Science*, 1980, *207*, 331–333.

Lehrke, R. A theory of X-linkage of major intellectual traits. *American Journal of Mental Deficiency*, 1972, *76*, 611–619.

Lewin, R. Is your brain really necessary? *Science*, 1980, *210*, 1232–1234.

Liebowitz, D., & Dubowitz, V. Intellect and behavior in Duchenne muscular dystrophy. *Developmental Medicine and Child Neurology*, 1981, *23*, 577–590.

Lipson, A., Beuhler, B., Bartley, J., Walsh, D., Yu, J., O'Halloran, M., & Webster, W. Maternal hyperphenylalaninemia: Fetal effects. *Journal of Pediatrics*, 1984, *104*, 216–220.

Maccoby, E. E., & Jacklin, C. N. *The psychology of sex differences*. Stanford, Calif.: Stanford University Press, 1974.

Marx, J. L. Autoimmunity in left-handers. *Science*, 1982, *217*, 141–142.

McLaurin, R. L., & McLennan, J. E. Diagnosis and treatment of head injury in children. In J. R. Youmans (Ed.), *Neurological surgery* (2nd ed.) Philadelphia: Saunders, 1982.

Money, J., & Alexander, D. Turner's syndrome: Further demonstration of the presence of specific cognitional deficiencies. *Journal of Medical Genetics*, 1966, *3*, 47–48.

Money, J., Lehne, G. K., & Norman, B. F. Psychology of syndromes. *American Journal of Diseases of Children*, 1983, *137*, 1083–1086.

Moskowitz, M. A., & Wurtman, R. J. Catecholamines and neurologic diseases. *New England Journal of Medicine*, Part I, 1975, *293*(6) 274–280; Part II, 1975, *293*(7), 332–338.

Neligan, G.A., Kolvin, I., Scott, D. McI., & Garside, R.F. *Born too soon or too small*. Philadelphia: Lippincott, 1976.

Oski, F. A., & Honig, A. S. The effects of therapy on the developmental scores of iron-deficient infants. *Journal of Pediatrics*, 1978, *92* (1), 21–25.

Ounsted, C., & Taylor, D. C. The Y-chromosome message: A point of view. In C. Ounsted & D. C. Taylor (Eds), *Gender differences—Their ontogeny and significance*. London: Churchill, 1972.

Pape, K. E., & Wigglesworth, J. S. *Haemorrhage, ischemia and the perinatal brain*. Philadelphia: Lippincott, 1979.

Paulos, M. A., & Tessell, R. E. Excretion of Beta-phenethylamine is elevated in humans after profound stress. *Science*, 1982, *215*, 1127–1129.

Potkin, S. G., Cannon, H. E., Murphy, D. L., & Wyatt, R. J. Are paranoid schizophrenics biologically different from other schizophrenics? *New England Journal of Medicine*, 1978, *298*, 61–66.

Potkin, S. G., Karoum, F., Chuang, L. W., Cannon-Spoor, H. E., Phillips, I., & Wyatt, R. J. Phenylethylamine in paranoid chronic schizophrenia. *Science*, 1979, *206*, 470–471.

Quinn, P. O., & Rapoport, J. L. Minor physical anomalies and neurologic status in hyperactive boys. *Pediatrics*, 1974, *53*, 742–747.

Read, M. S., & Felson, D. Malnutrition, learning and behavior (DHEW Publication). Washington, D.C.: National Institutes of Health, 1976.

Rimel, R. W., Giordani, B., Barth, J. T., Boll, T. J., & Jane, J. A. Disability caused by minor head injury. *Neurosurgery*, 1981, *9*, 221–228.

Ritvo, E. R., Freeman, B. J., Geller, E., & Yuwiler, A. Effects of Fenfluramine on 14 outpatients with the syndrome of autism. *Journal of the American Academy of Child Psychiatry*, 1983, *22*, 549–558.

Rose, R. J., Harris, E. L., Christian, J. C., & Nance, W. E. Genetic variance in nonverbal intelligence: Data from the kinships of identical twins. *Science*, 1979, *205*, 1153–1155.

Rosenberg, J. B., & Weller, G. M. Minor physical anomalies and academic performance in young school children. *Developmental Medicine and Child Neurology*, 1973, *15*, 131–135.

Sabelli, H. C., Fawcett, J., Gusovsky, F., Javaid, J., Edwards, J., & Jeffries, H. Urinary phenyl-acetate: A diagnostic test for depression? *Science*, 1983, *220*, 1187–1188.

Schaffer, J. W. A specific cognitive defect observed in gonadal aplasia (Turner's syndrome). *Journal of Clinical Psychology*, 1962, *18*, 405–406.

Stafford, R. E. Sex differences in spatial-visualization as evidence of sex-linked inheritance. *Perceptual and Motor Skills*, 1961, *13*, 428.

Thomas, H., Jamison, W., & Hummel, D. D. Observation is insufficient for discovering that the surface of still water is invariantly horizontal. *Science*, 1973, *181*, 173–174.

Tuber, D. S., Berntson, G. G., Bachman, D. S., & Allen, J. N. Associative learning in premature hydranencephalic and normal twins. *Science*, 1980, *210*, 1035–1037.

Turner, G., Till, R., & Daniel, A. Marker X chromosomes, mental retardation and macro-orchidism. *New England Journal of Medicine*, 1978, *299*, 1472.

Vandenberg, S. G. Genetic factors in human learning. *Educational Psychologist*, 1976, *12*, 59–63.

Volpe, J. J., & Pasternak, J. F. Parasagittal cerebral injury in neonatal hypoxic-ischemic en-cephalopathy: Clinical and neuroradiologic features. *Journal of Pediatrics*, 1977, *191*, 472–476.

Waber, D. P. Sex differences in cognition: A function of maturation rate? *Science*, 1976, *192*, 572–574.

Waber, D. P. Neuropsychological aspects of Turner's syndrome. *Developmental Medicine and Child Neurology*, 1979, *21*, 58–70.

Waldrop, M. F., Bell, R. Q., McLauglin, B., & Halverson, C. F. Newborn minor physical anomalies predict short attention span, peer aggression and impulsivity at age 3. *Science*, 1978, *199*, 563–565.

Weitkamp, L. R., Stancer, H. C., Persad, E., Flood, C., & Guttormsen, S. Depressive disorders and HLA: A gene on chromosome 6 that can affect behavior. *New England Journal of Medicine*, 1981, *305*, 1301–1306.

Weintraub, S., & Mesulam, M. M. Developmental learning disabilities of the right hemisphere: Emotional, interpersonal and cognitive components. *Archives of Neurology*, 1983, *40*, 463–468.

Whitehouse, P. J., Price, D. L., Struble, R. G., Clark, A. W., Coyle, J. T., & DeLong, M. R. Alz-heimer's disease and senile dementia: Loss of neurons in the basal forebrain. *Science*, 1982, 1237–1239.

Witkin, H. A., Sarnoff, A. M., Schulsinger, F., Bakkestrøm, E., Christiansen, K. O., Goodenough, D. R., Hirschhorn, K., Lundsteen, C., Owen, D. R., Philip, J., Rubin, D. B., & Stocking, M. Criminality in XYY and XXY men. *Science*, 1976, *193*, 547–555.

Yalom, I., Green, R., & Fisk, N. Prenatal exposure to female hormones: Effect on psychosexual development in boys. *Archives of General Psychiatry*, 1973, *28*, 554–561.

CHAPTER 12

The Science and Speculation of Rehabilitation in Developmental Neuropsychological Disorders

CATHY F. TELZROW

INTRODUCTION

The field of developmental neuropsychology has reached adolescence resting on its collective diagnostic laurels. Percent-correct classification has represented the staple of neuropsychological sophistication, and professional one-upmanship has focused on surpassing hit rates reported for earlier measures (Wedding, 1983). Despite the pleas of some experts that neuropsychology must address the implications of neurologic conditions, especially in view of such tools as the computed axial tomography (CAT) and positron emission tomography (PET) scans (Dean, 1982, 1985), in general neuropsychology remains arrested at the diagnostic level. Some of the major sources in the field published during the past five years make only passing reference to rehabilitation—presumably the end purpose for which clinicians engage in the rites of diagnosis. Those sources that at least acknowledge the issue of rehabilitation (Rourke, Bakker, Fisk, & Strang, 1983; Rutter, 1983) are fairly consistent in their conclusion that much of what is prescribed in the name of intervention is speculative (Gittelman, 1983; Hynd & Cohen, 1983; Rourke et al., 1983).

The present chapter attempts to address this critical omission in the neuropsychological literature by summarizing the available data pertinent to rehabilitation of brain-injured children. The three pediatric neurologic

CATHY F. TELZROW • Cuyahoga Special Education Service Center, Cleveland, Ohio 44137.

conditions to be addressed are those of highest incidence—developmental learning disorders, epilepsy, and head injuries. For each condition, a prototype of neuropsychological functioning will be presented, particularly, in keeping with the theme of this volume, as these are expressed in individual differences. Following each description, implications for educational and vocational rehabilitation suggested by the existing literature will be presented.

In preparing this chapter, it seemed relevant to reflect on the comments from contributor Charles Long quoted in the preface to this volume: "I do not understand it . . . it is questionable if anyone understands it . . . this area may be too complex for anyone to understand." It is certain that the science of rehabilitation, particularly with children, operates at a fairly primitive level. However, clinicians who see a good many neurologically impaired children in the context of educational and vocational planning are cognizant of the need to implement the best practices concurrent with testing new approaches. Specialists must be prepared to advise parents and educators who ask such questions as, "What can we expect?" and "What do we do?"; it is for this purpose that the present chapter was written.

SPECIFIC LEARNING DISABILITIES

Learning disorders vary widely and are characterized by numerous subtypes. Terminology meant to clarify sometimes confuses instead, as when the generic label "developmental learning disorder" subsumes such disparate conditions as mental retardation and specific genetic dyslexia. In the context of this chapter, the term *specific learning disabilities* refers to those conditions so defined under the federal (P.L. 94–142) criteria. Such conditions are identified on the basis of a demonstrable discrepancy between intellectual ability, as measured via an individual measure of intelligence, and academic achievement in such areas as reading, mathematics, or oral or written communication. Such diagnoses are made in most states through the application of various statistical formulas (Epps, Ysseldyke, & Algozzine, 1983; Telzrow, 1985), although other supporting data, including patterns of neuropsychological abilities, may be of instrumental value in the identification procedure (Cato & Rice, 1982; Hynd & Hynd, 1984).

NEUROPSYCHOLOGICAL CHARACTERISTICS

Learning disabilities may be manifested by disorders of reading, arithmetic, or understanding or using language. Even within each category, learning-disabled persons represent at least two (Bakker, 1979; Pirozzolo, Dunn, & Zetusky, 1983) or perhaps as many as five (Lyon & Watson, 1981) discrete subtypes. Such variability in the hallmark characteristics of this disorder compounds the problem inherent in diagnosis and complicates the selection of a prototype for illustrative purposes. Within the generic category of learning-disabled populations are those who have only reading and language disorders, only mathematics disorders, or a combination of both (Table 1). In addition, within each of these categories are subgroups of individuals who have specific profiles of disabilities associated with unique neuropsychological patterns of strengths and weaknesses. As Table 1 illustrates, the literature together with personal clinical experience suggest that these permutations may result in at least six general types of specific learning disabilities, with many students not clearly categorized as one or the other, but representing some hybrid of these subtypes. A brief description of the neuropsychological characteristics associated with each of the most common disorders of reading and mathematics follows.

Group 1: Auditory, Phonetic Dyslexia. Reading disabilities represent one of the largest categories of specific learning disabilities, and within this group, auditory phonetic dyslexics are disproportionately represented, having an incidence rate perhaps four to five times greater than other types (Boder & Jarrico, 1982; Pirozzolo, 1979; Telzrow, Century, Redmond, Whitaker, & Zimmerman, 1983). Such students are characterized by a higher Performance than Verbal IQ (Stoiber, Bracken, & Gissal, 1983; Telzrow et al., 1983); superiority on spatial relative to sequential processing (Bannatyne, 1978); and disorders of reading and spelling characterized by poor sound–symbol associations, difficulty in sound blending, and phonetic irregularities (Bannatyne, 1978; Boder & Jarrico, 1982). Such children may have a left-hand advantage on sensory and motor neuropsychological tasks such as finger tapping and finger tip number writing (Hartlage, 1981b; Telzrow et al., 1983), and other evidence of more efficient right hemisphere processing may be present (Bakker, 1979; Witelson, 1977; Zenhausern & Oexle, 1981). A family history of reading or spelling disorders may be present.

Group 2: Visuospatial Dyslexia. Whereas the incidence of visuospatial dyslexia is rather rare statistically and in personal clinical experience (Boder & Jarrico, 1982; Pirozzolo, 1979; Telzrow et al., 1983), it bears mentioning for completeness. The pattern of this disorder is in many respects the opposite of the condition just described. Visuospatial dyslexics do relatively better at sequential, linguistic tasks, and hence have superior Verbal IQ scores and do better on sequential than spatial clusters on the Wechsler Intelligence Scale for Children–Revised (WISC–R) (Hartlage, 1981b; Telzrow et al., 1983). Reading and spelling patterns demonstrate

TABLE 1

General Categories of Specific Learning Disabilities

Affected achievement area	Subtypes	Neuropsychological characteristics
Reading, spelling, written language	1. Auditory-phonetic dyslexia	P > V IQ Spatial > sequential abilities Poor sound–symbol associations in reading and spelling Left-hand advantage on sensory and motor tasks
	2. Visuospatial dyslexia	V > P IQ Overreliance on phonetic patterns Perceptual organization deficits
	3. Mixed dyslexia	P > V IQ Spatial > sequential abilities Higher incidence of left-handedness Left-hand advantage on sensory and motor tasks Spelling patterns show deficits in both visuospatial and auditory phonetic skills
Arithmetic	4. Mathematics computation disorder	Deficits in perceptual organization abilities Preserved reading and language abilities Directional confusion, spatial deficits
	5. Mathematics reasoning disorder	Associated with general language deficit
All basic academic	6. Pervasive learning disorder	Difficulty in dealing with symbol systems including time, money, reading, arithmetic Average IQ, decreases over time; often P > V IQ Spatial abilities a relative strength May have unique strengths in mechanics, drawing

an overreliance on phonetic patterns in conjunction with unique difficulty in sight-word acquisition and spelling phonetically irregular words (Boder, 1971; Boder & Jarrico, 1982; Hynd & Cohen, 1983). Such children may have relatively superior performance on right-handed motor and sensory abilities, indicative of stronger left cerebral hemisphere processing (Hartlage, 1981b; Telzrow et al., 1983).

Group 3: Mixed Dyslexia. The mixed dyslexic is more common than Group 2 (visuospatial type) although, fortunately, still a rare condition. As would be anticipated, mixed dyslexics demonstrate the reading deficiencies associated with both the subtypes described above, that is, they have deficits in both visuospatial and sequential processing of written language (Boder, 1971). Such children have been shown to have higher Performance than Verbal IQ scores, poorer sequential than spatial processing, a higher incidence of left-handedness, and a left-hand advantage on neuropsychological motor tasks (Telzrow et al., 1983). A family history of learning disorders may be present.

Group 4: Mathematics Computation Disorders. Although knowledge of mathematics disabilities is not so extensive as that of specific reading disorders, perhaps because of lesser attention to this phenomenon by educators (Rourke & Strang, 1983), a small number of children have been demonstrated to exhibit weaknesses specific to mathematical computation or reasoning, or a combination of both types of arithmetic deficits. A neuropsychological pattern has emerged in which discrete computation disorders are associated with neuropsychological weaknesses in perceptual organization abilities (Rourke & Findlayson, 1978), as would be construed from poor performance on such tasks as the Tactual Performance Test (TPT), the Beery, and WISC-R subtests loading on a spatial ability factor (e.g., Block Design, Object Assembly). The arithmetic paperwork of such children is characterized by poor column alignment, incorrect reading of computation signs, and directional confusion (Rourke & Strang, 1983). The reading and spelling abilities of such children may be within normal limits.

Group 5: Mathematics Reasoning Disorder. A unique and discrete disability in mathematics reasoning is a rare condition. Of greater likelihood is the expression of deficits in the ability to apply mathematics functions correctly, a disorder that is associated with more pervasive neuropsychological weaknesses in language processing. Rourke and Strang (1983) have suggested that the disabling effects of a general language impairment on mathematics performance might be exacerbated by lack of experience with arithmetic processes.

Group 6: Pervasive Learning Disorder. This condition is characterized by unique and extreme difficulty in processing most written symbols, which is reflected in pervasive reading and mathematics disabilities as well as associated problems with other symbol systems such as time and money. Students in this category tend to have average or low-average intellectual ability scores at early ages, although their IQ scores typically decrease over time until adolescence when scores may fall in the borderline or mildly retarded range. A relatively superior Performance IQ score is typical, although even this may be a standard deviation or more below the mean. Spatial abilities may fail within normal limits, and many of these students demonstrate discrete, preserved abilities in such areas as drawing and mechanics. A pattern of sensory and motor abilities favoring the left side (right cerebral hemisphere) frequently is observed. Students in this group may be literal nonreaders, despite years of educational intervention, and may be able to write only their name and perhaps their address. A family history of the disorder may be identified. Physical adeptness often remains intact, as do fundamental spoken language skills, and adaptive behavior for areas not associated with written language is age appropriate.

EDUCATIONAL RESPONSE

It is ironic that so much energy is invested in qualifying students for learning disabilities services when the value of such interventions for individual students has not yet been demonstrated unequivocally (Hynd & Cohen, 1983). Nevertheless, it is commonly accepted that specialized instruction, such as might be provided in a learning disabilities classroom, is desirable for children with specific learning disabilities. Depending on the type and severity of the condition, such intervention might be delivered in a resource room or in extreme cases, a self-contained special-education classroom where instructional strategies can be modified suitably. For children with pervasive learning disabilities, however, adjustment of educational objectives as well as teaching techniques may be warranted (Hartlage & Telzrow, 1983), which may require a specialized school or training program.

Whereas agreement is not unanimous (Balow, 1979; Gittelman, 1983; Sandoval & Haapanen, 1981), much research suggests that the optimal approach for learning-disabled children is one which provides instruction that capitalizes on existing neuropsychological strengths (Hartlage & Reynolds, 1981; Hartlage & Telzrow, 1984a; Maxwell & Zenhausern, 1983; Reynolds, 1981; Zenhausern & Markman, 1983; Zenhausern, Minardi, & Maxwell, 1983). Hartlage and Telzrow (1983), in a review of aptitude-treatment research, concluded that optimal outcomes were reported for intervention designs derived from neuropsychological test data that focused on intact abilities. This approach has been shown to result in comparatively greater gains for children (Gunnison & Kaufman, 1982; Hartlage & Reynolds, 1981; Reynolds, 1981), relative to controls.

Examples of specific educational applications for each of the learning-disabled subgroups described are summarized in Table 2. Omitted from Table 2 are Groups 3 (mixed dyslexic) and 6 (pervasive learning disability). Such children may be served more effectively via educational approaches that circumvent their pervasive learning disorders rather than attempt to remediate them. In their review of intervention research, Hartlage and Telzrow (1983) concluded that a small number of learning-disabled children—perhaps those categorized into Groups 3 and 6—do not show benefits from even intensive intervention. Such students are characterized by significant impairment in memory for symbols. Although apparently able to "read" a pool of words for a limited period following rehearsal, they cannot seem to retain such skills without continual drill. Spelling skills are similarly affected, and such individuals have been known to spell their own names incorrectly as adolescents or adults.

For these learning-disabled individuals, Hartlage and Telzrow (1983), as well as others (Kutsick, 1982; Minskoff, 1982), recommend a compensatory approach. Through an extension of the "capitalization of strengths" (Cronbach & Snow, 1977) concept described above, this approach requires a more restrictive educational environment because of the modifications necessary (Hartlage & Telzrow, 1983). In addition, there is strong likelihood that persons for whom compensatory approaches are necessary may not be educationally independent, even following many years of intervention (Cato & Rice, 1982), thus providing evidence of the chronic nature of specific learning disabilities (Compton, 1984). However, there is evidence that such individuals can become functionally independent (i.e., able to maintain effective relationships with others, to hold a job, and to manage day-to-day living) if appropriate prevocational and vocational objectives are pursued (Compton, 1984; Gottfredson, Finucci, & Childs, 1983; Schonhaut & Satz, 1983).

VOCATIONAL RESPONSE

The term *learning disabilities* was coined less than two decades ago (Mauser, 1981). Federal authorization for educational funding for learning disabilities services did not occur until 1969, and for many years following that date, high school services were available only on limited and often experimental bases. Experts were hopeful that elementary school services would eradicate the observed disabilities so that adolescents could function without need for specialized services. More recently, we have recognized that learning disabilities represent a lasting neuropsychological

TABLE 2

Illustrative Teaching Strategies Which Capitalize on Existing Neuropsychological Strengths

Group 1 Auditory-phonetic dyslexic	Group 2 Visuospatial dyslexic	Group 4 Mathematics computation disorders	Group 5 Mathematics reasoning disorders
• Whole-word, look–say approaches	• Auditory-phonetic, sound symbol strategies	• Auditory-verbal emphasis (naming numerals, auditory fact memoriation)	• Use of concrete objects (e.g., abacus, manipulatives, Montessori materials)
• Flash card drill	• Deep structure, emphasis on comprehension	• Written or oral sequence of steps to use as structure in performing computations	• Pictorial conversion of word problems to mathematical processes (e.g., "Jon had 7 balls and *lost* 2" converts to "7 minus 2")
• Word families	• Sequential approaches to spelling and decoding	• Templates to assist with column alignment in mathematics operations	• Use of arrows and visual cues to teach sequence of steps in mathematics processes
• "Chunking" of prefixes, suffixes, root words	• Segmentation of common word elements (prefixes, suffixes) to assist in decoding		
• Configuration clues			
• Multisensory, demonstration, experiential			
• Pictographic, rhebus approaches			

disorder that may well require lifelong adjustments and modifications. A major step in such acknowledgment occurred in 1981 with the recognition by the Rehabilitation Services Administration of specific learning disabilities as a legitimate disabling condition, hence making such individuals eligible for specific vocational training.

The need for systematic transitional programs from school to the world of work is critical for handicapped persons (Tindall, 1984). In 1984, Education Department Assistant Secretary Madeleine Will identified a need to emphasize realistic career goal setting and vocational training over academic remediation for learning-disabled adolescents (" Will, Let's Move Forward ...," 1984). A few months earlier, in remarks made while signing a proclamation designating the National Decade of Disabled Persons, President Reagan announced federal assistance in increasing job opportunities for the handicapped and in easing the now giant step between special education programs and successful employment ("President Declares Goal of Independence ...," 1984). Employment rates for learning-disabled adults may run as high as 76% (Brown, 1982; Szuhay, Newill, Scott, Williams, Stout, &. Decker, 1980), perhaps as a result of low knowledge of community resources ("Problems Plague Efforts ...," 1984). Evidence suggests that the most favorable outcomes are associated with higher IQ scores and socioeconomic levels (Compton, 1984; Gottfredson et al., 1983; Schonhaut &. Satz, 1983).

Vocational rehabilitation approaches that are effective for learning-disabled individuals in many ways represent a logical extension of educational intervention techniques. When applied to vocational rehabilitation, this may be described as a two-pronged approach: (a) matching existing functional abilities with the work environment (Hartlage &. Telzrow, 1984b; Witten, 1983); and (b) providing the individual with workable strategies and assistive devices to compensate for critical disabilities (Blalock, 1982; Witten, 1983).

Telzrow and Hartlage (1984) have described a model that addresses the first step in this two-pronged approach. They suggest that the ability-vocation matching process is facilitated by a theoretical job-sort, where the two dimensions are the student's age and profile of neuropsychological abilities. The career potential for any given individual can be depicted as a funnel where the mouth (top) of the funnel corresponds to a relatively young age (beginning of school, for example), whereas the spout (bottom) of the funnel represents the student's exit from a secondary education program. Career options enter the theoretical job-sort funnel at the top, where the pool of available alternatives is large. At various levels along the height of the funnel, job screens are placed, each of which corresponds to a formal evaluation or systematic decision-making point (e.g., choice of educational track before entering high school). These screen inserts, which increase in density from the top to the bottom of the funnel, serve to sort out vocations that require specific neuropsychological abilities not demonstrated by the student, allowing others without such prerequisites to continue through the student's job-sort funnel. Examples of neuropsychological abilities that might be associated with specific job requirements include general intellectual level, memory, spoken and written language skills, reading ability, and planning and organization skills. Presumably those vocations that emerge at the bottom of the funnel are most likely to match the student's functional abilities, although others requiring skills in which the student is deficient would be eliminated.

The second step in this two-pronged approach to vocational intervention incorporates required compensatory strategies for functional deficits that are still present even in work settings well matched to existing neuropsychological abilities (McGuire & Goyette, 1983; Tindall, 1984). An effective vocational rehabilitation program often is one that can identify techniques and assistive devices that permit an individual to succeed in the work environment despite the chronic nature of specific learning disabilities (Cato & Rice, 1982). A number of recent publications have provided illustrations of creative techniques used in the vocational rehabilitation field to maximize the career adjustment of learning-disabled persons (Tindall, 1984; Witten, 1983). Whereas some suggestions are adaptable to all work situations (e.g., using a digital watch for those unable to tell time), individually designed compensatory strategies may be most effective when developed in conjunction with a particular employment setting. In this way the compensations can be specific to the requirements of the job demands and personnel with whom the learning-disabled individual interacts. An example concerns a severely learning-disabled young man working in the role of custodian whose supervisors must be counseled to provide all tasks orally and by demonstration rather than in writing.

EPILEPSY

The incidence of epilepsy in the general population ranges from 1 to 4% (Wright, 1975), with the highest proportion of those afflicted developing their seizure disorders during the developmental period ("Plan for Nationwide Action . . . ," 1977). Of the major seizure types recognized, those most common in the pediatric population include absence seizures, generalized tonic-clonic seizures, and complex partial seizures (Batshaw & Perret, 1981). Estimates indicate that although the vast majority of children with epilepsy can be maintained nearly seizure free with anticonvulsant medication, a substantial number (15–20%) have regular seizure episodes despite pharmacological therapy (Hartlage, 1983).

NEUROPSYCHOLOGICAL CHARACTERISTICS

Epilepsy is not a unitary syndrome with characteristic symptoms, but a condition that is expressed in highly variable ways, ranging from mild, probably insignificant features (e.g., an occasional psychomotor spell) to severe, intractable seizures accompanied by significant impairment in mental and behavioral functioning. Because of this extreme variability in the expression of childhood epilepsy, it is difficult to generalize about the neuropsychological characteristics associated with this condition. However, some broad generalizations will be made to provide a basis for the discussion of educational and vocational responses.

A large number of individuals with epilepsy have some demonstrable impairment in neuropsychological functioning. Estimates suggest that one half ("Plan for Nationwide Action on Epilepsy," 1977) to three quarters (Rodin, Shapiro, & Lennox, 1976) of persons with seizure disorders have some degree of dysfunction in intellectual or academic functioning. There is some consensus that, as a group, the mean IQ score for persons with epilepsy is below average (Brittain, 1980). In a review of published studies reporting mean IQ scores of populations of children and adults with seizure disorders (Hartlage & Telzrow, 1984c), mean WISC, Wechsler Adult Intelligence Scale (WAIS), and Binet scores ranged between 72 and 102. When the results of all studies sampled are combined, representing a total N of 1115, the mean IQ score is approximately 87. If these subjects are considered to be representative of the epileptic population as a whole, it would appear that the mean IQ for persons with seizure disorders falls nearly a standard deviation below average. An earlier review (Halstead, 1957) reported that higher IQs are noted for children with idiopathic epilepsy and those with absence spells. Other evidence has suggested that IQ scores are lower for epileptic adults who demonstrate EEG abnormalities, and for generalized rather than focal seizures (Dodrill & Wilkus, 1967).

There is some evidence to suggest that the IQ score may be a fairly sensitive measure of the neurological integrity of persons with epilepsy. Dean (1983), for example, has reported significant negative correlations between the number of lifetime seizures and WISC-R IQ scores. These findings suggest that increased cortical impairment such as is associated with ongoing seizure activity is reflected in regressions in IQ test scores. Other evidence suggests that the intellectual impairment reflected by lower IQ scores may not be permanent. Seidenberg, O'Leary, Berent, and

Boll (1981), for example, reported significantly improved IQ scores relative to controls for adult epileptics who demonstrated seizure improvement over an 18-month period.

In addition to the level of intellectual performance deficits observed in populations of persons with seizure disorders, there is evidence that characteristic performance patterns are apparent for this group as well. Perceptual-motor deficits have been reported for a significant number—approximately one third—of epileptic children with IQs above 80 (Gastaut, 1964). Similar findings were reported by Dennerll, Broeder, and Sokolov (1964), who found relatively poorer perceptual organization than verbal abilities for epileptic children. Fedio and Mirsky (1969) reported that attention disorders and constructional dyspraxia are common neuropsychological disorders associated with generalized epilepsy in children. These authors (Fedio & Mirsky, 1969) also have reported that disorders associated with temporal lobe epilepsy are specific to the implicated hemisphere: left temporal foci were associated with verbal learning deficits, whereas right temporal lesions correlated with impairments in learning and recalling nonverbal information. Recent information has suggested that although left lateralized and generalized seizures were associated with performance decrements on verbal tasks, the corollary for nonverbal tasks was not apparent (Berent, Giordani, Sackellares, O'Leary, & Boll, 1983).

Other sources have identified a specific pattern of deficits that would appear to be associated with left cerebral hemisphere dysfunction. Cases of acquired aphasia subsequent to seizures in children have been described by Cooper and Ferry (1978), who noted this pattern occurs more often in males than females, and results in a generalized, severe language disturbance even after successful management of seizures. Although adults with partial seizures are more likely to exhibit normal language function following a transient aphasia or "speech arrest," which occurs in conjunction with the seizure episode (Gilmore & Heilman, 1981), such does not appear to be the case for children.

Learning problems, apparently of neuropsychological origin, have been identified for populations of children with seizure disorders. Rangaswami (1983) reported that 80% of children with epilepsy experienced school problems despite average ability levels. A study of 21 children with idiopathic epilepsy (Bolter, Berg, Ch'ien, Williams, Lancaster, & Cummins, 1982a) reported a Selz-Reitan Impairment Rating of 20.1, indicative of mild CNS impairment associated with groups of learning-disabled children. In a study of the relationship between tactile-perceptual scores (tactile-perception, finger localization, finger tip number writing, and form recognition) and Wide Range Achievement Test (WRAT) scores, Bolter, Berg,

Ch'ien, Williams, Lancaster, and Cummins (1982b) demonstrated significant negative correlations between these sets of abilities. Such results suggest that specific sensory dysfunction, such as these that neuropsychological tasks identify, are associated with poorer academic performance.

Recently increased attention has been directed toward the relationship between neuropsychological impairment and specific behavioral characteristics in children (Dorman, 1982). Most studies of the relationship between psychopathology and epilepsy in children have reported that psychiatric disturbance in such populations exceeds the incidence figures for nonepileptic children. Some authors suggest that as many as one fourth of school-aged children with epilepsy may exhibit some degree of psychopathology (Pond & Bidwell, 1960). A study of 21 children with idiopathic epilepsy determined that while as a group no significant psychopathology was observed, analysis of individual profiles identified approximately one third as displaying problems in social-emotional adjustment (Berg, Bolter, Ch'ien, & Cummins, 1984). An early study by Halstead (1957) identified 35% of a population of epileptic children as having aggressive or destructive behavior, with an additional 28% having less severe behavior problems characterized by oversensitive, sullen behavior. Lewis, Pincus, Shanok, and Glaser (1982) reported significant correlations between the number of psychomotor seizure symptoms and expressions of violence for a group of incarcerated male juvenile delinquents.

Rutter, Graham, and Yule (1970) reported that psychopathological disorders are three to ten times as common in children with epilepsy as in the general population, depending on the type of seizure disorder. Evidence for a neurologic rather than a functional etiology in such disorders is apparent from these authors' findings that physically handicapped children have an incidence of psychopathology that is half that of the epileptic group.

Several studies have examined the types of psychopathology exhibited by epileptic children. There is some evidence that psychiatric disturbances fall into two types, which can be categorized on the basis of IQ. Low-IQ epileptics have been reported to exhibit psychotic behavior and hyperkinetic symptoms, whereas the less-impaired group demonstrated such psychopathology as anxiety disorders and aggressive personality (Rutter et al., 1970). Hyperactivity is reported for many epileptic children (Ives, 1970; Rutter et al., 1970), especially those with lower IQs (Pond, 1961). Some studies have associated increased patterns of hyperactivity in subgroups of epileptic children, such as those who are younger (Dreifuss, 1975) or for boys (Stores, Hart, & Piran, 1978).

There appears to be at least some evidence that relates specific behavioral symptomatology to epileptogenic foci. Watts (1975) reported that bilateral amygdala lesions may be associated with violence and unique difficulty in controlling anger. Whereas Nuffield (1961) has reported a relationship between temporal lobe epilepsy and aggressive behavior in children, Bagley (1971) associated such behavior with nonspecific brain dysfunction rather than a temporal focus. Bear and Fedio (1977) have identified distinct behavioral differences between patients whose epileptic focus is in the left versus the right hemisphere. Although the former were characterized by a catastrophic reaction, whereby the individual perceives his or her condition as more hopeless than it may be, epileptics with right temporal foci demonstrated denial and emotive reactions characteristic of the *la belle indifférence* syndrome. The specificity with which behavioral expressions may be associated with discrete brain regions is suggested by the work of Hughes and Olson (1981), who described behavioral characteristics associated with eight different loci of temporal lobe epilepsies.

In concluding this section of the neuropsychological characteristics of persons with seizure disorders, it seems imperative to mention the potential effects of various anticonvulsant medications. Most experts agree that there are not yet available anticonvulsants that are completely therapeutic and at the same time free of side effects (Hartlage, 1983; Livingston, 1966). Phenobarbital, perhaps the most investigated of the anticonvulsants, has been associated with drowsiness and excitability (Livingston, 1966), significant psychomotor slowing (Hutt, Jackson, Belsham, & Higgins, 1968), short-term memory deficits (MacLeod, Dekaban, & Hunt, 1978), and decreased performance on various psychological (Thompson & Trimble, 1983) and neuropsychological tasks (Hartlage, 1981a). Enhanced memory performance has been associated with dosage reduction of phenobarbital and primidone (Oxley, 1979), although a concomitant increase in number of seizures was noted as well.

Other potential side effects of neuropsychological relevance that have been associated with various anticonvulsants include increased hyperactivity (Dreifuss, 1975), decrements in motor performance (Dodrill, 1975), disturbances of language (Wilson, Petty, Perry, & Rose, 1983), and lower IQ scores (Trimble, 1979). Of particular interest is a report by Bellur and Hermann (1984) that a significant reduction of deviant Minnesota Multiphasic Personality Inventory (MMPI) scores occurred following discontinuation of anticonvulsants. The authors suggest that some of the behavioral characteristics long ascribed to the existence of an "epileptic personality" may be more accurately attributed, ironically, to the anticonvulsants themselves. Although the now-common practice of monitoring anticonvulsant blood levels may minimize the possibility of severe drug side effects, there is evidence that significant impairment in neuropsychological functioning may be associated with even therapeutic dosage levels (Hartlage, 1981a; MacLeod et al., 1978; Reynolds & Travers, 1974).

EDUCATIONAL RESPONSE

Most experts agree that one of the biggest deterrents to good adjustment in educational settings by children with epilepsy is lack of understanding of the condition by professional educators (Ansbaugh, Gilliland, & Ansbaugh, 1980). Many myths surrounding epilepsy still exist, and whereas a knowledgeable and sensitive teacher can facilitate the adjustment of a child with epilepsy, the reverse is true as well (Ansbaugh et al., 1980). This factor suggests that a primary educational response is the provision of clear information about the nature, pattern, and severity of an individual child's seizure history to school officials. Although some parents may wish to withhold such information from the school with the belief that if school officials are informed about the student's epilepsy they will behave in a manner that discriminates against the child, there is evidence that open communication between the family and the school is most beneficial to the child (Ansbaugh et al., 1980).

A second educational response, which requires consideration of the individual child's seizure history, concerns the provision of an environment that is suitably protective. The nature of this protective setting is highly variable, depending on the nature of the child's seizures. Whereas for a child with absence spells no particular adjustment may be necessary, a child with major motor or tonic-clonic seizures several times a month may require a helmet, appropriate supervision while going to the restroom and on the playground, and a quiet place to rest following a spell. Although adjustments in the classroom environment require flexibility and effort on the part of school officials, most experts agree that maintaining a child with epilepsy in school is preferable to home-bound instruction (Hartlage, 1983).

Evidence that some children with seizures may demonstrate a variety of behavioral symptoms, including hyperactivity, may be of relevance in an educational setting. For some such children, environments that are structured, with clear behavioral expectations and immediate feedback, can mitigate the negative effects of such behavior. Behavioral intervention programs also might incorporate other aspects of concern to optimal adjustment of epileptic children, such as compliance with pharmacological and health regimens. Adolescents, in particular, may reject therapeutic anticonvulsant programs and neglect dietary and exercise demands important for optimal seizure control (Trostle, Hauser, & Susser, 1983). Educational intervention programs that provide information about the importance of such habits to seizure control, as well as incentives for compliance, can maximize the adoption of habits conducive to good maintenance of seizure-free status.

Also of possible relevance to educational programming for children with epilepsy is the high incidence of disorders of social and emotional adjustment cited earlier. There is evidence that adolescents with epilepsy may withhold information about their seizures from peers and significant others, such as teachers and coaches, in order to avoid rejection (Goldin, Perry, Margolin, Stotsky, & Foster, 1971; Kleck, 1968). Ironically, this coping strategy often leads to the afflicted individual's withdrawing in a self-imposed isolationism, thus producing the situation he or she wished to avoid. Dodrill (1981) has demonstrated that adults with 100 or more separate seizure episodes display significantly greater deficits in psychological functioning than other groups, including those who have experienced status epilepticus. He attributes these deficits, at least in part, to devastating emotional stress associated with these separate seizure episodes. Since seizure episodes are unplanned and often occur without warning, anticipation of a seizure, with its accompanying physical debilitation or social embarrassment, represents a significant psychosocial stressor. The unpredictable nature of seizures, which removes them from the individual's control, has been associated with degrees of anxiety disproportionate to that observed in other disabling conditions (Goldin & Margolin, 1975).

Since personality and social adjustment problems may have adverse effects on educational performance, it may be determined that addressing these concerns is appropriate within an educational context. Informational approaches, in which unreasonable fears and anxieties are confronted with factual information, have been effective with some groups of persons with epilepsy. Similarly, cognitive behavior modification or rational-emotive therapy approaches, which use a variety of self-talk methods and *in vivo* techniques to assist students in moderating the negative emotional effects associated with anxiety about epilepsy, may be effective.

In addition to providing information, general safety, and personal adjustment training, appropriate educational programs for children with epilepsy are individually tailored to the neuropsychological profile of the student in question. As was noted earlier, the mean IQ score for populations of children with epilepsy tends to be below average, and for this reason teachers' expectations regarding academic attainment may need to be modified accordingly. However, expectancy levels must be deter mined individually rather than based on group means, since many epileptic children have IQ scores in the superior range.

It is important to emphasize that establishing expectancy levels for children with epilepsy on the basis of IQ scores alone may be misleading. There is considerable evidence that the achievement levels of children with epilepsy are below expectancy based on IQ (Rangaswami, 1983; Rutter et al., 1970; Yule, 1980). Several explanations for this phenomenon have been cited. Bolter et al. (1982b) reported that specific neuropsychological deficits (e.g., sensory perceptual abilities) are significantly correlated with achievement test scores for a group of epileptic children with average IQs. Such findings suggest that discrete neuropsychological abilities, somewhat independent of IQ, which are requisite for academic achievement, may be impaired in children with seizure disorders. This hypothesis is supported by evidence that seizures represent a behavioral symptom of generally compromised functioning of the central nervous system (Dubinsky, Wilkening, & Minarcik, 1982).

The evidence that epileptic children perform poorly on sensory perceptual tasks (Bolter et al., 1982b; Morgan & Groh, 1980) is consistent with findings of uniquely poor performances in arithmetic (Green & Hartlage, 1971). Recent description of learning-disability subtypes (Rourke & Strang, 1983) suggests that deficits in perceptual organization abilities are associated with concomitant arithmetic learning disabilities. These findings, when considered together, may suggest that as a group epileptic children are more prone to math-related academic learning problems. Once again, individual appraisal of the pattern of strengths and weaknesses is necessary in order to plan an appropriate educational program.

VOCATIONAL RESPONSE

The employment statistics for persons with handicaps are abysmal. Despite federal mandates requiring equal opportunities in education and employment for handicapped persons, recent figures suggest that as many as 85% of disabled persons have annual incomes below $7,000, with half of these earning less than $2,000 per year (Cavanaugh, 1983). There is evidence that the rate of unemployment of persons with epilepsy is several times higher than the national average. Estimates are that even among persons whose seizures well-controlled, unemployment may run as high as 25% (Holmes & McWilliams, 1981). Generally this circumstance has been attributed to employer resistance, since studies have shown that worker skill, attendance, and safety records are no different for groups of persons with epilepsy than for the general population (Benson, 1977; Udel, 1960). Evidence suggests that employers who report more knowledge and experience with epilepsy are more likely to indicate a willingness to hire persons with a history of seizure disorders (Holmes & McWilliams, 1981).

In addition to employer attitudes, a major deterrent to the successful employment of persons with epilepsy is the absence of off-the-job skills relative to getting along with others and managing in the work setting. Such skills have repeatedly been identified among the most important variables in job success and yet children with epilepsy have been shown to have related prevocational skills ranked among the lowest of their adaptive behavior abilities (Green & Hartlage, 1971). There has been some speculation that poorer interpersonal skills are associated with the special stress of a seizure disorder, resulting in the individual's tendency to withdraw and retreat from others (Dodrill, 1981).

Another deterrent to the employment of epileptic persons concerns the logistical aspects of a seizure possibility and the manner in which this interferes with such pragmatic activities as traveling to and from work. Legal restrictions against driving may require some persons to use public transportation or rely on others for transportation. In addition, for some epileptic persons work environments that are associated with continual alertness necessary for safety might best be avoided.

In entering a vocational guidance program, a critical first step is a careful appraisal of seizure status (Lehtovaara, 1983). This assessment of the various aspects of the seizure history, including such data as type, frequency, time, postictal state, precipitants, and medication taken and side effects, is critical in order to identify areas for which some intervention is necessary and those which may require special vocational responses. Since potential side effects of anticonvulsant medications may have implications for vocational rehabilitation (Blank & Anderson, 1983), ongoing appraisal of medication effects is an especially important consideration. An example of a prevocational seizure status appraisal form that may be of use in assisting young persons with epilepsy make informed and realistic vocational decisions is included in Table 3.

When the information outlined in Table 3 is available, it can be used by the vocational counselor, together with the counselee, to plan desirable and attainable career goals (Hershenson, 1981). Optimal vocational outcomes that have been identified for handicapped populations in general also are relevant for persons with epilepsy. These guidelines suggest that ideally the chosen work setting should be one in which the individual can respond to job requirements effectively and efficiently, does not endanger self or others, and where work demands do not exacerbate the disabling condition (Foster, Szoke, Kapisovsky, & Kriger, 1979).

Given the high level of unemployment for persons with seizure dis-

TABLE 3
Prevocational Seizure Status Appraisal Form[a]

Name _____ DOB _____

Date _____ Age _____ Sex _____

1. Average number of seizures per month:	>20	10–20	5–10	<5 0
2. Number of seizures during past month:	>20	10–20	5–10	<5 0

3. Time of day when seizures generally
   occur:
   7–10 AM   10–12 noon   12–3 PM
   3–6 AM   6–10 PM   after 10 PM

4. Seizure precipitants, if any: _____

5. Warning signs of imminent seizure: Aura   Agitation   Headache
   Other _____

6. Characteristic postictal behavior: Deep sleep   Agitation   Drowsiness
   Weakness   Other _____

7. Seizure type(s):   _____

8. Medication(s) taken: Type: _____
   Dosage: _____
   Time: _____

9. Side effects noted: Loss of appetite   Drowsiness
   Motor slowness   Change of mood
   Other _____

10. Special dietary requirements: _____
    _____

11. Driver's license eligibility: _____
    _____

[a]Adapted from Foster et al., 1979.

orders, and the emphasis most employers place on work habits and attitudes, special emphasis in vocational rehabilitation efforts should be
directed toward job seeking and job survival skills (Foster et al., 1979). At
least one study (Forrest, 1961) reported that disclosure of seizure history
to prospective employers was associated with hiring difficulties, although
it should be emphasized that this occurred prior to the 1973 Rehabilitation
Act in which Section 504 prohibits hiring discrimination. Interestingly,
this study also noted that persons who disclosed their condition to the

employer prior to being hired were less likely to be dismissed following a seizure episode. Techniques such as simulations and role-playing, perhaps with videotape capability to permit later critique between the student and supervisor, can enable an adolescent or young adult to experience job seeking and interviewing skills, including rehearsal for employer hesitancy and ignorance about epilepsy. Mock situations which prepare young people for potential difficulties encountered on the job (e.g., how and when to inform co-workers of seizures) can be of great value to the vocational rehabilitation effort.

Several experts (Cavanaugh, 1983; Kallanranta, 1983) suggest that collaborative relationships between educational and vocational agencies can benefit both these systems, as well as the clients they serve. By working hand-in-hand, the strengths of both components are utilized to enhance the student's vocational adjustment, and resources are complementary rather than redundant. One example of a comprehensive approach to the long-term educational and vocational habilitation of persons with epilepsy is a project implemented by the Baltimore City Schools in 1978. This program integrated a variety of medical, educational, social, and vocational resources to insure that students received appropriate educational challenges, training in social skills and work experience, and vocational counseling. Early findings supported the value of such an approach, indicating that students who completed the program had employment rates three times those for program dropouts ("Baltimore Schools ...," 1983).

HEAD INJURIES

Accidents are the leading cause of death in children above age 1 year (Brink, Imbus, & Woo-Sam, 1980), and the majority of accidents are associated with some degree of head trauma. A prospective study of over 1200 head-injured patients in the central Virginia area reported that such injuries are disproportionately represented by younger persons, with 42% of the sample falling below age 20, and an additional 28% between ages 20 and 30 (Rimel & Jane, 1983). As many as 18,000 children and adolescents may experience debilitating head injuries per year from automobile accidents alone (Brink et al., 1980). When all sources and degrees of head trauma are combined, this figure may reach as high as one million children annually (Young, 1969). Evidence suggests that more children than adults survive serious head injuries (Levin, Benton, & Grossman, 1982), and that male children are two to three times more likely to sustain head injuries than females (Klonoff & Paris, 1974; Levin et al., 1982; Rimel & Jane, 1983; Winogron, Knights, & Bawden, 1983).

NEUROPSYCHOLOGICAL CHARACTERISTICS

Like the previous two conditions discussed, children with head injuries are difficult to describe because of the wide variety of characteristics and outcomes associated with such populations. Clinicians have just begun to understand the pattern of recovery from childhood head trauma, and some experts (Rourke *et al.*, 1983) have suggested that further research may reveal the existence of discrete neuropsychological subtypes in populations of head-injured children, much as has been shown for learning-disabled groups.

Some data have supported this viewpoint. Klonoff, Low, and Clark (1977) differentiated head-injured children on the basis of presence or absence of residual neuropsychological effects, and reported that these groups were significantly different at the time of initial hospitalization and at five-year follow-up. Additional support for the practice of identifying subtypes of traumatically brain injured comes from the work of Winogron *et al.* (1983), who evaluated 51 children identified on the basis of a multidimensional severity index into severe, moderate, and mild categories. Subjects in the three groups were equal in number and were matched on several variables, including sex, age of insult, and age at follow-up. Neuropsychological performance was interpreted utilizing both level and pattern methods. Significant differences among the three groups were demonstrated for Performance IQ scores, although not for Verbal or Full-Scale measures. Other significant differences in neuropsychological testing performance were shown for dominant hand Pegboard Test Time, Finger Tapping, TPT, and Verbal Fluency. Furthermore, classification by impairment index (the authors' Deficit Index) was consistent with severity rating determined by multidimensional neurologic indicators. Although finer discrimination was not possible on the basis of this study, the authors did report differences among the two extreme (i.e., severely and mildly impaired) groups. In general, the mildly and moderately impaired groups resembled one another on most performance areas, with the severely impaired group identified as a discrete category.

A number of studies have identified variables that are associated with eventual outcome following head injury. Klonoff *et al.* (1977) reported that the best predictors of neurologic sequelae (e.g., headaches, disorders of memory and personality) were Full-Scale IQ during initial hospitalization and number of minutes of unconsciousness. There is evidence that these two variables are not independent, since Brink, Garrett, Hale, Woo-Sam, and Nickel (1970) reported a direct relationship between length of coma and posttraumatic IQ level. Similar findings were reported by Winogron *et al.* (1983), who reported that deeper coma and unconsciousness of a longer duration were associated with poorer outcome.

Although there has been some speculation about the effects of age of onset on the subsequent pattern and quality of recovery, Klonoff *et al.* (1977) found no difference between younger (below 9 years) and older (above 9 years) children with regard to recovery of neuropsychological functioning. Brink *et al.* (1970) reported the same approximate correlation between IQ level and length of coma for both younger and older children, although younger children (below age 10) were more likely to experience shorter periods of coma. However, in apparent contradiction of this relationship, younger children experienced greater intellectual impairment, as has been shown in other studies (Klonoff & Low, 1974). Although the findings continue to be equivocal (Rutter, Chadwick, & Shaffer, 1983), there is increasing evidence that the commonly accepted premise that early traumatic insults tend to result in more favorable outcome may be part of the neuromythology lore (Levin *et al.*, 1982).

Establishing prognoses for head-injured children is complicated by findings that such individuals continue to show evidence of recovery as late as five years following onset (Klonoff *et al.*, 1977). Furthermore, since this is as long as most populations have been followed, it may be discovered that resumption of abilities continues indefinitely, although Long, Gouvier, and Cole (1984) suggest that deficits that are present five years posttraumatically are likely to be permanent. Neuropsychological performance has been shown to be an important predictor of recovery from head injury. Klonoff *et al.*, (1977) reported that a subgroup of head-injured children without deviant neuropsychological sequelae continued to show a steady gain in IQ over a five-year period and were not significantly different from controls at the end of that period. Different findings were reported by Brink *et al.* (1970) for their population of children with severe head injuries (average length of coma of seven weeks). The authors indicated that for their group improvement was ongoing for two to three years posttraumatically, although most gains were evidenced during the first year, with the rate of recovery slowing markedly thereafter.

There is evidence that despite often good neurologic recovery (Brink *et al.*, 1980), restitution of neuropsychological abilities in brain-injured children occurs more slowly. Brink *et al.* (1970) reported that the vast majority of their sample demonstrated independent functioning in areas of ambulation and self-care abilities, although most continued to display significant intellectual impairment. Similar findings were reported in a 1980 study (Brink *et al.*, 1980), where significant intellectual and personality impairments were observed even for children with negative neurologic findings. Klonoff *et al.* (1977) reported that 30% of their sample of children surviving head injury experienced serious school difficulties later. These included grade failure, special class placement, or withdrawal from school altogether because of repeated school failure, all in absence of premorbid school adjustment problems. In their follow-up of 52 children experiencing severe head injuries, Brink et al. (1970) reported that 26 of 34 students in school were enrolled in special education programs.

These results suggest that perhaps one consistent neuropsychological finding in populations of head-injured children is significant intellectual impairment. The level and pattern of the observed deficits have been shown to vary, perhaps as a function of severity of the injury. Winogron et al. (1983), for example, reported significantly different mean Performance IQ scores for children categorized on the basis of neurologic severity indicators as suffering severe (PIQ = 80), moderate (PIQ = 95), or mild (PIQ = 99) head injuries. A similar, although not statistically significant, trend was reported for Full-Scale IQ, with mean scores ranging from 82 (severely injured) to 96 (mild). Such results would appear to support findings that have suggested that Performance IQ scores are more vulnerable to the effects of head injury (Berger-Gross &. Shackelford, 1984; Chadwick, Rutter, Brown, Shaffer, &. Traub, 1981), and that these differences may persist as late as two years posttraumatically (Chadwick, Rutter, Shaffer, &. Shrout, 1981). In at least one study (Berger-Gross &. Shakelford, 1984), depressed Performance IQ was expressed in conjunction with significantly lower achievement in arithmetic. This relationship between perceptual organizational abilities and mathematics achievement has been demonstrated in the neuropsychological literature (Franco &. Sperry, 1977; Warrington, 1982) and is consistent with a specific subtype of learning disabilities described by Rourke and his colleagues (Rourke &. Strang, 1983).

In addition to general intellectual impairment, memory deficits represent one of the most severe and lasting of neuropsychological sequelae in brain-injured children (Levin et al., 1982). Greater memory impairment is associated with more severe injuries and longer periods of coma (Levin &. Eisenberg, 1979a,b), and deficits remain long after other abilities (e.g., motor skills) have recovered (Farr, Greene, &. Meyer, 1983; Fuld &. Fisher, 1977). There is evidence that memory deficits may remain indefinitely as a perennial reminder of the head injury, despite normal intellectual level (Levin et al., 1982).

Of relevance to the discussion of neuropsychological sequelae of head injury is mounting evidence that even mild head injuries may be associated with a variety of impairments that may affect adjustment at school and at work (Boll, 1983). In their study of persons sustaining minor injuries (Glasgow Coma Scale Score of 13 or higher), Rimel, Giordani, Barth, Boll and Jane (1981) reported that three quarters experienced loss of consciousness for 10 minutes or less. Only 8% were reported to have neurologic abnormality at the time of admission, and all showed normal neurologic evaluation at the time of discharge. In light of the minor nature of the injuries and absence of neurologic findings, results of the three-month follow-up of this population were startling. Seventy-eight percent reported frequent headaches, 59% reported changes in memory ability, and one sixth reported problems in daily living. Only one out of six of those followed reported no complaints. Of greatest import is the finding that 34% of persons who had been employed prior to the accident were no longer employed. Unemployment was not associated with the status of insurance coverage or litigation proceeding. Significantly higher levels of employment were demonstrated for older individuals and for those with higher levels of education, income, employment, and socioeconomic status. Nearly half the subjects classified as unskilled laborers remained unemployed three months posttraumatically.

Personality and behavior changes associated with head injuries represent another type of neuropsychological sequela of relevance to educational and vocational rehabilitation. There is some evidence to suggest that these disorders are greater deterrents to eventual adjustment than associated physical disabilities (Bond, 1975). Brink et al. (1970) have identified hallmark characteristics for younger (below age 10) and older (above age 10) brain-injured children. Such behavior as hyperactivity, aggressiveness, decreased attention span, impulsivity, and temper tantrums, were reported for the younger group, with poor judgment standing out as the most frequent characteristic observed in older children.

There is evidence that personality changes may represent the most difficult residual effect of the head injury for families (Brink et al., 1970; Lezak, 1978), who seem better able to cope with physical rather than behavioral sequelae. Levin et al. (1982) suggest that resumption of some obvious abilities (e.g., ambulation and self-care skills) may give the false appearance of greater than actual recovery, thus resulting in unrealistic expectations from parents and teachers and concomitant frustration as a result of the ensuing disparity between expectations and actual behavior. A similar phenomenon is discussed by Long et al. (1984), who describe a recovery sequence in which the head-injured patient moves from a "sick" role, where all responsibilities are removed, to a convalescent status, where although impairment still exists, obvious deficits have lessened, and hence the client is expected to begin to resume routine obligations. These authors suggest that the demands for resumption of a normal routine are greater for mildly injured patients, perhaps resulting in a higher incidence of adjustment problems in this group.

These findings suggest that one important variable in the optimal adjustment of the head-injured patient is the degree to which the client's family understands the probable course of recovery (Long et al., 1984).

However, the results of at least one study imply that experience with head injury may not predispose persons to a greater understanding of the residual effects of head trauma. In a survey of the attitudes of college undergraduates toward head injury (Novack, Alexander, Henking, & Long, 1983), those persons reporting personal experience with head trauma demonstrated a tendency to describe the effects as more like a physical condition than an emotional disorder. Persons unfamiliar with head injuries showed a greater tendency to evaluate the individual's functioning levels in a variety of settings (e.g., on the job, as a family member, self-image) as less impaired. Professionals asked to make similar judgments demonstrated findings consistent with the literature. The authors conclude that persons who have had experience with head injuries and those who have not both show perceptions about the sequelae of such trauma that are distorted relative to what the literature shows, although the nature of these distortions differ for the two groups.

EDUCATIONAL RESPONSE

The previous section has identified a variety of characteristics that may be evident in brain-injured children, including intellectual impairment (Levin et al., 1982); specific deficits in neuropsychological performance, particularly on measures sensitive to speeded fine-motor performance (Winogron et al., 1983); disorders of memory (Levin & Eisenberg, 1979a,b); and specific personality changes including hyperactivity, aggression, destructiveness, and poor judgment (Brink et al., 1970). Some evidence suggests that each of these characteristics may be represented along a continuum from mild to severe, and that some groups of head-injured children may display only minor impairment, although others may exhibit significant deficits. Increasing evidence suggests that groups of children may be categorized into mild or severe impairments, and that there is a relationship between outcome and severity of injury as measured by depth of coma and length of unconsciousness. In addition, there is anecdotal evidence that head injuries may exacerbate premorbid adjustment problems in children (Long et al., 1984), such that mild restlessness becomes extreme hyperactivity and minor acting-out yields to severe aggression.

In planning appropriate educational interventions for the individual head-injured child, careful appraisal of neuropsychological strengths and weaknesses is essential. Since a "characteristic" neuropsychological pattern subsequent to head injuries in children does not appear to exist, this assessment is necessary in order to identify residual areas of strengths that can serve as the foundation for remedial programs, as well as to identify critical areas of impairment that may interfere with good rehabilitation outcomes. This assessment, conducted prior to entering an educational rehabilitation program and at regular intervals thereafter, also can represent an important yardstick for recovery.

Evidence from the follow-up studies of brain-injured children suggests that the majority require some special education approach, and that even those who return to regular education classrooms do not perform at levels equivalent with premorbid achievement. When selecting initially appropriate educational programs, evidence is that optimal adjustment is associated with programs that to the degree possible can provide a safe, protective environment without undue stressors (Long *et al.*, 1984). Often this suggests a special education program, located in a rehabilitation center or a public school. Such programs typically are characterized by fewer students, lower adult–pupil ratio, a structured environment, and professionally trained staff who are sensitive to the learning needs of children with diverse neurologic impairments.

It should be noted, however, that most states do not have a special education category unique to head-injured children, and hence some description of the child's major educational need is required prior to placement. Individual brain-injured children may be served appropriately in a wide range of different educational settings, including classes with the following categorical labels: orthopedic and other health impaired; developmentally handicapped or mentally retarded (both mild and moderate); multihandicapped; learning disabled; severe behavior handicapped; and other low-incidence programs (e.g., visually handicapped). In determining the appropriate category of special education for a given youngster, school officials and parents need to attempt as close a match as is possible between functioning levels and major educational needs of the child and the capability of the program and the staff to respond to these needs. A number of children surviving severe head trauma have been reported to exhibit disorders of motor function, including spasticity and ataxia (Brink *et al.*, 1970). A youngster with such symptoms, who requires ongoing physical and occupational therapy, might best be served in a program for orthopedic/other health impaired or multihandicapped children, where these services are more readily incorporated into the educational program. In contrast, a youngster who has resumed adequate motoric and self-care behaviors and nevertheless continues to show significant impairment in memory and social judgment might be better educated in a classroom for children with behavior disorders or learning disabilities.

In general, change is difficult to manage for children with brain injuries. As a result, an optimal environment, especially for recently injured children, is a self-contained educational program rather than one that requires the student to change classes and adjust to new environments and personalities several times during the day. Because mainstreamed settings are more likely to be recommended for students who have suffered mild injuries, whose recovery apparently has been speedy, special precaution against too-rapid integration is suggested for this population. There often is the temptation on the part of encouraged parents and educators to attempt to resume normal programming for such children before they can manage it comfortably. When placed in such situations, children may exhibit negative adjustment problems, including depression, withdrawal, and acting-out behavior.

Regardless of what environment is selected as the optimal setting in which to deliver the educational rehabilitation program, the best outcomes for populations of head-injured persons have been associated with programs that are highly behavioral, incorporating principles of cuing and shaping (Ben-Yishay & Diller, 1983); demonstrate repetition of information and opportunities for practice (Miller, 1980); use a variety of cuing procedures to assist in generalization (Webster & Scott, 1983); and offer a structured, training-oriented environment with considerable positive feedback (Bolger, 1982). Furthermore, since the rate of learning may progress more slowly (Miller, 1980) and may fade to a greater degree than for other children, programs may need to be highly redundant (Silver, Ben-Yishay, Rattok, Ross, Lakin, Piasetsky, Ezrachi, & Diller, 1983).

Most experts agree that difficulties in attention and concentration represent major deterrents to rehabilitation of brain-injured persons (Levin et al., 1982). Recently, positive results in directing attention have been achieved through the use of verbal cuing, self-talk strategies (Bolger, 1982; Webster & Scott, 1983). Because in the majority of cases of head injury, language abilities remain reasonably functional even in the presence of sustained deficits in other areas (Levin et al., 1982), strategies that employ verbalization have been shown to be viable. Furthermore, because cortical control of attention may be indicated as a result of dysfunction of more automatic attention centers, the use of these cognitive behavior modification techniques may assist head-injured persons in maximizing rehabilitation efforts. Webster and Scott (1983) report that such procedures have been associated with improvement in memory performance and enhancement of daily living skills and return to gainful employment.

In identifying appropriate objectives of educational intervention programs, most experts agree that those functions that can permit the individual to resume as independent a lifestyle as possible are of highest priority, since these skills have been associated with optimal outcome. Residual higher level skills may be of little relevance to an individual who cannot walk to the store and home again without getting lost. Ben-Yishay (1981) has identified these three objectives of cognitive remediation as of

298

CATHY F. TELZROW

greatest relevance to successful adjustment: (a) daily living functions and self-care skills; (b) psychomotor, perceptual, and cognitive skills that relate directly to subsequent vocational abilities; and (c) social and interpersonal skills. For children, these general domains are equally relevant and might include such educational objectives as independent dressing, feeding, toileting, playing, and working; optimal perceptual and motor functioning; the acquisition of functional reading and math skills; and the ability to manage in one's family, neighborhood, and school environments.

VOCATIONAL RESPONSE

As increasing attention is devoted to the necessary partnership of special education and vocational training programs ("President Declares Goal of Independence . . . ," 1984), it is anticipated that transitions for head-injured children will be smoother and more productive. Ideally, vocational planning for head-injured children should be incorporated into educational intervention programs at early stages, so that the development of critical prevocational abilities comprises a major component of the youngster's individual educational plan (IEP).

Increasingly, emphasis is being placed on the relevance of neuropsychological assessment for vocational rehabilitation. In a study of the relationship between General Aptitude Test Battery (GATB) scores and performance on various neuropsychological variables, Cole and Long (1983) reported significant relationships between the two measures on selected factors. Measures sensitive to cognitive and motor abilities were shown to be related most consistently across the two batteries for a head-injured population. These results suggest that neuropsychological assessment data may be of critical relevance to vocational rehabilitation specialists, especially with regard to developing remedial or compensatory approaches for deficit skill areas.

Vocational training for the brain-injured adolescent or young adult appears to require characteristics similar to those associated with educational intervention, including structure, consistency, and intensity. One such program included a six-month period of intensive, remedial intervention for persons deemed to have reached a level of vocational rehabilitation readiness. The remedial programs were highly individualized, and provided trainees with occupational trials that simulated actual work settings. At the conclusion of the training effort, the following outcomes were reported: (a) 15% failed to complete the program; (b) 10% were unemployed, although the program was completed; (c) 30% were employed in settings such as noncompetitive sheltered or open environments; and (d) 45% were employed competitively part-time or full-time (Ezrachi, Ben-Yishay, Rattok, Ross, Lakin, Silver, Piasetsky, & Diller, 1983).

Vocational rehabilitation efforts for head-injured persons require ongoing supervision and monitoring. One method used a 10-point scale to rate the individual's employability level after consistency in performance had been established. The client was then placed in an actual work setting commensurate with the assigned employability rating, and employability status was reappraised at regular intervals. Results of follow-up indicated that 85% of the head-injured clients participating in this intensified, structured program were productively employed (Silver *et al.*, 1983). The authors reported that work ratings tended to remain stable over time for the majority of participants. The importance of follow-up is evidenced by the authors' experience that ongoing "maintenance" contacts with the brain-injured individual were necessary to sustain high rates of employment in this population.

Concern about the difficulty brain-injured clients exhibit in generalizing from one setting to another complicates the transfer of skills from vocational rehabilitation setting to work environment. Wechsler (1984) described a rehabilitation program that eliminates this concern by incorporating components of a cognitive retraining program into an actual work setting. Once again, highly intensive and ongoing feedback and monitoring features are characteristic of the best vocational rehabilitation programs for brain-injured persons.

In closing this section, it seems appropriate to reiterate mounting evidence (e.g., Rimel *et al.*, 1981) that even mild head injuries are associated with remarkably high unemployment rates. Unemployment is highest for persons in lower level positions and may reach as high as 50% for this category (Rimel *et al.*, 1981). These results suggest that adolescents and young adults with head injuries that are neurologically insignificant (i.e., none exhibited positive neurologic findings at the time of hospital discharge) nevertheless may be in need of assistance in coping with ensuing memory and personality changes that may interfere with successful employability. Furthermore, the need for ongoing rehabilitation throughout the chronic phase of recovery (Long *et al.*, 1984) and for periodic follow-up sessions, perhaps indefinitely (Silver *et al.*, 1983), have been indicated by the literature.

SUMMARY

Whereas the science of educational and vocational rehabilitation in neuropsychology operates at an elementary level relative to the more advanced status of diagnosis in the field, it is the former that is expected to represent the most viable contribution of neuropsychology over time (Dean, 1983, 1985). The present chapter identified hallmark neuropsychological characteristics associated with chronic neurologic conditions of highest incidence in a pediatric population: specific learning disabilities, epilepsy, and head trauma. The description of individual differences associated with each condition emphasized patterns of neuropsychological abilities relevant for educational and vocational rehabilitation: intellectual functioning, memory, verbal and visuospatial abilities, motor and sensory performance, and social and emotional functioning.

Optimal rehabilitation programs, whether implemented in educational settings (for children) or in vocational contexts (for adolescents and young adults), are characterized by training strategies that capitalize on existing neuropsychological strengths and, when necessary, provide alternative compensatory techniques. Ideally, intervention settings are designed to provide maximum protection and safety during acute periods and to encourage the acquisition of independent skills at optimal levels. Most successful programs have been described as those that are characterized by consistency, repetition, practice, and rehearsal in real-life environments.

Increasing evidence suggests that the conditions described in this chapter are chronic in nature, and thus may require lifelong adjustments. As a result, systematic interagency programs designed to ease the transition from the educational system to the vocational training setting to the world of work are especially critical for these special populations. Such cooperative efforts have been shown to result in most successful outcomes for persons with these chronic neurologic conditions.

REFERENCES

Ansbaugh, D. J., Gilliland, M., & Ansbaugh, S. J. The student with epilepsy. *Today's Education*, 1980, *69*, 78E–86E.

Bagley, C. *The social psychology of the epileptic child*. Coral Gables, Fla.: University of Miami Press, 1971.

Bakker, D. J. Hemispheric differences and reading strategies: Two dyslexias? *Bulletin of the Orton Society*, 1979, *29*, 1–7.

Balow, B. Biological defects and special education: An empiricist's view. *The Journal of Special Education*, 1979, *13*(1), 35–40.

Baltimore schools try to ease problems of epilepsy. *Education of the Handicapped*, 1983, *8*(3), 6.

Bannatyne, A. The spatially competent LD child. *Academic Therapy*, 1978, *14*, 133–155.

Batshaw, M. L., & Perret, Y. M. *Children with handicaps: A medical primer*. Baltimore: Paul H. Brooks, 1981.

Bear, D. M., & Fedio, P. Quantitative analysis of interictal behavior in temporal lobe epilepsy. *Archives of Neurology*, 1977, *34*, 454–467.

Bellur, S., & Hermann, B. P. Emotional and cognitive effects of anticonvulsant medications. *Clinical Neuropsychology*, 1984, 6(1), 21–23.

Benson, H. *Epilepsy & employment: Placement problems and technique.* Washington, D. C.: Epilepsy Foundation of America, 1977.

Ben-Yishay, Y. Cognitive remediation after TBD: Toward a definition of its objectives, tasks and conditions. In *Working approaches to remediation of cognitive deficits in brain-damaged persons. Rehabilitation monograph* (No. 62). New York: New York Medical Center, 1981.

Ben-Yishay, Y., & Diller, L. Cognitive remediation. In M. Rosenthal, E. Griffith, M. Bond, & J. Miller (Eds.), *Rehabilitation of the head injured adult.* Philadelphia: F. A. Davis, 1983.

Berent, S., Giordani, B., Sackellares, J. C., O'Leary, D., & Boll, T. J. Cerebrally lateralized epileptogenic foci and performance on a verbal and visual-graphic learning task. *Perceptual and Motor Skills*, 1983, *56*, 991–1001.

Berg, R. A., Bolter, J. F., Ch'ien, L. T., & Cummins, J. A standardized assessment of emotionality in children suffering from epilepsy. *The International Journal of Clinical Neuropsychology*, 1984, 6(4), 247–248.

Berger-Gross, P., & Shackelford, M. *Closed head injury in children: Intelligence and academic achievement.* Paper presented at the meeting of the International Neuropsychological Society, Houston, February, 1984.

Blalock, J. Residual learning disabilities in young adults: Implications for rehabilitation. *Journal of Applied Rehabilitation Counseling*, 1982, *13*(2), 9–13.

Blank, J. R., & Anderson, R. J. The effects of anticonvulsant drugs on rehabilitation and employment of epileptics. *Journal of Rehabilitation*, 1983, 49(2) 61–63.

Boder, E. Developmental dyslexia: Prevailing diagnostic concepts and a new diagnostic approach. In H. R. Myklebust (Ed.), *Progress in learning disabilities* (Vol. 2). New York: Grune & Stratton, 1971.

Boder, E., & Jarrico, S. *The Boder Test of Reading-Spelling Patterns—Manual.* New York: Grune & Stratton, 1982.

Bolger, J. P. Cognitive retraining: A developmental approach. *Clinical Neuropsychology*, 1982, 4(2), 66–70.

Boll, T. J. Minor head injury in children: Out of sight, but not out of mind. *Journal of Clinical Child Psychology*, 1983, *12*(1), 74–80.

Bolter, J. F., Berg, R. A., Ch'ien, L. T., Williams, S. J., Lancaster, W., & Cummins, J. *Emotional adjustment in children with chronic epilepsy.* Paper presented at the meeting of the National Academy of Neuropsychologists, Atlanta, October 1982. (a)

Bolter, J. F., Berg, R. A., Ch'ien, L. T., Williams, S. J., Lancaster, W., & Cummins, J. *Tactile-perceptual functioning and academic performance in children with chronic seizures.* Paper presented at the meeting of the National Academy of Neuropsychologists, Atlanta, October 1982. (b)

Bond, M. F. Assessment of the psychosocial outcome after severe head injury. *Ciba Foundation Symposium*, 1975, *34*, 141–159.

Brink, J. D., Garrett, A. L., Hale, W. R., Woo-Sam, J., & Nickel, V. L. Recovery of motor and intellectual function in children sustaining severe head injuries. *Developmental Medicine and Child Neurology*, 1970, *12*, 565–571.

Brink, J. D., Imbus, C., & Woo-Sam, J. Physical recovery after severe closed head trauma in children and adolescents. *The Journal of Pediatrics*, 1980, 97(5), 721–727.

Brittain, H. Epilepsy and intellectual functions. In B. M. Kulig, H. Meinardi, & G. Stores (Eds.), *Epilepsy and behavior '79.* Lisse, the Netherlands: Swets & Zeitlinger, 1980.

Brown, D. *Steps to independence for people with learning disabilities.* Washington, D. C.: Closer Look Parent's Campaign for Handicapped Children and Youth, 1980.

Brown, D. Rehabilitating the learning disabled adult. *American Rehabilitation*, 1982, 8, 3–11.

Cato, C. E., & Rice, B. D. *Rehabilitation of clients with specific learning disabilities*. Little Rock, Ark.: University of Arkansas, 1982.

Cavanaugh, R. M., Jr. Cooperative programming with the schools: A proposal. *Journal of Rehabilitation*, 1983, 49(1), 33–36.

Chadwick, O., Rutter, M., Brown, E., Shaffer, D., & Traub, M. A prospective study of children with head injuries. II: Cognitive sequelae. *Psychological Medicine*, 1981, 11, 49–61.

Chadwick, O., Rutter, M., Shaffer, D., & Shrout, P. E. A prospective study of children with head injuries. IV: Specific cognitive deficits. *Journal of Clinical Neuropsychology*, 1981, 3, 101–120.

Cole, J. C., & Long, C. J. *Interrelationship of neuropsychological and vocational assessments in neurologically impaired patients*. Paper presented at the meeting of the National Academy of Neuropsychologists, Houston, October 1983.

Compton, C. *Living with learning disabilities: A ten-year follow-up study*. Paper presented at the meeting of the National Association for Children with Learning Disabilities, New Orleans, February 1984.

Cooper, J. A., & Ferry, P. C. Acquired auditory verbal agnosia and seizures in childhood. *Journal of Speech and Hearing Disorders*, 1978, 43, 176–184.

Cronbach, L. J., & Snow, R. E. *Aptitudes and instructional methods*. New York: Irvington, 1977.

Dean, R. S. Neuropsychological assessment. In T. Kratochwill (Ed.), *Advances in school psychology* (Vol. 2). Hillsdale, N.J.: Erlbaum, 1982.

Dean, R. S. Neuropsychological correlates of total seizures with major motor epileptic children. *Clinical Neuropsychology*, 1983, 5(1), 1–3.

Dean, R. S. Perspectives on the future of neuropsychological assessment. In B. S. Plake & J. C. Witt (Eds.), *Buros-Nebraska series on measurement and testing: Future of testing and measurement*. New York: Erlbaum, 1985.

Dennerll, R. D., Broeder, J. D., & Sokolov, S. L. WISC and WAIS factors in children and adults with epilepsy. *Journal of Clinical Psychology*, 1964, 20(2), 236–240.

Dodrill, C. B. Diphenylhydantoin serum levels, toxicity, and neuropsychological performance in patients with epilepsy. *Epilepsia*, 1975, 16, 593–600.

Dodrill, C. B. *Effects of generalized tonic-clonic seizures upon intellectual, neuropsychological, emotional, and social functioning*. Paper presented at the meeting of the American Psychological Association, Los Angeles, August 1981.

Dodrill, C. B., & Wilkus, R. J. Relationships between intelligence and electroencephalographic epileptiform activity in adult epileptics. *Neurology*, 1967, 26, 525–531.

Dorman, C. Personality and psychiatric correlates of the Halstead–Reitan tests in boys with school problems. *Clinical Neuropsychology*, 1982, 4(3), 110–114.

Dreifuss, F. E. The nature of epilepsy. In G. H. Wright (Ed.), *Epilepsy rehabilitation*. Boston: Little, Brown, 1975.

Dubinsky, B. L., Wilkening, G. N., & Minarcik, C. J., Jr. *The effect of subclinical discharges on the cognitive performance of children with seizure disorders: The use of simultaneous EEG/CCTV monitoring and neuropsychological testing*. Paper presented at the meeting of the National Academy of Neuropsychologists, Atlanta, October 1982.

Epps, S., Ysseldyke, J. E., & Algozzine, B. Impact of different definitions of learning disabilities on the number of students identified. *Journal of Psychoeducational Assessment*, 1983, 1, 341–352.

Ezrachi, O., Ben-Yishay, Y., Rattok, J., Ross, B., Lakin, P., Silver, S., Piasetsky, E., & Diller, L. Rehabilitation of cognitive and perceptual deficits in people with traumatic brain damage: A five year clinical research study. In *Working approaches to remediation of cognitive deficits in brain damaged persons. Rehabilitation monograph* (No. 66). New York: New York Medical Center, 1983.

Farr, S. P., Greene, R. L., & Meyer, P. G. Changes in neuropsychological functioning in patients recovering from closed head injury. *Clinical Neuropsychology*, 1983, 5(1), 44–55. (Abstract)

Fedio, P., & Mirsky, A. F. Selective intellectual deficits in children with temporal lobe or centracephalic epilepsy. *Neuropsychologia*, 1969, 7, 287–300.

Forrest, J. W. Epileptics need not apply. *Journal of Rehabilitation*, 1961, 27(4), 21–24; 40–43.

Foster, J. C., Szoke, C. O., Kapisovsky, P. M., & Kriger, L. S. *Guidance, counseling, and support services for high school students with physical disabilities: Visual-hearing-orthopedic-neuromuscular-epilepsy-chronic health conditions.* Cambridge, Mass.: Technical Education Research Centers, 1979.

Franco, L., & Sperry, R. W. Hemisphere lateralization for cognitive processing of geometry. *Neuropsychologia*, 1977, 15, 107–114.

Fuld, P. A., & Fisher, P. Recovery of intellectual ability after closed head injury. *Developmental Medicine and Child Neurology*, 1977, 19, 495–502.

Gastaut, H. *Enquiry into the education of epileptic children.* Paper presented at the second seminar of the International Bureau for Epilepsy, Marseilles, France, 1964.

Gilmore, R. L, & Heilman, K. M. Speech arrest in partial seizures: Evidence of an associated language disorder. *Neurology*, 1981, 31, 1016–1019.

Gittelman, R. Treatment of reading disorders. In M. Rutter (Ed.), *Developmental neuropsychiatry.* New York: Guilford Press, 1983.

Goldin, G. J., & Margolin, R. J. The psychosocial aspects of epilepsy. In G. N. Wright (Ed.), *Epilepsy rehabilitaton.* Boston: Little, Brown, 1975.

Goldin, G. J., Perry, S. L., Margolin, R. J., Stotsky, B. A., & Foster, J. C. *The rehabilitation of the young epileptic: Dimensions and dynamics.* Lexington, Mass.: D. C. Heath, 1971.

Gottfredson, L. S., Finucci, J. M., & Childs, B. *The adult occupational success of dyslexic boys: A large-scale, long-term follow-up* (Report no. 334). Silver Spring, Md.: Center for Social Organization of Schools, 1983.

Green, J. B., & Hartlage, L. C. Comparative performance of epileptic and nonepileptic children and adolescents. *Diseases of the Nervous System*, 1971, 32, 418–421.

Gunnison, J. A., & Kaufman, N. L. *Neuropsychological approaches to educational intervention.* Paper presented at the meeting of the American Psychological Association, Washington, D. C., August 1982.

Halstead, H. Abilities and behavior of epileptic children. *Journal of Mental Science*, 1957, 103, 28–47.

Hartlage, L. C. Neuropsychological assessment in anticonvulsant drug toxicity. *Clinical Neuropsychology*, 1981, 3, (4) 20–22. (a)

Hartlage, L. C. Neuropsychological assessment techniques. In C. R. Reynolds & T. Gutkin (Eds.), *Handbook of school psychology.* New York: Wiley, 1981. (b)

Hartlage, L. C., & Reynolds, C. R. Neuropsychological assessment and the individualization of instruction. In G. W. Hynd & J. E. Obrzut (Eds.), *Neuropsychological assessment and the school-age child: Issues and procedures.* New York: Grune & Stratton, 1981.

Hartlage, L. C., & Telzrow, C. F. The neuropsychological bases of educational intervention. *Journal of Learning Disabilities*, 1983, 16(3), 521–528.

Hartlage, L. C., & Telzrow, C. F. Neuropsychological basis of educational assessment and programming. In P. E. Logue & J. E. Schear (Eds.), *Clinical neuropsychology.* Springfield, Ill.: Charles C Thomas, 1984. (a)

Hartlage, L. C., & Telzrow, C. F. Rehabilitation of persons with learning disabilities. *Journal of Rehabilitation*, 1984, 50(1), 31–34.(b)

Hartlage, L. C., & Telzrow, C. F. Neuropsychological aspects of childhood epilepsy. In R. Tarter & G. Goldstein (Eds.), *Advances in clinical neuropsychology* (Vol. 2). New York: Plenum Press, 1984.(c)

Hartlage, P. L. Neuropsychological aspects of epilepsy and the effects of medication on children's behavior. In C. R. Reynolds & J. H. Clark (Eds.), *Assessment and programming for young children with low-incidence handicaps.* New York: Plenum Press, 1983.

Hershenson, D. B. Work adjustments, disability, and the three R's of vocational rehabilitation: A conceptual model. *Rehabilitation Counseling Bulletin,* 1981, 25(2), 91–97.

Holmes, D. A., & McWilliams, J. M. Employer's attitudes toward hiring epileptics. *Journal of Rehabilitation,* 1981, 47, (2), 20–21.

Hughes, J. R., & Olson, S. F. An investigation of eight different types of temporal lobe discharges. *Epilepsia,* 1981, 22, 421–435.

Hutt, S. J., Jackson, P. M., Belsham, A., & Higgins, G. Perceptual-motor behavior in relation to blood phenobarbitone level: A preliminary report. *Developmental Medicine and Child Neurology,* 1968, 10, 626–632.

Hynd, G. W., & Cohen, M. *Dyslexia: Neuropsychological theory, research, and clinical differentiation.* New York: Grune & Stratton, 1983.

Hynd, G. W., & Hynd, C. R. Dyslexia: Neuroanatomical/neurolinguistic perspectives. *Reading Research Quarterly,* 1984, 19, 482–498.

Ives, L. A. Learning difficulties in children with epilepsy. *British Journal of Disorders of Communication,* 1970, 5(1), 77–84.

Kallanranta, T. Rehabilitation of epileptic patients. *Acta Neurologica Scandinavica,* 1983, 67(93), 67–70.

Kleck, R. *Self-disclosure patterns among epileptics.* Hanover, N.H.: Dartmouth College, 1968.

Klonoff, H., & Low, M. Disordered brain function in young children and early adolescents: Neuropsychological and electroencephalographic correlates. In R. M. Reitan & L. A. Davison (Eds.), *Clinical Neuropsychology.* Washington, D.C.: Hemisphere, 1974.

Klonoff, H., Low, M. D., & Clark, C. Head injuries in children: A prospective five year followup. *Journal of Neurology, Neurosurgery, and Psychiatry,* 1977, 40, 1211–1219.

Klonoff, H., & Paris, R. Immediate, short-term and residual effects of acute head injuries in children: Neuropsychological and neurological correlates. In R. M. Reitan & L. A. Davison (Eds.), *Clinical neuropsychology.* Washington, D. C.: Hemisphere, 1974.

Kutsick, K. Remedial strategies for learning disabled adolescents. *Academic Therapy,* 1982, 17, 329–335.

Lehtovaara, R. The estimation of working capacity in epileptic patients. *Acta Neurologica Scandinavica,* 1983, 67 (93), 60–66.

Levin, H. S., Benton, A. L., & Grossman, R. G. *Neurobehavioral consequences of closed head injury.* New York: Oxford, 1982.

Levin, H. S., & Eisenberg, H. M. Neuropsychological impairment after closed head injury in children and adolescents. *Journal of Pediatric Psychology,* 1979, 4, 389–402. (a)

Levin, H. S., & Eisenberg, H. M. Neuropsychological outcome of closed head injury in children and adolescents. *Child's Brain,* 1979, 5, 281–292. (b)

Lewis, D. O., Pincus, J. H., Shanok, S. S., & Glaser, G. H. Psychomotor epilepsy and violence in group of incarcerated adolescent boys. *American Journal of Psychiatry,* 1982, 139(7), 882–887.

Lezak, M. D. Living with the characterologically altered brain injured patient. *Journal of Clinical Psychiatry,* 1978, 38, 592–598.

Livingston, S. *Drug therapy for epilepsy.* Springfield, Ill.: Charles C Thomas, 1966.

Long, C. J., Gouvier, W. D., & Cole, J. C. A model of recovery for the total rehabilitation of individuals with head trauma. *Journal of Rehabilitation,* 1984, 50(1), 39–45.

Lyon, R., & Watson, B. Empirically derived subgroups of learning disabled readers: Diagnostic characteristics. *Journal of Learning Disabilities*, 1981, *14*, 256–261.

MacLeod, C. M., Dekaban, A. S., & Hunt, E. Memory impairment in epileptic patients: Selective effects on phenobarbital concentration. *Science*, 1978, *202*, 1102–1105.

Mauser, A. J. *Assessing the learning disabled: Selected instruments* (3rd ed.). Novato, Calif.: Academic Therapy Publications, 1981.

Maxwell, M., & Zenhausern, R. *Teaching reading to disabled readers by eliminating the necessity for grapheme to phoneme recoding*. Paper presented at the meeting of the Eastern Psychological Association, Philadelphia, April 1983.

McGuire, G. M., & Goyette, C. H. The development of a functional assessment for learning disabled adults: A preliminary analysis. *Journal of Rehabilitation*, 1983, *49*(4), 70–73.

Miller, E. The training characteristics of severely head-injured patients: A preliminary study. *Journal of Neurology, Neurosurgery, and Psychiatry*, 1980, *43*, 525–528.

Minskoff, E. H. Training LD students to cope with the everyday world. *Academic Therapy*, 1982, *17*, 311–316.

Morgan, A. M. B., & Groh, C. Visual perceptual deficits in young children with epilepsy. In B. M. Kulig, H. Meinardi, & G. Stores (Eds.), *Epilepsy and behavior '79*. Lisse, the Netherlands: Swets & Zeitlinger, 1980.

Novack, T. A., Alexander, P. C., Henking, B., & Long, C. J. *Attitudes towards individuals experiencing head trauma*. Presented at the meeting of the National Academy of Neuropsychologists, Houston, October 1983.

Nuffield, E. J. A. Neurophysiology and behavior disorders in epileptic children. *Journal of Mental Science*, 1961, *107*, 438–458.

Oxley, J. Drugs and brain function. *National Spokesman*, 1979, *12*(10), 7.

Pirozzolo, F. J. *The neuropsychology of developmental reading disorders*. New York: Praeger, 1979.

Pirozzolo, F. J., Dunn, K., & Zetusky, W. Physiological approaches to subtypes of developmental reading disability. *Topics in Learning & Learning Disabilities*, 1983, *3*(1), 40–47.

Plan for nationwide action on epilepsy (Vol. 1). Washington, D. C.: U. S. Department of H.E.W., 1977.

Pond, D. A. Psychiatric aspects of epileptic and brain-damaged children. *British Medical Journal*, 1961, *2*(1), 377–382, 1454–1459.

Pond, D. A., & Bidwell, B. H. A survey of epilepsy in fourteen general practices II. Social and psychological aspects. *Epilepsia*, 1960, *1*, 285–299.

President declares goal of independence for disabled persons. *Programs for the Handicapped*, 1984, *1*, 9.

Problems plague efforts to employ the handicapped, expert says. *Vocational Training News*, 1984, *15*(11), 2.

Rangaswami, K. Educational difficulties and adjustment problems of epileptic adolescents. *Child Psychiatry Quarterly*, 1983, *16*(1), 19–25.

Reynolds, C. R. Neuropsychological assessment and the habilitation of learning: Considerations in the search for the aptitude × treatment interaction. *School Psychology Review*, 1981, *10*(2), 343–349.

Reynolds, E. H., & Travers, R. D. Serum anticonvulsant concentration in epileptic patients with mental symptoms. *British Journal of Psychiatry*, 1974, *124*, 440–445.

Rimel, R. W., Giordani, B., Barth, J. T., Boll, T. J., & Jane, J. A. Disability caused by minor head injury. *Neurosurgery*, 1981, *9*(3), 221–228.

Rimel, R. W., & Jane, J. A. Characteristics of the head-injured patient. In M. Rosenthal, E. R. Griffith, M. R. Bond, & J. D. Miller (Eds.), *Rehabilitation of the head injured adult*. Philadelphia: F. A. Davis, 1983.

Rodin, E. A., Shapiro, H. L., & Lennox, K. *Epilepsy and life performance.* Detroit: Lafayette Clinic, 1976.

Rourke, B. P., Bakker, D. J., Fisk, J. L., & Strang, J. D. *Child neuropsychology.* New York: Guilford Press, 1983.

Rourke, B. P., & Finlayson, M. A. J. Neuropsychological significance of variations in patterns of academic performance: Verbal and visual-spatial abilities. *Journal of Abnormal Child Psychology,* 1978, *6,* 121–133.

Rourke, B. P., & Strang, J. D. Subtypes of reading and arithmetical disabilities: A neuropsychological analysis. In M. Rutter (Ed.), *Developmental neuropsychiatry.* New York: Guilford Press, 1983.

Rutter, M. (Ed.). *Developmental neuropsychiatry.* New York: Guilford Press, 1983.

Rutter, M., Chadwick, O., & Shaffer, D. Head injury. In M. Rutter (Ed.), *Developmental neuropsychiatry.* New York: Guilford Press, 1983.

Rutter, M., Graham, P., & Yule, W. *A neuropsychiatric study in childhood.* Philadelphia: J. B. Lippincott, 1970.

Sandoval, J., & Haapanen, R. M. A critical commentary on neuropsychology in the schools: Are we ready? *The School Psychology Review,* 1981, *10,* 381–388.

Schonhaut, S., & Satz, P. Prognosis for children with learning disabilities: A review of follow-up studies. In M. Rutter (Ed.), *Developmental neuropsychiatry.* New York: Guilford Press, 1983.

Seidenberg, M., O'Leary, D. S., Berent, S., & Boll, T. Changes in seizure frequency and test-retest scores on the Wechsler Adult Intelligence Test. *Epilepsia,* 1981, *22,* 75–83.

Silver, S., Ben-Yishay, Y., Rattok, J., Ross, B., Lakin, P., Piasetsky, E., Ezrachi, O., & Diller, L. Occupational outcomes in severe TBD's following intensive cognitive remediation: An interim report. In *Working approaches to remediation of cognitive deficits in brain-damaged persons. Rehabilitation monograph* (No. 66). New York: New York Medical Center, 1983.

Stoiber, K. D., Bracken, B., & Gissal, T. J. Cognitive processing styles in reading-disabled and a matched group of normal children. *Journal of Psychoeducational Assessment,* 1983, *1,* 219–233.

Stores, G., Hart, J., & Piran, H. Inattentiveness in school children with epilepsy. *Epilepsia,* 1978, *19,* 169–175.

Szuhay, J. A., Newill, B. H., Scott, A. J., Williams, J. M., Stout, J. K., & Decker, T. W. *Field investigation and evaluation of learning disabilities.* Scranton, Pa.: University of Scranton, 1980.

Telzrow, C. F. Best practices in reducing error in learning disability qualification. In J. Grimes & A. Thomas (Eds.), *Best practices manual,* 1985.

Telzrow, C. F., Century, E., Redmond, C., Whitaker, B., & Zimmerman, B. The Boder Test: Neuropsychological and demographic features of dyslexic subtypes. *Psychology in the Schools,* 1983, *20,* 427–432.

Telzrow, C. F., & Hartlage, L. C. A neuropsychological model for vocational planning for learning disabled students. In W. M. Cruickshank & J. M. Kliebhan (Eds.), *Early adolescence to early adulthood, Vol. 5, The best of ACLD.* Syracuse, N.Y.: Syracuse University Press, 1984.

Thompson, P. J., & Trimble, M. R. Anticonvulsant serum levels: Relationship to impairments of cognitive functioning. *Journal of Neurology, Neurosurgery & Psychiatry,* 1983, *46*(3), 227–233.

Tindall, L. W. Seven steps to employment for learning disabled students. In W. M. Cruickshank & J. M. Kliebhan (Eds.), *Early adolescence to early adulthood, Vol. 5, The best of ACLD.* Syracuse, N.Y.: Syracuse University Press, 1984.

Trimble, M. Drugs and I.Q. *National Spokesman*, 1979, *12*(10), 7.

Trostle, J. A., Hauser, W. A., & Susser, I. S. The logic of noncompliance: Management of epilepsy from the patient's point of view. *Culture, Medicine & Psychiatry*, 1983, *7*(1), 35–56.

Udel, M. The work performance of epileptics in industry. *Archives of Environmental Health*, 1960, *1*, 257–264.

Warrington, E. L. The fractionation of arithmetic skills: A single case study. *Quarterly Journal of Experimental Psychology*, 1982, *34*(A), 31–51.

Watts, G. O. *Dynamic neuroscience: Its application to brain disorders*. Hagerstown, Md.: Harper & Row, 1975.

Webster, J. S., & Scott, R. R. The effects of self-instructional training on attentional deficits following head injury. *Clinical Neuropsychology*, 1983, *5*(2), 69–74.

Wechsler, F. S. The work environment as a cognitive retraining laboratory. *Clinical Neuropsychology*, 1984, *6*(1), 86. (Supplement)

Wedding, D. Clinical and statistical prediction in neuropsychology. *Clinical Neuropsychology*, 1983, *5*(2), 49–55.

Will: let's move forward to improve special education. *Education of the Handicapped*, 1984, *10*(5), 7–8.

Wilson, A., Petty, R., Perry, A., & Rose, F. C. Paroxysmal language disturbance in an epileptic treated with clobazam. *Neurology*, 1983, *33*(5), 652–654.

Winogron, H. W., Knights, R. M., & Bawden, H. N. *Neuropsychological deficits following head injury in children*. Paper presented at the meeting of the International Neuropsychological Society, Mexico City, February 1983.

Witelson, S. Developmental dyslexia: Two right hemispheres and none left. *Science*, 1977, *195*, 309–311.

Witten, B. J., Rehabilitation and learning disabilities: A new challenge for counselors. *Journal of Applied Rehabilitation Counseling*, 1983, *14*(3), 59–64.

Wright, G. N. Rehabilitation and the problem of epilepsy. In G. H. Wright (Ed.), *Epilepsy rehabilitation*. Boston: Little, Brown, & Co., 1975.

Young, W. M. Poverty, intelligence and life in the inner city. *Mental Retardation*, 1969, *7*(2), 24.

Yule, W. Educational achievement. In B. M. Kulig, H. Meinardi, & G. Stores (Eds.), *Epilepsy and behavior '79*. Lisse, the Netherlands: Swets & Zeitlinger, 1980.

Zenhausern, R., & Markman, S. *Hemispheric cognitive style and processing strategies in verbal learning*. Paper presented at the meeting of the International Neuropsychological Society, Mexico City, February 1983.

Zenhausern, R., Minardi, A., & Maxwell, M. *The remediation of reading disability: A new approach*. Paper presented at the meeting of the Eastern Psychological Association, Philadelphia, April 1983.

Zenhausern, R., & Oexle, J. E. *Differential hemispheric activation in good and poor readers*. Paper presented at the meeting of the of the International Neuropsychological Society, Atlanta, February 1981.

CHAPTER 13

Synthesis of Neuropsychological Bases of Individual Differences

LAWRENCE C. HARTLAGE and CATHY F. TELZROW

As mentioned in the introduction to this volume, a conscious attempt was made by the editors to preserve the flavor of respective chapter contributions, although at the same time adopting some commonality of style throughout the text in order to facilitate readability. This final chapter serves to provide further integration of the discrete but interdependent topics addressed in the 12 substantive chapters of *The Neuropsychology of Individual Differences*, as well as offering a summary statement that synthesizes the major conclusions of the respected contributors to this volume.

The role of the neuropsychological bases of individual differences is inherent in Dean's description of neuropsychology as a science involving attempts to relate observable behavior to the functional efficiency of the central nervous system. When we consider that the nervous system of the average human being contains some 10 billion neurons and approximately 10 times that number of glial cells, the potential for near-infinite numbers of permutations and combinations of central nervous system organizational schemata becomes apparent. When to this near infinity of possible individual differences attributable to brain organization we add the fact that neurodevelopmental phenomena associated with different stages of cortical differentiation can be interrupted or delayed by insults to the central nervous sytem from the instant of conception through progressive levels of subsequent development, with differential behavior se-

LAWRENCE C. HARTLAGE • Department of Neurology, Medical College of Georgia, Augusta, Georgia 30902. CATHY F. TELZROW • Cuyahoga Special Education Service Center, Cleveland, Ohio 44137.

quelae associated with insults at various ages, the potential for individual neuropsychological variation becomes even greater.

The assessment of the interaction of neuropsychological substrates of behavior with environmental phenomena, although representing a potentially fruitful area for providing greater understanding of the neuropsychological bases of individual differences, is fraught with formidable methodological problems. In an attempt to clarify the implications of developmental neuropsychology for interindividual and intraindividual variability, Bolter and Long trace a number of lines of research involving both normal and neurologically damaged children. As they point out, this is an area of considerably greater complexity than is encountered with comparable studies involving adults, in that both structural and biochemical variation concerning such diverse phenomena as age-related changes in axonal and dendritic organization, myelination, synaptogenesis, neurotransmitter concentration, and protein and nucleic acid production are related to brain maturation. Furthermore, this maturational pattern may vary both between hemispheres and intrahemispherically in a complex and multilevel way. The fact that development of brain structures and behavior are mutually interactive presents the researcher with the need to study a variety of factors whose interactions with other potentially related variables are largely unknown. As Bolter and Long emphasize, there is special need for a model of brain development, such as that proposed by Luria, to serve as a basis for conceptualizing relevant research questions, with a longitudinal design representing perhaps the most viable approach for testing and refinement of the model. When we consider the variety, complexity, and range of abilities to be sampled and the measurement techniques and limitations unique to each developmental level, it is not surprising that no study or group of studies has been conducted comparing development in normal and neurologically impaired children over a sufficient span of time to help clarify which, if any, model may be most productive. In spite of the complexity of the issue, the conclusions drawn by Bolter and Long state succinctly the current status of knowledge in the field and what areas still need further clarification, conceptualization, and research.

Perception has long represented one of the dependent variables that has provided especially valuable data concerning individual differences in brain–behavior relationships. However, as Melamed and Melamed point out in their opening comments, perceptual science has not had an influential role in formulating the conceptual basis of neuropsychological assessment. Although much of the historical lack of influence of perception research on neuropsychological theory may be due to the multiple definitions of perception and the abstruseness of many theories in per-

SYNTHESIS   311

ception, the Melameds help overcome many of the obstacles imposed
by these factors by their subsequent systematic discussion of discrete
issues. Their special focus on visual perception reflects that of traditional
human neuropsychology and places the historic nativism–empiricism
controversy in perspective as it relates to the contributions of modern
perceptual science to neuropsychology. Of special relevance to applied
aspects of neuropsychology is the authors' perspective on current use
of perceptual constructs in neuropsychology and their translation into
such neuropsychological batteries as the Luria-Nebraska and Reitan-
Indiana, other discrete measures such as the Benton and Beery scales,
and subscales of the McCarthy and Illinois Test of Psycholinguistic Abilities tests. Their concluding segment on key areas of perceptual development research for child neuropsychology demonstrates the potential
for research, conducted either by investigators with dual expertise or via
collaborative research implemented by experts sophisticated in either
perception or neuropsychology, for making important contributions toward increased understanding of neuropsychological bases of individual
differences in perception.

     The interaction of internal regulators and external feedback systems
is perhaps nowhere more pronounced than in the realm of temperament
and the development of self-regulation, and yet this is an area that traditional neuropsychology appears to have ignored in favor of more "hard
wiring" emphases. As Rothbart and Posner observe, just as inborn programs of self-regulation modulate individual responsivity, the reactivity
of the developing child influences the nature and effect of phenomena
that will facilitate or inhibit the development of given aspects of temperament, and these reciprocal and interactive forces have substantial
implications for a general theory of neuropsychological bases of individual
differences in both normal and more traditional clinical populations. Such
temperamental factors as extroversion and introversion offer heuristic
potential for relating cortical arousability and electrophysiological measures of neuropsychological functioning to behavioral measures of individual variation in a normal population, as well as providing possible
insights into underlying physiological substrates of classical clinical neuropsychological descriptions of "la belle indifference" versus "catastrophic
reaction" types of response to unilateral cerebral insult. As Rothbart and
Posner integrate classical research involving lower (e.g., reticular) systems
with more recent research involving the psychopharmacology of neurotransmitter roles on attention and arousal, the contingent negative variation, and split-brain findings, and relate learning-theory conceptualizations of temperament to the reinforcing roles of the dopamine,
norepinephrine, and opioid systems and the punishment system involving

serotonin, there is a sense of gestalt unifying these apparently diverse systems of psychology as they are focused on individual differences under the unifying concept of neuropsychology.

The focus of much applied neuropsychology traditionally has involved some aspect of general cognitive ability, and second-generation neuropsychological assessment batteries have incorporated conceptual and theoretical aspects of cognitive factors into their empirical approach to neuropsychology. In his approach to the general topic of the neuropsychology of individual differences in general cognitive ability, Vernon traces the historical evolution of general cognitive theory from the monistic theory of Spearman to modern foci on the nature and structure of general intelligence. Current work involving reaction time, inspection time, and speed of short- and long-term memory processing is integrated into the evolutionary development of cognitive theory based on biological bases of intelligence, topics that share as common ground neuropsychological approaches to individual differences. Vernon's demonstration of the close relationship between neural adaptability and intelligene elaborates this commonality, and he further incorporates biochemical substrates into his overview of current approaches to the nature of general intelligence, paving the way for his concluding proposed model for individual differences in mental ability. The concept of neural efficiency that Vernon describes serves to synthesize traditional conceptualizations of intelligence with current neuropsychology and provides a promising heuristic model for a neuropsychological basis of individual differences in general cognitive abilities. This discussion prepares the reader to focus on discrete aspects of cognitive abilities such as language and learning disorders, the topics of the two succeeding chapters.

Lasky's perspectives on language development precede the chapter on learning disabilities in adherence to the pedagogic dictum that first focus is on normal development followed by study of pathological or deviant variations from normal. Her early introduction of approaches to defining language sets the stage for clarifying how conceptualizations of the nature of language provide structure to what will be studied, and thus influence both subsequent research and the interpretation of data. Given this structure, Lasky begins with distinguishing between such aspects of language as comprehension and production, with careful attention to the neurological structures underlying these discrete processes of language development. From the neural substrates of such comprehension phenomena as pragmatics and production phenomena such as phonology, with emphases on their internal and environmental interactions, she progresses through semantics and their categories into relational terms, increasing complexities of syntax and metalinguistic skills, with continued focus on individual differences among these variables at each stage of development. Lasky's meticulous tracking of the sequential development of discrete aspects of language from infancy through school readiness provides both a context for understanding neuropsychological substrates of individual variation in language development and a basis for approaching the study of disorders in language development as they are reflected in difficulties in learning.

Pirozzolo and Harrell approach what constitutes for clinical child neuropsychologists a common referral problem and for developmental neuropsychological theorists a means for studying individual differences in the development of specific aspects of langauge, learning, and reasoning schemata. Their focus on the neuropsychology of learning disabilities begins with a recognition of the problems for definitive research in learning disability that are imposed by the ambiguity of both definition and conceptualization of the condition. They then begin a systematic evaluation of its pathophysiology, as inferred from cytoarchitectonic, biochemical, hemispheric asymmetry, and electrophysiological studies. Moving from anatomic and physiologic approaches, the authors explore perceptual and information-processing strategies, with focus on auditory, visual, and intersensory modalities. They conclude with a recognition of the heterogeneity of learning disabilities as a meaningful diagnostic entity, and note the emerging trend toward neuropsychologically based subtypes of learning disabilities as an approach with promise for helping elucidate possible bases of individual differences in learning capabilities.

From its earliest history, neuropsychology in the United States has been concerned with attempts to identify possible neuropsychological components of psychopathology. Golden and Sawicki, recognizing this tradition, begin with an evaluation of the various schizophrenic syndromes, with special attention to diagnostic issues as they relate to such neuropsychological substrates as disorders in cognition, perception, language, and sensory and praxic functions. In a novel conceptual approach, they relate these disorders to the neuropsychological functional model of Luria, especially reminiscent of his descriptions of behavioral sequelae of damage to frontal areas, thus providing an argument for brain dysfunction as an underlying component of schizophrenia. Because of the possible depressing effects of associative thought disorder on neuropsychological function, and reciprocal depression of associative thinking imposed by neuropsychological impairment, the authors explore a series of studies using such neuropsychological measurement approaches as the Wechsler Scales, Halstead-Reitan Neuropsychological Battery, and the Luria-Nebraska Neuropsychological Battery and such neuroanatomical measures as pneumoencephalography, computer-assisted transaxial tomography, electroencephalography, cerebral blood flow, and positron emission tomography. Although not totally conclusive, results tend to support suggested brain impairment among schizophrenics, as inferred by both neuropsychological and neuroanatomical test findings. Focusing next on affective disorders, Golden and Sawicki apply the same sequence of investigation with similar measures, citing evidence that, although not so comprehensive as with schizophrenics, is compatible with some potential neuropsychological bases for this form of psychopathology. In overview, their conclusion that there exists at least a subgroup of schizophrenics who show significant indicators of neuropsychological etiology represents a potentially potent focus for both clarifying and enhancing understanding of major forms of psychopathology.

Developmental psychology has long recognized the importance of sex differences, but it is only in recent years that neuropsychological research has become attuned to possible sex differences in neuropsychological organization. Languis and Naour approach this issue by the use of a vector model, beginning with the role of sex differences in cerebral hemispheric asymmetry. They present a variety of results from anatomic studies involving both the cerebral hemispheres and the corpus callosum, which suggest that not only do females have less anatomic asymmetry of the cerebral hemispheres, but also demonstrate significantly richer interhemispheric connections than males. The authors' interpretation of these differences addresses such issues as possible bilateral language representation in females and increased lateral specialization in males as this might be reflected in conditions ranging from autism to stuttering. Next Languis and Naour approach sex differences in neuropsychological functioning from a hormonal perspective, with focus addressed on studying whether hormonal differences may exert a developmental influence on cortical asymmetry. From the research on levels of circulating androgens during *in utero* development, they address differential sexual patterns in innateness versus acquiredness of given behaviors, and construct a continuum for the expression of such personality variables as compliant-dominant and for such cognitive variables as verbal-visual-spatial. Recognizing that hormonal differences represent only a portion of the tapestry of sex differences, the authors explore possible developmental interactive patterns that might influence the shape and expression of anatomic differences as a stratum of the development of sex differences in neuropsychological organization and function.

Completing the spectrum of developmental variation, Hartlage addresses the topic from the perspective of a pediatric neurologist accustomed to dealing with the nervous system in disease rather than in health. Beginning with congenital influences on neuropsychological differences, she touches on the burgeoning literature relating X chromosome genetic loci to a variety of both global and specific intellectual impairments, and covers the spectrum of various genotypic combinations of sex chromosomes that are associated with various intellectual and neurological deficits, as well as related hereditary inborn errors of metabolism that have known neuropsychiatric correlates. Moving to developmental structural and physiological differences, Hartlage reviews such conditions as dyslexia, Gerstmann's syndrome, and mathematical giftedness in terms of these substrates. Attention is then given to intrauterine environmental influences such as alcohol, mechanical disruptions, and infections and how their occurrence or effects at given stages of intrauterine development can result in variation on a number of neuropsychological variables. Hartlage then describes postnatal influences on the developing brain, such as head injury, nutrition deficits, and biochemical disorders with emphasis on the relationship of the timing of such insults to their potential neuropsychological sequelae. In conclusion, she emphasizes the essential human quality of uniqueness, and discusses how current and anticipated advances in medical science and technology, in collaboration with surgical and behavioral neurosciences, may help in the further measurement and understanding of individual differences.

In keeping with the scientific tradition that diagnosis precedes treatment, the concluding chapter is the first to address intervention. Although presumably the goal of description, assessment, and evaluation is some form of treatment, there has been, as Telzrow points out, an apparent trend in neuropsychology toward a functional autonomy of classification, with previous work focusing on treatment or rehabilitation tending to be speculative. She focuses attention on three conditions (developmental learning disorders, epilepsy, and head injuries) with a relatively high incidence and presumed potential for amelioration as the basis for a survey of the science and speculation of rehabilitation in developmental neuropsychological disorders. For developmental learning disorders, a capitalization-of-strengths model appears most promising, but there is no compelling body of research that can be considered to provide conclusive proof of its utility. With epilepsy, no single rehabilitation approach has been documented to be uniquely effective, although a number of models stressing multifaceted and multidisciplinary strategies appear to effect results better than those typically reported for single-focus rehabilitation approaches. For head injury, those variables most associated with favorable outcome appear to be related more to the characteristics and extent of injury rather than to specific rehabilitative approach, although as with learning-disabled children, a behaviorally oriented capitalization-of-strengths approach based on neuropsychological assessment appears to be the most viable intervention strategy. In conclusion, Telzrow reiterates Dean's premise that whereas the science of educational and vocational rehabilitation in neuropsychology operates at an elementary level relative to the status of diagnosis in the field, such rehabilitation approaches eventually may be expected to represent the most viable contribution of neuropsychology.

There appear to be a number of themes relevant to neuropsychological bases of individual differences that appear among the various approaches. Anatomic cerebral asymmetry, for example, is recognized by scholars with different perspectives as having considerable relevance for individual differences, but more comprehensive understanding of genetic and biochemical bases of such asymmetry is necessary for clarification of the causes and potential modifiability of such asymmetry and its effect on individual functioning. There is suggestive evidence in several chapters that environmental interaction may play a role in the development of internal neuropsychological structures and certainly in the expression of behaviors derived from neuropsychological bases. Diverse approaches suggest a crucial role for neurotransmitters as both determinants of and reactive to self-regulation and environmental feedback, and the growing research literature in this field and the increasing sophistication of technological approaches for its study appear to offer promise for contribution to increased understanding of individual variation in neuropsychological organization and function. Similarly, the rapid progress in neurological and electrophysiological sciences promises greater refinement of biological measurement criteria for the assessment of effects of both biochemical and behavioral manifestation of underlying neuropsychological organization, which serves as the central focus for a conceptual approach to study and understanding of the individual, who hopefully shall remain as both the first word and the first concern of those who study the fascinating panorama of individual differences.

Author Index

Abenson, M. H., 215
Abrams, R., 207, 208, 220, 221
Ackerman, P. T., 191, 192
Acredolo, L. P., 64, 76, 77
Adams, R. D., 206
Ahn, H., 189, 256
Aiken, L. S., 74
Ainsworth, M. D. S., 107, 160
Alavi, A., 217
Albert, M. L., 42, 46, 48, 54
Alexander, D., 255
Alexander, P. C., 295
Algozzine, B., 184, 272
Allard, F., 25
Allen, J. N., 259
Allen, L., 116
Allen, M., 215, 218
Almli, C. R., 42, 45, 48, 54
Alpert, M., 207
Als, H., 111
Altman, J., 114
Amadeo, M., 205
American Psychiatric Association, 204
Ames, L. B., 116
Anderson, E. S., 162
Anderson, M., 132
Anderson, R. J., 288
Andreasen, N. C., 214
Anglin, J. M., 166
Annet, M., 27, 32
Ansbaugh, D. J., 285
Ansbaugh, S. J., 285
Anselmo, V. C., 31
Appelle, S., 75
Arena, J. M., 258
Ariel, R. N., 216

Asano, N., 212
Aschkenasy, J. R., 75
Ashton-Jones, G., 102
Aslin, R. N., 75
Atkins, G., 186
Attneave, F., 67
Ayers, F. W., 188

Baade, L. E., 209
Backman, D. S., 259
Baddeley, A. D., 134
Bagley, C., 284
Baird, H., 189
Baisel, E., 112
Baker, S. W., 242
Bakker, D. J., 24, 42, 52, 85, 187, 271, 273
Bakkeström, E., 255
Ballenger, J. C., 262
Balow, B., 276
Banich, M. T., 103
Banks, M. S., 75
Bannatyne, A., 273
Barbizet, J., 31
Barlow, P. W., 255
Bardin, C. W., 31
Barrell, R. J., 208
Barrett, P., 128, 140, 142, 145
Bartels, P. H., 189
Barten, S., 107, 108
Barth, J. T., 42, 49, 50, 52, 260, 293
Bartlett, F., 256
Bartley, J., 258
Bates, E., 163, 175
Batshaw, M. L., 280
Baum, M. J., 31
Baumgardner, M. J., 174

Bawden, H. N., 290, 291
Bayer, S. A., 114
Bear, D. M., 284
Beaumont, J. G., 27
Beck, J., 67
Becker, B. C., 208
Behan, P., 245
Bell, G. L., 20
Bell, R. Q., 260
Bell, S. M., 107
Bellak, L., 204
Bellur, S., 284
Belmont, L., 71, 193
Belsham, A., 284
Benbow, C., 245, 257
Benjamin, J., 108
Benson, H., 287
Benton, A. L., 32, 188, 189, 290, 292
Ben-Yishay, Y., 297, 298
Berent, S., 282
Berg, R. A., 213, 216, 282, 283
Berger, P., 211
Berger-Gross, P., 293
Berlin, D., 244
Berndt, R. S., 153, 178
Berntson, G. G., 259
Beuhler, B., 105, 258
Bever, T. G., 174
Bidwell, B. H., 283
Bigelow, L. B., 208
Bigler, E. D., 66
Bijur, P., 217
Binet, A., 2, 128
Binge, K., 193
Birch, H. G., 95, 106, 193
Birns, B., 107, 108
Bishop, A., 76

318

Bishop, R. J., 221
Bjerring, J., 9
Bjorklund, A., 109
Blakemore, C., 195
Blank, J. R., 288
Blank, M., 194
Blass, J. P., 255
Blazer, D. G., 116
Bloch, S., 213
Bloom, L., 163, 168
Bloom, R. E., 102, 133
Bobbitt, B., 135
Boder, E., 72, 196, 273, 275
Bogen, J. E., 24
Boies, S., 134
Bo-Lassen, P., 215
Boldrey, E., 29
Bolger, J. P., 297
Boll, T. J., 8, 10, 42, 46, 49,
  50, 52, 260, 282, 293
Bolter, J. F., 282, 283, 287
Bond, M. F., 294
Boring, E. G., 128
Bornstein, M. H., 74
Botwinick, J., 116
Bowlby, J., 112
Bracken, B., 273
Bradshaw, J. L., 240, 241,
  242, 243, 244
Brain, L., 32
Brand, C. R., 132
Brann, A. W., 15, 18, 21
Brase, D. A., 186
Brazelton, T. B., 110, 111,
  160
Bridger, W., 107, 108, 194
Bridges, K. M. B., 105
Brink, J. D., 290, 291, 292,
  293, 294, 295, 296
Brittain, H., 281
Broca, P., 4, 7, 24
Brockington, I. F., 218
Broeder, J. D., 282
Broen, P. A., 162
Brogen, J. H., 24
Bronson, G., 111
Brown, A. L., 127
Brown, D., 256
Brown, D., 273
Brown, D. R., 74

Brown, E., 293
Brown, J., 25
Brown, R., 152, 170, 171
Bruinincks, R., 190
Brumback, R. A., 220, 263
Bruner, J. S., 22, 25, 152,
  153, 160
Brunner, R. L., 114
Bryan, T., 191
Bryant, N. D., 128
Bryden, M. P., 25, 153, 154,
  240
Buchanan, J. M., 31
Buchsbaum, M. S., 186,
  215, 216
Buffery, A. W., 51, 243
Bunney, W. E., 217, 262
Burns, G. W., 193
Burt, C., 126
Burton, L. A., 103
Buss, A. H., 95
Butters, N., 42

Cabanac, M., 107
Campanella, D. J., 26
Campbell, B. A., 109
Campos, J., 95, 112
Cannon, H. E., 262
Cannon-Spoor, H. E., 262
Caplan, P. J., 27
Cappelletti, J., 217
Caramazzo, A., 153, 178
Cardano, C. B., 186
Carlton, P. L., 110
Carpenter, B. N., 219, 220,
  221
Carroll, J. B., 117
Carson, G., 187
Carver, D. H., 49
Cato, C. F., 272, 277, 280
Cattel, J., McK., 128
Catterall, J. F., 31
Caudill, W., 111
Cavanaugh, R. M., Jr., 287,
  290
Century, E., 273, 275
Chadwick, O., 217, 292,
  293
Chandler, M. J., 47
Chapandy, A., 174

Chapman, L. F., 211
Chapman, R. S., 161, 172,
  173
Chase, W. G., 133
Chelune, G. J., 26, 42, 208,
  260
Chess, S., 95
Chi, J. G., 23
Chi, M. T. H., 127
Ch'ien, L. T., 282, 283
Childers, D. G., 189
Childs, B., 189, 277
Chipman, S. F., 74
Chomsky, C., 152, 167, 168
Christensen, K., 26
Christian, J. C., 254
Christiansen, E., 255
Christman, D. R., 217
Chuang, L. W., 262
Cicone, M., 176
Clark, A. W., 262
Clark, C., 291
Clark, E. V., 166, 167, 175,
  176
Clark, H. H., 133
Clarke, R., 23, 187, 240
Clements, S. D., 184, 191,
  192
Coffman, J., 213
Cohen, M., 188, 271, 275,
  276
Cohen, Y., 118
Cohen, R., 77
Cohen, S. M., 218
Colarusso, R. P., 61, 66
Cole, J. C., 292, 302
Cole, P. R., 160
Coleman, M., 186
Coltheart, M., 257
Compton, C., 277, 279
Connors, C. K., 191
Cooper, J. A., 282
Corballis, M. C., 76
Cordero, J. F., 258
Corning, W. C., 256
Coyle, J. T., 262
Craik, F. I. M., 138
Creutzfeldt, O. D., 144, 214
Crinella, F. M., 141
Crockett, D., 9

Cronbach, L. J., 277
Cross, T. G., 162
Croughan, J., 218
Crowley, T. J., 207
Crowley, W. F., Jr., 209, 258
Cummins, J. A., 282, 283
Czudner, G., 191, 192

Damasio, A., 29
Das, J. P., 126
Davidson, H. L., 116
Davis, L., 106
Davis, P. A., 221
Davis, S., 215
Davis, W. E., 220
Davison, A. N., 11
Dawson, M. E., 100
Dax, M., 4, 26
Dean, R. S., 8, 9, 10, 12, 24, 25, 27, 28, 32, 299, 309
Deary, I. J., 132
Decina, P., 220
Decker, T. W., 279
deHirsch, K., 192
DeKaban, A. S., 284
deLacoste-Utamsing, C., 240, 244
Delong, M. R., 262
Denckla, M. B., 189, 256
Dennerll, R. D., 282
Dennert, J. W., 214
Dennis, M., 26, 259
Derryberry, D., 93, 95, 96, 104, 105, 118
Dessetto, L., 193
Deuel, R. K., 3
DeVellis, R. F., 133
deVilliers, J. G., 164, 170, 171, 175
deVilliers, P. A., 164, 170, 171, 175
DeVivo, D. C., 257
DeVoogd, T. J., 52
DeWolfe, A. S., 208
Dikman, S., 26
Diller, L., 297, 298
Dirksen, J. W., 216
Dobbing, J., 11

Dodge, P. R., 11, 13, 15, 18, 19
Dodrill, C. B., 281, 284, 286, 288
Doehring, D., 191
Dollimore, J., 215
Donnelly, E. F., 210, 213
Donovan, W. L., 107
Dooling, E. C., 23
Dorman, C., 283
Doty, R. W., 23
Douglas, D., 113, 114
Douglas, R. J., 113, 114
Douglas, V. I., 113, 118
Drake, W. E., 184, 185
Dreifuss, F. E., 283, 284
Dubinsky, B. L., 287
Dubowitz, V., 254
Duchan, J. F., 162, 173, 174
Duffy, F. H., 189, 256
Dugas, J. L., 133
Dunn, K., 273
Dunn, T. L., 215
Durant, W., 64
Dykman, R. A., 191, 192

Easton, P., 256
Ebbin, A. J., 255
Edds, M. V., 53
Edwards, J., 262
Edwards, M. L., 159
Edwards, P., 26, 42, 260
Ehrfurth, J. W., 66
Ehrhardt, A. A., 242, 258
Eichelman, W., 134
Eidelberg, D., 185, 186, 293
Eilers, R. E., 155, 156, 157
Eimas, P., 155
Eisenberg, H. M., 295
Eisenson, T., 192
Emde, R. N., 107, 108, 111, 112
Epps, S., 184, 272
Escourolle, R., 49
Essock, E. A., 75
Eysenck, H. J., 94, 126, 128, 140, 145
Ezrachi, O., 297, 298

Fantz, R. L., 73, 74
Fariello, G. R., 76
Farkas, T., 217
Farr, S. P., 293
Fass, B., 52
Fawcett, J., 262
Fedio, P., 282, 284
Fenelon, B., 190
Fenton, G. W., 215
Fenwick, P. B. C., 215
Ferdinandsen, K., 74
Ferrier, L. J., 175
Ferry, P. C., 282
Fesback, S., 194
Fillmore, C. J., 168
Filskov, S. B., 46, 48
Fineman, M., 69
Finger, S., 53
Finlayson, M. A. J., 275
Finley, K. H., 221
Finucci, J. M., 277
Fischer, W. F., 193
Fisher, C. B., 74
Fisher, P., 293
Fishman, R., 218
Fisk, J. L., 42, 85, 271
Fisk, N., 258
Fitz, C. R., 259
Flax, M., 194
Flechsig, P., 11
Fleer, R. E., 133
Fleischer, S., 106
Fletcher, J. M., 10, 26, 42, 48, 83, 84, 85
Flood, C., 255
Flor-Henry, P., 207, 208, 210, 215, 217, 218, 220, 221
Flynn, R. W., 217
Folch, J., 11
Foldi, N. S., 176
Foote, S. L., 102
Ford, F. R., 13, 20
Forgus, R. H., 70
Forrest, T., 191, 289
Forsell, T., 216
Foster, J. C., 286, 288, 289
Fowler, J. S., 217
Fox, S. S., 144
Franco, L., 293

Fraser, C., 162
Freeman, B. J., 262
Freedman, D., 72
Freeman, J. M., 15, 19
Freeman, R. B., 18, 35
Friedrich, F., 102, 104
French, J. H., 72
Freunal, P. C., 194
Frodi, A. M., 107
Fromm-Auch, D., 207, 217

Gadea Ciria, M., 216
Gaensbauer, R. J., 107
Gaensbauer, T., 112
Galaburda, A. M., 3, 185, 245, 256
Gale, A., 215
Galton, F., 1, 128
Gambini, O., 207
Gandelman, R., 242
Garcia-Coll, C. G., 115
Gardner, E., 25
Gardner, H., 176
Garner, W. R., 74
Garrett, A. L., 291
Garside, R. F., 261
Garvey, C., 163
Gasser, B., 220
Gastaut, H., 282
Gavin, W. J., 157
Gazzaniga, M. S., 11, 12, 15, 24, 100, 101, 103
Geller, E., 262
Gellhorn, E., 106, 108
Gerall, A. A., 241
Gerard, R. W., 204
Gerson, I., 256
Gertman, D., 189
Geschwind, N., 3, 20, 22, 23, 26, 27, 187, 245
Gesell, A., 116
Geyer, L. H., 80
Gibson, E. J., 16, 22, 23, 62, 69, 73, 75, 80, 84
Glbson, G. E., 255
Gibson, J. J., 65, 68
Gilles, F., 23
Gilliland, M., 285
Gilmore, R. L., 282
Giordani, B., 282, 293

Gissal, T. J., 273
Gittelman, R., 271, 276
Glaser, G. H., 283
Glaser, R., 127
Gleitman, H., 76, 177
Gleitman, L., 177
Goebel, R., 24
Goldberg, A. M., 186
Goldberg, H., 188
Goldberg, H. K., 187, 191
Goldbert, R. A., 135
Golden, C. J., 26, 71, 208, 209, 210, 211, 213, 216, 221
Golden, G. S., 262
Goldin, G. J., 286
Goldman, J. M., 46
Goldman, P. S., 12, 13, 45, 55
Goldsmith, H. H., 95
Goldstein, G., 209
Goldstein, L., 221, 222
Gonzalez, E. R., 262
Goodenough, D. R., 255
Gottesman, I. I., 256, 263
Gottfredson, L. S., 277, 279
Gottlieb, G., 46
Gottlieb, J., 215
Gottlieb, L. S., 116
Gottman, J. M., 110
Gouvier, W. D., 292
Goy, R. W., 32, 241, 242
Goyen, J., 191
Goyette, C. H., 280
Graber, B., 211, 213, 216
Gradijan, J., 215
Graham, F. K., 108
Graham, P., 283
Grandrud, C. E., 75
Grassi, J., 191
Gray, J. A., 94, 95, 111, 113, 114, 243
Green, J. B., 12, 287, 288
Green, R., 258
Greenberg, A. S., 186
Greenberg, F., 258
Greenberg, J. H., 217
Greene, R. L., 293
Greenough, W. T., 52, 54
Grisell, J., 215

Groh, C., 287
Gross, C. G., 74
Grossman, R. G., 290, 292
Gruber, J., 168
Gruzelier, J., 209
Guerra, F., 191
Gunnison, J. A., 277
Gusovsky, F., 262
Guthrie, J. T., 189, 191, 211
Guttman, L. A., 126
Guttormsen, S., 255

Haapanen, R. M., 276
Haaxma, R., 21
Hake, J. L., 64, 76
Hakes, D., 174, 175
Hale, W. R., 291
Halliday, M. A. K., 161
Halsey, J. H., 187
Halstead, H., 281, 283
Halverson, C. F., 260
Hamilton, L. W., 110
Hamm, A., 23, 187, 240
Hammeke, T. A., 210, 211
Hammill, D. D., 61, 66, 83
Hansch, E. C., 187, 195
Hardyck, C., 24
Harkness, S., 162
Harley, J. P., 26
Harmany, T., 256
Harmon, R. J., 107
Harris, E. L., 254
Harris, G. J., 133
Harris, L. J., 244
Harris, P. L., 76
Hart, J., 283
Hart, P. N., 186
Harter, M. R., 190
Hartlage, L. C., 3, 8, 10, 21, 80, 273, 275, 276, 277, 279, 281, 284, 285, 287, 288
Hartlage, P. L., 8, 10
Haug, J. O., 212
Hauser, W. A., 286
Hawkins, H. H., 118
Hayes-Roth, F., 68
Hays, P., 215
Haywood-Nash, D. C. F., 259

Heaton, R. K., 207, 208, 209
Hebb, D. O., 3, 29
Hecaen, H., 25, 42, 46, 48, 54
Hedrick, D. L., 159
Heffner, T. G., 109
Heilman, K. M., 46, 48, 282
Heller, A., 109
Heller, W., 103
Helmholtz, H., 65
Hendrick, E. B., 259
Hendrickson, A. E., 128, 142, 143, 144, 145
Hendrickson, D. E., 128, 142, 145, 146
Henking, B., 295
Herdt, J. R., 213
Hermann, B. P., 284
Hermann, K., 257
Hershenson, D. B., 288
Hertzig, M. E., 95
Hick, W., 131
Hicks, R. E., 28
Hier, D. B., 258
Hiers, D. B., 187
Higgins, G., 284
Hijada, D., 186
Hill, A., 69
Hillenbrand, J., 157
Hiller, V. F., 218
Hillyard, S. A., 100, 101
Himwich, W. A., 11, 15
Hirsch, S. R., 215
Hirschhorn, K., 255
Hiscock, M., 25
Hochberg, J., 65, 68
Hochschild, A. K., 115
Hoffman, H. J., 259
Holloway, R. L., 240, 244
Holmes, D. A., 287, 288
Holmes, L. B., 258
Holzman, P. S., 204, 205, 206
Honig, A. S., 262
Honzik, M. P., 116
Hood, L., 168
Hopkins, D. A., 45
Horvath, T. B., 211
Howell, V. V., 255
Hsu, W., 215

Hua, M. S., 24, 25, 27
Huber, G., 212
Hughes, J. R., 188, 189, 205, 284
Hull, E., 257
Hummel, D. D., 257
Humphreys, R. P., 259
Hunt, E., 128, 257, 284
Hunter, J. R., 258
Hurbec, Z., 218
Hurt, S. W., 205
Hutt, C., 255
Hutt, S. J., 42, 47, 284
Hutton, J. T., 195
Hynd, C. R., 28, 272
Hynd, G. W., 28, 187, 188, 271, 272, 275, 276

Ilg, F. L., 116
Imbus, C., 290
Ingram, T. T. S., 22, 168
Ingvar, D. H., 187, 216, 217
Isaacson, R. L., 19, 20, 21, 26, 42, 47
Isenberg, D., 187, 188
Itil, T. M., 215
Izard, C. E., 105

Jablensky, A., 218
Jacklin, C. N., 258
Jackson, J. H., 7, 24
Jackson, P. M., 284
James, L. M., 258
Jamison, W., 257
Jane, J. A., 260, 290, 293
Jansky, J. J., 192
Janson, A. J., 80
Jarrico, S., 273, 275
Javiad, J., 262
Jefferson, J. S., 218
Jeffries, J. R., 262
Jenkins, J. J., 151
Jensen, A. R., 2, 126, 128, 131, 132, 133, 135, 136, 137, 139, 141, 254
Jick, H., 258
John, E. R., 189, 256
John, M., 256
Johnson, C. E., 162
Johnson, D., 42, 45, 48, 54

Johnson, J. L., 217
Johnson, K. L., 113, 114, 209
Johnston, J., 73
Johnston, L., 195
Jones, R. K., 65, 68, 69

Kagan, J., 115
Kahneman, D., 96, 97
Kairim, R., 257
Kallanranta, T., 290
Kaman, M., 193
Kane, R. L., 211
Kapisovsky, P. M., 288, 289
Karmel, B. Z., 74, 256
Karoum, F., 262
Katz, J., 153
Katz, K., 188
Kaufman, N. L., 277
Kavale, K., 60
Kaye, H., 189, 256
Kaye, K., 110
Keating, D. P., 133, 135
Keele, S. W., 118
Kellas, G., 133
Kemler, D. G., 74
Kemper, T. L., 185, 245, 256
Kendall, R. E., 218
Kendler, H. H., 25
Kendler, T. S., 25, 42, 43, 188
Kennard, M. A., 42, 43, 188
Kern, C. A., 159
Kershner, J. B., 28
Kessler, R., 216
Ketchum, G., 188
Kiessling, L. S., 256
Kiev, A., 212
Kiloh, L. G., 221
Kilroy, M. C., 74
Kimble, D. P., 19, 114
Kimura, D., 24
King, A. C., 217
Kinsbourne, M., 24, 25, 27, 28, 118, 196, 257
Kirk, S. A., 191
Kirk, W. D., 191
Kirsch, J. T., 189
Kleck, R., 286

Kleiman, M. B., 49
Klonoff, H., 9, 290, 291, 292
Klopp, K., 161, 163
Klopper, J. H., 109
Knights, R. M., 290, 291
Knott, J. R., 188, 189
Koffka, K., 66, 67
Kohler, W., 127
Kohn, B., 26
Kolata, G. B., 31, 257, 258
Koles, Z. J., 215
Kolvin, I., 261
Konick, A. F., 138
Kopin, I. J., 262
Koranyi, L., 109
Korn, S., 95
Korner, A. F., 107
Koslowski, B., 110, 111, 160
Kosslyn, S. M., 76
Kotake, C., 109
Kraft, R. H., 244
Krakow, J. B., 113, 114
Kramer, K., 191
Kraut, A. G., 99
Krawciw, N., 222
Kriger, L. S., 288, 289
Kruszewski, S., 222
Kubovy, M., 67
Kuennapas, T., 80
Kuhl, P., 157
Kutsick, K., 277
Kuypers, H. G. J. M., 21

Laatinen, L. V., 114
Lahey, M., 163
Lake, C. R., 262
Lakin, P., 297, 298
Lally, M., 128, 132
Lamb, M. E., 107
Lancaster, W., 282, 283
Landau, B., 76
Languis, M. L., 238, 240, 244, 249
Lansdell, H. C., 30, 187
Larsen, S. C., 83
Lashley, K. S., 53
Lasky, E. Z., 153, 161, 162, 174, 312, 313
Lassen, N. A., 216

Laughery, K. B., 80
Lawrence, D. G., 45
Lawson, K. R., 106
Lawson, L., 188
Lawson-Kerr, K., 26
Leander, R., 188
Leavitt, L. A., 107
Lecours, A. R., 15, 18, 48, 158
Lee, D., 220
Lee, J., 186
Lee, L., 172
Lefford, A., 193
Lehman, R. A., 208
Lehne, G. K., 259
Lehtinen, L. E., 10
Lehtovaara, R., 288
LeMay, M., 187
Lemke, R., 212
Lemmon, V. W., 128
Lenneberg, E. H., 25
Lennox, K., 281
Leonard, L., 168, 169
Leong, C. K., 188
LeTendre, J. B., 76
LeVere, T. E., 53, 54
Levin, H., 63, 69, 84, 290, 292, 293, 294, 295, 297
Levinson, J. Z., 66
Levitzky, W., 3, 23, 24, 187
Levy, D. L., 32, 103, 205
Levy, J., 26, 28, 244, 247
Levy, L., 106
Lewin, R., 259
Lewis, D. O., 283
Lewis, G., 211
Lewkowicz, D. J., 106
Lezak, M. D., 48, 294
Liebowitz, D., 193, 254
Lifshitz, K., 215
Lightbown, P., 168
Lindvall, O., 109
Lipson, A., 258
Lipton, E. L., 108
Lishman, W. A., 49, 218
Livingston, S., 284
Loh, H. M., 186
Lohman, D. F., 133
Long, C. J., 292, 294, 295, 296, 298, 299

Lonnum, A., 212
Loofbourrow, G. N., 106
Lorber, J., 259
Loren, I., 109
Low, M., 291, 292
Lowrey, G. H., 15
Luchins, D. J., 213
Ludlow, C., 186
Lumsden, C. J., 248
Lund, N. J., 162, 173, 174
Lundsteen, C., 255
Luria, A. R., 12, 21, 30, 46, 47, 48, 53, 55, 57, 84, 85, 104, 113, 114, 204, 206, 210, 225, 227
Lyle, J. G., 191
Lyon, R., 72, 273

Mabry, P., 109
Maccoby, E. E., 32, 258
Macfarlane, J., 116
MacGregor, R. R., 217
MacLean, P. D., 12, 15, 18
MacLeod, C. M., 284, 285
MacLusky, N. J., 31, 32
Madsen, S., 258
Main, M., 110, 111, 160
Maisel, E. B., 74
Maiti, A., 213
Malec, J., 206, 208, 209
Manfield, P., 186
Mann, L. S., 217
Manning, R. G., 217
Marcel, T., 188
Marcus, M. M., 140
Margolin, R. J., 286
Markman, S., 276
Marr, D., 70
Marsden, C. D., 102
Marshalek, B., 133
Marshall, J. R., 218
Martz, M. J., 207
Marx, J. L., 257
Matarazzo, J. D., 207
Mateer, C. A., 153, 154
Mathura, C. B., 51
Matthews, C. G., 26
Mattis, S., 72, 196
Mattson, D., 60
Mauser, A. J., 277

Maxwell, M., 276
Maxwell, S. E., 117
Mazurky, G., 138
McCarthy, J. J., 192
McCauley, C., 133
McComas, A. J., 221
McEwen, B. S., 32, 241, 242
McGee, M. J., 243
McGill, H. C., 31
McGlone, J., 243
McGue, M., 184
McGuinness, D., 94, 95, 96, 109
McGuire, G. M., 280
McGuire, I., 106, 107
McKeever, W. R., 188
McLaughlin, B., 260
McLaurin, R. L., 260
McLennan, J. E., 260
McLeod, P., 117
McReynolds, L. V., 191
McWilliams, J. M., 287, 288
Mednick, S., 209, 215
Megaw-Nyce, J., 73
Melamed, L. E., 70, 81, 83, 310, 311
Melnechuk, T., 213
Meltzer, H. Y., 205, 220
Mendelson, M. J., 74
Menyuk, P., 158, 177
Mesulam, M. M., 263
Meyer, P. G., 293
Meyer-Bahlburg, H. F., 258
Miccinati, J., 84
Mikkelsen, E. J., 186
Miller, E., 297
Miller, F. E., 109
Miller, G. A., 138
Milner, B., 30, 48
Minarcik, C. J., Jr., 287
Minardi, A., 276
Minkowski, A., 10, 11, 13
Minskoff, E. H., 277
Miranda, S. B., 74
Mirsky, A. F., 282
Moffit, A. R., 156
Molfese, D. L., 153, 157, 178
Molfese, V. J., 18, 23, 25, 157

Monakhov, K., 221
Money, J., 255, 259
Moore, J. M., 156
Moran, C. C., 3
Moreau, T., 106
Morgan, A. M. B., 287
Morgan, C. T., 11, 29
Morris, R., 72
Moskowitz, M. A., 263
Moses, J. A. Jr., 211
Muehl, S., 188, 189
Munro, E., 2
Murphy, D. L., 262
Musso, M. R., 190

Naftolin, F., 31, 32
Naglaki, J., 28
Nance, W. E., 254
Nauta, W. J. H., 114
Neligan, G. A., 261
Nelson, K., 152, 153, 154, 165, 166
Neophytides, A. N., 210
Netley, C. T., 259
Nettlebeck, T., 128, 132, 241, 242
Nettleton, N. C., 240, 243, 244
Newill, B. H., 279
Newlin, D., 206, 207, 211, 213
Nickel, V. L., 291
Nielson, H., 193
Nishihara, H. K., 70
Norman, B. F., 259
Norrie, E., 257
Nottebohm, F., 32, 187
Novack, T. A., 295
Nuffield, E. J. A., 284

Oakley, G. P., 258
O'Brien, J. H., 144
Obrzut, J. E., 28, 187, 188
Ochs, S., 29
Odom, R. D., 75, 84
Oexle, J. E., 273
O'Halloran, M., 258
Ojemann, G., 27, 154, 178, 187
O'Leary, D., 282

Oller, D. K., 155, 156, 157, 158, 159
Olsen, S. A., 214
Olson, G. M., 108
Olson, S. F., 284
Orme, J. E., 220
Orton, S. J., 26, 27, 192
Osborne, K., 215
Osgood, C., 191, 192
Oski, F. A., 262
Osselton, J. W., 221
Ounsted, C., 255
Overman, W. H., 23
Overton, D. A., 205
Owen, D. R., 255
Owens, D. H., 74
Owsley, C. J., 73
Oxley, J., 285

Packouz, K., 113, 114
Palermo, D., 37
Pallie, W., 23, 187, 240
Pankey, W., 111
Pape, K. E., 260
Paris, R., 290
Park, G. E., 188
Parsons, C., 157
Parsons, O. A., 47, 211
Pasternak, J. F., 260
Pastore, N., 65
Pate, J. L., 20
Paulos, M. A., 262
Pavlov, I. P., 113
Peak, H., 128
Pearlson, G. D., 221
Peiper, A., 11, 18, 20, 22, 23, 25
Penfield, W., 12, 29, 30
Perlo, V. P., 187
Perret, Y. M., 280
Perris, C., 221
Perry, A., 284
Perry, N. W., 189
Perry, S. L., 286
Persad, E., 255
Peters, J. E., 191, 192
Petrie, B. F., 27
Pettersen, L., 75, 240
Petty, R., 284
Phelps, C. P., 109

Philip, J., 255
Philipson, L., 187
Phillips, I., 262
Phoenix, C. H., 241
Piaget, J., 7, 18, 22, 23, 25, 51
Piasetsky, E., 297, 298
Pick, A. D., 69
Pick, H. L., 76
Pien, D. P., 113, 114
Pieri, E., 207
Pincus, J. H., 283
Piran, H., 283
Pirozzolo, F. J., 26, 187, 188, 195, 196, 273
Pizzamiglio, L., 27
Plomin, R., 95
Poirier, J., 49
Pollin, W., 218
Pomerantz, J. R., 67
Pond, D. A., 283
Poppen, R. J., 192
Porges, S. W., 108, 109
Posner, M. I., 95, 96, 97, 101, 102, 103, 104, 117, 118, 134, 135, 138, 311
Post, R. M., 262
Potkin, S. G., 262
Powell, J. S., 125, 127, 146
Pradham, S. N., 109
Prather, E. M., 159
Prechtl, H. F., 19
Preston, M. S., 189
Pribram, K. H., 94, 95, 96, 109
Price, D. L., 262
Prichep, L., 189, 256
Prinz, P. M., 175
Proctor, L. R., 205
Purisch, A. D., 210, 211

Quage, M. A., 216
Quinn, P. C., 260

Rabinovitch, M., 187
Rabinovitch, R., 188
Rafael, R. O., 102, 104, 118
Rakic, P., 23
Ramsay, D., 25
Randall, J., 186

Rangaswami, K., 282, 287
Rapin, I., 72
Rapoport, J. L., 186, 260
Rattok, J., 297, 298
Rayner, K., 187, 188, 195
Redfield, J., 298
Redmoud, C., 273, 275
Reed, E. J., 65, 68, 113
Reed, M., 26
Rees, E., 127
Reinisch, J. M., 242
Reitan, R. M., 8, 30
Reivich, M., 217
Resnick, J. S., 115
Reynolds, C. R., 10, 25, 276
Reynolds, E. D. R., 47
Reynolds, E. H., 285
Rice, B. D., 272, 277, 280
Richmond, J. B., 108
Rieder, R. O., 213
Rieser, J. J., 76
Rimel, R. W., 260, 290, 293, 299
Ringland, J. T., 110
Risberg, J., 187
Ritvo, E. R., 262
Roberts, L., 30
Roberts, N., 162
Robins, E., 218
Robinson, A., 208
Robinson, J., 107, 108, 111
Robinson, R. J., 19, 20, 21
Rock, I., 60, 69
Rodin, E., 215, 281
Rogers, L., 242
Rose, D., 114
Rose, F. C., 284
Rose, R. J., 254
Rosen, J., 42
Rosenberg, J. B., 259
Rosenberger, P. B., 187
Rosenkilde, C. E., 114
Rosenthal, R., 208
Rosina, A., 144
Rosner, B. S., 53
Rosner, J., 190
Ross, B., 297, 298
Ross, E. D., 217
Ross, J. J., 189
Ross, P., 158

Roth, E., 128
Rothbart, M. K., 93, 95, 96, 104, 105, 113, 114, 118, 311
Rothlisberg, B. A., 28
Rourke, B. P., 42, 46, 77, 85, 191, 192, 271, 275, 287, 291, 293
Rousey, C., 205
Routtenberg, A., 96
Rubin, D. B., 255
Rudel, R. G., 43, 44, 45, 50, 51, 52, 55, 57, 76
Rudnick, M., 193, 194
Ruedrich, S. C., 221
Ruff, H. A., 73
Rugg, 27, 28
Rugle, L., 81, 83
Rush, A. J., 217
Rutter, M., 42, 49, 271, 283, 287, 292, 293

Saarni, C., 115
Sabatino, D. A., 184
Sabelli, H. C., 262
Sackallares, J. C., 282
Sackheim, H. A., 220, 282
Saletu, B., 215
Sameroff, A. J., 47
Sanders, T., 238
Sandini, G., 189, 256
Sandoval, J., 276
Sarnoff, A. M., 255
Sarsikov, S., 12, 18
Satz, P., 10, 23, 24, 25, 26, 27, 28, 42, 48, 72, 83, 84, 277, 279
Scarone, S., 207
Schafer, E. W. P., 128, 140, 141
Schaffer, H. R., 111
Schaffer, J. W., 255
Schankweiler, D., 193
Schell, A. M., 100
Schlesinger, I., 168
Schmeck, H. M., 31
Schmidt, R. H., 109
Schneider, G. E., 42, 44
Schneirla, T. C., 106
Schonhaut, S., 277, 279

Schopflocher, D., 207
Schulsinger, F., 209, 255
Schulte, F. J., 11, 19, 20
Schwartz, A., 112
Schwartz, E., 256
Schwartz, N. H., 27
Schwartz, S., 135
Scott, A. J., 279
Scott, D. M., 261
Scott, M. L., 221
Scott, R. R., 297
Segall, P. E., 116
Segalowitz, S. J., 153, 154
Seiden, L. S., 109
Seidenberg, M., 281
Seidman, L. J., 212, 213, 214, 215, 217
Selman, R., 115
Selz, M., 71
Semmes, J., 26
Senf, G. M., 194
Shackleford, M., 293
Shaffer, D., 217, 292, 293
Shagass, C., 205
Shankweiler, D., 30
Shannon, C. E., 67
Shanok, S. S., 283
Shapiro, H. L., 281
Shapiro, I., 195
Shatz, M., 163
Shaywitz, R. A., 109
Sheridan, P. J., 31
Sherman, T., 108
Shields, J., 256, 263
Shriberg, L. D., 159
Shrout, P. E., 293
Silbergeld, E. K., 186
Silver, S., 297, 298, 299
Silverstein, M. L., 220
Simon, T., 2, 128
Slater, D., 257
Smith, A., 26
Smith, C. M., 190
Smith, L. B., 74
Smith, L. S., 27
Smith, M. R., 188, 214, 220
Snider, R. S., 213
Snow, C. E., 162
Snow, R. E., 133, 277
Sokolov, E. N., 106

Sokolov, S. C., 217, 282
Spaner, F. E., 208
Sparrow, S., 23
Spearman, C., 125
Spelke, E., 76
Sperry, R. W., 3, 9, 12, 13, 22, 23, 24, 25, 26, 293
Spiegel, F. S., 242
Spiegel, M. R., 128
Sroufe, L. A., 105, 111
St. James-Roberts, I., 42, 47, 52, 53
Stancer, H. C., 255
Stanley, J., 4, 245, 257
Stark, H., 192
Staton, R. D., 220, 263
Steger, J. A., 193
Stein, D. G., 42, 47, 54
Stein-Schneider, A., 108
Stergachis, A., 258
Stern, D., 110
Sternberg, D. E., 262
Sternberg, R. J., 125, 127, 133, 134, 136, 139, 146
Sterritt, G. M., 193, 194
Stewart, A. L., 47
Stewart, M., 135
Stewart, N., 72
Stocking, M., 255
Stoiber, K. D., 273
Stores, G., 283
Stork, D. G., 66
Stotsky, B. A., 286
Stout, J. K., 279
Strang, J. D., 42, 85, 271, 275, 287, 293
Strauss, A. A., 10
Strock, B. D., 108
Struble, R. G., 262
Sugar, J., 259
Sugar, O., 26
Susser, I. S., 286
Swartzburg, M., 222
Sweet, J. J., 211
Szoke, C. O., 288, 289
Szuhay, J. A., 279

Tamasy, V., 109
Taylor, D. C., 255
Taylor, M., 207, 208, 221

Taylor, R., 134
Telzrow, C. F., 21, 80, 272, 273, 275, 276, 277, 279, 281
Tenuissen, J., 24
Tessell, R. E., 262
Teuber, H. L., 42, 43, 44, 45, 50, 54, 57, 213
Thatcher, R., 256
Thoman, E. B., 107
Thomas, A., 116
Thomas, H., 257
Thompson, P. J., 126, 284
Thorndike, E. C., 6
Thurstone, L. L., 126
Tipps, S., 238
Toro, A., 256
Torres, F., 188
Torrey, E. F., 210, 213
Trepetin, M., 189
Trevarthen, C., 110, 164
Trimble, M. R., 284
Tronick, E., 111
Trostle, J. A., 286
Tuber, D. S., 259
Tucker, D. M., 101, 103, 114
Turkewitz, G., 106, 107
Tzeng, O. J., 24

Udel, M., 287
Ullman, S., 68
Umiker-Seboek, D., 163
Uttal, W. R., 63, 65

Valdes, P., 256
Valenstein, E. S., 29, 46, 48
Valsiner, J., 178
Van der Vlugt, H., 18, 22, 24
Van Deventer, A. D., 188
Van Kammen, D., 217, 262
Van Nostrand, G. K., 23
Vaughan, H. G., 144
Vellutino, F. F., 193
Vernon, P. A., 126, 127, 128, 131, 132, 135, 136, 137, 139, 312
Veroff, A. E., 221
Vickers, D., 132

Vilkk, J., 114
Von Knorring, L., 221
Vygotsky, L. S., 18, 22, 55

Waber, D. P., 25, 32, 244,
    255
Wada, J., 23, 25, 187, 240
Wainwright, S., 218
Waldman, I. N., 210, 213
Waldrop, M. F., 260
Walk, R. D., 75
Walker, A. S., 73
Walker, J., 102, 104, 218
Walker, R. F., 116
Walsh, D., 258
Wang, W., 24
Warrington, E. L., 257, 293
Waters, R. N., 217
Watkings, M. J., 138
Watson, B. L., 193, 273
Watson, C. G., 208, 220
Watson, E. H., 15
Watts, C. O., 284
Weaver, W., 67
Webb, E. M., 188
Weber, G. Y., 84
Webster, J. S., 297
Webster, W., 258
Wechsler, F. S., 299
Wedding, D., 271
Weed, W., 28, 188
Weider, S., 194
Weinberger, D. R., 210, 213
Weingartner, H., 186
Weinstein, E. A., 104
Weinstein, H., 111
Weintraub, P., 31
Weintraub, S., 263
Weitkamp, L. R., 255

Weller, G. M., 259
Welner, A., 218
Wender, E. H., 186
Wender, P. H., 186
Wepman, J., 192, 196
Wertheim, G., 127, 191
West, R. L., 84
Wexler, D., 188
Whitaker, B., 27, 273, 275
Whitaker, H. A., 187
White, S. H., 22
Whitehouse, P. J., 262
Wiens, A. N., 207
Wigglesworth, J. S., 260
Wilkening, G. N., 287
Wilkus, R. J., 281
Williams, J. M., 110, 279
Williams, S. J., 282, 283
Williams, T. M., 74
Williamson, P. A., 101, 114
Wills, E. L., 187
Willson, R. J., 132
Wilshire, C., 186
Wilson, A., 284
Wilson, E. D., 248
Wilson, E. M. A., 187
Wilson, J., 216
Wilson, M. G., 255
Wilson, N., 263
Wilson, W. R., 156, 157
Winogron, H. W., 290, 291,
    295
Wissler, C., 128
Witelson, S., 23, 32, 187,
    240, 243, 244, 273
Witkin, H. A., 255
Witten, B. J., 279, 280
Wittig, M. A., 240
Wohlwill, J. F., 85

Wolf, A. P., 217
Wolff, H. G., 212
Wood, N. E., 191
Woo-Sam, J., 290, 291
Wright, G., 11
Wurtman, R. J., 263
Wyatt, R. J., 210, 213, 262

Yager, R. D., 109
Yakovlev, P. I., 15, 18, 23,
    48
Yalom, I., 258
Yasillo, N. J., 203
Yeni-Konshian, G., 187,
    188
Yeudall, L. T., 207, 215, 220
Yonas, A., 75
Young, W. C., 241
Young, W. M., 290
Ysseldyke, J. E., 184, 272
Yu, J., 258
Yule, W., 283, 287
Yuwiler, A., 262

Zahn, T. P., 186
Zalik, M. C., 76
Zangwill, O. C., 27, 28, 195
Zata, L. M., 211
Zegans, L. S., 109
Zegans, S., 109
Zeigler, B. L., 108
Zenhausern, R., 273, 276
Zetusky, W., 273
Ziegler, M. G., 262
Zimmerman, B., 273, 275
Zuckerman, M., 94, 95,
    115
Zurif, E. B., 153, 178, 187
Zusne, L., 80

Subject Index

Abstract reasoning, 23, 78, 87
Affective disorders, 217–222, 228–229
Age-related variation, 9–10, 14, 16–17, 18, 27, 41–50, 55, 74–75, 76, 81–82, 99, 101, 116, 159, 177–178, 192, 205, 223–224, 226, 260–261, 291–294, 310
Aphasia, 191, 282
Arborization, 11
Arousal, 96–99, 102
Attention, 95–96, 97, 99–100, 102, 103, 104, 117–118, 261, 297
Attention deficits, 117–118, 186, 191
Auditory processing, 190–192
Autism, 262

Behaviorism, 2
Bender-Gestalt Test, 66, 71, 72
Benton Visual Retention Test, 71, 87
Brain damage, effects of, 8, 26, 29, 42–53, 101, 103, 104, 176–177, 183, 206, 207, 222–223, 224–225, 263, 281–285, 291–295
Brain electrical activity mapping (BEAM), 189

Cerebral asymmetry, 3, 26, 187–188, 240–241
Cerebral blood flow, 154, 214, 215–216, 256–257
Cholinergic, 109, 186
Chronogenetic localization, 55–56
Computed tomography (CT), 3, 187, 211, 212–214, 221, 224, 264, 271

Developmental Test of Visual-Motor Integration, 71, 72, 79

Developmental Test of Visual Perception, 66
Diagnostic and Statistical Manual of Mental Disorders, 3rd ed. (DSM-III), 117, 204, 218
Dichotic listening, 28, 187–188, 191, 246
Dyslexia, 26–27, 72, 185–186, 187–196, 243–244, 256–257, 272–275

Educational interventions, 85–89, 276–277, 285–287, 295–298
Electroencephalography (EEG), 25, 97, 146, 185, 188–190, 214–215, 221–222, 224, 256
Encephalitis, 10
Environment, influence of, 2, 9, 10, 27, 52, 56, 76–77, 110–111, 157, 160–162, 249, 259, 310
Epilepsy, 260, 280–290
Equal potentiality, 24–25
Ethnic differences, 137
Evoked potentials, 128, 140–141, 144–145, 157, 189–190
Eye movements, 194–196, 205

Fetal alcohol syndrome, 257–258
Florida Kindergarten Screening Battery, 71
Frontal lobe, 29, 45, 46–47, 103–104, 114, 206, 208, 217, 223, 224, 228, 229

Gerstmann's syndrome, 257
Gestalt perception, 66–68, 127

Halstead-Reitan Neuropsychological Battery, 50, 71, 72, 209–210, 211, 220–221

Head injuries, 43–45, 49–50, 52, 104, 260–261, 290–299
Hemispheric specialization, 24, 25–26, 153–154, 157, 178, 187, 244, 247, 263
Hippocampus, 19–20, 113, 114
Hydrocephalus, 259
Hyperactivity, 19, 112, 186, 259–260, 261–262, 283–285, 294

Illinois Test of Psycholinguistic Abilities, 71, 192
Inspection time, 132–133
Intrauterine effects, 257–258

Kennard principle, 42–43
Kent Perceptual Processing Inventory Copying Test (KPPI-C), 80–85

Language, 12, 18, 21, 22, 23, 24, 25, 26, 27, 28, 30, 46, 48, 151–178, 187, 205, 242–244
Laterality/lateralization, 13, 22, 23–24, 26–28, 32, 103, 187, 247–248
Lateral preference, 27
Learning disability, 183–196, 244, 272–280, 313
Left-handedness, 28, 185, 245, 257, 273–275
Leiter International Performance Scale, 141
Limbic system, 12, 19, 20, 94–95, 114, 262
Localization, 8, 12, 24, 28–31, 41, 48, 178, 185, 222–223, 228, 262
Luria-Nebraska Children's Battery, 71
Luria-Nebraska Neuropsychological Battery, 210–212

Manic depressive psychosis, 256
Mathematics, 25, 29, 245–246, 257, 273–275, 293
McCarthy Scales of Children's Abilities, 71
Memory, 24, 31, 61, 85, 86, 97, 133–135, 137–139, 192, 291, 293
Minnesota Multiphasic Personality Inventory (MMPI), 220
Motor Free Visual Perception Test, 61, 66, 71, 86

Motor function, 12, 21
Motor strip, 21, 29
Muscular dystrophy, 254
Myelination, 11, 20–21, 158, 260, 310

Nerve cell, 11, 46, 309
Neurological development, 10–23, 46
Neuropsychological assessment, 41, 50, 71–72, 78–79, 80–89, 208–212
Nuclear magnetic resonance tomogram (NMR), 264–265
Nutrition, 261

Occipital lobe, 30

Parietal lobe, 29–30, 104
Parkinson's disease, 102, 262
Peabody Picture Vocabulary Test, 141
Perception, 1, 61–79, 84–88, 192–193, 310–311
Plasticity, 26, 244, 260
Pneumoencephalogram (PEG), 212–213
Positron emission transaxial tomography (PETT), 214, 216–217, 271
Premorbid functioning, 9, 52, 205
Primary projection areas, 11

Reaction time, 98–99, 116, 128–132, 135–137
Reading, 22–23, 30, 184–196, 214–215, 272–275
Recovery of function, 53–55
Reflexes, 18, 19
Reye's syndrome, 253, 260

Schizophrenia, 203–217, 222–228, 256, 262
Sex differences, 27, 31–32, 51, 237–249, 254–255, 257–258, 314
Sex hormones, 115–116, 238, 241–243, 245–246, 257, 258–259, 314
Simultaneous-sequential processing, 126
Split-brain research, 3, 24, 101–103
Stanford Binet, 141

Temperament, 93–118
Temporal lobe, 30–31
Tourette's syndrome, 256
Turner's syndrome, 255

Visual closure, 61
Visual system, 15, 194–195
Vocational intervention, 277–280, 287–
    290, 298–299

Wechsler Adult Intelligence Scale (WAIS),
    133, 145, 208–209, 219–220, 273–
    274
Wepman Auditory Discrimination Test,
    71